Harold Nicolson at the Paris Peace Conference, 1919

HAROLD NICOLSON

Diaries and Letters 1930-1939

EDITED BY
NIGEL NICOLSON

Collins

ST JAMES'S PLACE
LONDON
1966

Dedicated to

BENEDICT NICOLSON

by his father and brother

Contents

CONTENTS

CONTENTS

Illustrations

Introduction by Nigel Nicolson

Harold Nicolson[1] began to keep a regular diary from the moment when he resigned from the Foreign Service at the end of 1929. The first entry is dated 1st January, 1930. There were no earlier diaries apart from that which he kept in 1919 during the Paris Peace Conference and which he later edited for publication in *Peacemaking*.[2] Having once started the diary afresh he maintained it without a single break until 4th October, 1964, when the emptiness of his days left him with too little to record. He typed it every morning after breakfast on both sides of loose sheets of quarto paper, slipping one completed page after another into a folder which at the end of the year was filed in a steel cabinet at Sissinghurst, never, or almost never, to be looked at by him again. When he was particularly busy or public events became of great importance, he would dictate the diary, and sometimes he would insert the carbon copy of a letter, a menu-card or some pages torn from *Hansard*. On an average day he would type half a page, on occasion extending it to two or three pages or reducing it to a few lines. The diary for the year 1938, for example, covers 95 double-sided sheets and contains about 105,000 words. The entire diary is some three million words long.

In October 1964, when the idea of editing this version was first mooted, my brother and I asked him why he had kept it day after day for over 34 years. 'Oh, because I thought I would', he replied. 'Come', we said, 'that's not good enough. You didn't write it for publication?' 'No, that never entered my head.'[3] 'You never showed it to anybody?'

---

[1] In order to minimise personal intrusion by the editor, I shall refer to my father throughout by his full name, and as H.N. in the footnotes. Similarly, my mother will be referred to as V. Sackville-West or V.S-W., the maiden name under which she always wrote.

[2] Constable. 1933.   [3] But see p. 420, note 1.

'Never.' 'You never re-read it yourself?' 'Very, very rarely, when I
wanted to check a name or a date.' 'Then why did you take such
trouble?' 'Because I thought that one day it might amuse you and
Ben.' And that was all that we could get out of him. Six months
later, lunching alone with him at Sissinghurst, I repeated my question.
He replied that the diary became a habit. 'Like brushing your teeth?'
'Exactly.'

Reading the diary for the first time, I was reminded by it of a
conversation in August 1938, when he told us that the diary 'is not a
work of literature or self-revelation, but a mere record of activity put
down for my own reference only.' But it is clear from the diary itself
and a knowledge of his personality and books that there were other
motives, other impulses. Writing always came very easily to him:
his typewriter was an extra tongue. It put no additional strain on him
to type this daily record once a slot had been established for it in his
morning's time-table. Leading so full and interesting a life, he thought
it a waste of experience to allow conversations, impressions and ideas
to fade beyond recollection. He had an acutely historical sense. The
conflict between principle and ambition in a person's nature, the role
that chance plays in great events, the subtleties of race and class distinctions, are central themes in his diary as they are in his many books and
articles. He recorded his life daily as an exercise in contemporary
history. It amused him; but there can have been little doubt in his
mind that the diary might one day be of interest to more than just
'you and Ben'. Besides, while he was not much given to self-analysis
in his conversation and letters, his diary received the fantasies of his
ambition and the dregs of his despair. In it he would talk to himself,
reassure himself, scold himself, take stock of what he had become and
hoped to be, and play around with themes for possible future books.
The diary was an anthology of his daily experience; but it also traced
the oscillations of an unusually active and sensitive mind.

'It is not a work of literature.' This is true in the sense that it was
hurriedly written and never revised. But nor was it merely an annotated
engagement-book. He wrote, as he spoke, with a cadence that became
instinctive to him. He would illustrate his sketches of people by describing not only what they said, but their gestures, dress and tone of voice,
and of places by mixing his colours as if on a palette. His own attitudes
emerge very clearly from the admiration or contempt which he
expresses for the attitudes of others. The diary, in short, is what he

said it was not, 'self-revelation', and to that extent, it is also a work of literature.

It is, however, more solemn than his other writings. He gave to it the most serious side of his mind. When I handed him the edited version to read in typescript, I waited rather anxiously in the next room for his first reaction. Half-an-hour later I heard through the closed door a dreadful yawn. But later, as he came to relive the political events of the 1930's, in which all his faculties and deepest emotions had been engaged, his indifference vanished, and he read it through at a sitting, asking me afterwards to make but a single excision, from a passage where he had described an acquaintance, now long dead, as 'a rabbit-toothed fool'. This incident illustrates another characteristic of the diary. It is rarely malicious. There is gossip in it, certainly, in the sense of contemporary rumour about prominent people, and he could become passionate in his antipathy to political ninnies and trouble-makers. But on the whole the diary is discreet and well-disposed. In selecting for publication barely one-twentieth part of the original, my problem has been to save space rather than to avoid offence.

I have included in this volume[1] a reproduction of part of a page of the original diary alongside the edited text. Comparison between the two will show that I have retained what seemed to me significant additions to other published records of those days, or passages which throw a special light on Harold Nicolson's personality, and left out what in retrospect seemed otiose or repetitive. I have mingled public matters with family matters in roughly the same proportion as in the original. I have made slight changes to the grammar in order to render the sequence of two separated passages intelligible, and I have corrected spelling mistakes and a few errors of fact. Apart from that, I have omitted one or two passages which I had wished to include, because people mentioned in them have told me that their views were seriously misrepresented; and I have very occasionally been forewarned against the possibility of defamation or political indiscretion.

The first volume covers the period from the beginning of the diary in 1930 until the outbreak of war. A second volume will deal with the war years, and a third with the years from 1945 to 1964. When the last volume has been published, the whole original diary will be deposited in the library of Balliol College, Oxford, at Harold Nicolson's request and with the consent of the Master and Fellows.

[1] on p. 357.

II

These pages are, I believe, of historical importance in the picture they give of literary, political and social London in the 1930's. But they also form the portrait of a marriage.

When they were apart, Harold Nicolson and V. Sackville-West wrote to each other every day, from the time of their engagement in 1911 until her death in 1962, and each kept all the other's letters. His side of the correspondence was not simply a repetition of the diary, although he typed the letter each morning immediately after completing his journal of the day before. The letter was often a longer or more vivid description of the same events. He would elaborate the incidents which he knew would amuse her, and abbreviate, except in moments of great crisis, the purely political record, adding the usual domestic details about his health, the garden or the times of trains. I have used the letters to supplement the diary, and having had the happy choice between them, I have chosen the more illuminating. Occasionally I have added one of her replies in order to suggest the unbroken rhythm of strophe and antistrophe in their correspondence, and to indicate the effect of his letters on her and of hers on him.

V. Sackville-West was not, however, a good letter-writer, at least to her husband. While he would write to her with the tone and almost at the speed of conversation, she in her replies was curiously constrained. She was unable to match his exuberance, and was humbly shy of the comparative dullness of her life. 'Another quiet day at Sissinghurst' became a family joke in which she shared. From her letters I have usually chosen those which suddenly caught fire with excitement or indignation, but these moods were rarely communicated. It was much more often a brief recital of who had come, what she had read (never what she had written) and what plants had blossomed. If none of her other writings had survived, she would have been judged from these letters as gentle but rather colourless, like the shadow of a flower. I am very conscious that she does not emerge from this volume as she really was, but to have included more of her letters would only have deepened the false impression that they give.

Others knew her much better than I did. She kept private from her family whole sides of her life and nature. We would tease her by saying that we only really knew what she was thinking when we opened her latest novel. We never tried to penetrate her privacy, and she never demanded confidences from her sons, telling us that filial affection was something that grew with independence, and could be killed by forced intimacy. Our relationship became one of mutual trust and respect, but because there was an acknowledged reserve on each side, there could also be misunderstanding. An incident in the mid-1930's well illustrates what I mean. She paused one evening at the bottom step of her staircase, turned to me shyly, and said: 'I have written a new poem, and I would like to dedicate it to you.' 'Oh, don't do that', I replied unthinking. 'You know that I don't really understand your poetry.' She went up the tower without a word, and when she came to dinner I saw that she had been crying. By this incomparably cruel remark I had meant, 'Your poetry is the side of you that I have never shared, and cannot claim to share. I don't deserve the dedication. It would be a form of intrusion.' But that was not what I said, and she was as distressed by the heartlessness of my words as I was by the remorse which I immediately felt, and still feel, for having uttered them. I was then 17. Later, after the University, the war, politics and business had intervened, our mutual understanding increased. I was able to talk to her of things of which she had no experience, and she would be amused, as any biographer or novelist would be amused, to see a new casement opened on the foam of life. But still our relationship was one of reaching out with finger-tips to grasp what can only be grasped by the whole hand. Almost my last memory of her is when I arrived at Sissinghurst one summer evening in 1962 and she tried to rise from her chair to greet me (me, her son!), only to fall back in exhaustion. Two days later she died.

But my brother and I understood her better than we would reveal. We understood her masculinity, her enduring regret that she was not born a boy, a boy who would have inherited Knole (Knole was like a lover to her, and that is why houses and the idea of inheritance play such an important part in her books), a boy who would have been sent to schools and a University, who would have learned Greek and Latin, and of whom it would have been assumed throughout his life that he could do things which girls could not do. She believed that she had had to struggle for recognition more than a man. When a reviewer referred to her as an 'authoress' or 'poetess', she would raise her fists in the air with rage that was not diminished by our amusement. 'If I'm anything', she expostulated, 'I'm an *author*, a *poet*. Nobody ever talks about a "gardeness". Why on earth, then, a "poetess"?' Her strong masculinity came out in a number of ways: in her dislike of the institution (not the fact) of marriage, as if from that moment onwards the woman 'belonged' to the man—she never introduced Harold Nicolson as 'my husband', nor he her as 'my wife'; in the mettle of her character and the marked independence of her life; in her indifference to discomfort—she spent every penny she could spare on the garden at the expense of the house; and even in her dress, for in the last twenty years or more she always wore breeches and gaiters in winter and loose linen trousers in summer, and claimed that she did not even own an evening-dress. One was found in her wardrobe after her death: it dated from 1927.

But for all that she was a woman too. She had an extraordinary tenderness with people who were lonely or in trouble. She would show superhuman patience with those who became a burden to her, writing to them daily letters which she knew would only feed the appetite for more. And though she had a great gift for a few very intimate friendships, like that with Virginia Woolf, she found mere acquaintanceship difficult. She was shy, feeling ill at ease in the company of clever people unless she had known them for years, and she hated 'society' with a loathing that was partly due to her contempt for its superficiality and the need to dress up, but also because (as she wrote of a character in one of her novels) she feared that she would not be able to catch the ball when it was thrown in her direction. She became increasingly devoted to her garden, her books and her few close friends. If she were obliged to come to London, she would stay there for the shortest possible time, taking the last and most uncomfortable train rather than endure a night away from home.

V. Sackville-West was well aware that although she looked in with resentment at the world of men, she had no real desire to share it. Politics and business did not interest her. Nor had she the gift of logical reasoning. In her prose works the development of a story was as nicely balanced as a pendulum; in her poetry she could always find the surprising but inevitable word. But when she turned these gifts to examine the everyday world, they deserted her. The simplicity of her reactions rendered her almost inarticulate. She would repeat over and over again certain basic beliefs: God must be either a knave or a fool; the trouble with the world is its lack of compassion; Germans are always dangerous; aeroplanes always crash; Churchill is the greatest man of our times; the monarchy is our most valuable institution. But if one attempted to apply these ideas to any current situation (that aeroplanes, for example, are shown statistically to be less lethal than motor-cars), she was not really interested, and it was unkind to pursue the subject further.

Shortly after her death I found in a locked cupboard a seventy-two page autobiography which she had written at the age of 28. 'July 23rd, 1920', it begins. 'I start writing, having spent no consideration upon this task. Shall I ever complete it? and under what circumstances? begun as it is in the margin between a wood and a ripe cornfield, with the faint shadow of grasses and ears of corn falling across my page. Unkernelled nuts hang behind me along the fringe of the wood; I lie on green bracken, among little yellow and magenta wild-flowers whose names I don't know. I lie so close to the ground that my only view is of tall corn, so crisp that in the breeze it stirs with a noise like the rustle of silk.' She wrote of her girlhood at Knole:

> I made a great deal of being hardy, and as like a boy as possible. I know I was cruel to other children, because I remember stuffing their nostrils with putty and beating a little boy with stinging-nettles, and I lost nearly all my friends in that kind of way, until none of the local children would come to tea with me except those who acted as my allies and lieutenants ... I was always grubby and in tatters; my dogs, absorbingly adored; my rabbits, who were used to 'course' in secret with my dogs, and whose offspring I used to throw over the garden wall when they became too numerous; the trenches I dug in the garden during the war[1]; the 'army' I raised and commanded among the terrorised children of the neighbourhood; my khaki suit, and the tears of rage I shed because I was not allowed to have it made with trousers—no, not so much as a proper kilt; my first play, whose rehearsal was remorselessly scattered by Mother after all my pocket-money had gone in muslin. All this, I suppose, made my childhood very much like that of other children, but to me it stands out now so vivid, that I see myself in the garden, feel the familiar cut of my pocket-knife into the wooden table of the summer-house where I did my lessons; see the little cart into which I used to harness three ill-assorted dogs; see myself plain, lean, dark, unsociable, unattractive —horribly unattractive!—rough and secret.

This was the South African War. She was born at Knole in 1892.

She was an only child. Her mother, Lady Sackville, whom she was later to describe so sympathetically in *Pepita*, frightened her because she knew that she disappointed her, and with her father, a quiet, conscientious, country gentleman, she felt more at ease. They shared a distaste for weekend parties, and she would escape to the attics, to write:

When I was about twelve I started to write (it was *Cyrano de Bergerac* that first initiated me to the possibilities of literature!), and I never stopped writing after that—historical novels, pretentious, quite uninteresting, pedantic, and all written at an unflagging speed: the day after one was finished, another would be begun. I think that between the ages of thirteen and nineteen I must have been quite dreadful. I was plain, priggish, studious (oh very!), totally uninspired, unmanageably and lankily tall—in fact, the only good thing that could be said of me was that I wouldn't have anything to do with my kind. Seeing that I was unpopular (and small wonder, for a saturnine prig), I wouldn't court popularity. I minded rather, and used to cry when I went to bed after coming home from a party, but I made myself defiant about it. I don't mean this to sound in the least pathetic; I wasn't unhappy, only solitary, but I don't pretend that I minded solitude, I rather chose it. (Looking back, I think I maligned myself rather by calling myself totally uninspired: I had flaring days, oh yes, I did, I did!, when I thought I was going to electrify the world; it was like being drunk, and I can find traces of it now in the margins of all those ponderous, interminable books I wrote—two little letters, V.E., which stood for 'very easy', and I look at them now, and re-read the leaden stuff which they are supposed to qualify, and take on trust that those moments were full of splendour.)

In 1910, when she was aged 18, she first met Harold Nicolson:

I 'came out'—a distasteful and unsuccessful process—but the death of Edward VII saved me many festivities. Thus can the tragedies of great Kings be turned to the uses of little people. It was just then, however, that I first met Harold. He arrived late at a small dinner-party before a play, very young and alive and charming, and the first remark I ever heard him make was, 'What fun!', when he was asked by his hostess to act as host. Everything was fun to his energy, vitality and buoyancy. I liked his irrepressible brown

Lady Sackville in 1905,
by J. S. Sargent

Vita Sackville-West and her parents, Lord
and Lady Sackville, at Knole in 1911

curls, his laughing eyes, his charming smile, and his boyishness. But we didn't become particular friends. I think he looked upon me as more of a child than I actually was, and as for myself I never thought about people, especially men, under a very pleasant aspect unless they made friendly advances to me first.

They became engaged during 1911, at first secretly, and were married in the chapel at Knole in October 1913. After a honeymoon in Italy and Egypt, they went to live in Constantinople, where Harold Nicolson was serving in the British Embassy.

For sheer joy of companionship, I think the years that followed were unparalleled or at least unsurpassed. I was really gentle, self-sacrificing; I was *too* good, if anything. We were a sort of by-word for happiness and union. We never tired of one another. God, how we adored one another! Harold was like a sunny harbour to me. It was all open, frank, certain. . . .

The correct and adoring young wife of the brilliant young diplomat came back to England in June 1914. I remember a divine voyage by sea from Constantinople to Marseilles, through the Aegean, a second honeymoon. Then we went to Knole. War was declared on the 4th August, and Ben was born on the 6th. We spent the winter in London and I became quite sociable. I was, in fact, thoroughly tamed. That was the only period of my life when I achieved anything like popularity. I was no longer plain, I took adequate trouble to make myself agreeable, Harold was loved by everyone who met him—we were, in fact, a nice young couple to ask out to dinner. Oh God, the horror of it!

Harold Nicolson was exempted from war-service because of his work in the Foreign Office, and they passed the war-years in their house at 182 Ebury Street in Pimlico, and at Long Barn, the cottage they bought at Sevenoaks-Weald, near Knole.

In our personal life there was nothing except moving to London for the winter, to the cottage for the summer, watching Ben grow and learn to speak, and for me, writing. I should think it was hardly possible for two people to be more completely and unquestionably happy. There was never a cloud, never a squabble. I knew that if Harold died, I should die too; it all made life very simple. In the winter Nigel was born.[1]

[1] On 19th January, 1917, at Ebury Street.

These extracts from her scribbled autobiography reveal better than anything what sort of person V. Sackville-West was, although she was not yet thirty when she wrote it. They reveal in particular the quality and depth of her love for Harold Nicolson. They were, on the face of it, wholly unsuited to each other. She was anti-social, passionate, romantic, secret and undomesticated. He was gay, immensely sociable, ambitious, phil-Hellenistic and profoundly interested in the ways and politics of the world. In a sense she was the stronger character of the two. When distressed, she would grow harder, he softer. She could be intimidating. Almost from the moment of their first meeting it was evident that the differences in their characters would lead either to early disaster or to one of the strangest and most successful unions that two gifted people have ever enjoyed. There was a crisis in their relationship in 1920, but the narrowness of their escape frightened both of them, and from that moment onwards their concern for each other became the dominating thought of their lives. It would not be true to say that they were unhappy whenever apart, but the moment of reunion was for each of them the light at the end of the street. When that moment came, their pleasure was not demonstrative. An on-looker might have thought it no more than contentment at being together again. When alone, they did not talk profoundly or cleverly; theirs was no Webb or Sitwell relationship. They talked about the events of the last week or the next week, about the garden or the children or the dogs. Harold Nicolson would sometimes discuss the book that he was writing or reviewing; she almost never. In the letter which he would write her next day on returning to London, he would say what he had not felt able to say to her directly, and she would sometimes reply in the same key. 'When with each other', he wrote, 'we relax completely. Thus we get the maximum satisfaction out of a static relationship. Yet our relations are also dynamic. We stimulate each other. . . . I think it is the perfect adjustment between these two elements, the static and the dynamic, which creates such harmony in our lives.'[1] And then again: 'Viti is not a person one can take for granted. She is a dark river moving deeply in shadows. She really does not care for the domestic affections. She would wish life to be conducted on a series of *grandes passions*. Or she thinks she would. In practice, had I been a passionate man, I should have suffered

[1] See page 92.

tortures of jealousy on her behalf, have made endless scenes, and we should now have separated, I living in Montevideo as H.M. Minister and she breeding Samoyeds in the Gobi desert.'[1] Two years later he wrote to her: 'My faith (in life and integrity and human nature) is something which you alone really understand, and to replenish which I rush to you like a petrol-filling station. We never talk about it, since we never talk about the really vital links between us. But that is where you help.'[2]

III

Harold Nicolson was by temperament an aristocrat. So was V. Sackville-West, but she had been sickened by the ostentation of life at Knole during her girlhood, feeling it to be a betrayal of the house, and she came to despise what she had no wish to share. He, on the other hand, never rejected his upbringing. He was born in 1886 in Tehran, Persia, the third son of Sir Arthur Nicolson (later Lord Carnock) who was then Chargé d'Affaires of the British Legation. Sir Arthur, as Harold Nicolson wrote in his biography of his father, was 'neither imaginative nor intellectual: he was merely intelligent, honest, sensible, high-minded and fair'. His mother, Catherine Rowan Hamilton, a younger sister of the Vicereine Lady Dufferin, 'although descended from one of the most excessive of Irish rebels, was herself a gentle little loyalist'. Thus although there was no literary tradition in his parentage, there was a very strong sense of patriotic duty, and this he absorbed. His boyhood and early youth were spent in his father's legations and embassies at Constantinople, Sofia, Tangier, Madrid and St Petersburg, or at the great Ulster houses of his mother's relations while on holiday from his private school at Folkestone, from Wellington College and from Balliol. Only at the last of these did he become happy and industrious. He achieved only a Third, but it was at Balliol that he learned to work and began to sense the power and pleasure of literature and friendship. In 1909 he passed into the Foreign Office second only to Eustace Percy in the most competitive examination of the day, and in the next year he met V. Sackville-West.

His first impact on her has already been described in her own words. He was, and remained, the most companionable of men. 'Only one

[1] See p. 158.   [2] p. 267.

person in a thousand is a bore', he once said to me, 'and he is interesting because he is one person in a thousand.' This maxim may give the false impression that he was unselective in his choice of friends, but it is true in the sense that he found other people's shop-talk fascinating for a short while, and that he would take great pleasure in identifying the quirks of human behaviour, the conceits and other small touches that betray class or profession or culture. I remember him standing at the window of a London nursing-home where I was recovering from an operation in 1933, and describing to me in a brilliant running-commentary the actions of a man getting out of a taxi in the street below. From my bed I could imagine not only the scene exactly, but the character and whole background of this unfortunate stranger, and I became suddenly aware of what I had always assumed, his amused outlook on the world, and his gift, his impulse, to nail down fleeting impressions in words, almost as if they had not happened until recorded.

This small incident also illustrated for me the standards that he applied in his judgement of people. He naturally believed them to be the highest, the only possible, standards. He summarised them in describing the character of the ideal diplomatist in his *Diplomacy*[1]: 'Truth, accuracy, calm, patience, good temper, modesty, loyalty. "But", the reader may object, "you have forgotten intelligence, knowledge, discernment, prudence, hospitality, charm, industry, courage and even tact." I have not forgotten them. I have taken them for granted.' They are an amalgam of the Greek, Roman and European 18th-century virtues, and the man in the taxi, when measured against this formidable scale, did not emerge a hero, for there was something missing from the list—sympathy.

In the facile sense Harold Nicolson was a most sympathetic person. He was generous, affable to the young and shy, and he had a capacity for pity. The account of his association with the Lindberghs, for example, is among the most compassionate sections of this volume, and he would take endless trouble over misfits. He was something of a sentimentalist. He would say, 'He is a dear man', when he did not think so at all. But he was not always very charitable. He knew that he belonged to an élite, an élite more of intelligence and achievement than of birth, and he tended to feel that people outside that élite had something wrong with them: business-men, for example, the humbler type of schoolmaster or clergyman, most women, actors, most

[1] Oxford University Press. 1939.

24

Americans, Jews, all coloured or Levantine peoples, and the great mass of the middle and working classes. Dullness or duplicity of mind irritated him. He felt sorry for them, but he had no real wish to understand them, and a single false note in their conversation or even their pronunciation, an ugly ornament on the mantelpiece, a doily under the plate or a grapefruit on it, were enough to render them uninteresting to him and he could suddenly turn cold. Until I read his diaries and letters I never imagined that he was even aware of this trait. But there is a passage describing his meeting in Pittsburgh with some foolish American women in which he analyses it precisely:

It was not merely that I had a longing to contradict them, [he wrote to his wife that night]; it was also that I was conscious of a temptation to cause pain. When I feel that angry sword within me, I understand why people think I am a cruel person. I could have smashed and bashed their silly heads. I merely sat there glum and silent. I know that it might be possible to excuse my feelings in terms of intellectual impatience or hatred of the sham. But it was more than that. It was something almost brutal which rose up in me. I feel rather ashamed of it looking back. But I see that there is in me a vein of intellectual brigandage, a rather mean little hawk swooping on the doves, and it is that, I think, of which people like Hugh Walpole are conscious and which gives the impression that I am unkind. I must try to work it out of my system. It is not a pretty thing.[1]

With people whose tastes he shared and who stimulated him, he was the most entrancing companion. 'Buoyancy' was V. Sackville-West's word, and it is a good one. He would aerate the conversation by the quickness and unexpectedness of his turns of phrase, his use of analogy and allusion, his extraction of the maximum pleasure from every situation and idea, his skill as a raconteur, his enjoyment of giving and receiving new information, his sense of urgency and of fun. He was dubbed witty and urbane, and though he grew to hate the latter word, both were apt. When, for example, an earnest American reporter asked him whether he and V. Sackville-West had ever collaborated on anything, he replied, poker-faced, 'Yes, we have two sons.'[2] In answer to Cyril Joad, who asked him in 1938 whether he did not agree that Neville Chamberlain's mind had broadened recently, he said, 'Yes, in the same way that a darning-needle is broader than a sewing-needle.'

[1] See pp. 189–90. [2] p. 140.

I was in the same car at the time, and I can remember Joad's shout of laughter, 'Oh *how* I wish I had said that!' Several people subsequently did, and Harold Nicolson achieved the flattering but somewhat unenviable reputation as a performer, enhanced by his popular wireless talks and articles. As a guest he was usually expected to take the conversational lead. But he knew when to shut up. He was never in any sense a comic. He had an acute sense of occasion, and his diplomatic training made him alert to changes of conversational gears and variations of speed. As a host he was curiously nervous, being clumsy at the practical things of life and needing a ready-made frame and canvas for the full display of his talents.

Those who knew him only as a broadcaster (the majority of English people in the period covered by this volume) thought of him as more of a dilettante than he really was. He was fundamentally a serious man. His knowledge of literature and foreign policy was professional. As an author he was an expert craftsman; as a journalist he was meticulous and punctual. His political beliefs were deep-rooted. He worked, always, extremely hard, finding his greatest pleasure in *la difficulté vaincue* (a phrase of Alain which he often quoted to his sons), despising those who made no use or bad use of their time equally with those who disdained the company of other people because they had too much to do. But although there can be no question that as a writer and diplomatist he was preeminent, as a politician he never quite found his feet. This brings me to the second of the two failings to which he would on occasion admit.

He was politically rather soft, or, as a friend put it, 'too fastidious and too critical to have the essential faculty of belief in democracy'.[1] 'I lack a lust for battle', he wrote to Robert Boothby; 'I have no combative qualities.'[2] He would even claim that he lacked ambition, but this was not quite true. His attitude to it is best summed up in one of the few pieces of advice that he remembered receiving from his father: 'Never ask for a job, and never refuse one.' His unusual upbringing and early career abroad had cut him adrift from his own countrymen. The only England he knew was the world of weekend parties, exclusive luncheons, Bloomsbury and the Travellers Club. He had never known Leicester, nor any other town like it, when he became its Member in 1935. He was ill at ease at its social functions and working men's clubs, and only really came to know his constituents

[1]See p. 205. [2]p. 402

26

when he quarrelled with them over Chamberlain's policy of appeasement. Then he felt despair that they should comprehend so little. He should have been the Member for one of the University seats, or gone to the House of Lords. He was never a party-man. He was very willing to accept leadership, but he could not decide for more than short periods at a time which leaders to follow, and he could never bring himself to believe that loyalty is among the chief of the political virtues, nor that of two opinions on an issue one was bound to be wrong. In the House of Commons, though personally very popular and respected for his knowledge and intelligence, he was regarded as a brilliant man gone astray, as a dissenter without the pugnacity to press home his dissent. He found himself instinctively drawn to rebels, perhaps because they were men in whom he recognised qualities which he lacked and because they cut across the party lines. But when they became fierce, he became nervous, and tried to mollify their excesses. There is one passage in his diary which is so typical of him that I laughed aloud with remembered affection when I first read it. He was talking to Sir Oswald Mosley in 1931 about the new 'trained and disciplined force' by which Mosley intended to bolster up his crumbling New Party. 'We discuss their uniforms', the diary records. 'I suggest grey flannel trousers and shirts.'[1]

With his family he was invariably gentle and affectionate. All the worries of the London week would be smoothed out when he returned home. His recitation of events would be touched by that self-depreciatory humour that he reserved for us; and our intimate attention, though we could contribute little to his ideas, would stimulate them afresh. This process of unwinding would take perhaps an hour, and then with the inevitable phrase 'Well, I must go and work', he would shut himself up in his room, pull out the typewriter and write steadily till dinner-time. His life at Long Barn and at Sissinghurst was regulated like clockwork. Breakfast at 9, work from 9.30 till 1, an hour's reading after lunch and then gardening, followed by a further two hours' work before dinner, and an early bed. It was a perfect life. As the other three of us were also reading and writing throughout most of the day, our shared industry seemed to multiply the available hours by four, and we would meet at mealtimes, without, I hope, any overt signs of self-satisfaction, to compare notes.

His attitude to his sons was one of open enthusiasm for anything that

[1] See p. 91.

27

we were doing. He read, for instance, the whole of Aeschylus' *Seven Against Thebes* because it was my set-book at school. He hired a boat to visit the islands which I bought in the Outer Hebrides. He encouraged us to discuss with him anything that amused, interested or worried us. I once wrote to him from Eton about the problem of switching from surname to Christian-name terms with my close friends. He replied from the United States in a six-page letter of advice, the gist of which was to smother the explosive word: 'Don't begin by saying, "James, have you borrowed my Latin dictionary?" Say, "Oh by the way, James, have you borrowed my Latin dictionary?" ' This was exactly the sort of small problem that delighted him. He always claimed that it was impossible for a father to transmit experience, but in fact he did so, for his advice was always very practical, and by understanding the exact nuances of our dilemmas, he dissipated them. Mixed with our deep affection for him was growing admiration, for in time we tried to do what he did, writing and speaking and organising, and realised that what came to us stodgily, to him was as effortless as ping-pong balls dancing on a fountain at a fair.

What I think we failed to appreciate was his adventurousness. Reading these diaries, all of which cover a period which I remember well, for I was already nearly 13 when the first page was written, I understood for the first time what risks our parents took—his resignation from the Foreign Office, exchanging their comfortable house near Sevenoaks for the ruined castle at Sissinghurst, renouncing the allowance which Lady Sackville owed them as a legal right—and in many other ways their lives were boldly creative. Perhaps the best example of it is the garden at Sissinghurst, where they found nothing except some old apple-trees when they bought the place in 1930, and before the outbreak of war had created one of the largest and most imaginative gardens in England, which is still improving with maturity. All this they did during a period of continual financial strain and desperately hard work. It did not occur to them to save, nor even to economise. Their investment was in present extravagance for future enjoyment. They lived hand-to-mouth until Lady Sackville's death in 1936 made them financially secure, and though they worried, they never for one moment despaired. Nor did they ever falter. 'It's the things that you haven't done that you regret in life', Harold Nicolson was fond of saying to us: 'never the things that you have done.' Though he was conscious that a more careful man would have organised his life differently, he felt no remorse. When he reached the age of fifty, he wrote in his diary:

'I have dispersed my energies in life, done too many different things, and have no sense of reaching any harbour. I am still very promising and shall continue to be so until the day of my death. But what enjoyment and what interest I have derived from my experience! I suppose that I am too volatile and fluid. But few people can have extracted such happiness from fluidity, and when I look back upon my life, it is as gay as an Alpine meadow patinated with the stars of varied flowers. Would I feel happier if I had stuck to a single crop of lucerne or clover? NO.[1]'

IV

In the 1920's Harold Nicolson rapidly climbed the diplomatic scale. He had served on the British Delegation to the Paris Peace Conference in 1919, and for his work there and on the League of Nations he was awarded the C.M.G. at the unusually early age of 34. In the same year, 1920, he wrote his first book, a biography of *Paul Verlaine*, at the suggestion of Michael Sadleir of Constable's. From 1920 to 1925 he was back with the Foreign Office in London, and found time to write a novel, *Sweet Waters* (1921), and three literary biographies, *Tennyson* (1923), *Byron, the Last Journey* (1924) and *Swinburne* (1926). In 1925 he went to Tehran as Counsellor, returning to the very building where he had been born. In 1927 he joined the Embassy in Berlin as its second-ranking official. In the interregnum between two Ambassadors, he became Chargé d'Affaires.

V. Sackville-West did not go with him to his foreign posts. Great as was their distress at being separated for such long periods, even greater was her horror of exile and of the social role that she would be expected to play. She remained at Long Barn, writing, writing, writing. Her first book, a three-act drama on the life and death of Chatterton, had been privately printed as early as 1909 when she was 17, but it was not until 1917 that she achieved genuine publication with *Poems of West and East*.[2] Her first novel, *Heritage*,[3] was published in 1919, and several more followed in quick succession in the early 1920's.

[1] See pp. 288. [2] John Lane, the Bodley Head. [3] Collins.

In 1926 came *The Land*,[1] her long poem (awarded the Hawthornden Prize) which she wrote partly at Long Barn and partly in Persia:

> *That moon, that star, above my English weald,*
> *Hung at that hour, and I not there to see.*

It was in Persia, where she joined Harold Nicolson for two short holidays, that she found her greatest happiness abroad and much of the inspiration for her two gardens. I remember the orange labels, *Passenger to Tehran*, dangling from her luggage in the hall: I can see her now at her sitting-room table at Long Barn writing *The Land*, looking up over her spectacles as we burst in, patient with our interruption, but closing the blotter on the manuscript, which only now, forty years later, have I seen for the first time. I remember above all the visits from and to Virginia Woolf at the period when *Orlando* was in its crucible, visits that even to a child were full of drama, for she would cross-question us about our simple lives, and hand back, glittering, what we had imparted so dully. ('What happened this morning?' 'Well, after breakfast ...' 'No, no, no. Start at the beginning. What woke you up?' 'The sun.' 'What sort of sun?' And so on. It became a game, but it was really a lesson.) The whole time the letters flowed nose to tail between Kent and Persia, the first arriving as the twentieth was being written, passing an equivalent stream flowing through Moscow in the opposite direction.

H.N. TO V.S-W.   *28th June, 1926*
                                                         Gulahek, Persia

I added a scribble to my letter on Saturday (No. 48) to say that Raymond[2] had arrived. I showed him the article-thing I had done for my new book.[3] He said that I must rewrite it, as it read like A. P. Herbert or A. A. Milne. My buoyancy will have to come to the rescue.

---

[1] Heinemann.   [2] Raymond Mortimer, then aged 31.

[3] This was the origin of *Some People* (Constable. 1927). It was only with the greatest difficulty that V.S-W. persuaded him not to cancel publication when the proofs arrived. He thought the book unbearably trivial, and likely to harm his diplomatic career.

H.N. TO N.N. *(aged 9)*   *16th July, 1926*
                                                      Gulahek, Persia

I do hope that you won't make Mummy nervous by being too wild. Of course men must work and women must weep, but all the same, I hope you will remember that Mummy is a frightful coward and does fuss dreadfully about you. It is a good rule always to ask before you do anything awfully dangerous. Thus if you say, 'Mummy, may I try and walk on the roof of the greenhouse on my stilts?', she will probably say, 'Of course, darling', since she is not in any way a narrow-minded woman. And if you say, 'Mummy, may I light a little fire in my bed?' she will again say, 'Certainly, Nigel'. It is only that she likes being asked about these things beforehand.

H.N. TO V.S-W.   *21st July, 1926*
                                                      Gulahek, Persia

Today is the Achoura, the feast, that is, of the martyrdom of Hussein. It dawned like other days, a pearl light among the plane trees flushing to pink and then to gold. I bathed early, and we left at 7. At the northern end of the great square we could hear a confused murmur, and at 8 o'clock the front ranks of a procession could be seen with wide banners half in black shade and half in glaring sun. A flute began to play a strange Theocritean elegy like the lament for Adonis. It was answered by a sinister drum. The procession swayed forward, like a Breton funeral. Then suddenly the whole movement and colour altered from a sedate slow-moving block to rhythmic agitated naked forms. A group of butter-coloured torsos, thin and muscular, their palms beating in unison flat upon their breasts.

Out they jerked into the sunlight, and then, the pace quickening to a crescendo, there was a culminating yell and a hundred swords flashed in the sun. Bald and shaven heads spurted with blood: they raised their left hands and smeared the blood over their faces—great gobbets of it splashed upon their white aprons. They were followed by half-naked flagellists. They must have begun earlier to cut themselves, as their white robes were crimson to the foot, not splashed as previously, but a scarlet wet dabble. Three or four collapsed as they passed us. The sweet hot smell of blood came up

31

to us in warm eddies. The flutes died away into the street. It was silent again except for the cooing of doves. It was nice to return to the clear cool garden at Gulahek.

V.S-W. TO H.N.   *28th October, 1927*
Long Barn

I have had Virginia [Woolf] here all day, and she has just gone. We had fun this morning. We went up to Knole and chose pictures for *Orlando*. We chose obscure pictures, out of which we will take bits. That book sounds more fantastic the more I hear of it!

By that time Harold Nicolson had moved to Berlin, where in two years he achieved a position that promised a brilliant future in diplomacy. Instead, he decided to resign. As it was the major turning-point in his life and the immediate preface to the diary that follows, his decision needs some explanation.

Fundamentally, the reason was the enforced separation, for years on end, between two people who loved each other deeply. One of them would have to give up his or her way of life before they could be permanently reunited. As V. Sackville-West would have been as unhappy as a caged lark if she had been forced into the diplomatic life, the sacrifice would have to be made by him. But it was not quite so much of a sacrifice as all that. He loved his work, and he knew that it would be regarded by his friends in the Foreign Service as a betrayal to leave it at the age of 43. The next step in his profession would logically be Minister in a minor Legation, with the certainty of an Embassy at the end of his career. He did not, however, particularly desire this. He genuinely hated the pomp of high position, and the interest of the work would be little greater than that which he had already enjoyed in Tehran and Berlin. If he could be brought home as head of a department of the Foreign Office in London, that would provide a temporary solution, but the problem would arise again, perhaps in an acuter form, within a few years. V. Sackville-West, because she was so much else, was not adaptable to the role of Ambassadress. Friends in England, notably Virginia and Leonard Woolf, told him that he was wasting his talents. He should be a writer; or he should enter politics. They advised a clean break with his past, and he was impressed by their argument.

Benedict and Nigel Nicolson with their parents at Long Barn, 1929

*Long Barn, two miles from Knole, the house where the Nicolsons
lived from 1915 until 1930*

Returning to Berlin from leave in June 1929, he found a letter from V. Sackville-West which was among the most heart-broken that she ever wrote:

V.S-W. TO H.N. *25th June, 1929*
Long Barn

What is so torturing when I leave you at these London stations and drive off, is the knowledge that you are *still there*—that, for half an hour or three-quarters of an hour, I could still return and find you; come up behind you, take you by the elbow, and say 'Hadji'.

I came straight home, feeling horribly desolate and sad, driving down that familiar and dreary road. I remembered Rasht and our parting there; our parting at Victoria when you left for Persia; till our life seemed made up of partings, and I wondered how long it would continue.

Then I came round the corner on to the view—our view—and I thought how you loved it, and how simple you were, really, apart from your activity; and how I loved you for being both simple and active in one and the same person.

Then I came home, and it was no consolation at all. You see, when I am unhappy for other reasons, the cottage is a real solace to me; but when it is on account of *you* that I am unhappy (because you have gone away), it is an additional pang—it is the same place, but a sort of mockery and emptiness hangs about it—I almost wish that just *once* you could lose me and then come straight back to the cottage and find it still full of me but empty of me, then you would know what I go through after you have gone away.

Anyhow, you will say, it is worse for you who go back to a horrible and alien city, whereas I stay in the place we both love so much: but really, Hadji, it is no consolation to come back to a place full of coffee-cups[1]—there was a cardboard-box lid, full of your rose-petals, still on the terrace.

You are dearer to me than anybody ever has been or ever could be. If you died suddenly, I should kill myself as soon as I had made provision for the boys. I really mean this. I could not live

[1] The empty coffee-cup which one finds on the table after saying goodbye to a much-loved guest. Hence any sad reminder of this sort.

if I lost you. I do not think one could conceive of a love more exclusive, more tender, or more pure than I have for you. I think it is immortal, a thing which happens seldom.

Darling, there are not many people who would write such a letter after sixteen years of marriage, yet who would be saying therein only one-fiftieth of what they were feeling as they wrote it. I sometimes try to tell you the truth, and then I find that I have no words at my command which could possibly convey it to you.

I believe that it was this letter, out of many thousands, that made up his mind. He often referred to it later. But there were other reasons. He had come to hate Berlin, particularly its Sundays, when his walks between the sad pines of the Tiergarten accentuated his loneliness. And then there was the current row with Lady Sackville. Her always impetuous nature had suddenly turned sour. She accused her daughter and son-in-law of the most dreadful crimes, attempting inexcusably to gain the support of her young grandsons for her campaign of calumny against their parents. She said that the Nicolsons had stolen her money, her jewels, her furniture; that they had not allowed her wreath to be placed on Lord Sackville's grave; that she was ruined by having to pay their debts. She wrote these things to all their friends, but as she simultaneously told them that the house which she intended to build at Streatham would be 20-foot higher than St Paul's, it is not surprising that she was not believed. But Harold Nicolson came to the conclusion that peace could not be restored unless they cut themselves off financially from her. Under a trust-settlement, Lady Sackville was paying her daughter £1,600 a year, and it was this that they were now determined to renounce. They could not possibly afford to do so on Harold Nicolson's salary as a civil servant. He must find a better-paid job in London.

For all these reasons cumulatively, he was receptive to an invitation which he suddenly received from Lord Beaverbrook, through Bruce Lockhart, on 22nd July, 1929. 'Beaverbrook', wrote Lockhart, 'is looking for a man of your ability and your knowledge of men and affairs, and would offer a very considerable inducement for his services. His job would be to write and edit a page like the Londoner's Diary in the *Evening Standard*. I have already suggested your name to Beaverbrook, and he would be glad to "capture" you.' The salary would be £3,000 a year, which could be supplemented by outside literary work.

It was a very tempting offer. For two months, in their daily exchange of letters, they examined it from every angle:

H.N. TO V.S-W.   *26th August, 1929*
                                     British Embassy, Berlin

You say in your letter that Ernest Gye[1] must have upset me by telling me not to leave the Service. No, my sweet, my perplexities and hesitations are deeper than that. You see, diplomacy really does give me leisure to do literary work of my own, and it *does* have advantages such as leave, nice people etc. Moreover (and this is the essential point), if I stay in diplomacy I am certain of being 'successful', or in other words of getting to the top. You say, with justice, that it is not a very glorious top. I quite agree. Yet I have sufficient knowledge of human nature to realise that it is more satisfactory to succeed on a small scale than to fail on a big one. If I end up as Ambassador, I shall always feel (and say) what a wonderful career I could have made for myself in the open market. But if I climb down into the open market and then fail to make good there, I shall regret bitterly not having remained in my armchair and ended as an Ambassador. I shall feel that I was absolutely mad to chuck a certainty for an uncertainty.

Naturally I put against this (i) B.M.[2]; (ii) being separated from you. In the end these two factors will probably be determinant. Whatever decision I take will not have been taken without hours and hours of very anxious thought. If I were ten years younger, the whole thing would be different.

Next day he wrote to Sir Ronald Lindsay, who had been his Ambassador in Berlin until 1928 and was now Permanent Under Secretary of State at the Foreign Office. He told him what was passing through his mind, and Lindsay replied that he must make his own decision. He came home on his last leave in September, and then the decision was taken. He accepted Lord Beaverbrook's offer, not without strong misgivings. He had the *Evening Standard* and *Daily Express* posted to him in Berlin, in order to accustom himself to his new life and outlook. Already he was appalled.

---

[1] Ernest Gye entered the Foreign Office in 1903, and became Minister in Tangier 1933-36.
[2] 'Bonne Mama'. Their name for Lady Sackville.

35

H.N. TO V.S.-W. *14th November, 1929*
British Embassy, Berlin

I have been reading three-days-worth of the *Express* and *Standard*.
They really fill me with alarm. I shall simply be unable to write
the sort of sob-stuff they want. They seem to have an unerring eye
for just the sort of thing I loathe. What shall I do in such a *galère*?
I shall be thought high-brow and cloacal. For this I shall be glad
when my *Express* and *Standard* reach me by post in small doses.
I really feel ill when I consume a whole fid of them at a time.

But the decision was now irrevocable. His resignation had become
official. There were farewell parties, and he sold his car to the
Australian Ambassador. He packed up. On 20th December he finally
left Berlin, and twelve days later the diary begins.

May 1966 *Sissinghurst Castle,*
Kent

1930

H.N. leaves the Foreign Office and starts work with the 'Evening Standard' – Beaverbrook and Winston Churchill – with Ramsay MacDonald at Chequers – 'The Edwardians' – purchase of Sissinghurst Castle – G. B. Shaw – holiday in Italy – H. N.'s growing unhappiness in journalism – Cliveden and Oxford – Sir Oswald Mosley's New Party

On 20th December, 1929 Harold Nicolson returned to England from Berlin, where he had been Counsellor at the British Embassy since 1927. On 1st January, 1930 he joined the staff of the 'Evening Standard'. The diary therefore begins on the day when he abandoned his career in diplomacy for an occupation which he found increasingly distasteful. As the year advanced, his misgivings about his suitability for Fleet Street journalism grew to the point where his eventual resignation clearly became inevitable. His task was to write in collaboration with Robert Bruce Lockhart about fifteen paragraphs a day of social, political and literary gossip for the Londoner's Diary. He found it trivial and debasing. In addition, he soon began to write weekly book-reviews for the 'Daily Express', and to broadcast a series of topical talks for the B.B.C. under the title 'People and Things', which were to make him for the first time a nationally known figure. In the same year he published 'Lord Carnock', the biography of his father, which he had completed during his last few months in Berlin, but he did not embark upon any new book until 1932. At the back of his mind was the intention to enter politics, and each of the three major parties approached him in turn. In the end, he joined none of them, but opened his political career by standing as a candidate for Sir Oswald Mosley's New Party in 1931.

V. Sackville-West was writing 'The Edwardians', a novel based on memories of her girlhood at Knole. It was to become the greatest popular success of any book which either of them ever wrote. In the early months of 1930 she and Harold Nicolson stayed for most of the week in his chambers at 4 King's Bench Walk, Inner Temple, where he continued to live in London until after the end of the war. At weekends they returned to Long Barn, Sevenoaks-Weald, their small fifteenth-century house two miles from Knole. Because they were so often together, the letters exchanged between them during this period were few, and even the diary was scrappy compared to later years, perhaps because Harold Nicolson derived so little pleasure from his new life as Lord Beaverbrook's employee.

In January 1930 he was aged 43 and V. Sackville-West 37. Of their

39

two sons, Benedict (aged 15) was at Eton, and Nigel (12) at Summer Fields, Oxford.

DIARY   *1st January, 1930*

Saw the New Year in at Penns.[1] Ethel Sandys, Desmond MacCarthy,[2] Francis Birrell. We listen to the wireless and then to the notes of Big Ben. I feel glad that 1929 is over. Not a very happy year for me, since it has entailed being separated from Vita and living a rather hugger-mugger existence in Berlin. But there have been compensations. In the first place I have worked hard at father's book[3] and completed it before the year was out. In the second place I was able to perfect my knowledge of the German character: in other words, to make quite certain that I did not understand them in the least. In any case, for better or worse, the end of 1929 marks the end of my career as a diplomatist. What will 1930 bring? I shall try at least to keep a fuller diary and shall type it on single sheets and then get it bound. See how that works.

H.N. TO V.S-W.   *2nd January, 1930*
                                   Evening Standard, 47 Shoe Lane, E.C.4
Came up with Desmond MacCarthy who was very charming and full of talk. Rather too full of talk, as I wanted to do my lessons, which now consist in reading all the papers in the hope of finding a good paragraph. I suppose that I shall get into the way of finding these paragraphs leaping ready-armed to the mind. At present they are rather a bother to think of, rather a bother to write, and terribly feeble when written. But I shall settle down in time.

Got here soon after ten. Found Bruce Lockhart fussing about in a rush as usual. Rather like all this rush business. Read French and German newspapers. Wrote three paragraphs. Fiddled about.

DIARY   *8th January, 1930*
Work fruitlessly superficially futilely upon the Londoner's Diary. The difficulty is that the only news I get is from my friends and that is just the news that I can't publish.

---

[1] Penns-in-the-Rocks, Withyham, Sussex, which belonged to Dorothy Wellesley, the poet, later Duchess of Wellington.
[2] Editor of *Life and Letters*, and the foremost literary critic of the day.
[3] *Lord Carnock, A Study in the Old Diplomacy.* Constable. 1930. Carnock died in 1928.

Lunch with Sibyl Colefax.[1] The Rudyard Kiplings and the Lloyds[2] there, also the Oswald Birleys.[3] Rudyard Kipling's eyebrows are really very odd indeed. They curl up black and furious like the moustache of a Neapolitan tenor. He has a slightly Anglo-Indian voice, with notes of civil service precision in it, and his conversation is twisted into phrases like his writing. He spoke of Cecil Rhodes and [Theodore] Roosevelt. He admired them both. He assured me that Rhodes did not drink: he looked as if he did, but that was due to a weak heart.

DIARY   23rd January, 1930

I was to have dined with Gwen[4] but was summoned by Lord Beaverbrook and chucked. I arrived at Stornoway House to find him alone writing a cross letter to his son about bills. In a few minutes Winston Churchill slouched in. Very changed from when I had last seen him. A great round white face like a blister. Incredibly aged. Looks like pictures of Lord Holland. An elder statesman. His spirits also have declined and he sighs that he has lost his old fighting power.

They talk the whole time about Empire Free Trade. Winston says that he has abandoned all his convictions and clings to the conviction of free trade as the only one which is left to him. But he is clearly disturbed at the effect on the country of Beaverbrook's propaganda. He feels too old to fight it. 'Thirty years ago', he said, 'I should have welcomed such a combat: now I dread it.' He seems to think Baldwin[5] absolutely hopeless, and no instructions have been given to the provincial candidates and agents as to the line that decent Conservatives should adopt. It is quite clear that this Empire free trade is going to split the Conservative and possibly the Liberal Parties. Winston complains pitiably: 'But Max, Max, you are destroying my party.' Beaverbrook uses every wile to secure if not his support then at least his agreement not to oppose. Winston agrees to the exploitation of the crown colonies and to 'tariffs for negotiation', but he will not agree to

[1] Lady Colefax, who then lived at Argyll House, Chelsea, was a life-long friend of the Nicolsons. She and Lady Cunard were the two leading hostesses of literary and political London.
[2] The first Lord Lloyd, High Commissioner for Egypt and the Sudan, 1925–29.
[3] The portrait painter.
[4] H.N.'s younger sister, then Mrs St Aubyn, later Lady St Levan.
[5] Stanley Baldwin had been leader of the Conservative opposition since his defeat in the General Election of May 1929.

anything in the shape of a tax on food. He would prefer freight subsidies. Beaverbrook, I must say, is rather impressive. Young and nervous he walks about the room piling argument on argument and statistic on statistic. There is no question but that he is passionately sincere and has really studied his subject.

DIARY   22nd February, 1930

Motor down to Chequers with Vita. A lovely day. Arrive at 1.15 and met by Ishbel MacDonald—a sturdy sensible humorous lassie. The Prime Minister[1] appears in Lovat plus-fours carrying an axe in one hand and a log of wood in the other. Then the son[2] appears and we go in to luncheon. All very simple and cheerful. Look at the house afterwards and then go a walk with the P.M. up on to the downs. There is a walk there, called the Prime Minister's quarter-deck, from which one can see right away almost to Oxford. The P.M. inveighs against the neglect into which Baldwin has let the place fall. He loves it with passionate affection.

DIARY   27th February, 1930

Lunch with Desmond MacCarthy at Gatti's. He is reading Maurois' *Byron* and we discuss it. He tells me a story about Keir Hardie. Looking down on the 1905 House of Commons a friend remarked to him how few members there were from the working classes. 'Yes, it will take the British working man twenty years to learn to elect his equals to represent him. And then it will take him another twenty years not to elect his equals.' This is true. I saw it with Ramsay MacDonald the other day—his longing to get hold of the young university men. His feeling that the *cadets de bonne famille* were the people he wanted.

DIARY   4th March, 1930

Vita finishes her novel on the Edwardians.[3] We hear that Cookes, the poultry people, have bought Westwood, the farm next to Long Barn.

This development led rapidly to the decision to leave Long Barn, where they had lived since two years after their marriage seventeen years before. As it turned out, the threat to the neighbouring fields did not materialise,

[1] Ramsay MacDonald.   [2] Malcolm MacDonald.
[3] *The Edwardians.* Hogarth Press. 1930.

but the hint of it threw them into a panic. At first they tried to buy the fields, but the price was too high. So they began to search the Weald of Kent and Sussex for another house where they would be unmolested by chickens or commuters, and where they could make a new garden. They found Sissinghurst Castle.

The decision to buy Sissinghurst, at first more resolute on V. Sackville-West's side than on Harold Nicolson's, was extraordinarily bold. Their financial position, with little capital and two sons at expensive schools, was insecure, and the place was in ruin. There was not a single room which they could immediately occupy in what remained of a great Tudor and Elizabethan mansion, and the garden was worse than nonexistent: it was a rubbish dump. The castle had been deteriorating since the middle of the eighteenth century, when Horace Walpole described it as a 'house in ruins and a park in ten times greater ruins', and four years after his visit it was leased to the Government as a prison for French sailors captured during the Seven Years War. Sissinghurst never recovered from that experience. A large part of it was pulled down in about 1800, and the remaining buildings were used for nearly sixty years as the parish work-house. Since 1854 it had been a romantic, if neglected, adjunct to a farm. Some of the surviving buildings were used as stables and out-houses, others as makeshift dwellings for a few farm-labourers. But the sturdiness of the original construction, and the faded beauty of the great brick tower which rose from the centre of this battered compound, aroused all their adventurous feelings. They would buy the place; they would gradually make some of the buildings habitable; they would clear away the old wire-netting and rusted bedsteads, the nettles and the docks; and even if it took them years, they would make a garden between the isolated fragments of the house.

DIARY   *20th March, 1930*

Mrs Taylour has offered to sell us the whole of Westwood for £16,000. Vita wishes to offer her £13,000. I have my doubts. I feel that this occasion should be taken to leave Long Barn and that to spend all that money would be to hamper ourselves in the future. The whole thing together would represent a capital outlay of some £23,000 and for that sum we could obtain an almost perfect place anywhere else. Long Barn will not improve in amenity as the district gets built over, and it is neither architecturally nor in any other way really ideal. The great advantages of being near Knole and near London are now less important than they were.[1] And I do feel that we could find another place which would be more amusing for the boys and in the end more satisfactory to ourselves. On the other hand there is our affection for Long Barn and our disinclination to leave a place where we have been so happy for fifteen years. It is a great problem.

DIARY   26th March, 1930

On to the *Daily Express* office about books. I see an intolerable man who treats both me and literature as if they were dirt. I am so depressed by the squalor of this interview that I return home in a nerve-storm. To make it worse, I am sent out to represent the *Standard* at the Knights of the Round Table dinner. There is no seat for me and I creep away in dismay and humiliation. I never foresaw that writing for the Press would be actually so degrading. What I dread is that I may get to like it: the moment I cease to be unhappy about it will be the moment when my soul has finally been killed.

DIARY   4th April, 1930

Ben arrives back from Eton. I take him to lunch at the Savoy and then on to a movie of *Disraeli*. When we get home Vita telephones to say she has seen the ideal house—a place in Kent near Cranbrook, a sixteenth-century castle.[2] Take Ben to watch me broadcast.

DIARY   5th April, 1930

Go down to Staplehurst with Ben. We are met, after some delay, by Vita, Boski,[3] Niggs,[4] and all the dogs. We then drive to Sissinghurst Castle. We get a view of the two towers as we approach. We go round carefully in the mud. I am cold and calm but I like it.

---

[1] Because Lord Sackville, V.S-W.'s father, had died in 1928 and the Nicolsons now had a flat in London.

[2] Sissinghurst is two miles north-east of Cranbrook in the Weald of Kent. V.S-W. had been told about it by a local land-agent and went there with her younger son, Nigel, and Dorothy Wellesley. She wrote in her own diary that evening: 'Fell flat in love with it.'

[3] Miss le Bosquet, V.S-W.'s secretary.   [4] Family name for Nigel.

HAROLD AND VITA NICOLSON decide that the Victorians were the only people who knew how to bring up their children. So they adopt the manner.
—

A drawing made by Harold Nicolson in
about 1928 to amuse his children

DIARY   *6th April, 1930*

The boys misbehave by bullying little Miss Barnes.[1] I am absolutely furious and curse them as I have never cursed them before. I do detest cruelty in any form. Vita and I then go off feeling ruffled and unhappy to revisit Sissinghurst. My great anxiety had been that the main wing would be too narrow to build in. But we measure and find that we get eighteen feet. We then go round the buildings carefully, and finally walk round the fields to the brook and round by the wood. We come suddenly upon the nut-walk and that settles it. From that moment we decide to buy. A happy day, except for the boys.

DIARY   *10th April, 1930*

Vita hears from Pemberton[2] that we can raise the money. A lovely day. Go down after luncheon [to Long Barn] and work at books as well as my wireless talk. The spring has really come and the hedges are beginning to get green. One freak iris is out in the border. Otherwise only daffodils and aubretia. The double peaches are just beginning. Many letters about my father's book.[3] I gather that some people are shocked at its detachment. Well, let them be. The book is solid enough to stand on its own and I really do not mind in the least about what reviews I get.

DIARY   *13th April, 1930*

A wet cold day. Work in the morning, and in the afternoon go over to Sissinghurst. It is raining and there is an icy wind. Mummy[4] preaches discouragement and foresees heavy expenses and heavy taxation. We are so depressed with the weather that we begin to agree with her. It all looks big, broken-down and sodden.

[1] This was a disgraceful and long-remembered incident: we threw stones at the weak-minded daughter of the gardener at Long Barn.
[2] The family solicitor.
[3] *Lord Carnock* had been published on 3rd April. The reviews had been good, and until the publication of *George V*, H.N. would say that it was the book with which he was most satisfied.
[4] Lady Carnock, then aged 73.

DIARY   *14th April, 1930*

Wake up feeling more confident again about Sissinghurst. In the morning I go to the plenary session of the Naval Conference.[1] A large drawing-room has been set apart for the journalists and we sit in dryad chairs smoking cigarettes and listening to the speeches through loud-speakers. Very luxurious. In the afternoon go to the House of Commons to hear Snowden[2] introduce his Budget. A packed House, and that strange yellow glare. Snowden dapper and frail; he fingers the edge of the box for a moment and then settles down to his task. I leave after a few minutes as the crush is intolerable.

DIARY   *17th April, 1930*

Down by the 1.15 train. Get out at Tonbridge where I am met by Vita and the boys and go on to Sissinghurst. A cold April day. We measure a bit and then walk down to where I want to make a lake. Then into the wood. Very lovely. I have a long talk to Vita about what we shall do about it. I am terrified of socialist legislation, of not being able to let the fields, of finding that the place is a huge hole into which we pour money, of finding that the whole thing is far more bother than it is worth. On the other hand, it would suit us splendidly and could with money be made perfectly beautiful. We are worried and depressed about it all, and Long Barn is very nice and pretty.

H.N. TO V.S-W.   *24th April, 1930*
                                              4 King's Bench Walk, E.C.4

My view is:

(a) That it is most unwise of us to get Sissinghurst. It costs us £12,000 to buy and will cost another good £15,000 to put it in order. This will mean nearly £30,000 before we have done with it. For £30,000 we could buy a beautiful place replete with park, garage, h. and c., central heating, historical associations, and two lodges r. and l.

(b) That it is most wise of us to buy Sissinghurst. Through its veins pulses the blood of the Sackville dynasty. True it is that it comes through the female line[3]—but then we are both feminist and, after

---

[1] The Five Power Naval Conference (Great Britain, United States, France, Italy and Japan) which eventually reached agreement on the relative strengths of their navies.
[2] Philip Snowden, Chancellor of the Exchequer in MacDonald's Government.
[3] Cecily Baker, daughter of Sir John Baker who owned Sissinghurst in the reign of Henry VIII, married Sir Thomas Sackville, first Earl of Dorset.

all, Knole came in the same way.[1] It is, for you, an ancestral mansion: that makes up for company's water and h. and c.

(c) It is in Kent. It is in a part of Kent we like. It is self-contained. I could make a lake. The boys could ride.

(d) We like it.

They decided to buy.

DIARY   *6th May, 1930*

After dinner we are rung up by Beale.[2] He says that they accept our price. I sit there while Vita answers the telephone: 'Quite' ... 'Yes, of course' ... 'Oh naturally!' She puts down the receiver and says, 'It is ours'. We embrace warmly. I then go and get the plans and fiddle. Vita thinks we had better build a small wing for ourselves abutting on to the tower and joined to the main building on the north side by a huge loggia. She has given up all ideas of leaving the court-yard open to the north.

H.N. TO V.S-W.   *7th May, 1930*
                                                          4 King's Bench Walk, E.C.4

See you tomorrow. Still excited about Sissinghurst and not as appalled as I thought I should be. Oh my dear dear love—what fun the Mars[3] have! Please don't die.

The first building which they made habitable was the tower, but such was the state of its internal dilapidation that it was not until 12th July that they were able even to picnic in its first-floor room, and their first night was spent there (on camp beds) on 18th October. They continued to live at Long Barn but went over to Sissinghurst most weekends and began to plan, clear and plant. By the end of the year the South Cottage was ready for them and the lake was made.

The diary continues to reveal a certain listlessness. Harold Nicolson scarcely mentions his work for the 'Evening Standard', the 'Daily Ex-

---

[1] Only in the sense that Knole was given to Sir Thomas Sackville by his cousin, Queen Elizabeth I.

[2] The land-agent.

[3] 'Mar' was the name by which V.S-W.'s mother, Lady Sackville, always called her. H.N. came to use it too, and they referred to each other jointly as 'the Mars'. Later they applied the nickname to their sons, and by inference, to any children and even to any thing that was small or vulnerable.

Harold Nicolson in June 1930 at Sissinghurst Castle, which was purchased in the previous month. One of their first restorations was to open up the brick archway in the centre

Sissinghurst Castle from the air in 1932. A beginning has been made on the garden. The South Cottage is beyond on the right

press' or the B.B.C. Daily he records where he lunched and dined, but seldom is there much more than a list of the other guests. His social life was varied and immensely active, for he was naturally gregarious and needed material for his hated column. His life was therefore lived on three planes: his work; his literary, political and diplomatic friends; and Sissinghurst.

'The Edwardians' was published on 29th May by the Hogarth Press, and within a month it had sold twenty thousand copies in England and was chosen as the Book of the Month in America. V. Sackville-West had already begun to write 'All Passion Spent', the best of her novels and almost as great a public success as 'The Edwardians'. She, too, was broadcasting regularly, but she spent most of her time at Long Barn and Sissinghurst, where her three most frequent visitors were Hilda Matheson (Director of Talks at the B.B.C.), Virginia Woolf and Dorothy Wellesley.

DIARY   30th May, 1930

Lunch with Hazel Lavery.[1] Austen Chamberlain,[2] G. K. Chesterton,[3] Donegall[4] there. Austen tells a characteristically conceited story. He introduces it by way of praising Crowe.[5] He tells us how once when he was ill he was unable to go to Geneva. The Under Secretary had to go himself. The latter came to him and said, 'I shall feel completely lost without you. What am I to do if the Germans try to steal a march on us?' 'Read Crowe's minutes to them', Austen answered. He was nice about my book. He looks ever so much stronger. A different man. Frederick Voigt[6] dines. Broadcast afterwards.

DIARY   5th June, 1930

Dine with Beaverbrook at Stornoway [House]. He is in a good temper. The chill of that house—no flowers, just newspapers and telephones—is appalling. The Brownlows,[7] Dicky Adair, Mrs

[1] Wife of Sir John Lavery, the portrait-painter.   [2] Foreign Secretary, 1924–29.
[3] The Roman Catholic writer. Then aged 56.
[4] The sixth Marquess Donegall. An active journalist.
[5] Sir Eyre Crowe. Permanent Under Secretary of State at the Foreign Office from 1920. Died 1925.
[6] Political author and journalist. Editor of Nineteenth Century and After, 1938–46. Died 1957.
[7] Lord Brownlow was to become Personal Lord-in-Waiting to Edward VIII.

Norton.[1] The McKennas[2] come in afterwards. They are just as frightened of Lord Beaverbrook as all the other people. There is an atmosphere of sycophancy about it all which I find distressing. Have some talk with Beaverbrook after. I tell him I think the Londoner's Diary is getting dull. He denies it—and gives some good suggestions. He thinks that the *Daily Herald* will only last a year. He says that once a modern paper begins to lose, it loses hand over foot.

DIARY   *6th June, 1930*

I go to William Rothenstein[3] to have a drawing done. He tells me that [Oscar] Wilde had a red face, grey lips and very bad teeth. He was so ashamed of his teeth that he used to put his hand over them when he spoke, giving an odd furtive expression to his jokes. Rothenstein did a drawing of Wilde which the latter always took with him. He lost it in Naples after the trial. It was probably stolen. That was about the only portrait of Wilde ever made.

DIARY   *22nd June, 1930*

Talk to Stephen Spender.[4] He is an intelligent young man with wild blue eyes and a bad complexion. He takes his work and poetry with immense seriousness, and talks for hours about whether he is more fitted to be a poet than a novelist. He is not conceited so much as self-preoccupied. He is absolutely determined to become a leading writer. A nice and vital young man whom we both liked.

DIARY   *2nd July, 1930*

Dine at Sovrani's with Bob Boothby.[5] The Archie Sinclairs[6] and the Harold Macmillans[7] there. Bob tells me that when someone asked Ramsay MacDonald whether he, Bob, was about to join the Labour Party, Ramsay replied, 'No, Bob is no Labour man: it is merely that

---

[1] Wife of Richard Norton, later Lord Grantley.
[2] Reginald McKenna. Home Secretary, 1911–15. Chancellor of the Exchequer, 1915–16.
[3] The portrait-painter. Principal of the Royal College of Art.
[4] The poet, then aged 21.
[5] Later Lord Boothby, then aged 30 and Conservative M.P. for East Aberdeenshire since 1924.
[6] Sir Archibald Sinclair, leader of the Liberal Party after 1935.
[7] Then aged 36. He had lost his seat in the 1929 Election but regained it in 1931.

he has a deep personal admiration for myself.' That is characteristic of the man's diseased vanity. I talk to Macmillan. He says that the old party machines are worn out and that the modern electorate thinks more of personalities and programmes than of the pressure put upon them by an electoral agent. He thinks that the economic situation is so serious that it will lead to a breakdown of the whole party system. He foresees that the Tories may return with a majority of 20 and then be swept away on a snap vote. No other single party will form a Government and then there will be a Cabinet of young men. He was kind enough to include me in this Pitt-like Ministry.

DIARY   5th July, 1930

Down to Wilton with Vita. A large party. The Winston Churchills, Duff and Diana Cooper,[1] the Cranbornes,[2] Maurice Baring,[3] Malcolm Bullock,[4] Christopher Sykes.[5] Watch the lads bathe. A lovely evening. After dinner go with Pembroke[6] to the Palladian bridge and look back on the house all lit up with the Van Dykes showing in the Double Cube [Room]. After that a dash into Salisbury for the last night of the carnival. Torches and processions and community singing. Great fun.

DIARY   6th July, 1930

Winston talks long and sadly about Beaverbrook's Empire free trade campaign which he sees is ruining the country. He says it will hand over South America to the Yanks, split the Empire for ever, and shatter the Conservative Party into smithereens. He is writing three books: one a last volume of the *World Crisis*[7]; one a life of the Duke of Marlborough[8]; one of reminiscences of his own.[9] He is in gentle and intelligent form. He goes a long walk with Vita and tells her his troubles and hopes. He spoke of his American tour. The difficulty of food and drink. One never got real food, only chicken. He had been

---

[1] Duff Cooper, later Lord Norwich, was then aged 40. He had lost his seat in 1929, but was re-elected in 1931. In 1930 he was writing his biography of Talleyrand.
[2] Later fifth Marquess of Salisbury. Then Conservative M.P. for South Dorset.
[3] The author and journalist, 1874–1945.   [4] Conservative M.P. since 1923.
[5] Author. Then aged 23. Honorary Attaché to H.M. Embassy, Berlin, 1928–29.
[6] Fifteenth Earl of Pembroke and Montgomery, 1880–1960.
[7] This was the abridged and revised edition, published in 1930.
[8] In four volumes, published 1933–38.   [9] *My Early Life*, published in 1930.

given a dozen champagne by Barny Baruch[1] and paid it back to him
at the cost of £30. He was happy there.

DIARY   *10th July, 1930*

Dine with Sir Henry Norman—a man's dinner. Bernard Shaw,[2] Sir
John Simon,[3] Lutyens,[4] Lord Dawson,[5] A. A. Milne.[6] I sit next to
Shaw.

He is amazingly young-looking: his shoulder blades at the back
stick through his dinner-jacket like those of a boy who has not finished
growing. His hair is dead-white but thick. His cheeks as pink as a
girl's. His eyes as simple and unmalicious as those of an animal. And
yet behind their simplicity is a touch of reserve. He talks with a faintly
effeminate voice and a soft brogue. He had a special menu of excellent
vegetables.

He was asked whether Boanerges in *The Apple Cart*[7] was meant to
be John Burns. He said no, that he had really modelled it on Bradlaugh
and his type, and that John Burns never entered his head. But that
when he had seen the thing on the stage he realised that it *was* John
Burns to the life. He was asked whether the politician in *John Bull's
Other Island*[8] was meant to be Haldane. 'No,' he answered, 'he wasn't.
I only put Haldane into one of my parts, and that was the waiter in
You Never Can Tell.'

He spoke with horror of Pitoeff's rendering of Joan of Arc. He
called it 'dreadful'. She tried to awake pity—a thing that Joan would
never have done. He talked of Laurence.[9] Said he was a born actor.
Spoke of him with real admiration.

Afterwards we went upstairs and there were some young girls to
amuse the old man. Sir John Simon was charming about my book.
Ned Lutyens was even sillier than usual.

DIARY   *11th July, 1930*

Ben comes up for Long Leave. He has grown again and I really
believe that he is taller than I am. He was very sweet and charming as

[1] Bernard Baruch. American statesman, 1870–1965.
[2] Then aged 74.   [3] Foreign Secretary, 1931–35.
[4] Sir Edwin Lutyens, architect, an intimate friend of Lady Sackville.
[5] Lord Dawson of Penn, Physician-in-Ordinary to Kings Edward VII, George V,
   Edward VIII and George VI.
[6] Author and journalist.   [7] First produced in 1929.   [8] First produced in 1904.
[9] Sir Laurence Olivier, then aged 23.

usual. Peter Howard,[1] the rugby footballer, and Keith Winter[2] come to luncheon. Howard wants a job with Beaverbrook. He is charming and forceful but terribly immature. I go to the Eton and Harrow match for a moment, feeling rather out of it in my trilby hat. What a ghastly show.

Broadcast in the evening. Gerald Heard[3] comes with me. He is as fascinating as ever on medical questions. He thinks that before they discover a cure for cancer it will have ceased to be a mortal disease. He also thinks that when they do discover a cure for cancer they will have discovered the source of life.

We go on afterwards to the Woolfs.[4] Hugh Dalton[5] is there. I attack the nomination board at the Foreign Office, not on the grounds that it rejects good men, but on the grounds that its very existence prevents good men from coming up for fear they may be ploughed for social reasons. The awkward question of the Jews arises. I admit that is the snag. Jews are far more interested in international life than are Englishmen, and if we opened the service it might be flooded by clever Jews. It was a little difficult to argue this point frankly with Leonard there.

The Edwardians is still booming. They are within sight of 22,000.

DIARY   *21st July, 1930*

Dine at Emerald Cunard. A ghastly dinner supposed to be literary. George Moore,[6] the two Sitwells,[7] Evelyn Waugh,[8] Robert Byron.[9] I do not enjoy it and a gloom hangs over the whole party. George Moore talks rubbish about all great writers having lovely names, instancing Shelley, Marlowe, Landor. I ask him what about Keats? 'Keats', he answers, 'was not a great writer.' What a silly old man! We hate our party.

In August they went on a motoring holiday to Italy. Nigel had just left

---

[1] Captain of the England Rugger XV in 1931. Journalist and New Party candidate. Later a prominent supporter of Moral Rearmament and, after Frank Buchman's death, its leader. He died in 1965.
[2] Novelist and dramatist.
[3] Scientific and philosophical writer.   [4] Leonard and Virginia Woolf.
[5] Labour M.P. since 1924. In 1930, Parliamentary Under-Secretary, Foreign Office.
[6] The novelist and literary critic.   [7] Osbert and Edith.
[8] Then aged 27. He had just published *Vile Bodies*.
[9] Writer, mainly on art and architecture, 1905–41.

Summer Fields, and was to go to Eton in September: Ben had been at Eton for two years and was finding it difficult to settle down and discover his real interests. The holiday was therefore more for the benefit of both boys than to give their parents a rest. They took their work with them. In five days at Portofino Harold Nicolson wrote his only play, 'The Archduke', which never found a producer and was never published; and V. Sackville-West simultaneously wrote a large part of 'All Passion Spent'. They drove across France to Portofino on the Italian Riviera and started their return journey by motoring to Pisa, Florence and Bologna, where Harold Nicolson left them to return to England by train. V. Sackville-West and the boys continued home by car. This enforced separation after so happy and productive a holiday led to the exchange of the following letters, which illustrate something of their quadrilateral relationship. The first two letters were written on the same day and almost at the same moment, within an hour or two of their parting.

H.N. TO V.S-W.   *22nd August, 1930*
                                              In the train, Bologna–Milan

Oh dear, that black and dusty bundle holds everything in life for me, and shortly it will come humming along that very road under this plate-glass sun. Darling, *why* did I consent to this bloody scheme? I do so hate it for you. The road looks like white ashes, all hot. Dust and ashes. But at least it looks straight, and when you get to where I am looking now, you will be only a little way to Piacenza and can sleep there.

Darling, I wonder if other people mind being separated quite as much as we do? It's too silly. Today week we shall be reunited. Exactly at this hour. Yet I feel as if we had been parted for ever. I always retreat at such moments into the cool orchard of my gratitude. 'For nearly seventeen years', I say, 'we have been so happy. Nothing, not even death, can take that away from us.' If you died or I died, we should not feel any wastage. We should merely feel that we had been too happy for it to last.

V.S-W. TO H.N.   *22nd August, 1930*
                                                                  Parma

We have an awful story to tell you. Listen. We got to Modena at 11.30. We stopped. We asked if your train halted there. The first man (who was a fool) said no. We persevered. The second man

54

(who was bright) said yes. He showed me exactly where the 1st class carriages drew up. We spaced ourselves out in a row down the platform like this

_____

_____

    •   •   •

   Nigel   **Ben**   *Me*

(the parallel lines represent the *binari*), and we waited. The train was due at 11.35. It arrived actually at 11.45. We were frightfully excited. We ran up and down looking for a curly head peeping out at Modena station. There was no curly head. Most of the compartments had their curtains drawn. We said, Damn those curtains. We ran up, and down, and up again. The engine shrieked, and off it went—bearing, presumably, a Daddy immersed in a room of his own. We remained disconsolate and thwarted on the platform as the behind of the *fourgon* disappeared. We nearly cried with disappointment.

Can't tell you how disappointed and distressed we were about Modena. We console ourselves by thinking that you are having a delicious lunch on the train (*Ben*). This is not much consolation (*V.*). I suppose you are about Milan now. Getting further and further away from your beloved family who chase after you in a dust-white motor. Mummy is looking very lovely and being very sweet, and I can assure you that we are attempting to support her in all perplexities (*Nigel*).

H.N. TO V.S-W.   *24th August, 1930*
                                 Evening Standard, E.C.4

I opened your telegram from Milan first, and then I kept all your letters and postcards till the end. My darling, what lovely letters. They made me feel warm and wanted instead of cold and unwanted. How silly about Modena station! But I had pulled down the blinds— or was in the restaurant car or something. I am glad I didn't see you, as I should have felt miserable. You can't think how anxious I feel about you all. It is like toothache.

I loved the little additions and scribblings of the boys. How sweet they are! I feel this trip has done them a world of good. Especially Ben. It was pretty grim, I can tell you, getting back to the office. They didn't seem in the least pleased to see me. So unlike the F.O.

or an Embassy. That's what happens when one works with bedints[1]: they are all so tied up and *manquent d'amabilité*. Not hostile exactly, but always on the defensive.

DIARY   *12th September, 1930*

Go over to Sissinghurst with Reggie Cooper. We decide, on his advice, to make the bowling-green longer and to reach right down to the moat. Our general line is to keep the whole thing as green and quiet and simple as we can.

During the remainder of 1930 the impending switch from journalism to politics and literature becomes increasingly apparent.

DIARY   *5th October, 1930*

Motor to Chequers. On passing through Bromley we half-see a poster blown by the wind which looks like 'Airship destroyed'. We stop later and buy a paper. We find that the R.101 has crashed near Beauvais[2] and that Thomson and some 43 other people have been burnt alive. We then drive on to Chequers.

When we arrive we find that the P.M. [Ramsay MacDonald] is up in London and is expected back later. Ishbel [MacDonald] says he will be in a dreadful state. He arrives about 1.30. He looks very ill and worn. Bennett, the Prime Minister of Canada, is there. Ramsay begins to introduce him to Vita but forgets his name. He makes a hopeless gesture, his hand upon his white hair: 'My brain is going', he says, 'my brain is going.' It is all rather embarrassing. He then tells us that the telephone beside his bed had rung that morning and he had lifted the receiver. He was told it was the Air Ministry. He was told of the disaster. He dashed up to London in 55 minutes and went to the

---

[1] The word 'bedint', used as an adjective or noun, is difficult to explain. It comes from the German *bedienen*, to serve, and 'bedints', in Sackville language, originally meant 'servants'. But 'bedint' also meant 'vulgar' or 'genteel' or 'lacking in standards'. It is in the latter sense that the word is used here.

[2] The airship, R.101, was contracted by the Government in 1925 as a sister-ship to R.100, built in the previous year. Both were designed to carry a hundred passengers at 70 mph on Commonwealth and trans-Atlantic routes. The R.100 first flew successfully in July 1930 to Montreal, but the R.101 crashed on a hill-top near Beauvais, France, on 5th October, killing forty-six people, including Lord Thomson, the Minister for Air. There were only seven survivors. The R.100 was subsequently scrapped.

Air Ministry. There were only a few clerks about. Salmond[1] was got hold of and sent across to France. Baldwin[2] came to see him. They agreed that no man's health could stand being Prime Minister. The King was in a dreadful state. Ramsay seemed more worried about the King's dismay than about anything else.

We then go into luncheon. All very beautifully and excellently done. Afterwards we go up to the long gallery. The women look at Cromwell's head.[3] The P.M. pours out to Vita the miseries of his soul: he cannot sleep: 'Two hours a night is all I get.' He can do no work: 'The moment I disentangle my foot from one strand of barbed wire it becomes entangled in another.' 'If God were to come to me and say, "Ramsay, would you rather be a country gentleman than a Prime Minister?", I should reply, "Please God, a country gentleman." ' He is a tired, exhausted man. Bless him.

DIARY   *14th October, 1930*

Lunch with Ernest Benn[4] at the Reform to meet Henry Ford.[5] He is not the same as I imagined. His eyes blaze and blink with faith and his large mouth twists sensitively into all variations of approval, obstinacy, pity and contempt. A quiet courteous man. Very yellow about the face.

DIARY   *18th October, 1930*

Feeling very depressed with life. Can't make out whether it is mere middle-aged depression or whether it is really that I loathe journalism so much that it covers all my days with a dark cloud of shame. I feel that I have no time to add to my reputation by doing serious work and that my silly work day by day diminishes the reputation I have already acquired. I have become 'famous' as a radio comedian, and shall never be able to live down the impression thus acquired. In fact I feel a pretty feeble creature, just a soppy superficial humourist. I would give my soul to leave the *Standard* but I daren't risk it because of the money. Middle-age for a hedonist like myself is distressing in any case, but with most people it coincides with an increase of power and income. With

[1] Marshal of the Royal Air Force, Sir John Salmond, then Chief of the Air Staff.
[2] Stanley Baldwin, Leader of the Opposition.
[3] The famous life-mask of Oliver Cromwell.
[4] Sir Ernest Benn, publisher. Chairman of Ernest Benn Ltd, 1924–45.
[5] The American motor pioneer, 1863–1947.

me I have lost all serious employment, sacrificed my hopes of power, and am up against the anxiety of having not one penny in the world beyond what I earn. Is it this that makes me so perpetually unhappy? I have never been unhappy like this before. Till this year I have, except in rare periods of some definite worry or misery, woken each morning with the zest of being alive. Today each morning comes to me as a renewal of humiliation. It may be that I am overworked. I certainly mind things more than I should if my nerves were in order. I loathe getting fat for instance, and yet at my age I can't expect to be young. Perhaps all this is good for me. Life has been an easy thing for me till this year 1930. And yet I shouldn't mind if I were in a position to fight my difficulties with what is best in me. What depresses me is that I can only live by exposing what is worst in me to the public gaze. I feel a fake: and it is that which humiliates and saddens me.

In the afternoon I go to Staplehurst and am met by my darling. She had been sleeping all alone at Sissinghurst for two whole nights. Brave woman. We mark out the garden by the cottage. A lovely evening. We sleep in the top room of the tower on two camp beds. We read by candles.

DIARY   *28th October, 1930*

Lunch with Sibyl [Colefax]. Only Noel Coward[1] and Willie Maugham.[2] Noel abuses me for being a journalist: he feels that this constant emptying of my accumulators upon futile energies may end by sapping the source of energy itself, and that when I eventually leave and try to settle down to serious books the force will have gone out of me. I fear he may be right. But what am I to do? I can't sacrifice Viti and the boys merely for my own convenience. It is not as if the *Standard* were intolerable: it is perfectly tolerable. It is only that I am losing my literary reputation and shall never be taken seriously again. And all this for money!

DIARY   *5th November, 1930*

Dine with Beaverbrook and Esmond Harmsworth.[3] Beaverbrook goes on to see Neville Chamberlain afterwards. I remain behind and

---

[1] Noel Coward was then aged 31 and already well-known as a playwright. His *Bitter Sweet* was produced in 1929 and *Private Lives* in 1930.

[2] Somerset Maugham, the novelist, then aged 56.

[3] Chairman of the *Daily Mail*. He succeeded his father as the second Viscount Rothermere in 1940.

sleep on a sofa. The others go. At 12.30 B. returns. He is not pleased with his conversation with Chamberlain. He feels that Baldwin is in for another five years. He talks to me as a father about my political career. He urges me not to be a Liberal. Begs me to become a Tory. Indicates that Tom Mosley will form a new party and that then I shall be free. He is in his best, most serious, least petty, mood.

DIARY   *6th November, 1930*

Lunch with the Mosleys. Tom talks afterwards about the future. He is evidently thinking of leading some new party of younger Nationalists. He is not certain what to do or when to do it. If he strikes now he may be premature. If he delays he may be too late. 'If,' he says, 'I could have £250,000 and a press I should sweep the country.' By the press he means Beaverbrook. I warn him against the impulsive character of Lord B. I tell him that so long as there is a battle on, B. will behave as a great and loyal fighter. But that once the battle is over and victory is assured, B. will get bored and will create battles, if necessary in his own party. His pugnacity destroys both his judgement and his decent feeling. If they ally themselves with B. they must think of some bone to give him later which will keep him busy. He lives only by opposition: if he cannot find an opposition he creates one. Tom, I think, agreed. I said I would be with him all the time. He begs me to do nothing till December. I shall hold my tongue, and hold my cards. I want to be in real things again, and not to feel that my batteries are wasted playing the spillikins of the Press.

DIARY   *25th November, 1930*

Lunch with Sir John Tudor Walters at the Reform. He tells me he is resigning his seat as Liberal Member for Penryn and Falmouth. Will I take it on? A safe Liberal seat with a running organisation. It will cost me £1,000 for the election and £250 a year in subsequent subscriptions. The electorate is largely Wesleyan and old-fashioned. I am much tempted by the offer and say that I shall think it over.

In the afternoon I go down to Oxford for the St Catherine's dinner at Balliol. Stay with the Master.[1] My health is proposed by the senior scholar, Mackenzie,[2] in an amusing speech with a strong Scotch accent. I reply by telling them how unhappy I was at Balliol and why. By

[1] A. D. Lindsay, later Lord Lindsay of Birker, Master of Balliol 1924–49.
[2] W. J. M. Mackenzie, later Professor of Government at Manchester University.

saying that once a Balliol man, always a Balliol man, and how fond I am of it now. By ragging the dons. And by urging the young men to avoid sets and to work. The speech is not a success. It falls between two stools. The young men expected me to be witty and the dons expected me to praise them. I disappointed both. Kenneth Bell[1] was the only man who liked it. But it may have done some good perhaps to one or two shy young men like myself, who feel they are doomed to failure, and see me, who felt the same as they did, at least a guest of honour. If this has got home even to one diffident soul, I do not mind the others thinking it a frost.

DIARY   *28th November, 1930*

To Noel Coward's *Private Lives* and on to supper with Noel at 17 Gerald Road. An elaborate studio. Noel very simple and nice. He talks of the days when his mother kept lodgings in Ebury Street and he himself had a top back room. Gradually he began to make money and took the top floor for himself, finally descending to the first floor and ejecting the lodgers. 'As I rose in the world I went down in the house.' Completely unspoilt by success. A nice eager man.

DIARY   *29th November, 1930*

Down to Cliveden.[2] A dark autumnal day. Thirty-two people in the house. Cold and draughty. Great sofas in vast cathedrals: little groups of people wishing they were alone: a lack of organisation and occupation: a desultory drivel. The party is in itself good enough. Duff and Diana [Cooper], Tom Mosley and Cimmie.[3] Oliver Stanley[4] and Lady Maureen, Harold Macmillan and Lady Dorothy, Bracken,[5] Garvin,[6] Bob Boothby, Malcolm Bullock. But it does not hang together. After dinner, in order to enliven the party, Lady Astor dons a Victorian hat and a pair of false teeth. It does not enliven the party.

[1] Fellow and tutor in History at Balliol 1919–41.
[2] The great house of the Astors, near Maidenhead, Berks.
[3] Cynthia Mosley, daughter of Lord Curzon of Kedleston. They were married in 1920 and she died in 1933. She was Labour M.P. for Stoke 1929–31.
[4] Son of Lord Derby. Later he held several offices in pre-war and war-time Conservative Governments.
[5] Brendan Bracken, Conservative M.P., 1929–45. Then aged 29.
[6] J. L. Garvin, Editor of *The Observer*, 1908–42.

DIARY   *30th November, 1930*

Dawdle all morning. Go a damp walk with Hilda Matheson. In the afternoon over to Eton. The boys are well and Ben seems more self-confident. Have tea at Fuller's and return to Cliveden. In the evening after dinner a discussion starts on the future of England. Philip Kerr —now Lothian[1]—says that democracy and Empire cannot go together, Garvin inveighs against the politicians, and especially Baldwin and Ramsay. The others join in. The main conclusion is that Parliament, though susceptible to dealing with politics, is hopeless at finance and economics. That we are about to enter the worst crisis in our history. And that unless the economic situation can be dealt with on undemocratic lines, i.e. independent of votes, we shall go smash. Not even Holland, but worse than Holland.

Tom Mosley tells me that he will shortly launch his manifesto practically creating the National Party. He hopes to get Morris[2] of Oxford to finance him. He hopes to get Keynes and similar experts to sign his manifesto. He hopes that [Oliver] Stanley and Macmillan will also join. He hopes to get the support of Beaverbrook. I doubt whether many of these hopes will be realised, but his conversation is convincing enough to decide me to write to Tudor Walters declining his offer to stand for Falmouth. That is one boat burnt.

DIARY   *22nd December, 1930*

Bertram Mills gives a luncheon for 1,100 people at Olympia. I am about to enter when I hear a voice behind me. It is Ramsay MacDonald. He says, 'Well, this is my one holiday of the year. I love circuses.' At that moment they hand him a telegram. He opens it. He hands it to me with the words, 'Keep this, my dear Harold, and read it if ever you think you wish to be Prime Minister.' It is a telegram from some crank society abusing him for attending a luncheon in honour of a circus proprietor—since performing animals are cruel. He is disgusted and his pleasure is spoiled.

---

[1] He had succeeded his cousin as eleventh Marquess of Lothian earlier in 1930. Ambassador to the United States, 1939–40.
[2] Later Lord Nuffield.

Thus ends the year 1930. Such an odd year. We buy Sissinghurst; we make a vast sum of money from our books; we increase our fame and lower our reputation; we prepare for the future. Viti has been very well and happy except for her back. Ben has been unhappy at Eton but is doing better. Niggs is bored by his first half at Eton but will probably settle down. I have quite found my feet in the *Standard* office—and Beaverbrook likes me. But that is all very well. I was not made to be a journalist and I do not want to go on being one. It is a mere expense of spirit in a waste of shame. A constant hurried triviality which is bad for the mind. Goodness knows what I shall do next year. I am on the verge of politics. I am on the verge of leaving the *Evening Standard* and either writing books of my own or sitting in the House of Commons. 1931 assuredly will be the most important year, for good or ill, in my whole life.

Whatever happens, let me, on this last day of 1930, record my gratitude for what I have had. Few men have been so spoiled by fortune as I have. But all of it—money, fame, health—is of little weight against the scale of my home life. Viti, Ben, Nigel, home, Sissinghurst, books. These, I hope, will always remain what I really care for.

1931

---

*With Ramsay MacDonald at No. 10 – H.N. joins the New
Party – H. G. Wells and Maynard Keynes – planning policy
with Mosley – Harold Macmillan's attitude – H.N.'s choice
between Beaverbrook and Mosley – discussion with Churchill
and Lloyd George on Mosley's movement – John Strachey's
resignation from the New Party – James Joyce – H.N. edits
Mosley's paper 'Action' – growing fascist tendencies of the
New Party – A. E. Housman – General Election – H.N.
forfeits his deposit as New Party candidate for the Combined
Universities – 'Action' ceases publication – 'of all my years
this has been the most unfortunate'*

1931 was the year of the New Party experiment. It is difficult for those who now associate Sir Oswald Mosley's name only with his headlong descent into fascism and offensive slogans chalked on a wall to visualise the brilliant flowering of his youth. In 1931 he was thirty-five years old. Born the heir to a baronetcy, married to Lord Curzon's daughter, handsome, rich, eloquent, determined, he frequently changed his party allegiances but it did not hamper the growth of his reputation. He was first elected to Parliament in 1918 as a Conservative. By 1922 his views had moved leftwards, and he sat for Harrow as an Independent. Two years later he joined the Labour Party, and when Ramsay MacDonald formed his Government in June 1929 he appointed Mosley Chancellor of the Duchy of Lancaster, with special responsibility for unemployment under J. H. Thomas, the Lord Privy Seal.

It was one of the key jobs in the new Government. Labour had come to power, with the Liberals holding the balance, on a policy of radical Socialist change and the forecast that once the country were free of Tory misrule, unemployment would drop rapidly. They were not able to fulfil either promise. The number of workless rose from just over one million in 1929 to two-and-a-half million by the end of 1930 and approached three million during the course of 1931. MacDonald, Snowden and Thomas had no answer to the problem except small-scale public works and the hope that something would happen internationally to put things right. There were no Socialist remedies for such a situation, and the bulk of the Party's Election programme must be put in suspense until times improved. They had no money to spare, and they were dependent for everything they did on Liberal support.

Mosley refused to accept so passive and pessimistic a policy. He considered that the Cabinet, and MacDonald in particular, were out of touch with opinion in the Parliamentary Party, and that only dynamic leadership could restore the country's finances and the reputation of Labour. He proposed to Thomas a series of measures to relieve unemployment, including public utility schemes such as slum clearance and agricultural reconstruction, the stabilisation of prices through bulk purchase, the '*scientific*' *regulation of tariffs, the public control of banking and the expansion of home purchasing power. Thomas rejected his schemes as impracticable. In May 1930 Mosley therefore resigned from the Government to be succeeded as Chancellor of the Duchy by Clement Attlee, and put his ideas forward, in direct challenge to MacDonald, at the Party's conference in October. His speech made a great impression on the conference, and he was only narrowly defeated. On 27th January, 1931 he renewed his challenge at a special meeting of the Parliamentary Labour Party, and again party loyalties just outweighed the admiration aroused by Mosley's passionate advocacy of his cause. It was then that he finally decided to found his New Party. The National Executive of the Labour Party expelled him on 10th March for 'gross disloyalty in seeking to create a new party ... with Parliamentary candidates in opposition to Labour members'. Mosley was now on his own, a formidable threat to all three major political parties, from whom he hoped to attract many recruits. Harold Nicolson, being partyless, was one of the first to join him.*

A national organisation was soon created, with Allan Young as Secretary, and Mosley began to place his candidates at bye-elections as the best means of putting his case before the people. The results were disappointing. As the economic crisis mounted, the New Party seemed less and less relevant to the seriousness of the situation—paradoxically, for it had been created for no other purpose—and the Press chose to ignore its efforts. More serious was Mosley's inability to attract the open support of more than a handful of prominent people. Men like Aneurin Bevan, Hore-Belisha, Oliver Baldwin and Maynard Keynes would let him understand that they were with him 'in spirit'. But those who openly sided with him were a motley group of second-rank politicians, some notable intellectuals and sportsmen, and a strong contingent of University and back-street youth. From the Parliamentary Labour Party he attracted John Strachey and Dr Robert Forgan: from the Conservatives, W. E. Allen and, at least temporarily, Colonel Moore-Brabazon; from the intellectuals, Harold Nicolson, the Sitwells and Cyril Joad. Peter Howard, then a rugger hero at Oxford, and 'Kid' Lewis, the professional boxer, rallied hundreds of their kin.

Harold Nicolson's importance to Mosley, apart from the increasing pulling-power of his name, was his close connection with Beaverbrook. Mosley hoped to gain the support of the Beaverbrook press. For some months it seemed that his hopes were not ill-founded, but Beaverbrook

*soon drew away into open hostility towards the New Party, and by the
early summer of 1931 considered that 'the movement has petered out'.
Although Beaverbrook behaved generously towards him, Harold Nicolson
was placed in a difficult position. Writing a daily column, largely
political, for one of Beaverbrook's own newspapers, he could hardly
advocate support for a party of which Beaverbrook disapproved, and
felt obliged to request Beaverbrook's assent before standing for Parliament
in its name. The final breach came in August, when he resigned from the
'Evening Standard' to edit Mosley's own weekly paper 'Action'. Meanwhile the strain of reconciling his dual loyalties became a heavy one,
and it was not eased by the cynicism of his friends and the knowledge
that V. Sackville-West, then busily writing novels in the country,
thought the whole Mosley venture insane.*

DIARY   *28th January, 1931*

Down to the House to see the division on the second reading of the
Trade Disputes Bill. Churchill has just finished the wittiest speech
of his life and the House is still chuckling. The division bell rings and
they troop out. Pause of suspense while sounds of singing from the
lobbies: *Auld Lang Syne* and the *Red Flag*. Troop back and figure
announced. Unexpected Government majority. People troop out.
I follow.

Walking across St Stephen's Yard I observe a small figure in front
of me with collar turned up. He turns to see who is behind him and I
see it is Ramsay MacDonald. I say, 'Hullo, sir. How are you?' He
greets me warmly. We walk across to Downing Street and people
take off their hats as he passes. The traffic is stopped. He talks about
Vita's broadcast on Persia: the best he has ever heard. He asks me to
come in and have a drink. We reach the door of No. 10. He knocks.
The porter opens and stands to attention. Ramsay asks him, 'Is Berry
in?' 'No, sir, he has gone.' 'Is Ishbel in?' (not 'Miss Ishbel'). 'Yes,
sir.' 'Would you ask her to bring two glasses to my room?' We
then go upstairs. The room has an unlived-in appearance. Turners
over the fireplace. Ishbel is there. He asks her to get us a drink. She
goes out and returns with two tooth-glasses and a syphon. Says she
can't find any whisky. Ramsay says it is in the drawer of his table.
He finds it. 'What about some champagne', he says, 'to celebrate the
victory?' I say I will not have champagne. Malcolm [MacDonald]
comes in. 'A cigarette?' I say I will. 'Malcolm, we have got cigarettes,

haven't we—in that Egyptian box?' Malcolm goes to search for the Egyptian box. Then there are no matches.

He shows me the Turners. There is also a De Wint and a Wilson, both his own. And an early Turner also his own. He is pleased. He then says that he has made a deal with Lloyd George to score off the Tories. The Liberal resolution about unemployment has been so drafted that it forestalls any similar resolution by the Tories and is yet not a vote of censure. He tells me that Winston on leaving the House met him behind the Speaker's Chair. 'You'll get three months hard for tonight's work', he said. At which Ramsay raised his glass: 'Here's to our three months hard.' He complains of overwork and bother. He sees me out. Nothing will convince me that he is not a fundamentally simple man. Under all his affectation and vanity there is a core of real simplicity.

DIARY   4th February, 1931

Cimmie [Mosley] lunches at Boulestin. She tells me that Tom is about to found a new party. I promise to join.

DIARY   15th February, 1931

At Savehay.[1] Oliver Stanley, Harold Macmillan and other M.P.s come over including Margesson.[2] Play rounders. I fall into the stream. Tom is organising his New Party. Poor Cimmie cannot follow his repudiation of all the things he has taught her to say previously. She was not made for politics. She was made for society and the home. He wants me to sit on the Party's publicity committee. I say that he must ask Beaverbrook, but as the latter is so busy with his East Islington Election he will not listen.

DIARY   16th February, 1931

Go to see Roger Fry's pictures. Mere whispers from a variegated artistic past. Vita returns from Sissinghurst. She says that this week Beale will finish the boys' cottage,[3] fill the two lakes and knock out the central arch. Then we shall be finished with all our immediate labours, and with all that we can at present afford.

---

[1] The Mosleys' country house.
[2] David Margesson, became Conservative Chief Whip in November 1931.
[3] The isolated building known as the Priest's House. See Appendix.

DIARY   *3rd March, 1931*

Lunch with Enid Jones.[1] Find myself between Margot Oxford and
Violet Bonham Carter who both abuse me for my review of Elizabeth's novel,[2] for joining the Mosley Party, and in fact for being
myself in any way at all. Feel as if I have been massaged by two Kurds.

H.N. TO SIR OSWALD MOSLEY   *4th March, 1931*
                                                Evening Standard

My Dear Tom,

I spoke to Max [Beaverbrook] about joining your party. He was
most appreciative. Striding about the room he explained to me how
far, far more remunerative it would be for me to attach myself to
some more established machine. He became eloquent upon the
constituencies and jobs which could be conquered and acquired under
the tattered banners of the old parties. And when I, sitting there glum
and obstinate, remarked that I did not care for the old parties, he said,
'Go to Hell with ye—and God bless ye'.

After which he expressed admiration for yourself and deep sympathy
with me in my obstinacy and wrong-headedness. He said I had his
blessing (his sorrowed blessing) in joining you. I might serve on any
of your committees if I wished. I must not boost you unduly in the
Evening Standard. Nor must I devote to the New Party the time that
I ought to devote to the *Standard*. Nor must I proclaim on the house-
tops my conversion to the faith. But short of that I might do what I
liked.

I am sorry you are ill. For God's sake take care.

I have told Peter Howard, if he sees you at Oxford, to accost you
boldly and say, 'I am Peter Howard.' Please be nice to him.

DIARY   *15th March, 1931*

A heavenly day at Sissinghurst. Cut down more willows. Sow
seeds. Viti prunes pear trees. I read her new novel *All Passion Spent*[3]
—a lovely book.

[1] Enid Bagnold, the novelist and playwright, wife of Sir Roderick Jones, Chairman
of Reuter's.
[2] *Portrait of Caroline*, by Elizabeth Bibesco.
[3] Published by the Hogarth Press on 27th May. Less than a week later she started to
write her third novel in two years, *Family History*.

69

H.N. TO LORD BEAVERBROOK

22nd April, 1931
Sissinghurst

Dear Lord Beaverbrook,

The Central Office of the New Party approached me yesterday with an enquiry as to whether I would be prepared to contest a bye-election which they anticipate may be held within the next few weeks in one of the London suburbs. I informed them that I would have to obtain your approval before giving them any definite answer.

I understand that it would entail a fortnight's intensive work, during which I should have to take my leave of absence from the newspaper. I should probably, however, be able to do the books during that period.

Once I was either thoroughly in or thoroughly out, I could resume my ordinary work with the newspaper, if you have no objection.

Will you let me know your views? Naturally I shall abide without question by any decision you come to.

I hope you are enjoying your holiday.

Yours sincerely,

LORD BEAVERBROOK TO H.N.

24th April, 1931
Hotel Adlon, Berlin

Dear Harold,

Replying to your letter.

I think you would be mad to contest the bye-election, which, I presume is Brentford and Chiswick.[1] I am convinced you would make no appeal to the working-classes there. And I am certain you would make no appeal to the aristocracy.

But the decision rests with you, and I have no objection so far as concerns the newspaper work.

Yours ever,
M.B.

DIARY

27th April, 1931

Leave luncheon early to catch a train for Manchester, arriving there about 7 p.m. Go to the Midland Hotel, where I find Tom and Cimmie,

---

[1] He was correct. The Chiswick division was represented by a Conservative, Lt. Col. Walter Grant-Morden, who was expected to retire shortly. He died the following year.

Allan Young and Joad, Maureen Stanley, Eckersley, Bruce [Lockhart] and other hangers-on. We drive down to Ashton-under-Lyne where they have taken the Artillery Hall which is packed by some 6 to 7,000 people. They tell me that the canvass vote shows a 50 per cent vote for Young[1] and if this is so, it means that he should have a large majority over the other two. Tom himself has little confidence in these canvass votes but seems certain now that we shall get in above Labour. If this is so, it would be an enormous triumph.

The audience in the hall is at first rather sticky and heavy and we begin by answering questions. Most of the questions bear upon tariffs, unemployment and pensions. Tom then gets up to make his speech and profits enormously by a few interruptions from Labour supporters. He challenges Arthur Henderson[2] to meet him tomorrow in open debate and this stirs the audience to enthusiasm and excitement. Having thus broken the ice, he launches on an emotional oration on the lines that England is not yet dead and that it is for the New Party to save her. He is certainly an impassioned revivalist speaker, striding up and down the rather frail platform with great panther steps and gesticulating with a pointing, and occasionally a stabbing, index, with the result that there was real enthusiasm toward the end and one had the feeling that 90 per cent of the audience were certainly convinced at the moment.

DIARY   *29th April, 1931*

H. G. Wells talks to me after lunch about Beaverbrook. He says that he is really alarmed lest B. should have hardening of the brain. He contends that he is showing the first symptoms, namely a dislike of contradiction and an avoidance of all people who are likely to contest anything that he says. Wells had been down there lately and stated that he had returned with the determination never to visit Cherkley again, since one came away with a vague sense of humiliation and an acute sense of disquiet.

Dined with Clive Bell.[3] Keynes[4] and Maclagan[5] there. Keynes is

---

[1] The Ashton-under-Lyne bye-election was a key test of the New Party's strength. Allan Young, the Party's Secretary, was opposed by Labour and Conservative candidates. The result, announced on 1st May, was: Conservative, 12,420; Labour, 11,005; New Party, 4,472.

[2] The Foreign Secretary.   [3] The writer on art and literature.

[4] John Maynard Keynes, the economist, 1883–1946.

[5] Sir Eric Maclagan, Director of the Victoria and Albert Museum, 1924–45.

very helpful about the economics of the New Party. He says that he would, without question, vote for it. The attitude of the Labour Party on the Sunday Cinema Bill, as well as that on Free Trade, has disgusted him. He feels that our Party may really do an immense amount of good and that our programme is more sound and certainly more daring than that which any other party can advance. I asked his advice about commodity boards and whether it would be possible to institute them with the present Civil Service machinery and without necessitating a whole bureaucracy of its own. He says that he thinks it would. He points out that England is really richer than she has ever been before; that it is complete rubbish for André Siegfried[1] to say that we are lazy and unintelligent, since we are actually succeeding in bearing a burden of taxation, debts and standard of living which is at least twice as good as that of any other country. France is sacrificing everything to stability; that stability may become rigidity. What is wrong with us is that owing to circumstances we are only putting forth two-thirds of our productive power. He feels that the New Party, if intelligently directed, may mobilize the remaining third. He gives the whole pig industry as an instance. There is no reason at all why our bacon etc. could not be produced in this country. I returned with a bad cold in my head but greatly cheered by Keynes' approval of our programme.

DIARY   4th May, 1931

Go with Leonard and Virginia Woolf to see the French talking-film, Le Million.[2] The theatre is crowded with intellectuals, from which it is evident that this form of intelligent talkie has a great future before it. The French talent for amusing dialogue finds an enormous scope in this rapid motion and will render American films completely old-fashioned.

Walked back with Leonard Woolf. He bitterly regrets that Mosley should have left the Labour Party since he feels that within the Party itself he could have done such an enormous amount of good. It is not a question of the policy of the New Party, which he confesses is by far the best put forward, but he fears that the personal animosity raised by Mosley's action will prove too heavy a burden for us to carry.

---

[1] The French scholar. He had just published La Crise britannique au XXe Siècle.
[2] Directed by René Clair.

DIARY   *5th May, 1931*

Lunch with Tom Mosley at the Carlton Grill. John Strachey there. Tom had just had his first fencing practice since his illness and was feeling rather giddy. He recovered immediately upon having cider and asparagus. He is quite determined that I must stand for Chiswick, but he is not quite certain as yet whether Grant-Morden is going to resign. It is possible that he may be able to put his affairs in order[1] and retain the seat until the next General Election. If that happens, we are in a difficulty. There is no other bye-election coming along which offers so good a chance of making a show. Tom does not wish to waste his money upon any bye-election where we were unlikely to get under 2,000 votes but wishes rather to concentrate upon a dramatic bye-election like Chiswick where he hopes to get 6 to 7,000.

I urged him strongly to concentrate not so much on details of policy as upon a new attitude of mind. In the first place, any policy for dealing with the economic situation is of necessity too intricate to be understood by the electorate, and in the second place, all the best items in our programme are certain to be filched by other parties. I feel certain that our appeal will have to be an intellectual appeal to a new attitude of mind. Naturally, we would have to have a firm programme, but the item in that programme which would be most valuable would be that of the reform of the House of Commons. That is a question that no other party would have the face to filch from us.

DIARY   *6th May, 1931*

Dine with the Colefax's. A large dinner in honour of the Lamonts.[2] Keynes, Garvin, Wells, and Mosleys. Sit next to Garvin who discourses on gestures in speaking. He states that Gladstone made the most extraordinary gestures: he would bend at the knees and stoop down quite low while raising his huge arms and simian hands straight above his head. He told me that Joseph Chamberlain was the best voice-producer he had ever heard, having the curious faculty of being able to get a whisper across the widest hall. He thinks that the only sure rules about gestures and speaking are never to make a gesture

---

[1] Grant-Morden was in imminent danger of being declared a bankrupt, in which case he would have been obliged to surrender his seat.
[2] Thomas Lamont, Chairman of J. P. Morgan and Co., New York.

below your waist and never to show the audience the back of your hand.

When the women had gone, Keynes, Mosley, Garvin and I had a fierce political discussion. Both Keynes and Garvin are very sympathetic to Tom's programme but object deeply to his methods. 'Today', Garvin said, 'method is as important as ideas. Even if I agreed with all your ideas, I should be prevented from becoming an adherent to your Party since I disagree with all your methods.' Keynes' view is that it is almost impossible, with these vast constituencies of today, to get across an economic programme when the only arguments the electorate can understand are the simple political slogans. They are all agreed that Chiswick will be a very important election, but none of them imagines for one second that I shall get in.

Tom and I go on to the Embassy Club to meet Portal[1] and Moore-Brabazon.[2] We are late, and in running up the steps from the cloak-room, we push into someone whom I at first take to be a slouching ex-prize fighter but then recognise as the Prince of Wales.[3] He flicks cigar-ash at me with a rather sly smile. I do not think he recognises me, as we have not met for three years. Moore-Brabazon, as an ex-member of the Tory Government, is considered a prize by the New Party, and they are endeavouring to push him over the edge. I do not think they have succeeded.

DIARY   11th May, 1931

Literary Fund dinner. Duke of York[4] in the chair. Speakers: the Master of Wellington and Frazer[5] of the *Golden Bough*. The latter has written out his speech in his own handwriting and when it gets to the point, he can scarcely read it. There are vast, appalling pauses during which Lady Frazer, at his side, looks up with the bright smile of anticipation adopted by people who are completely deaf. She is always armed with a portable wireless which she wears on her bosom.

[1] Possibly the first Viscount Portal (1885–1949), who became Minister of Works in Churchill's wartime Government.

[2] Lt.-Col. John Moore-Brabazon, a pioneer motorist and aviator, formerly Conservative M.P. for Chatham and Parliamentary Secretary to the Ministry of Transport. He lost his seat in the 1929 Election, but regained it (for Wallasey) in October 1931.

[3] Subsequently King Edward VIII.   [4] Subsequently King George VI.

[5] Sir James Frazer (1854–1941), the anthropologist and authority on folk-lore. His *Golden Bough* was first published in 1890.

When I sat next to her once at dinner, this machine gave out strange sounds of jazz interspersed with vague and distant talks on poultry farming. It took me some time to discover what had happened.

DIARY   *28th May, 1931*

Shaw was at luncheon. He talked a great deal. He said that when he started to write a play, he never worked out the plot beforehand. What happened was that he had an idea for a play and started at once writing the first act. Subsequently, of course, he was aware, while writing, of the limitations of the stage, and he presumed that some censor was at work within him modelling what he wrote into dramatic form. After *Methuselah*, he had determined to write no further plays, but one day he had said to his wife that he was feeling growing-pains and a desire to write further. 'Why,' she said to him, 'do you not write about St Joan?' He replied, 'I will', and he started writing immediately. In the same way, *The Doctor's Dilemma* was taken entirely from a chance visit to a London hospital and a conversation with Dr Almoth Wright.[1] He then spoke a great deal about St Joan saying that she was the first Protestant and the first nationalist in Europe.

Go and see Tom Mosley at his office. Have a long talk. He is finding some difficulty in restraining the more active members of the Party. They all feel that he must do something dramatic immediately if the movement is not to stagnate. I beg him not to listen to such imprudent counsels. He tells me that the main response which we are getting, and which is very encouraging, comes from the younger Conservative group and is distinctly fascist in character. We discuss the present danger of the Party attracting eccentrics and people with a grievance. He thinks that it is unavoidable at first but that gradually, if we keep our heads, we shall attract more serious people. He is thinking of starting a weekly paper as the official organ of the Party. He fully realises that it may entail a heavy financial loss. He thinks that the Chiswick Election will come on in the second week of July.

H.N. TO V.S-W.   *28th May, 1931*
                                          4 King's Bench Walk, E.C.4

Darling, I am worried about Chiswick and us. You said it would make you hate me. Of course I know it was a joke. But it will be

[1] Sir Almoth Wright (1861–1947), the originator of anti-typhoid inoculation.

rather bad luck if my martyrdom in the cause of cleaner politics is to land me in a mess at home. My sweet, sweet looney. I do love you so.

DIARY   *30th May, 1931*

Down to Oxford. Meet Harold Macmillan in the train. He takes the usual young Tory view that his heart is entirely with the New Party but that he feels he can help us better by remaining in the Conservative ranks. He does not hesitate to admit that if we could obtain a certain number of seats in Parliament, most of the young Tories, all the Liberals and a large proportion of the youngish Labour people would come over to us. He anticipates the present Government being in power for another two years, followed by a Tory administration lasting some three years. He feels that five years from now, the New Party will have its great opportunity.

DIARY   *1st June, 1931*

Motor down late to Trent. Philip[1] is alone in the house, a slim, Baghdadi figure, slightly long in the tooth, dressed in a double-breasted, silk-fronted blue smoking-jacket with slippers of zebra hide. He has now finished the decoration of Trent and is a strange, lonely, un-English little figure, flitting among these vast apartments, removed from the ordinary passions, difficulties and necessities of life. He always seems to me the most unreal creature I have known. People who care over-much for the works of man end by losing all sense of the works of God, and even their friends become for them mere pieces of decoration to be put about the room.

DIARY   *8th June, 1931*

Go down to Oxford in the afternoon for the Annual Dinner of the Canning and Chatham Clubs. Philip Guedalla[2] on the train. I like him. He has a sharp mind and a modest temperament. He has almost finished his book about the Duke of Wellington and is evidently convinced that it is the best thing he has done.

---

[1] Sir Philip Sassoon. Conservative M.P. for Hythe from 1912 until his death in 1939. Under-Secretary of State for Air, 1924-29 and 1931-37. A man of great wealth and lover of the arts. Trent Park was his country-house near London.
[2] The historian. His book on the Duke of Wellington, *The Duke*, was published later in 1931.

Stay with John Sparrow[1] at All Souls. The dinner takes place at the Clarendon and David Cecil[2] takes the chair, having Winston Churchill on his right and myself on his left. On my other side is the secretary, young Ford.[3] There are about sixty or seventy people present and the whole thing is a great success. I have to make the first speech proposing the health of the Clubs and I am careful to keep it in a very light vein in order not to trespass upon Winston's subsequent oration. It was very well received. Winston makes a very set speech on the 'Wake up, England!' theme and after speaking with great intensity about our responsibilities in India, concludes rather lamely that we should accept the Simon Report. His speech is enthusiastically cheered by Bracken and young Randolph Churchill[4] but the applause of the other young men is rather perfunctory.

Oxford is looking very beautiful in the evening and John [Sparrow] and I walk about the quadrangle at All Souls agreeing that life, literature and politics are all three most agreeable things.

DIARY   *10th June, 1931*

Go to see Allan Young in the afternoon. He tells me that they are anxious for me to become a member of the [New] Party Council and to attend meetings as regularly as possible. I can see that he is most uneasy lest the Party should swerve too much to the right and be forced into Hitlerism. He considers that should a revolution break out in England, it would mean that the whole aim and objects of the Party have failed, as our central aim is to forestall and prevent such a happening. He does not approve of the idea that we should meet communist force with fascist force. He is deeply opposed to the Youth Movement, which, to his mind, is either meaningless or else means disciplined force. I wholly agree with him.

---

[1] One of H.N.'s closest friends, a scholar, literary critic and, for several years before and after the Second World War, a practising barrister. In June 1931 he was 24 years old. He was first elected a Fellow of All Souls in 1929, and became Warden of the College in 1952.
[2] Lord David Cecil, then aged 29, later Professor of English Literature at Oxford University.
[3] Edward (now Sir Edward) Ford. In 1946 he became Assistant Private Secretary to King George VI and subsequently to Queen Elizabeth II.
[4] Aged 20. Then an undergraduate at Christ Church, Oxford.

DIARY   *13th June, 1931*

Down to Sissinghurst. Discuss future plans with Vita and decide that
we shall make an enormous tree-border run down to the lake, backed
by may. Also decide to run a lime-walk around the top of the moat.
Draw designs in the evening for our new wing.[1] Our difficulty is
that we do not wish to fake a Tudor reproduction and yet anything
18th-century must look too grand for the rest of the building.

*The New Party was beginning to discover that it did not know what it
collectively believed in. Its policy on the current economic crisis was clear
enough, but beyond that there was no more than an offer of leadership,
discipline, courage and 'action' at home, and a vague internationalism
abroad. The attempt to define these principles more clearly soon led to
internal conflict. Mosley's imposition of his personal authority, his
impatience with the democratic processes, and differences on the Party's
attitude to Russia, resulted within a month in the resignation of two of his
key lieutenants, John Strachey and Allan Young. The Party's momentum
was dropping. Those who should have joined, had not joined. It was
also short of money. Mosley's response was to step up the number, size
and drama of his public meetings, but the Press boycott of the New Party
continued and the mounting economic crisis engulfed it.*

*On 16th June Mosley invited Harold Nicolson to edit his Party journal
'Action'. He replied that 'there was nothing I should like more or undertake with greater zest'. But he was bound to Beaverbrook by contract
until the end of 1932, and in any case the Party could not afford to pay
him the salary which he received at the 'Evening Standard', and he could
not afford to take less. At that moment, Beaverbrook himself made a
curious approach to Harold Nicolson. In the most roundabout way, he
led him to believe that if he were to abandon the New Party and his
proposed candidature for Chiswick, he could have the editorship of the
'Evening Standard' for the asking. That evening Harold Nicolson
discussed the choice before him with his wife.*

DIARY   *18th June, 1931*

After dinner, I discuss with V. the situation raised by my luncheon
with Beaverbrook. Clearly I am likely to fall between two stools.
Were I to enquire further into Beaverbrook's offer, I might well be

[1] This was intended to join the tower to the north wall, but the idea was abandoned.

put in a position of authority on the *Evening Standard* which would mean not merely a very high salary, but also an opportunity of making a decent and influential paper out of it. There is no limit to the possibilities opened by such a prospect. B. is quite likely to become an invalid and to hand over the administration of all his papers to a Directing Board. It would be quite possible to evolve out of this a position of great influence and power. Alternatively, there is a chance that the New Party within five years would be in such a position as to force a coalition upon one of the other two parties. In such a coalition, I should certainly be able to ask for the Foreign Office, and here again, there is no limit to the avenue of extensive power. I said that possibly it might be open to me to tell B. that I would take on the editorship of the *Standard* on condition that he allowed me twice a month to devote a column to New Party news. This would reconcile my two allegiances. I could run the paper in the Party interest for say four years, and at the end of that period I might rejoin the Party openly and enter politics with greater authority and even greater prospects. I then elaborate these prospects with great force and imagination. For some time V.'s responses had become fewer and more far between. When I reach the point where I picture myself riding on an elephant at Delhi, I find that for the last half-hour she has been asleep.

DIARY   *19th June, 1931*

Tell Tom about my strange interview with Beaverbrook yesterday. He says I must decide entirely in my own interests. He is, however, extremely anxious for me to edit his new paper and insists that he will give me £3,000 a year for this. I must think it over during the weekend and decide on Monday. At the committee meeting, Tom informs us that he has heard that Beaverbrook himself is financing Grant-Morden in order to postpone an Election. He feels, therefore, that we should go very cautiously regarding Chiswick and that I should be prepared, if necessary, to stand somewhere else.

LORD BEAVERBROOK TO H.N.   *25th June, 1931*
                                       Cherkley, Leatherhead, Surrey

Dear Harold,
    I am very sorry to hear that you are getting more deeply involved in the New Party.
    I think the movement has petered out. It might be saved by immense

sums of money, and brilliant journalistic support, but of course there is a conspiracy of silence in the newspapers, except for the particular newspapers I am connected with.

I hope you will give up the New Party. If you must burn your fingers in public life, go to a bright and big blaze.

Yours sincerely,

B.

DIARY   *3rd July, 1931*

John Strachey yesterday addressed a meeting of the 'active forces' branch of the Youth Movement. A garbled version of what passed was published this morning in the *Daily Herald*. Tom is extremely angry at this and reprimands Strachey in terms which, if addressed to me, would have caused me the most acute embarrassment. I do not deny that I was impressed by the force of discipline in Tom's speech. It is quite evident that he will allow no independence to any member of the Party and that he claims an almost autocratic position. I do not myself object to this, since if we are to be the thin end of the wedge, we must have an extremely sharp point and no splinters. I wonder, however, how long other members of the Council will tolerate such domination.

DIARY   *17th July, 1931*

I think that Tom at the bottom of his heart really wants a fascist movement, but Allan Young and John Strachey think only of the British working man. The whole thing is extremely thin ice. Tom is good-tempered and amused. I talk to him afterwards about the paper and we decide we must start immediately and go ahead within the next ten days.

DIARY   *20th July, 1931*

Tom thinks it quite possible that Winston and Lloyd George tomorrow will approach us for a promise of support in the event of a National Government being formed to cope with the crisis. He feels that supposing Lloyd George heads such a Government and invites us to cooperate, we shall be placed in a highly awkward situation. To form a 'National Opposition' might merely be to wreck the last hope of orderly solutions and play straight into the hands of the communists. To enter a coalition under Lloyd George would be a trifle humiliating and might lead to John Strachey and Allan Young severing all connection with the Party. In other words, Tom would enter the Government in a dominating position while the rank and file of the Party, who in John Strachey's case at least have made heavy sacrifices to join, would be stranded high and dry. I believe that Tom has concealed from his own left wing the fact that he has a meeting tomorrow with Lloyd George and Winston. Probably nothing will come of it and we shall circle round each other in an atmosphere of amicable chaff.

DIARY   *21st July, 1931*

Venizelos[1] telephones and asks me to the Ritz. He has his old magnificent smile, that splendid gesture of wide oratory—head on one side, chest upright, and an arm flung wide open, as if motioning someone to pass through a door.

We motor down to Archie Sinclair's house at Coombe. In the car we discuss the future of our Party. Tom foresees a split with Strachey and Allan Young. He says that he does not wish that to occur till the autumn. In other words he wishes to use them a little more before he flings them aside.

We arrive to find Lloyd George and Megan assembled. Ll.G. is very polite about my wireless talks, and Megan says that he really did listen every Friday and loved it. Then Winston and Brendan Bracken arrive. Cimmie [Mosley], Mrs Winston. Dinner. Between Megan and Mrs Winston. Women retire.

When left alone, Ll.G. begins at once: 'Now, what about this National Government? We here must form a National Opposition. I have every reason to believe that Baldwin and Ramsay at the slightest drop in the pound will come together in a Coalition. That moment must find us all united on the front opposition bench, and' (this very significantly, tapping on the table) 'we shall not be there long. ....' Having said this, he switches off on to a long conversation about the economic crisis, tariffs, unemployment, throwing out little sparks of compliments to right and left, drawing Winston in, Bracken in, Tom in, never directly referring to the National Opposition—but assuming that it will materialise. 'Yes, on that we should ...' etc. Using the word 'we' as indeterminate whether it meant 'I and my Party' or 'You and me'. The impression was that of a master-at-drawing sketching

<hr>

[1] Eleutherios Venizelos (1864–1936), the Cretan rebel, and in 1931 again Prime Minister of Greece, whom H.N. had first met at the Paris Peace Conference of 1919.

in a fig-leaf, not in outline, but by means of the shadows around it. Winston is very brilliant and amusing but not constructive. We all part on the assumption that although nothing has been said, the Great Coalition has been formed. Tom, I think, is pleased.

Lloyd George, in discussing the world economic crisis, stated that the Treaty of Versailles was at the time of its framing regarded as little more than 'a temporary measure of a nature to satisfy public opinion in the belligerent countries'. 'Even Clemenceau', he added, 'thought that.'

DIARY   23rd July, 1931

I am working at the *Evening Standard* office when, at about 11 a.m., Tom rings me up and says will I come round at once. He had at that moment received letters from John Strachey and Allan Young resigning from the Party. I go round at 12.30 and find the Council gathered together in gloom. We try to get hold of our two delinquents but they are out and will not return till 6. As 6 is the hour at which they announced their intention of communicating their resignation to the Press, that is not of much value. We adjourn for luncheon.

Back to the office. I begin drafting statements to the Press in order to meet John's impending announcement. While thus engaged, a letter comes in containing that announcement. It says that they have resigned because Tom, on such subjects as the Youth Movement, Unemployment Insurance, India and Russia, was adopting a fascist tendency.

At 5.30 we at last find they have returned to 7 North Street. Bill Allen[1] and I dash round in a cab. Allan Young descends to the dining room looking pale and on the verge of a nervous breakdown. We say that Tom suggests that they should not openly resign at this moment, but 'suspend' their resignation until 1st December, by which date they will be able to see whether their suspicions of our fascism are in fact justified. Allan might have accepted this, but at that moment John Strachey enters. Tremulous and uncouth he sits down and I repeat my piece. He says that it would be impossible for him to retain his name on a Party while taking no active direction of that Party's affairs. He would feel that in his absence we were doing things, with his name pledged, of which he would deeply disapprove. He then

[1] W. E. D. Allen, M.P. Resigned from the Conservative Party in 1931 to join the New Party.

begins, quivering with emotion, to indicate some of the directions in which Tom has of late abandoned the sacred cause of the worker. He says that ever since his illness he has been a different man. His faith has left him. He is acquiring a Tory mind. It is a reversion to type. He considers socialism a 'pathological condition'. John much dislikes being pathological. His great hirsute hands twitched neurotically as he explained to us, with trembling voice, how unpathological he really was.

Undoubtedly the defection of John and his statement that we were turning fascist will do enormous electoral harm to the Party. Politically however, it will place Tom in a position where, with greater ease, he can adhere to Lloyd George and Winston. I think that Tom and Allan are inspired with passionate sincerity. Subconsciously, however, Tom's autocratic methods and biting tongue have frayed their vanity and their nerves. I see us from this moment heading straight for Tory socialism.

DIARY   *24th July, 1931*

Tom conceives of great mass meetings with loud speakers—50,000 people at a time. One or two of our organisers and speakers have resigned but others have rallied to the cause. Walk back with Joad. I say that I have joined the Party since I felt it was the only party which gave to intelligence a position above possessions or the thoughts of Karl Marx. He says he left the Party because he felt it was about to subordinate intelligence to muscular bands of young men. I don't believe it. But he is a nice, nice man.

DIARY   *30th July, 1931*

To luncheon with the Huntingtons[1] to meet James Joyce.[2] We await the arrival of this mysterious celebrity in a drawing-room heavy with the scent of Madonna lilies. There are the Huntingtons (Gladys a little nervous), Lady Gosford and Desmond MacCarthy. We make conversation apprehensively. Suddenly a sound is heard on the staircase. We stop talking and rise. Mrs Joyce enters followed by her husband. A young-looking woman with the remains of beauty and an Irish accent so marked that she might have been a Belgian. Well dressed in

[1] Chairman of Putnam, the publishers.
[2] James Joyce (1882–1941), the Irish novelist, author of *Dubliners, Ulysses, Finnegans Wake*, etc.

the clothes of a young French bourgeoise: an art-nouveau brooch. Joyce himself, aloof and blind, follows her. My first impression is of a slightly bearded spinster: my second is of Willie King[1] made up like Philip II: my third of some thin little bird, peeking, crooked, reserved, violent and timid. Little claw hands. So blind that he stares away from one at a tangent, like a very thin owl.

We go down to luncheon. Gladys Huntington in her excitement talks to Joyce in a very shrill voice on the subject of Svevo.[2] She bursts into Italian. I address myself to Mildred Gosford, speaking of Eton and whether boys under twenty should be allowed to fly. With my left ear, however, I catch the fact that Joyce is contradicting Gladys pretty sharply, and withal with bored indifference. My conversation with Lady G. peters out about the same time as the Svevo subject. Desmond then weighs in with a talk on Charles Pace and the Partridge murder. I describe the latter with great verve and acumen. 'Are you', I say to Joyce, hoping to draw him into conversation, 'are you interested in murders?' 'Not,' he answers, with the gesture of a governess shutting the piano, 'not in the very least.' The failure of that opening leads Desmond to start on the subject of Sir Richard and Lady Burton. The fact that Burton was once consul at Trieste sends a pallid but very fleeting light of interest across the pinched features of Joyce. It is quickly gone. 'Are you interested', asks Desmond, 'in Burton?' 'Not', answers Joyce, 'in the very least.' In despair I tell, not him but Desmond, that I have not been allowed to mention *Ulysses* in my wireless talks. This makes Joyce perk up. He actually asks, 'What talks?' I tell him. He says he will send me a book about Ulysses which I can read and quote. He asks if I have read *Les Lauriers sont coupés* by a man to whom Moore dedicated *The Lake* and whose name, if I recollect aright, was Du Jardin,[3] and that the latter, a broken old man, came to visit Joyce with tears in his eyes. His description of this incident is human enough, in spite of the odd corner-look behind his spectacles. He is not a rude man: he manages to hide his dislike of the English in general and of the literary English in particular. But he is a difficult man to talk to. 'Joyce', as Desmond remarked afterwards, 'is not a very *convenient* guest at luncheon.'

[1] William King, the leading authority on Sèvres porcelain.
[2] Italo Svevo, author of *Confessions of Zeno*, etc.
[3] Edouard Dujardin. *Les Lauriers sont coupés* (1886) was the first 'stream of consciousness' novel.

The political and economic crisis, of which Harold Nicolson himself wrote the classic account in 'George V: His Life and Reign',[1] mounted to a climax in mid-August 1931. The scale of the crisis was such that the New Party ceased to be of any significance thereafter, and Mosley's paper 'Action', which was launched under Harold Nicolson's editorship in October, died by the end of the year. These events altered the entire direction of their political lives. In order to link and explain the following extracts, it is therefore necessary briefly to summarise the political background.

The failure of the Credit Anstalt of Vienna in June 1931 led to a rapid loss of confidence throughout Europe, and by July heavy withdrawals of capital from London were threatening the security of the pound sterling. There was imminent danger of a galloping inflation in England, such as had already ruined millions of people in Germany, France and Italy. The pound could only be saved by obtaining large credits in Paris and New York. These credits would only be given if the British Government produced a balanced budget, and the budget could not be balanced except by making heavy increases in taxation and cuts in expenditure. Among the latter, the foreign bankers expected to see reductions in unemployment pay. This was the crux. If the Labour Government did not make at least a 10 per cent cut in the dole, they would get no loans: if they did, they would be accused of breaking faith with the class which had brought them to power.

On 22nd August, the day when Harold Nicolson left Beaverbrook's employment for Mosley's, the Cabinet agreed by a majority that the cuts were necessary, but on the 23rd, when it was seen that the American banks were stepping up their pressure, the voting was only eleven in favour and nine against. MacDonald declared that he could not continue to lead a Cabinet so deeply divided and intended to place all their resignations in the hands of the King. He did so on 24th August, but to the astonishment of his colleagues, he returned from Buckingham Palace to Downing Street to announce that he had agreed with the leaders of the Opposition parties to form a Coalition Government, with himself as Prime Minister, in order to press through Parliament the necessary economic legislation, including a 10 per cent cut in unemployment pay. As soon as the immediate crisis was over, there would be a General Election.

His announcement created consternation. MacDonald found himself deserted by all his Cabinet except J. H. Thomas, Lord Sankey and a

[1] Constable. 1952.

most reluctant Philip Snowden. The others not only resigned their offices, but formed themselves into a Labour Opposition Party under Arthur Henderson, the former Foreign Secretary. They never forgave MacDonald. To them his action was a gross betrayal both of the Party and of the whole working-class: he had been tricked by the Conservatives and Liberals and surrendered to the foreign bankers: he had abandoned his colleagues for the sake of remaining Prime Minister himself. To the country at large he was represented as a patriot who had placed national above party interests.

During the whole of this period Harold Nicolson was planning the first issues of 'Action'. Beaverbrook released him from his contract with the 'Evening Standard', and even before he officially assumed his editorial chair in the Action offices, he was in constant conference with printers, designers and advertising men, preparing dummies, commissioning authors, supervising a New Party film, as well as sending periodic bulletins on the crisis to Oswald Mosley, who was on holiday in the South of France.

The first issue of 'Action' appeared on 8th October, 1931. It was a weekly political journal, openly identified with the New Party, of 32 pages and costing 2d. It bore the stamp of its editor's temperament and the world from which he came and in which he moved. It was reflective, intellectually subtle, journalistically rather amateurish: it attempted to reconcile propaganda for a political party with a faint air of distaste for all party politics: and the seriousness of the political pages was not well balanced by the jauntiness of the articles on sport and women's clothes. Those who wrote for it were, on the one hand, Harold Nicolson's friends like Peter Quennell, Osbert Sitwell, Francis Birrell, Christopher Hobhouse, Gerald Heard, and inevitably V. Sackville-West on gardening; and on the other, Party stalwarts like Oswald Mosley (the Leader always wrote the leader), Peter Howard and Dr Forgan. Harold Nicolson himself wrote the Notes of the Week and the book-reviews. It lacked, as he later came to admit, a consistent style, a clearly defined audience, a punch. For that reason among others, it failed. The first issue sold 160,000 copies: the last barely 15,000.

DIARY   *12th August, 1931*

Back to King's Bench Walk and discuss our layout with Hamlyn[1] and Joseph.[2] We agree: (1) To start with Notes of the Week. (2) To have three and not two columns. (3) To go in for pictures wildly.

[1] The General Manager of *Action*.   [2] Assistant-Editor.

86

(4) To base our policy on absolute outspokenness even about our own finances. (5) If possible to give them 32 pages for the first six weeks, financing that out of our promotion expenses and saying we are doing so. (6) To aim at a 100,000 circulation.

On to see Raymond.[1] He has been talking to [Maynard] Keynes. The latter thinks that a general breakdown is inevitable. America will revert to a Texas type of civilisation. France and Germany will go to war. Russia will starve. And we, though impoverished, may just survive. What has happened is that that little item 'profit' has dropped out of world economics. Food will be cheap and thus riots not too serious.

DIARY   *14th August, 1931*

Lunch with Gerald Heard. He agrees to contribute to the paper for a nominal fee. He is very keen on the Party and will be a most valuable asset, especially as Morgan Forster[2] described him on the wireless yesterday as one of the most penetrating minds in England. H. G. Wells is at the club. Ill and a trifle tipsy. But what a darling man. I tell him that he is to write for us, for nothing, an article on class distinctions. He says he will do so since he loves me dearly. Then on to see Hamlyn. He has got out several tenders for printing, some of which are very fair and reasonable. He and Joseph have at the same time knocked up a dummy lay-out, which is very brisk. Dine at the club and write a long letter to Tom Mosley reporting progress.

H.N. TO SIR OSWALD MOSLEY   *21st August, 1931*
    (*at Cap d'Antibes*)   *Sissinghurst*

My main worry is whether or not you should return immediately. On the one hand the other parties may be flooding the Sunday Press with manifestoes and statements and your silence may be misinterpreted. I recognise also that people may say that at the gravest crisis in present political history, you prefer to remain upon the Mediterranean. On the other hand, I do not see what you would do were you here at this moment, and I feel that it is more dignified to be absent and aloof, than to be present and not consulted.

---

[1] Raymond Mortimer, the literary critic, and H.N.'s lifelong friend.
[2] E. M. Forster, the novelist.

DIARY   *22nd August, 1931*

My last day at the *Evening Standard*. I have learnt much in this place. I have learnt that shallowness is the supreme evil. I have learnt that rapidity, hustle and rush are the allies of superficiality. My fastidiousness has been increased and with it a loathing of the uneducated. I have come to believe that the gulf between the educated and the uneducated is wider than that between the classes and more galling to the opposite side. I have not been popular in the office. I make perfunctory farewells. As I leave the building I shake my shoes symbolically.

Take the 2 pm. train from Victoria to Paris.

DIARY   *24th August, 1931*

Leave Paris at 10 am. At Dover meet [David] Margesson who does not think there will be a General Election. Take the train to Ashford. Get the *Star* there and read that Ramsay MacDonald has resigned and will form a Cabinet with Baldwin and the Liberals. The National Government. Am met by a car and drive to Sissinghurst. Pours with rain. All very sodden and cold.

DIARY   *26th August, 1931*

Round to meet Box[1] who says that Press people are to meet Mosley at Victoria. Decide to forestall them and to go to Dover. Arrive just after the boat is in. Meet Lady Salisbury and David Cecil. Tom is the last to get off the boat. Travel up with him in a coupé. He feels that we should build up rather than cut down. That the Tories and Socialists have both dished themselves, the former by giving way on a tariff, the latter by placing party above country. He feels that it would be impossible for us, having been the first to preach crisis, to cease our lonely voice now that the crisis has come. He will not therefore join with Henderson but go straight ahead on the New Party programme. He recognises that this will entail some readjustment of seats since we shall address our appeal to the upper and lower middle-classes. He thinks that we may possibly get some six members into the House, provided the General Election does not come before February. He fully foresees, however, that we may fail completely and in that case he would retire from public life for ten years. 'After all,' he says,

[1] F. M. Box, Chief Agent of the New Party.

'I have never led a civilised life at all since I entered politics as a boy. I can well afford to wait ten years, to study economics, and even then when I return I shall be no older than Bonar Law was when he first entered politics.'[1]

DIARY   31st August, 1931

Lunch with Tom at the Carlton Grill. He tells me that young Randolph [Churchill] came to see him fresh from his father at Biarritz. It was clear that he had been sent on a mission by Winston. The latter asked whether Tom would join him and the Tory toughs in opposition. The assumption is that neither the present Coalition nor the Labour Opposition will be anything more than sheep—able perhaps to balance the immediate budget but unable to cope with the industrial difficulties by which the deficit has been produced. In other words, they will succeed in taking from the capital of the nation such sums as they require to fill the gap. We wish to fill the gap by intensive work. Tom asked Randolph why his father did not combine with Lloyd George and Horne[2] to form an Opposition of his own. Randolph replied, 'Oh, because without you, he will not be able to get hold of the young men.' Tom is very pleased with that.

SIR OSWALD MOSLEY TO H.N.   4th September, 1931
                                                                    London

All the reports are at present remarkably encouraging. The most experienced of our speakers appraise the rise in our stocks in both working-class and middle-class areas since the crisis at 30 or 40 per cent, and of course it has only just begun.

Re the Youth Movement, yes, I think Williams[3] is a very remarkable man with an extraordinary flair for working-class movement and organisation. He realises what the bourgeois never can realise—that the working-class have practically no sense of being ridiculous in the way that we have, and that their very drab lives give them a great thirst for colour and for drama: hence the excesses of the cinema.

[1] Bonar Law was 42 when he first entered Parliament in 1900. Mosley would be 45 in 1941.
[2] Sir Robert Horne. Conservative M.P., 1918–37. Chancellor of the Exchequer, 1921–22.
[3] The New Party Youth organiser.

It should not be impossible to hold the balance now that we are rid of the pathological element[1] and can settle the question by inquiring not whether Germans, Italians or Russians have done the thing before, but whether the said thing is likely to attract the average Englishman or to make him laugh at us. I agree very much with you that Williams' line is much less likely to excite ridicule if it is introduced under cover of clubs, sporting and otherwise. The club institution has such a great grip in this country and his idea of working through the common-room of working-mens' clubs is quite excellent.

On the whole, however, I think that Peter Howard is just the man to hold the right balance. He must see that Mr Kid Lewis is invariably accompanied on his tours by Mr Sacheverell Sitwell—in a Siamese connection they might well form the symbol of our Youth Movement!

H.N. TO V.S-W.   *8th September, 1931*
                                              'Action', 5 Gordon Square, W.C.1
Madam,

I understand that you are prepared to contribute to this journal a weekly article containing hints to the amateur gardener.

This article should contain 650 words, and the ms of the first article should be received at this office not later than September 22nd.

The fee payable to you for this contribution will be £0. 0. 0.

Yours sincerely,
Harold Nicolson

DIARY   *12th September, 1931*
I walk miserably to Trafalgar Square. London is drenched in a fine driving scotch mist. We have been warned that the communists intend to break up our meeting. Nobody in such a damp cloud could break up anything. When I get there I see the tiny figure of Sellick Davies[2] high up on the plinth flanked with lions. He is shouting at a damp crowd of umbrellas. In a few minutes Tom appears escorted by the Youth Movement and guarded by Mr Kid Lewis. He climbs on to the plinth. He launches out into one of 'My Friends' speeches— eloquent, demagogic and brave. Then there are questions. The crowd is packed with communists and they try to get him to commit himself. He is very skilful. I and Bill Allen and some of the pioneers

[1] By this Mosley meant men like Strachey and Joad.
[2] Treasurer of the New Party.

stand shivering behind him with drenched marigolds in our button-
holes. The buses lumber up and around the National Gallery. The
crowd of some three hundred show wet faces looking up at us. Behind,
a few miserable sandwichmen slouch about with sodden posters
Take Action: Out October 8. At seven I dash to a chemist and take a
dose of ammoniated quinine. Then to K.B.W.,[1] a hot bath, and a
rub of camphorated oil. Then dine off cold mutton at the Cannon
Street Hotel. Then the 8.42 down to Sissinghurst. Gloom: damp:
fear: worry: perplexity: depression.

DIARY   *21st September, 1931*

The papers are full of a razor attack made on Tom at Glasgow. On
getting to the office I find Peter [Howard] back from there. He tells
me that the meeting was really rather a success. 20,000 people. The
speech was got across all right by loud-speakers. During the meeting a
note was passed up: 'Be careful when you go—the Reds have got
their razors'. When all the questions had been asked and answered,
Tom faced the crowd: called out, 'Now, boys': stepped from the
platform and advanced towards the little group of communists who
had created the disturbance. They turned and fled. Tom passed through
the crowd. The communists formed behind and attacked them from
the rear. A stone was thrown and hit Tom lightly on the head. A man
attacked him with a life-preserver but was seized in time. Peter
Howard was thrown and rose to knock a man down. They escaped
to their cars.
     We have a meeting of the Party. Tom says that this forces us to be
fascist and that we need no longer hesitate to create our trained and
disciplined force. We discuss their uniforms. I suggest grey flannel
trousers and shirts.

DIARY   *22nd September, 1931*

Party-meeting at 11.30. We discuss *fascismo*. Tom says the young
Tories are forcing on an Election for October. He is being approached
on all sides to join some combination. The increase in communism
will be rapid and immense. But can we counter this by fascism? And
will not the Conservative element be represented not by dynamic force
but by sheer static obstruction? The worst of it is that the communists
will collar our imaginative appeal to youth, novelty and excitement.

[1] 4 King's Bench Walk, Inner Temple, H.N.'s chambers.

We decide to call the youth movement the Volts (vigour—order—loyalty—triumph).

DIARY   *23rd September, 1931*

Tom is gloomy about our Election prospects, and is thinking almost of abstaining from Parliament. It is distressing that with so little time before us our leader should in fact be so uncertain of his views. He may do a deal with the National Party. His line is, 'The movement is more important than the Party.'

DIARY   *26th September, 1931*

Vita goes off by Folkestone this afternoon for a hiking tour in Provence. Going up in the train I think what it is that makes us so indispensable to each other. I think it is this. (a) That we each respect in the other some central core of reality. (b) Neither of us would find it easy to define that core, but we are aware of it and the other knows that it is there and recognised. This produces a feeling of not having to strive or posture. It is not a question of insincerity or sincerity. It is merely that when with each other we relax completely. Thus we get the maximum satisfaction out of a static relationship. (c) Yet our relations are also dynamic. We stimulate each other. We are not merely intellectual chairs to each other, we are intellectual exercise. I think it is the perfect adjustment between these two elements, the static and the dynamic, which creates such harmony in our lives. No one else knows or understands. Oh my precious, my gentle, my magnificent Viti!

Down to Cambridge with old Gaselee.[1] We walk about the colleges. He then shows me my room at Magdalene. Panelled walls, silver candlesticks, virginia creeper. We dress for dinner. Black tie. We assemble. A. E. Housman[2] and a don disguised as a Shropshire Lad. We have 1789 Madeira and Haut Brion and tripe and oysters and grouse-pie and mushrooms. The firelight flits on the silver of the smaller combination room and there are red shades, highly inflammable, to each candle. Housman is dry, soft, shy, prickly, smooth, conventional, silent, feminine, fussy, pernickety, polite, sensitive, tidy,

---

[1] Sir Stephen Gaselee (1882–1943). Librarian at the Foreign Office since 1920. Fellow of King's College, Cambridge.

[2] A. E. Housman (1859–1936), the poet, was Professor of Latin at Cambridge University and a Fellow of Trinity. *A Shropshire Lad* was first published in 1896.

greedy, and a touch of a toper. 'What is this, my dear Gaselee?' 'This is Estrella 1789.' 'A perfect wine.' Yet not eighteenth-century and still less 1890. *A bon bourgeois* who has seen more sensitive days. He does not talk much except about food. And at 10.30 he rises to take his leave. All his movements are best described in such Trollope expressions. Gaselee tells me afterwards that MacDonald had offered Housman the O.M. and that he had refused. A gymnophobic attitude on the part of the old poet. The other don, whose name I never heard, tells me that Housman was at school in Worcestershire and that it was to him an unhappy school. Shropshire meant the unattained and the liberated. He had scarcely been there. It was known to him only as an occasional jaunt. He made topographical mistakes in the poems. That is why he is so sensitive about being asked Shropshire questions.

An interesting evening. A strange island in the flux around me.

DIARY   *1st October, 1931*

Lunch with Sibyl Colefax. A good party. Lady Castlerosse, Diana Cooper, Charlie Chaplin, George Lloyd, H. G. Wells, Tom Mosley. We discuss fame. We all agree that we should like to be famous but that we should not like to be recognised. Charlie Chaplin[1] told us how he never realised at first that he was a famous man. He worked on quietly at Los Angeles staying at the athletic club. Then suddenly he went on holiday to New York. He then saw 'Charlie Chaplins' everywhere—in chocolate, in soap, on hoardings, 'and elderly bankers imitated me to amuse their children'. Yet he himself did not know a soul in New York. He walked through streets where he was famous and yet unknown. He at once went to a photographer and had himself photographed as he really is.

Tom tells me that he has had a secret meeting with Neville Chamberlain. The Tories are anxious to get some of us in and are prepared to do a secret deal. Box is to see their Chief Agent tomorrow to see what sort of bargain can be struck. I doubt whether they will give us anything worth having.

---

[1] The great comic actor was then aged 42.

4th October, 1931

Talk to Gielgud,[1] who is a fine young man. He does not want to specialise on juvenile parts since they imply rigidity. He takes a high view of his calling. I think he may well be the finest actor we have had since Irving. His voice and figure are excellent. Read Virginia Woolf's *The Waves*[2]—a magnificently audacious experiment. It is very beautiful and luminous.

Polling Day in the General Election of 1931 was on 27th October. Ramsay MacDonald went to the country as the head of a National Government, which included members of all three parties, but fewest from his own. He asked for an extension of the 'Doctor's Mandate' to do what was necessary for the country's rehabilitation, and his appeal was backed by the Conservatives under Baldwin and by a section of the Liberal Party, although Lloyd George stood aloof. MacDonald therefore found that the main body of his opponents came from his own former Party, and the contest between them was very bitter. Although he won overwhelmingly, it seemed that the Labour Party had destroyed itself. Only one of his former colleagues who had opposed him in the Labour cabinet, George Lansbury, was re-elected: men like Arthur Henderson, J. R. Clynes and Herbert Morrison went down with 200 others of the Parliamentary Labour Party. The Conservatives picked up what Labour lost. When the new Parliament assembled there were 556 supporters of the National Government, of whom 472 were Conservatives; and an Opposition of 56.

Within this great drama was enacted the minor drama of the New Party. Mosley put up twenty-four candidates. His policy was to act as a gadfly to the National Government, and gradually to evolve under his own leadership an effective alternative to the communist revolution which he considered inevitable. He proposed an inner Cabinet of five members who would virtually rule the country. Harold Nicolson put it thus in his own Election Address: 'I am not an alarmist, yet I am convinced that we may be faced within measurable distance by a proletarian revolt. The widespread dissatisfaction prevalent in these islands may at any moment become inflamed. If this danger is to be averted we shall require . . . the Corporate, the Organic, State.' The British electorate did not take kindly to these ideas. Of the twenty-four New Party candidates,

[1] Later Sir John Gielgud, the actor, then aged 27.
[2] Published by the Hogarth Press in 1931.

all, *including its leader, were defeated: twenty-two forfeited their deposits. Mosley himself obtained 10,500 votes at Stoke, his wife's former seat, but was bottom of the poll: eighteen others secured less then 1,000 each. Kid Lewis obtained 157 at Stepney. Harold Nicolson, as the New Party candidate for the Combined English Universities, came fifth of five candidates with 461.*

The combined English Universities was a two-member seat and the only one in this Election to be contested on the basis of proportional representation. Graduates of Sheffield, Leeds, Manchester, Liverpool, Birmingham, Durham, Reading and Bristol Universities voted by post. As the electorate was so dispersed there could be no meetings, no canvassing: the candidates appealed to their electors solely through their Election Addresses. This left Harold Nicolson free to speak for other New Party candidates and to edit 'Action'. The only incident in his own campaign arose out of his happy discovery that Sir William Jowitt, the Attorney General and one of his chief rivals, had supported the proposal to abolish University representation only a few months before. Sir William was enraged by Harold Nicolson's description of his candidature as 'brilliant adaptability'. 'A man votes against the construction of a bridge over a river', wrote Sir William to the 'Manchester Guardian': 'notwithstanding his opposition, the proposal is carried and the bridge is built. Is he guilty of brilliant adaptability if he makes use of it to cross the river?' Harold Nicolson replied: 'Sir William had at his disposal no less than 615 bridges. Why should he have chosen the one bridge which eight months ago he condemned as unsound? I fear I must stick to my word "adaptability". But after reading Sir William's letter, I readily withdraw the epithet "brilliant".' Sir William was not elected as one of the two members for the constituency.

DIARY   *28th October, 1931*

Wake up to read the Election returns. A panic swing towards the Tories. Henderson and most of the Labour Ministers are out. The whole thing is so absurd and sensational that there is little to be said about it. From the purely selfish point of view I am glad of the Tory landslide since it will restore momentary confidence and its very immensity covers up our own discomfiture. Tom is out at Stoke and we have done hopelessly all along the line. We have lost our deposits in all but two seats. Even the communists have done better than we have. The National Government will have a majority of some five hundred and the Socialists are reduced to fifty. Considering that the Labour Party have polled nearly seven million votes to the fourteen million of the National Government, this proportion is absurd. It really is most disquieting that at this crisis of our history we should have a purely one-party House of Commons and no strong Opposition. I view the situation with grave disquiet, and feel more than ever glad that I should have courted disaster with the New Party than achieved success under this Tory ramp. The King in the evening visits *Cavalcade*[1] and is exposed to a jingo demonstration. This was a grave mistake.

DIARY   *30th October, 1931*

On to the Savoy to meet Tom Mosley. He keeps me waiting some time and when he eventually arrives is rather exhausted. He is worried about Party funds but not worried about our eclipse. He realises that we have been swept away in a hurricane of sentiment and that our time is yet to come. He thinks he may get in at a bye-election in eighteen months and that meanwhile the paper is our central hope. We have some £14,000 still left on which to run the paper. Otherwise our funds are very low. He wants to keep Box, Eggleston, Sellick [Davies], Forgan and Peter Howard. That costs him about £1,000 a month. Poor Tom.

DIARY   *2nd November, 1931*

Holmes[2] rings up from Birmingham at 12.30. I have got 461 votes, thus forfeiting my deposit. But it is not a bad vote, considering. Lunch with Bruce Lockhart at Boulestin. He tells me that Beaverbrook is femininely jealous of Tom: his rhetoric, his disbelief in immediate success, his disregard of Max Beaverbrook.

On to Virginia Woolf. Life is a busy but I am glad to say mottled business. Hell! Heaven! I am going through a bad period. A period of ill success. I am so used to being successful that failure gives me indigestion. This does not arise from my forfeiting my deposit in the Election. I had foreseen that. It arises from my having been unable to control Hamlyn or run the paper in a really efficient manner. The fact

[1] By Noel Coward.
[2] Allen Holmes, H.N.'s Election agent. The Combined Universities was the last result to be announced. The successful candidates were Eleanor Rathbone (Independent, and one of the two sitting Members) and Sir R. Craddock (Conservative).

is that I am not a journalist and as such not well suited to be a man who runs a weekly. I see both sides of every question. That is a mistake. Joseph thinks I am a good editor. That is a confusion, on his part, of thought. What he really means is that I am rather a nice man. This quality is, I fear, a very different thing. Yet I should like to make something of this paper. The difficulty is that I am backed and financed by a political party. And even then it is not a party but a rather sly little movement. I am loyal to Tom since I have an affection for him. But I realise that his ideas are divergent from my own. He has no political judgement. He believes in fascism. I don't. I loathe it. And I apprehend that the conflict between the intellectual and the physical side of the N.P. may develop into something rather acute.

DIARY   *24th November, 1931*

I beg Tom not to get muddled up with the fascist crowd. I say that fascism is not suited to England. In Italy there was a long tradition of secret societies. In Germany there was a long tradition of militarism. Neither had a sense of humour. In England anything on those lines is doomed to failure and ridicule. He answers that he will concentrate on clubs and on cells within clubs: that a new movement cannot be made within the frame of a parliamentary party. I beg him to examine himself carefully and to make certain that his feelings are in no sense governed by anger, disappointment or a desire to get back on those who have let him down. I admit that disasters such as he has experienced in the last year are sufficient to upset the strongest character, but I contend that the strength of his own character is to be tested by the patience and balance with which he takes the present eclipse. He says he feels no resentment: that he had expected that the effect of his defeat would be to throw him into a life of pleasure: on the contrary, he feels bored now with night clubs and more interested than ever in serious things. I say that he must now acquire a reputation for seriousness at any cost. That he is destined to lead the Tory Party (at this, Cimmie, who is violently anti-Tory, screams loudly) and that he must rest in patience till that moment comes, and meanwhile travel and write books.

DIARY   *11th December, 1931*

Dine with Tom Mosley in his Ebury Street studio. He asks me to arrive early as he has something to say. That something is that Rothermere wishes to place the whole of the Harmsworth Press at his disposal. Tom, curiously enough, is cautious. He says that he wants to lie low for a bit but would be grateful for it later. He also tells me that Winston has been urging him to stand at the Westminster bye-election and promises to come out in his support. Here again Tom thinks he had better wait till the reaction against the National Government assumes a more definite shape.

The guests at this stage begin to arrive. Cimmie, who is profoundly working-class at heart, does not at all like this Harmsworth connexion. Tom pretends he was only pulling her leg. Cimmie wants to put a notice in *The Times* to the effect that she dissociates herself from Tom's fascist tendencies. We pass it off as a joke. The Hutchinsons[1] and Keynes arrive. Lydia[2] is very full of the ballet season which she wants to arrange next June. She says that Bloomsbury are old-fashioned. 'Why?' we ask. 'Their morals', she answers.

Maynard Keynes talks about the future of Great Britain. He thinks that we shall survive. He thinks that the National Government in some form or other will survive. He thinks that one morning Darby of No. 10 and Joan of No. 11 will wake up to find that they have both been kicked out and that Neville [Chamberlain] rules in their stead. He thinks that prices will rise and that gradually people will find that their dividends are being paid again. He thinks that if the Government were active and intelligent we could have prosperity, real prosperity, in ten years. He then talks of the ultimate future of this machine-fed civilisation. He says that we are reaching the stage when boots will cost 1d and wireless-sets 3d. Everybody will be rich on £100 a year. He admits, however, that the transition between a battered capitalism and the organized State will be slow and bitter. But he portends no disasters. A pleasant evening.

DIARY   *22nd December, 1931*

At the printers in the morning. Then to Olympia with Viti for the opening of the circus. A large luncheon. Sit next to Charles Graves.[3] Back to a Party meeting which lasts from 3 pm. to 8 pm. The first part is taken up with our endless disputes with regional organisers, who have all run us into debt and threaten bankruptcy or writs. The

[1] St John Hutchinson K.C. (1884–1942).
[2] Lydia Lopokova, the famous ballerina, who married Maynard Keynes in 1925.
[3] The author.

second part with the paper. We agree that we must close down on 31st December. The one remaining point is, shall we fuse with the *Saturday Review*[1] or not? We meet again at 10 pm. at the Savoy Grill. Randolph Churchill there. There may just be a chance of fusing with the *Saturday*, but only just a chance. Back to K.B.W. feeling crushed and fussed. Randolph told me that Max Beaverbrook had said that I was 'cracked'. An awful thought strikes me that he may be right.

DIARY   23rd December, 1931

A gloomy day spent in giving notice to the staff. I only hope there will be money enough to pay them good compensation. Viti visits my bank and extracts an unwilling loan from them. My future financial prospects are so black that I groan to gaze into the abyss. I feel irreparably shallow.

DIARY   24th December, 1931

Lunch with Sibyl Colefax at Boulestin. She tells me that she has made £2,000 last year by her own sole efforts.[2] She gets up by candle-light and fusses till midnight. A brave woman.

DIARY   31st December, 1931

Of all my years this has been the most unfortunate. Everything has gone wrong. I have lost not only my fortune[3] but much of my reputation. I incurred enmities: the enmity of Beaverbrook; the enmity of the B.B.C.[4] and the Athenaeum Club; the enmity of several stuffies. I left the *Evening Standard*, I failed in my Election, I

---

[1] The *Saturday Review* agreed to carry articles by Mosley 'from time to time' and to insert announcements of New Party activities. The reasons for closing down *Action* were financial, not political: its circulation, and therefore its advertising revenue, had slumped disastrously since the Election. The paper was losing £340 a week, and its initial capital had been no more than £17,000, part of which had been diverted to Party funds. The thirteenth, and last issue, was published on 31st December, 1931.

[2] Lady Colefax had founded a highly successful interior-decoration business, and was joined by John Fowler as her partner in 1938.

[3] He meant by this his 'good luck', since he never had any money apart from what he earned, and therefore had none to invest in *Action* or the New Party.

[4] This was a row over Sir John Reith's refusal to allow him to mention *Ulysses* in a series of talks about modern literature. His contract for *People and Things* was then terminated by the B.B.C. A selection of the talks was published by Constable under the same title.

failed over *Action*. I have been inexpedient throughout. My connexion with Tom Mosley has done me harm. I am thought trashy and a little mad. I have been reckless and arrogant. I have been silly. I must recapture my reputation. I must be cautious and more serious. I must not try to do so much, and must endeavour to do what I do with greater depth and application. I must avoid the superficial.

Yet in spite of all this—what fun life is!

1932

Visit to Rome and Berlin – financial worries – end of the New Party and H.N.'s break with Mosley – 'Public Faces' – 'Peacemaking' – making the garden at Sissinghurst – discussion with Lloyd George – embark for America

In the whole of Harold Nicolson's life, there had never been, and would never be again, a year so depressing as 1931. With the failure of 'Action' and the obliteration of the New Party as a political force, his association with Mosley might have come to an immediate end, but it lingered on for another four months. It required first-hand experience of fascism to make clear to both of them that their paths must diverge, the one to embrace it, the other to recoil from it, and thereafter a period for Harold Nicolson to steel himself to break with a friend for whom he still felt affection and regard.

They had intended to go together to both Rome and Berlin, but Mosley was obliged to call off his German trip at the last moment, and Harold Nicolson went there alone. But they met in Rome. Their proposed pilgrimage had already aroused comment in England, given the known tendencies of the New Party, and in the last issue of 'Action' an 'Explanation' was inserted to this effect: 'We intend to study ... new political forces born of crisis, conducted by youth and inspired by completely new ideas of economic and political organisation. This does not mean that we wish to import Italian or German methods and practices into this country. .... We go to collect information, so that if and when this country comes to pass through great events, a few of us may be prepared.' The Explanation did not do much to reassure Harold Nicolson's friends.

In January 1932 Mussolini had been in power for ten years and Hitler still had one year to wait. Although the Duce had not been able to bring real prosperity to Italy and there were 600,000 unemployed, the people were still captivated by his flamboyant policies at home (such as the draining of the Pontine Marshes) and his truculence abroad, and there was no serious opposition to the régime.

In Germany, by contrast, there was turmoil. Brüning had become the most unpopular Chancellor that Germany had ever had, and President Hindenburg, now 84 years old, was losing his grip on the politics, if not on the affections, of his countrymen. He had met Hitler for the first time in October 1931. The President had not been impressed by the

'Bohemian corporal', as he called him, and did not need much persuasion, even at his advanced age, to run for a second seven-year term of office in order to keep Hitler out. On 22nd January, the day when Harold Nicolson arrived in Berlin, Hitler announced that he too was a candidate for the Presidency. He knew that Hindenburg was almost unbeatable, but not to run would be a greater confession of weakness than a defeat at the polls. On 10th April, 1932 the results were declared: Hindenburg had gained 53 per cent of the votes, Hitler 36·8 per cent, and Thaelmann, the communist candidate, 10·2 per cent.

DIARY   *1st January, 1932*
                                                                        Paris

Walk up to the Arc de Triomphe through the Tuileries gardens. Memories of my past life: the toy shop in the Rue de Rivoli when we stayed at the Embassy in 1892[1]: the time that Reggie[2] and I stayed at Versailles and bicycled into Paris every morning leaving our bicycles at the Gare St Lazare: then the successive times at Jeanne[3]: the walk along the Avenue des Acacias learning French vocabularies: the Peace Conference. Thinking on these things I see children scudding little chips of ice over the round pond. They swirl and tinkle. The fountain clears a space for itself on the pond, blowing sideways. *J'ai plus de souvenirs que si j'avais mille ans.*[4]

I walk thus, *parmi les avoines folles,*[4] to the Hôtel Napoléon. I am taken up to Tom's room. He is in blue pyjamas having only just arisen from sleep. He had spent *réveillon* at the Fabre-Luces and had been kept up doing *jeux de société* till 8 am. He looks pale. Walk down the Avenue Friedland and the Faubourg St Honoré. Again these incessant memories—the insistence of which shows me how much I regret the past. The tricolor in the January sun. The swept courtyards of the Embassy. The tug always at my heart of diplomacy in all its forms.

To the Gare de Lyon. The Rome Express, magnificently aligned, waits to receive me and me alone. I occupy the whole of one coach

---

[1] When H.N. was six, he stayed with his uncle, Lord Dufferin, then British Ambassador in Paris. The visit is described in *Helen's Tower* (Constable. 1937).

[2] Reginald Cooper, H.N.'s oldest friend. They had first met as boys at Wellington College.

[3] Jeanne de Hénaut, who presided over a private academy for young Foreign Office candidates. She is described in *Some People* (Constable. 1927).

[4] Paul Verlaine, whose biography H.N. had written in 1921. It was his first book.

and a very little Frenchman occupies the whole of another coach. Read. Dine lonelily and well. Sleep.

DIARY

2nd January, 1932
Rome

Wake up in the early dawn and pull the blind. Night like a blank wall stands in front. I open the window wide. The train roars through the night. Suddenly the roaring is hushed. What I had taken for the blank wall of night was the blank wall of a tunnel. When we leave it, there is first an impression of silence, a hush like entering an Oxford quadrangle. And then in this silence emerge steel stars and great amphitheatres of iron mountains ribbed under a tiny moon of ice.

Get to Rome at 7.45. Christopher[1] there to meet me. He has been to Munich and is full of Hitler and his men. He says the Nazis think that we of the New Party have tried to do things too much on the grand. We should have begun in the alleys, not in Gordon Square. They think the fact that Tom is not a working man will be a disadvantage to us. They say Hitler has a genius for crowd psychology. I have a bath and then Gladwyn[2] comes. We dine with him at his flat, which looks out over the Castel S. Angelo.

DIARY

5th January, 1932
Rome

Tom talks to me about his impressions. He feels that one of our disadvantages as compared with these people is actual costs. In Italy you can run even a daily paper on almost nothing. Our own compositors' union is so exacting that we can never compete with the great combines. He believes therefore in the future of our clubs. He feels that we should have two categories: one the Nupa[3] clubs, and the other, Young England clubs. The latter would be wholly unpolitical. The former would correspond to the S.S. or *Schutzstaffel* organisation of the Nazis. Christopher [Hobhouse] insists that the movement should be working-class. I insist that it should be constitutional and

---

[1] Christopher Hobhouse, the author. He had first met H.N. in 1931, when he was an undergraduate at Oxford and a supporter of the New Party. They formed a close friendship which lasted until Hobhouse's death in 1940.

[2] Gladwyn Jebb, later Lord Gladwyn, then aged 31, and serving in the British Embassy, Rome.

[3] The Youth Movement of the New Party.

that Tom should enter Parliament. He thinks he could do so with the backing of Winston and the Harmsworth press.

DIARY   6th January, 1932
                                                                              Rome

Spend most of the day reading *fascisti* pamphlets. They certainly have turned the whole country into an army. From cradle to grave one is cast in the mould of *fascismo* and there can be no escape. I am much impressed by the efficiency of all this on paper. Yet I wonder how it works in individual lives and shall not feel certain about it until I have lived some time in Italy. It is certainly a socialist experiment in that it destroys individuality. It also destroys liberty. Once a person insists on how you are to think he immediately begins to insist on how you are to behave. I admit that under this system you can attain to a degree of energy and efficiency not reached in our own island. And yet, and yet. . . . The whole thing is an inverted pyramid.

Tom cannot keep his mind off shock troops and the roll of drums around Westminster. He is a romantic. That is a great failing.

We dine up high by the Trinità dei Monti. A lovely flat with a view one way to the Villa Medici and the other way all over Rome. Signora Sarfatti[1] is there. She is the friend of Mussolini whom we met at the Embassy yesterday. A blonde questing woman, the daughter of a Venetian Jew who married a Jew in Milan. It was there that she helped Mussolini on the *Popolo d'Italia*, right back in 1914. She is at present his *confidante* and must be used by him to bring the gossip of Rome to the Villa Torlonia. She says that Mussolini is the greatest worker ever known: he rides in the morning, then a little fencing, then work, and then after dinner he plays the violin to himself. Tom asks how much sleep he gets. She answers, 'Always nine hours'. I can see Tom doing sums in his head and concluding that on such a time-table Musso cannot be hard-worked at all. Especially as he spends hours on needless interviews.

DIARY   7th January, 1932
                                                                              Rome

Start early to visit the reclamation of the Pontine Marshes. Pick up Gladwyn [Jebb], Murray and McClure at the Embassy and drive out

[1] Margherita Sarfatti. She was Mussolini's constant companion at the time of the March on Rome in 1922.

to Ninfa. A grey day. We go to Gelasio Gaetani's house amid the waters and the ruins. Lunch in his big room. Then on to below Sermoneta. And thus for hours across white roads and ponds seeing cranes, lorries, electric trams, new houses, canals.

Back in time to see Tom off to Mussolini. He finds him affable but unimpressive. He advises Tom not to try the military stunt in England.

DIARY   *9th January, 1932*
                                                                        Rome

Go to Campidoglio and look down upon the Forum. Decide that I must evolve a theory of ethics which will give consistency to all my impulses. Just being jolly is not enough, especially when one gives a simultaneous impression of being unkind. A lovely evening. The lights come out on the Janiculum. The motors squeak and grate in front of the Palazzo Venezia. I return slowly. Slowly I descend the steps. Rome is below me. The clouds, now wisps of purple, scud across a sunset sky. And on observing me, the two wolves which are kept in a hutch on the Capitoline Hill raise their twin snouts towards the west and let forth an ululation of such sustained misery that I smile. At least I am not captive. I descend the steps to the accompaniment of that animal howl: Yooo-yoo-yooo-yoah-youah-yoo. I feel a second Romulus weaned by wolves. A good omen for *La Vita Nuova*, a good ending for *La Nuit de Rome*.

DIARY   *18th January, 1932*
                                                                      London

Go to see Tom on his return from Italy. He was much inspired by Milan which he found Greek and bracing. He says that Mussolini sent him a message telling him to call himself Fascist. He does not want to do anything at present. What he would like, would be to lie low till the autumn, write a book, then rope in Winston Churchill, Lloyd, Rothermere and if possible Beaverbrook, into a League of Youth. Then launch an autumn campaign. He fears however that the Harmsworths, being restless folk, cannot be kept on ice for so long as the autumn and that we may be forced to do something violent in the spring. It is a bore being thus dependent on the prima donnas of the Press.

DIARY   *22nd January, 1932*
                                                                  Berlin

Arrive Berlin in a misty dawn. Go to see Rumbold.[1] He tells me that
he thinks the Hitlerites have missed the boat and are losing ground
every day. Go and see Lady Rumbold. She takes me and Christopher
[Sykes] in her car to see Mrs Carpenter. Brücken Allee.[2] Memories and
half-regrets. I was obscurely respectable then, now I am blatantly
well known.

DIARY   *24th January, 1932*
                                                                  Berlin

My general impression is that Hitler has missed the boat. There was a
moment when he stood at the crest of a national emotion. He could
then have made either a coup d'état or forced a coalition with Brüning.
He has missed that moment. The intelligent people feel that the
economic situation is so complicated that only experts should be
allowed to deal with it. The unintellectual people are beginning to
feel that Brüning and not Hitler represents the soul of Germany. In
Prussia, it is true, Hitler is gaining ground. But he is losing it in
Bavaria and Würtemberg which are comparatively prosperous.
Hitlerism, as a doctrine, is a doctrine of despair. I have the impression
that the whole Nazi movement has been a catastrophe for this country.
It has mobilised and coordinated the discontented into an expectant
group: Hitlerism can never satisfy these expectations: the opinion
they have mobilised may in the end swing suddenly over to communism. And if that be a disaster (as to which I am still not certain),
then Hitler is responsible. The Ambassador [Rumbold] feels that
anything may happen and that the only certain thing is uncertainty.

DIARY   *30th January, 1932*
                                                                  London

Telephone to Tom. He says that Rothermere will not back him
before the autumn. I am delighted by this procrastination. I want Tom
to lie low, since I feel that the New Party is as dead as a doornail and
must be allowed a decent burial. No exhumation. Down to Sissinghurst.

[1] Sir Horace Rumbold, British Ambassador in Berlin, 1928–33.
[2] H.N.'s flat when he was Counsellor at the British Embassy, 1927–29.

The question now arose what Harold Nicolson was to do, not only with the next few months, but with the second half of his life. He had cut his ties with diplomacy, journalism, and at least temporarily, with politics. He must earn his living, and quickly, for his income had dried up, and his way of life was in the circumstances highly extravagant. The Nicolsons were now running three houses: King's Bench Walk, Long Barn and Sissinghurst. They had two secretaries, a cook, a lady's maid, a chauffeur, a valet and three gardeners. They had two sons at Eton. It would never occur to Harold Nicolson to give up his agreeable social life in London, or to appeal for help to Lady Sackville, whose manner towards them and to all her former friends was becoming increasingly odd: she was issuing writs as fast as she received them, claiming that honourable men like Sir Edwin Lutyens had 'stolen' works of art that she had given him in lieu of architectural fees, and that every tradesman's bill was an outrage and a deceit. She nicknamed her house at Brighton, with pathetic jocularity, the Writs Hotel.

It therefore seems strange that a further two months were to pass before Harold Nicolson settled down again to serious work, and a further nine months before they took the obvious step of letting Long Barn and moving permanently to Sissinghurst. During this period he was emotionally exhausted by his experience of the New Party, from which he was gently trying to shake himself free, and was writing no more than the occasional article and lecture. Several offers of regular employment came to nothing: he rejected with disgust a proposal that he should edit the gossip column of the 'Sunday Dispatch': the idea that he might become literary editor of the 'New Statesman' greatly appealed to him, but it did not mature: there were inconclusive approaches from the 'Sunday Times', from a group of provincial dailies, and even from Lord Beaverbrook, who at one moment suggested that he should write the weekly book-reviews for the 'Sunday Express'. The only firm commitment was a joint lecture-tour of the United States that he and V. Sackville-West were to undertake in the first months of 1933. But that was still almost a year ahead.

DIARY   31st January, 1932

There is a dead and drowned mouse in the lily-pool. I feel like that mouse—static, obese and decaying. Viti is calm, comforting and considerate. And yet (for have I not been reading a batch of insulting press-cuttings?) life is a drab and dreary thing. I had a great chance. I have missed it. I have made a fool of myself in every respect.

Surely there was a time I might have trod
The sunlit heights, and from life's dissonance
Struck one clear chord to reach the ears of God?[1]

Very glum. Discuss finance. Viti keeps on saying that we have got enough to go on with. But when one goes into it, that enough represents only two months. I must get a job. Yet all the jobs which pay humiliate. And the decent jobs do not pay. Come back to Long Barn. Arrange my books sadly. Weigh myself sadly. Have put on eight pounds. Feel ashamed of myself, my attainments, and my character. Am I a serious person at all? Vita thinks I could make £2,000 by writing a novel. I don't. The discrepancy between these two theories causes me some distress of mind.

DIARY   *2nd February, 1932*

Go to see Beaverbrook at Stornoway House. He welcomes me with twin opening hands. 'My dear Harold, it *is* good to see you again.' He asks me about Germany. He asks me about Tom's personal finances. He says that Tom is an ambitious man, whereas he (Beaverbrook) is not an ambitious man. He says that Tom committed errors of tactics which have done him harm. He does not think that this harm is permanent. He thinks that Tom really ought not to go to the public parties given by Lord Castlerosse. 'I', he says, 'would never go to any of Valentine's parties.' He thinks that Tom should try to discover a real point of difference between him and the National Government and hammer at that difference at meetings in the provinces. He says that it would be a mistake for any of us to retire to the country and lick our wounds. He thinks that I should write a biography of Curzon. He thinks that I exaggerate when I feel that I have lost prestige. He indicates that I might do books for the *Sunday Express*. He exercises his charm which is vital and vivid. He says that we must meet often and again.

DIARY   *23rd February, 1932*

On to the Savoy Grill with Tom, Cimmie, Viti and Hilda [Matheson]. Viti loathes Tom. He gives her the creeps. She tells me that Leonard Woolf has an idea that I should take on the literary editorship of the *New Statesman*. I should like that.

[1] Oscar Wilde, lines prefixed to his *Poems*, Paris edition, 1903.

DIARY   *28th February, 1932*

Peter Howard and John [Sparrow] come. We play football. It is the first and last time that I shall ever play football against the ex-captain of England. I knock him down. 'Did I hurt you, Peter?' 'No, Harold, you did *not* hurt me.' In the evening Eddy[1] and Raymond [Mortimer] come over. We play the truth game. The boys[2] now fit in absolutely to our social life and are an unending joy.

DIARY   *2nd March, 1932*

Lunch with T. S. Eliot and Jim Barnes[3] at the Spanish restaurant in Swallow Street. We discuss the making of a symposium on modern politics. I say that unless we tell our contributors that the book is New Party or fascist in tendency we are not playing fair. And that if we do tell them this we shall not get good contributors. I thus propose that Jim should write an Introduction showing where Tom has made mistakes, that he should send Tom that Introduction, and that on the basis of that Introduction he should invite Keynes etc. to contribute. Eliot agrees. He is very yellow and glum. Perfect manners. He looks like a sacerdotal lawyer—dyspeptic, ascetic, eclectic. Inhibitions. Yet obviously a nice man and a great poet. My admiration for him does not flag. He is without pose and full of poise. He makes one feel that all cleverness is an excuse for thinking hard.

Then on to see Lutyens' drawings for the Liverpool Cathedral.[4] I cannot fully make them out, being a fool about ecclesiastical architecture. I am sure it is all magnificent, but I cannot see. He shows us the Delhi photographs. A real work of genius. Christopher[5] walks back exclaiming to the March sunshine upon the genius of Edwin Lutyens. 'Gosh!' he says, 'Gosh!'

---

[1] Edward Sackville-West, the author and music-critic, V.S-W.'s first cousin.
[2] On Long Leave from Eton.
[3] The son of Sir Hugh Barnes. He led an adventurous political life on the European Continent.
[4] Sir Edwin Lutyens' designs for the vast Roman Catholic Cathedral at Liverpool had been published in September 1930, a few months after the official opening of the Viceroy's House, New Delhi, on which Lutyens had been working for seventeen years. The foundation-stone of the Cathedral was laid on 5th June, 1933.
[5] Christopher Hobhouse was now sharing H.N.'s flat in King's Bench Walk.

DIARY   *6th March, 1932*

Louise[1] during the day has been spreading out the carpets which Viti brought from Streatham.[2] They are moth-eaten but superb. It is typical of our existence that with no settled income and no certain prospects we should live in a muddle of museum carpets, ruined castles, and penury. Yet we know very well that all this uncertainty is better for us than a dull and unadventurous security. After dinner we discuss the front of Sissinghurst. We decide to plant a wall of limes framing the two gables and the arch, and following on to a poplar avenue across the fields. That is our life. Work, uncertainty, and huge capitalistic schemes. And are we wrong? My God! we are not wrong.

DIARY   *14th March, 1932*

Feel more happy and healthy than I have felt in my life. This is due to violet rays at Sissinghurst, plus lack of unsuccessful occupation. I am doing nothing, therefore I do not fail. I am about to do many things, therefore I am on the verge of success. I know that this verge will not be a very sharp or productive verge. But until I reach it, I feel it will be magnificent, remunerative and calm.

DIARY   *15th March, 1932*

Tom has seen David Margesson, the Tory Whip, who is anxious for him to come back to St Stephen's in the shape of a National Independent. This means the end of the New Party. Tom does not wish to end it, being still obsessed by Mussolinian ideas. We suggest that Nupa can keep *fascismo* alive in this country and that the New Party can now acknowledge its own death. Peter Howard is summoned and speaks out in this sense with an openness which neither Bob Forgan nor I have as yet dared to assume. An important meeting, in that the death of the New Party has now been frankly discussed and the ice broken. Down to Long Barn.

DIARY   *20th March, 1932*

A lovely day. Dry and warm. Over to Sissinghurst. The Hayters have dug the places for the limes, have cut down the miffy little trees at the end of the moat walk, and prepared for the line of hornbeams

---

[1] Louise Genoux, V.S-W.'s French lady's-maid.
[2] One of Lady Sackville's houses, which she was then selling.

which is to join, frame and integrate that perspective. Vita and I measure the kitchen-garden[1] to discover how much paling will be required to make it square. I fiddle about with this vista problem. Obviously what would be good in a teleological sense would be to put the end of the main nuttery walk at the end of a main vista running from the new angle of the kitchen-garden, past the cottage garden and thus perspectively to what is now a gate into a field but which one day will be a classic statue erect among cherry trees. Only this cuts angularly across the holly hedge in our own little cottage garden and fits in obtusely with the rest of the design. That is what is such a bore about Sissinghurst. It is magnificent but constantly obtuse.

Disturbed by these considerations we weed the delphinium bed. A sedentary occupation which gives us the reward of finding one or two delphiniums sprouting among the crow's foot. It is very odd. I do not like weeding in any case. I have a cold coming on. I cannot get a job and am deeply in debt. I foresee no exit from our financial worries. Yet Vita and I are as happy as larks alone together. It is a spring day. Very odd.

DIARY   *30th March, 1932*

Down to Wellington College with Raymond [Mortimer]. I have not been there for twenty-seven years. I go up to my old room. I find in the woodwork of the partition the slit I cut for shoving notes through to Dainty. My memory is only vaguely stirred. I get a sudden revival at seeing the tiles over the mantelpiece of the dining-room—a pan-athenaic festival which I had forgotten. It gives me a stir like some forgotten smell. Talk to the boys. I find them more enlightened and less gawky than we were. This is due to the better atmosphere at home. We were always strangers to our parents. But the old segregation between the houses and the old athletic fetish still persists. The masters are progressive. I have no affection for the school whatsoever and no pride in it. I feel a grievance against it for having retarded my development. But I should have been happier there now than I was then. It is more human.

---

[1] Which became the rose-garden. It was then an allotment for cabbages.

DIARY   *5th April, 1932*

We decide to dissolve the New Party as a political or electoral organisation and to keep on with Nupa on a reduced basis. This means sacking Peter Howard. I say that I do not approve of the Party being transformed into Nupa. I quite see that that organisation may have its uses as a militant branch. But I am not militant in the least, and if we are too closely identified with these fascist bands, not only I, but others of the intellectuals, will become alien and even adverse to the whole movement. Tom takes it well. I say that our aim is to get him back to Parliament without undue loss of prestige. Therefore the sooner we allow the New Party to die a natural death, the better. He agrees.

H.N. TO DR ROBERT FORGAN   *15th April, 1932*
                                                                Sissinghurst

The difficulty about the New Party is that it is no longer new and no longer a party. The ideas which we stood for have been bagged by other people and are being adopted, though not with sufficient energy, by the present Government.

I joined the Party for two reasons. (1) Personal affection and belief in Tom. (2) A conviction that a serious crisis was impending and that our economic and parliamentary system must be transformed if a collapse were to be avoided. Now I feel that the New Party as such has become too much identified with Hitlerism.

I do not think that you or I can accuse ourselves of any lack of loyalty to Tom, since we have seen him through his worst period. On the other hand I do not believe in fascism for England, and cannot consent to be identified with anything of the sort. I do not think, moreover, that it will in practice be possible to ride two horses—mastering the young filly of the King's Road[1] and at the same time driving the old cab-horse of liberal intellectualism. The cab-horse simply will not budge. He will lie down in the road with all his four feet in the air.

If Tom would follow my example—retire into private and studious life for a bit, and then emerge fortified and purged—he will still be Prime Minister of England. But if he gets entangled with the boys' brigade he will be edged gradually into becoming a revolutionary—and to that waste land I cannot follow him.

[1] Nupa's headquarters, and later the headquarters of the British Union of Fascists.

I go to the New Party meeting in Great George Street. There are crowds at St Stephen's as Neville Chamberlain is introducing his Budget. Tom says he has been asked by Margesson to rejoin the Tory Party, and that he has been asked by Kenworthy[1] to lead the Labour Party. He will do neither of these things. He wishes to coordinate all the fascist groups with Nupa and thus form a central fascist body under his own leadership. I say that I think this is a mistake. He says that it would be impossible for him to re-enter the 'machine' of one of the older parties. That by doing so he would again have to place himself in a strait-waistcoat. That he has no desire for power on those terms. That he is convinced that we are entering a phase of abnormality and that he does not wish to be tarred with the brush of the old régime. That he thinks, as leader of the fascists, he could accomplish more than as a party back-bencher, and that in fact he is prepared to run the risk of further failure, ridicule and assault, rather than to allow the active forces in this country to fall into other hands. I again say that I do not believe that this country will ever stand for violence, and that by resorting to violence he will make himself detested by a few and ridiculed by many. He says that may be so, but he is prepared to take the risk. I say that on such paths I cannot follow him.[2]

The argument, though painful, is perfectly amicable. The ice cracks at no single moment. Nor do I think that Tom was hurt or imagined for one moment that I was deserting him.

Yet I hated it all, and with battered nerves returned to Cannon Street and took the train home.

That, except for mopping up, was the end of the New Party. Harold Nicolson had already begun to write 'Public Faces', which he was to

---

[1] J. M. Kenworthy succeeded his father as Lord Strabogli in 1934. He was Liberal (and after 1926, Labour) M.P. for Central Hull, 1919–31.

[2] Sir Oswald Mosley, on being shown in 1965 all the passages which refer to him, commented: 'It seemed to me that we had the clear choice of organising to overcome the violence or of closing down; our only effective means of spreading our ideas was public meetings. The decision so to organise created an intelligible and honourable difference of opinion, which led to the departure of old friends, including Harold Nicolson, who throughout these troubles was a most loyal colleague at considerable personal sacrifice. I do not think it is fair therefore to accuse me of loving violence, as some have done.'

finish within three months. This novel, the only one he wrote apart from 'Sweet Waters' (1921), was a satirical account of a political crisis in the year 1939. By setting his story in the not too distant future he was able to allot to his friends new roles: Winston Churchill was destined to head a coalition Government with Oswald Mosley in 1936, Philip Noel-Baker and Brendan Bracken to become successive Foreign Secretaries, and Robert Boothby Secretary of State for War. Diplomatic friends were awarded equivalent promotion. The less agreeable characters were fictional. Not only was the novel extremely amusing and revealed as no previous novelist had ever done what went on behind the scenes of diplomatic life, but it contained an astonishing prophecy which boosted its sales thirteen years later: it foretold, by name and function, the atomic bomb. The crisis stemmed from the discovery that a new mineral, found only on an island in the Persian Gulf over which the British had concessionary rights, 'might produce in large quantities an element so unstable that beside it radium would be as dull as lead'. A single bomb made of this substance, no bigger than an inkstand, 'could by the discharge of its electrons destroy New York'. For sufficient scientific jargon to make the idea sound plausible, but not for the idea itself, Harold Nicolson was indebted to Gerald Heard.

He wrote the book at Sissinghurst at the rate of 5,000 words a day, and as his mind stretched, his spirits slowly rose.

DIARY   *11th April, 1932*

I have been thinking during the last few days about my book. I have now had three good months of quarantine, and feel that I have at last got the poison of journalism out of my system. I can now settle down to write a book. What book? Historical or literary books are not in question, firstly because I have not with me my works of reference,[1] and secondly because I must make money. It thus comes down to doing either a sequel to *Some People* or a novel on a large scale. I have toyed with the former idea, and written or begun one story which picks up some people just as I plough in the lorry through the waters of Babylon.[2] Yet I am not happy about it. Sequels are in every case bad things. I expended upon *Some People* the best of my autobiographical experience, and the sense of development which gave unity to that book could not be reproduced again in a book dealing only with

[1] They were still at Long Barn.
[2] On his way to join the staff of H.M. Legation, Tehran, in 1925.

my middle life. Again, the note of *Some People* is good-humoured irony plus a certain youthful irreverence: I could not, at my age, recapture the exact mood in which it was written, and if I did, the repetition of that mood might prove ungainly and false. In the third place, I have nothing to write about which interests me on the scale of *Some People* things: I could write of Reza Shah and Hindenburg, but I do not think it would work out in the right key.

I shall try, therefore, to write a novel. About what? I think that it should be a dramatic, even a romantic, novel. Dealing with diplomacy and character. A central figure, intense as Charles Siepmann,[1] who might be a Private Secretary. A dispute, say with Persia. A Secretary of State such as Joynson Hicks[2]—unctuous, evangelical, insincere. A woman Under-Secretary of the type of Hilda Matheson. All this could work up into a play eventually. So much for the scaffold: but I must choose a material and a design. There must be a central intellectual theme: and a central emotional theme. I must choose one out of many 'ideas' and concentrate on that: the individual versus the democratic machine; something like that. But apart from all this, it is the *key* which I find difficult—whether ironical or romantic or angry.

DIARY   *12th April, 1932*

Viti and the boys go over to Brighton.[3] I stay at home and begin my novel. I work out a heroic figure introduced in the Galerie des Glaces just after the signature of the Treaty of Versailles. It won't do at all. It is not in my key. Go down to the wood, collect fox-gloves in the pram, and plant them in the nuttery. Decide while doing so that this heroic business is not my line of country. *Le grandiose échappe à ma dent.* Decide to go back to poor old Peabody and make him Private Secretary at the F.O.[4]

---

[1] Director of Talks at the B.B.C. in succession to Hilda Matheson, 1932–35. Then aged 33.

[2] William Joynson Hicks, later Lord Brentford (1865–1932). Home Secretary, 1924–29.

[3] To see Lady Sackville, who then lived at White Lodge, Roedean.

[4] *Public Faces* opens with Peabody lying in his bath.

DIARY   *18th April, 1932*

I shall try to be ironical—which is the only tone of voice of which I am capable, but at the same time avoid being just sneery. With this in mind I alter the name of Mr Bullwinkle to Mr. Bullivant.[1]

DIARY   *21st April, 1932*

Finish chapter 1. People are getting more real. Jane Campbell—sort of Hilda [Matheson] plus Gertrude Bell—will clearly take charge of the plot herself. A competent woman.

DIARY   *26th April, 1932*

Lunch at the Jardin with Alan Pryce-Jones[2] who is back from Kenya and Uganda. He says that people in Kenya drink, fornicate, absorb heroin, and wear suède, blue-leather shorts and belts of rattle-snake skin. He is very charming and clever.

A drunken down-and-out, who calls me a 'pukka sahib', comes to K.B.W. I am polite to him and give him £1 which I can ill afford. He also drinks my Vermouth. He then says that his wife is waiting outside. Will I allow him to introduce her? And will I (since this is the point) take off my hat? I accept both these exigencies. She is a wobbly and precise harlot. She bows like Mrs Baldwin. I go on to Cannon Street feeling that life is highly tragic and very diverse.

DIARY   *6th May, 1932*

Read the first two chapters of my novel, and am filled with overwhelming disgust. An idle chatter they are—no more. Depressed. Plant water-lilies in the lower lake.

DIARY   *27th May, 1932*

In the middle of [André] Maurois' lecture yesterday, an idea occurred to me: 'The action of your novel must be compressed within twenty-four hours.' Well, well ... that means re-writing everything I have

---

[1] The name had to be altered again to Bullinger at proof-stage, as the publisher's reader pointed out that Walter Bullivant was a leading character in one of John Buchan's novels.

[2] Author and literary critic. Then aged 23. Assistant Editor of the *London Mercury*, 1928–32. Editor of the *Times Literary Supplement*, 1948–59.

done so far.[1] My lumbago precludes such energetic thoughts. It is like toothache in the back.

DIARY   *22nd June, 1932*

V. goes to London. Gladwyn [Jebb] comes over. Am revising the first eight chapters of my novel. It is foul.

DIARY   *6th July, 1932*

Read Viti's *Family History*[2] in proof. Very competent and moving, but not exactly her type of thought.

DIARY   *19th July, 1932*

This lovely summer is amazing. Work hard at chapter 12. Finish *Secretary of State* at 10.40 pm.

DIARY   *22nd July, 1932*

Up to London. Get a photograph of Whitehall from Aerofilms and take it to Constable as my dust-cover. Michael[3] says the title *Secretary of State* has already been used by Stephen McKenna.[4] Alter it to *Public Faces* on the basis of Auden's lines.[5]

Within a week of finishing 'Public Faces', he embarked on his history of the Paris Peace Conference of 1919. 'Public Faces' was published on 6th October, a few days before V. Sackville-West's novel 'Family History'. 'Peacemaking' was actually written in a single month, 8th November to 8th December, but the research occupied him throughout August, September and October. At the same time he had begun to write a weekly book-review for the 'New Statesman'. That a 370-page book on so complicated a theme could be completed so quickly was due to a number of reasons. He was thoroughly familiar with the subject, since he had himself served on the British delegation in 1919; nearly half the book was an edited version of the diary which he had kept at the time; he was able to work almost uninterrupted at Sissinghurst; and for the first time

[1] By then he had written five chapters of *Public Faces* out of twelve. The action of the novel in fact covers four days, 2nd–5th June, 1939.
[2] Hogarth Press. 1932.
[3] Michael Sadleir (1888–1957), author and publisher. Director of Constable.
[4] His novel *The Secretary of State* was published in 1927.
[5] *Private faces in public places*
   Are wiser and nicer
   Then public faces in private places.

in three years he was feeling profoundly contented with his life and work.

These were also the months when Sissinghurst began to assume its present shape. As a relaxation from literature, Harold Nicolson planned the vistas, walls and hedges, and sited the garden statuary and pots, which in combination with V. Sackville-West's imaginative planting, have rendered the mature garden one of the most famous in England. She later described the process of their collaboration in these words:

'I could never have done it myself. Fortunately I had, through marriage, the ideal collaborator. Harold Nicolson should have been a garden-architect in another life. He has a natural taste for symmetry, and an ingenuity for forcing focal points or long-distance views where everything seemed against him, a capacity I totally lacked. We did, however, agree entirely on what was to be the main principle of the garden: a combination of long axial walks . . . and the more intimate surprise of small geometrical gardens opening off them, rather as the rooms of an enormous house would open off the arterial corridors. There should be the strictest formality of design, with the maximum informality in planting.'[1]

They had now owned Sissinghurst for two years. They had cleared the soil of the accumulated rubbish of centuries and formed the two main courtyards. Now was the time to extend the garden into the cabbage patches and open fields around the house, and in the evenings Harold Nicolson would sit down with squared paper, rulers and india-rubber, and sometimes send his sons out after dark to check a measurement by torch-light. The White Garden, then known as the Rose Garden, was laid out first, then the avenues of poplars to the front entrance and down to the lake, next the lime-avenue with the spring-border and the circular yew-hedges of the present rose-garden, and finally the vista from the tower steps through the orchard to the moat. By the end of the year the Castle had been wired for electricity (they had lived hitherto by the light of oil-lamps), and they were adding to the South Cottage a bedroom for Harold Nicolson, a book-room and a garden-room, all of which he designed himself.

This activity restored his cheerfulness and self-respect. At the end of the year, in his cabin on board the German liner 'Bremen' in mid-Atlantic, he was able to write, 'I do not expect that I shall ever love a year so much as this year.' He and V. Sackville-West were on their way to a three-months' lecture-tour of the United States.

[1] *Journal of the Royal Horticultural Society*, vol. lxxviii, November 1953.

DIARY   29th July, 1932

Rains. Start my book on the Peace Conference.

DIARY   14th August, 1932

Go over to Rottingdean to lunch with the Roderick Joneses. As we
arrive a rich car containing Sir William and Lady Jowitt draws up.
I have not seen him since the unfortunate incident of the Combined
Universities Election.[1] Instead of bearing me a grudge he is as decent
as possible both to me and the boys. A good mark. Bernstorff[2] and
Ustinov[3] of the Wolf agency there. Also a pretty French girl—Mlle
de Chaume. A good luncheon. Ustinov afterwards does imitations
of Queen Victoria.

   We then go off to Rodmell to visit Leonard and Virginia Woolf.
V. is ill, and takes my V. up to her room. Talk to Leonard about my
Peace Conference book. Look at the garden. Their sky is as wide and
clear as the sky above the downs. We come back to Rottingdean
feeling as usual lightened and inspired.

DIARY   13th September, 1932

Mark out new hedges with Ben. A lovely warm night. We walk out
to meet Viti. The [electric-power] cable approaches nearer.

DIARY   26th September, 1932

Motor up to London with Viti. Lunch with Leo Kennedy.[4] He tells
me that Ramsay MacDonald is breaking up. He tries to find out
whether I would return to the Foreign Office. He has evidently been
asked to do so by Vansittart.[5] I reply that I would in no circumstance
go back to diplomacy until I attain Ambassadorial rank. I have two
books to do before I return to public service. But if in November
next they were still to offer me a chance to re-enter the F.O., I might
accept it gladly.

[1] See p. 95.
[2] Albrecht Bernstorff, German diplomatist, who had been at the German Embassy
   in London since 1922. He was murdered by the Nazis in 1945.
[3] Iona von Ustinov, father of Peter Ustinov, the playwright and actor, who was born
   in 1921.
[4] A foreign correspondent of *The Times*.
[5] Sir Robert Vansittart, Permanent Under-Secretary of State for Foreign Affairs,
   1930-38.

DIARY   *6th October, 1932*

Paving across the courtyard finished. They begin upon the windows in the porch. Viti and I plant lupins at the end of the moat walk. *Public Faces* published.

DIARY   *19th October, 1932*

A lovely day. Round to the *New Statesman*. Kingsley Martin[1] indicates that he wants me to become the literary editor when Ellis Roberts goes. That is all very well. But I get £600 a year already from my articles and could not expect to make more than £1,000 a year as Lit. Ed. This would mean that I should gain only £400 a year net and that sum would be absorbed by loss of time and the need to live in London for four days in the week. Besides, I think that Raymond [Mortimer] should have that £1,000 a year.

On to Constable's to see Michael Sadleir. He talks about my Peace Conference book. He agrees that it should be in two parts and that the second part should be my diary as it stands. He says that *Public Faces* is going very well. I say, 'How well?' He says that it sold 1,600 copies before publication. I say that Viti's *Family History* sold 6,000 copies before publication. He says, 'But then she has broken through.' I say, 'Broken through what?' He says, 'The middle-class belt.' Buy a pair of shoes at Fortnum and Mason.

DIARY   *21st October, 1932*

Over to Churt to see Lloyd George. Motor there with Copper[2] at the wheel. Arrive at 1 pm. Gate-piers with Welsh emblems. Cystus and rosemary. A small house. A parlour-maid. A puff of hot air as I enter. Ll.G.'s study. Ceiling up to the roof. Comfortable arm-chairs. Photograph of A. J. Balfour on his writing table, and an engraving of Bonar Law above it. He rises from a hard Windsor chair. He waddles powerfully as of old.

He says that the last time we met was at Archie Sinclair's when we discussed the National Opposition.[3] He says that it was the first time he had ever heard of the formation of the National Government. 'Winston knew, of course, and he would not believe that I did not know. But I didn't know. Nor did Samuel. He would have told me,

[1] Editor of the *New Statesman and Nation*, 1931-60.
[2] Jack Copper, the Nicolsons' chauffeur from 1931 onwards.   [3] See p. 81.

I am sure.' He talks of Tom Mosley. His lack of judgement, his wasted
opportunities, his courage. He talks of his early speeches. 'Nobody
listened to him, but I did. I knew that that young man always had
something to say.' About fascism in England, he is not so sure it may
not become possible. 'I do not know at this moment what our condition really is. On the surface all seems right enough. But what is
happening at this moment underneath? I had Seebohm here the other
day. You know—Seebohm Rowntree.[1] He said things were getting
better. I asked why. I said, "Look here, supposing you were a trustee
and had £5,000 to invest, where would you put it? Steel? No.
Shipping? Certainly not. Cotton? Wool? Coal? Railways? No,
no, no. Then where? Artificial silk?" ' 'No,' he concluded. 'We do
not know.' I suggest that he is well out of it for the moment. 'No', he
says, 'one is never well out of it. One is just out of it.'

We go into luncheon. He discusses bores: says that a man who finds
any other man a bore is a fool: no man, once you are alone with him,
is a bore: he has always something which he knows better than other
people: it is only when he interrupts other and more vital informants
that he becomes a bore. He talks of Asquith; his inability to face facts
except under pressure. Of Grey; his sham honesty. Of Edward VII;
his dignity and his shrewdness; how he never treated Ll.G. as monarch
to subject, but as an old man to a young man. 'He was irresistible.' Of
Gladstone; his terrifying eyes. We talk Peace Conference. I go with
him back to the study. I produce my thirty questions which I have
prepared. He answers glibly. His answers will all be embodied in my
book. The main new thing is that he thinks that President Wilson
had something like a stroke in March 1919. After 1st April he fell
entirely under the influence of Clemenceau.

Ll.G. is on the surface as hearty and brilliant as ever. But one feels
it is an effort. I felt he was glad that I did not stay too long.

DIARY   23rd October, 1932

It pours and blows. Work at my lecture for Leeds. Lunch with the
Drummonds.[2] They are giving us two balls. Of stone. Nice people.

---

[1] The manufacturer and social scientist, 1871–1954.

[2] Major-General Lawrence Drummond (1861–1946), who lived at Sissinghurst Place,
less than a mile from the Castle. He and his wife, their son Lindsay Drummond,
the publisher, and his wife Cynthia ('Bunny'), became intimate friends of the
Nicolsons.

Lindsay and Bunny there. I like them all. A happy day in pouring rain. We are so happy here: it is absurd. Darling Viti: she is the eternal sun for me.

DIARY   *2nd November, 1932*

Plant the five acacias round the Sissinghurst Crescent. Plant out Buddleia at the end of the moat. Plant the two *Souvenir du Docteur Jamain*.[1] Plant the poplars down to the lake. A good day's work. Also do Peace Conference. Weight 11 st. 4 lbs.

DIARY   *13th November, 1932*

A still, dark day. The chestnut leaves hang, one or two, motionless. Go a walk in the wood up to Olive Rinder's[2] bungalow. It is dark and glum and autumnal. I feel absurdly happy. The dogs bark in the woods.

DIARY   *14th November, 1932*

Revise the first three chapters of my Peace Conference book. It seems all right. Barnes[3] comes over and begins prodding the border. Beale[4] comes and we decide details about my new bed-room etc. Again ridiculously happy. Feel that I could do anything. A catastrophe must be very near.

DIARY   *9th December, 1932*

To a party where I meet Mrs D. H. Lawrence.[5] She is much less *hausfrau* than I had supposed. A sharp questing little nose, a bright inquisitive impression, a sense of silliness somewhere, and excess. She talks quite naturally about Lawrence and is clearly pleased at his being the hero of legend. She has a sort of *Egeria* look which must be put on. She says that Lawrence said, 'Frieda, if people really knew what you were like, they would strangle you.' I say, 'Did he say that angrily?' She said, 'No—very quietly, after several minutes deep thought.' She talked of how ghastly it was to see all this Lawrence

[1] An old Hybrid Perpetual rose which V. S-W. found growing against the office wall of a derelict nursery and restored to horticultural circulation.
[2] She wrote the women's page in *Action*, and was a close friend of V. S-W.
[3] The gardener from Long Barn.
[4] The local builder, who did most of the reconstruction work at Sissinghurst.
[5] D. H. Lawrence, the novelist, had died in 1930 at the age of 44. He married Frieda von Richthofen in 1914.

worship now, and then realise that if only this fame had come to him in his lifetime he might have been spared. 'We were so poor,' she said. 'So poor!' 'Surely,' I said, 'you could not have been so very poor at the end?' She laughed. 'No,' she said, 'that was not true what I said just now. We were not poor in the end.'

DIARY   *11th December, 1932*

Sibyl [Colefax], Gwen and Sam [St Aubyn] come over. A dark day. A happy day. God! if only life were ten times longer.

DIARY   *31st December, 1932*
On board 'Bremen' in mid-Atlantic

A fine sun-swept day with great towers of waves hurtling past us and mantling on the horizon. Too rough to work. We lie on our beds and read. Eat huge meals. It gets calmer in the evening. An attempt at *réveillon*—consisting mostly of balloons. We received radio messages of happy new year. We retire to bed at 10 pm. which is midnight at home. Thus ends 1932.

A lovely year for which I thank life heartily. I have got rid both of journalism and of politics. All the horrors of 1931 are behind me. I enjoyed writing *Public Faces* and it has had a certain success. I have enjoyed my articles for the *New Statesman* which have also helped my reputation. I have loved working on my book on the Peace Conference. Viti, except for overwork in the summer, has been well and happy. Rebecca[1] has come into our life. Ben has left Eton[2] having recovered his self-esteem there and managed to make good. Niggs is as sensible and hard-working and sweet as ever, and Sissinghurst has become for us the real home which we shall always love. I do not expect that I shall ever love a year so much as this year. And I render thanks.

[1] A wire-haired terrier.
[2] He went to Balliol College, Oxford in 1933.

1933

H.N. and V. Sackville-West on a three-month lecture-tour of the United States and Canada – New York – H.N.'s opinion of America and the Americans – Washington – storm in Chicago – a happy interlude in Charleston – Los Angeles – Hollywood – Smoke Tree Ranch, California – Grand Canyon – return to England in April – 'Curzon, the Last Phase' – Italian holiday – Nigel's illness – Auden and T. E. Lawrence – H.N.'s relationships with V. Sackville-West and her mother, Lady Sackville – uncertainty of H.N.'s future

It was the first time that either of them had been to America. Harold Nicolson was to go often again: V. Sackville-West never. The trip started badly. Their Atlantic passage in the 'Bremen' was delayed by the worst gale for thirty years. Their arrival in New York coincided with the greatest economic crisis in American history. Roosevelt succeeded Hoover as President in March, but the situation remained so grave that they were advised to transfer to Britain all the money they earned from the lecture-tour in case the dollar were devalued, and at one time there was talk of cancelling the tour itself. They completed their arduous programme nonetheless. Towards the end, Harold Nicolson, who was amused by such statistics, worked out that between them they had visited 53 different cities in the United States and Canada, spent 63 nights in the train, and covered 33,527 miles.

They were surprised to find that their names were better-known in America than in Britain. Everywhere they went, their audiences had read, or hurriedly started to read, 'The Edwardians', 'All Passion Spent', 'Some People' and 'Public Faces'. Harold Nicolson was billed as 'a robust, handsome Britisher, with a keen, witty face', as 'one of the cleverest men in England': V. Sackville-West as 'Junoesque', as 'Portia-like', as (inevitably) 'Orlando'. 'Virginia Sackville-West, the English noblewoman, novelist and poet', began a report in the 'Des Moines Register', 'has the glorious rosy skin that bespeaks more chapters written under the drifting petals of her apple-orchard at Long Barn, Kent, than in a leather-scented library.' For some reason the journalists never discovered Sissinghurst. 'Countess Vera Sackville-West', wrote another, 'spoke to an attentive audience for almost twenty minutes. Then she suddenly stopped, dropped her head and quietly said, "I have forgotten what I was going to say".' They adored her. They respected her shy dignity. They liked her clothes, 'the sort of clothes', Harold Nicolson remarked to a journalist, 'that Beatrice would have worn had she married Dante'. She lectured, over and over again, on half-a-dozen literary or social subjects, in Boston, in Chicago, in St. Louis, in Cincinnati, in Kansas City, in Newark, in Montreal, in Los Angeles, while Harold Nicolson filled other halls with 'The Future of Diplomacy', 'English Biography', and 'Europe and the Postwar Generation'. But by far the most successful of their lectures were those that they gave jointly. The two of them sat lonely on a stage and discussed before audiences of 2,000 or more, 'What we think about Marriage', 'Romanticism versus Classicism', How to bring up Children', 'Changes in English Social Life'. They had worked out these discussions with great care before leaving England, but they delivered them without notes and with such wit and apparent effortlessness that they became, during that particular season, the lions of the American lecture-circus.

It is not surprising that the lecturers should have taken a different view of the tour than their audiences. It was the worst possible way in which to see America for the first time. The adulated seldom take kindly to their adulators. The former seem to the latter like arrivals from another world; the latter seem to the former not only foolishly mistaken, but identical, city to city. Well-meant hospitality ('It must be so nice for you to be able to relax') soon began to cloy, and all the worst, as well as the best, of the American character was paraded before their eyes. They travelled from coast to coast and from Canada to the deep South, sometimes together, more often separated for a night or ten days at a time, writing to each other homesick letters when they were apart, reuniting in some hotel bedroom or sleeping-car when like a pair of skaters their different arcs again intersected. There were moments when they experienced great happiness—V. Sackville-West at Niagara, Harold Nicolson at Charleston, and together in Arizona—but mostly their lives were harassed by time-tables, exhaustion, the weather, worry about money and each other's health, the almost universal ignorance of European cultural values, and the need to be constantly polite.

DIARY   *2nd January, 1933*
                                        On board 'Bremen' in mid-Atlantic
A hurricane blowing. We have slowed to five knots and just keep enough steam to steer by. The waves hiss and foam around us. Viti tries to make out that it is all the Captain's fault. Anyhow it has convinced us both that we are excellent sailors. We have felt bruised, battered and exhausted but never sick.

5th January, 1933
New York

Wake up at 5.30. Dress and go on deck. It is warm with a faint rain. We are in the East River. The lights of Staten Island appear among thin trees. Quite dark. Go down to breakfast. When I come up there is a faint damp dawn. A church spire, some wooden houses in gardens, the bluff of a low escarpment. It is like the prints of early New York. Viti dresses. We are intercepted by reporters. They take us on deck and we are exposed to a regiment of cameras. By that time the sun has risen and we are alongside the dock at Brooklyn. We walk down the gangway and the first person we meet is Copley Amory.[1] Delighted to see him. We are then met by Mr Butterly, Colston Leigh's[2] publicity agent and also by Russell Doubleday and the sales-manager of Doubleday Doran.[3] We find our luggage under N and pass through easily. We drive through Brooklyn in a car. A lovely morning. All very like Berlin. Suddenly as we reach Manhattan Bridge the skyline indents itself for us. Up Broadway and Madison to the hotel. Nesting-boxes. As we enter the room the telephone rings. Press people arrive. Bootleggers ring up. Social hostesses ring up. There are two telephones, one in each room, and three publicity agents, that of the hotel, that of Doubleday and that of Colston Leigh.

The afternoon is a further procession of journalists, flowers, bell-hops, photographers, telephones. We have no time to unpack and change our clothes.

We then go to a suite at the Waldorf Astoria where we dine. The party consists of Mr and Mrs Redmond, Charles Lindbergh and his wife, Henry James (the nephew of Henry James and son of William James), Mr and Mrs Frederick King, Dr James Murphy and his wife, Mr and Mrs Barber, and Mr and Mrs Kermit Roosevelt.

Lindbergh is a surprise.[4] There is much more in his face than

[1] An old Boston friend.
[2] Colston Leigh Inc. was the lecture-agency which arranged their tour.
[3] V.S-W.'s American publisher. H.N.'s publisher was Houghton Mifflin, who brought out the American edition of *Public Faces* two days later.
[4] This was H.N.'s first meeting with Colonel Charles Lindbergh, who was to play a significant part in his life for the next four years. In 1927, at the age of 25, Lindbergh had been the first pilot to fly the Atlantic direct from New York to Paris, and he flew alone. He became America's hero. On 1st March, 1932 his baby son was kidnapped and the body was found months later in a wood.

appears in photographs. He has a fine intellectual forehead, a shy engaging smile, wind-blown hair, a way of tossing his head unhappily, a transparent complexion, thin nervous capable fingers, a loose-jointed shy manner. He looks young with a touch of arrested development. His wife is tiny, shy, timid, retreating, rather interested in books, a tragedy at the corner of her mouth. One thinks of what they have been through and is shy to meet them. Henry James is like an American in Henry James' books. Dr Murphy is on the Rockefeller Foundation and was a friend of Geoffrey Scott.[1] Kermit Roosevelt[2] is hearty, hunting, genial, original. We go on to the Empire State building. The lights of the great avenues sparkle like fire-flies. But there are great patches where there are no fireflies at all: the great water spaces. The shadows of huge buildings. Little cabs creeping like lice. Viti enjoyed herself in spite of being awake for twenty hours. To bed at 1 a.m. Not tired. Oh brave new world!

DIARY   *8th January, 1933*
                                                        New York

I go to Miss Marbury's. Find Mrs Vanderbilt there representing society. Van Loon[3] representing literature. Wylie representing journalism—he is the editor of the *New York Times*. Miss Marbury[4] is enormous, emphatic, civilised, gay. She says she is 76 and has never been so happy as in the last fifteen years. All passion spent. Van Loon is Dutch but very Americanised. Wylie is pure American.

Now, here were three people corresponding roughly to Garvin, Ethel Smyth and Maynard Keynes. And this, with infinite slowness, was one of the many stories that Wylie told: 'That', he said, 'reminds me of a story I heard the other day down town. A man is taken from speak-easy to speak-easy. He returns to his wife after having music of negro orchestras drummed into his ears. She says, "How are you feeling?" He says, "Rather syncopated." She looks up *syncopate* in her dictionary and finds it says "passing from bar to bar".' We laugh

---

[1] The writer and art-critic, V.S-W.'s friend of the 1920's. He died in 1929.

[2] Colonel Kermit Roosevelt, son of President Theodore Roosevelt; the soldier, explorer and shipping magnate.

[3] Hendrik Van Loon, the historian. Born in Holland and emigrated to the U.S.A. at the age of 21.

[4] Elisabeth Marbury, an author and authors' representative, was a well-known figure in New York society. She died on 23rd January, 1933, two weeks after this meeting with H.N.

politely. But it is incredible that such a story should be told to people who are really educated. It is this that I find so trying. They are so slow in conversation that it is like being held up by a horse-dray in a taxi. And then they never listen to what one says oneself. The depression is dreadful. All the hotels are bankrupt. Most apartments are empty. The great Rockefeller buildings, and the two theatres, are to close down. Rockefeller will lose some £3,000,000 a year by this venture. Four thousand architects are out of work in New York alone.

DIARY   *11th January, 1933*
                                                        New York

Get back [from Princeton] to find Vita arrived and not over-tired by her visit to Springfield and Yale. She is so touched by all their kindness to her, and so astonished by the many admirers whom she finds there. Above all she had loved Yale and the professors and the eager young faces. Her lectures at both places had been a great success.

DIARY   *24th January, 1933*
                                              Springfield, Massachusetts

Dining with the intelligentsia of Springfield, Mass., the conversation languished. An elderly lady dressed in an Assiut shawl and with hair arranged in silvery neatness, asked me how many *e*'s there were in the advertisement on a pack of Camel cigarettes. I asked if I might see a packet and count them. I counted twelve. There were really thirteen. 'Nobody', she said, 'ever gets it right; and I thought you were a clever man, Mr Nicolson.' 'What,' I asked her, 'is the catch?' 'Oh', she said, 'there isn't a catch. Only one always counts wrong. And it does make things *go* so.' She then discussed the higher education of women. She said that statistics had proved that the feet and hands of the modern American girl were two sizes larger than those of their mothers. 'How terrible for you', I said. 'What are you going to do about it? I suppose it's all these beastly games and gymnastics.' She said, not at all—they liked it. America would breed a race of giants. 'Bigger', I said, 'and better?' She adjusted her Assiut shawl upon her shoulder. 'Sure,' she said.

DIARY   *26th January, 1933*
                                              Boston—Washington

Leave Boston by the *Senator* at noon. We take the coast route. The beauty of the Massachusetts coast-line. Indented lagoons with little wooded islands and white houses and churches. Something hard and small and moving like the early settlers. Not a trace of vulgarity or emphasis.

Get to Washington at 9.55. Drive to the Embassy. Wilmot, *The Times* correspondent, has been dining. Philip Lothian there. Viti has recovered from her cold. We retire and read accumulated letters. Two lovely letters from Niggs. He has been happy at Sanary.[1]

DIARY   *27th January, 1933*
                                              Washington

Viti and I drive out to Mount Vernon.[2] We stop on the way to let me see the Lincoln memorial and the statue. It is impressive with its sunken eyes and heavy working-man's hands. But there is a look of angered despair in the face by which I am not surprised. The dramatic effect is heightened by a floodlighting in the roof. Then on along the grey Potomac in a gathering snow-storm. Mount Vernon is impressive in its simple magnificence. There is a park-like farm with a big estate feel about it. The ceilings and furniture indicate a high level of culture and taste.

Lunch at the Embassy.[3] Then on to the Senate. The Vice President[4] presides. A bleary, tobacco-drugged looking man. He has a wooden mallet which he holds by the hammer end, tapping irritably with it against the wood of the desk. Around the tribune sit little boys like the elder sons of peers on the steps of the throne.[5] They wear black plus-fours with black woollen stockings and shoes. They giggle and pick their noses. From time to time a Senator beckons to them and they run messages giggling back at their fellows. The desks for the Senators are arranged in a rough semicircle with a gangway down the middle.

[1] Aldous Huxley's house in the South of France, where Nigel had been staying during the Christmas holidays. Ben was learning French with a family near Tours.
[2] George Washington's house.
[3] The British Ambassador in Washington from 1930 to 1939 was Sir Ronald Lindsay, who had previously been Ambassador in Berlin, 1926–28.
[4] John N. Garner.   [5] In the House of Lords.

The room itself is rectilinear and scarcely decorated at all. Two brown-wood roll-top desks are pushed against the wall. There is a hard top-light from the glass ceiling and busts along the cornice. A woman Senator, the only woman Senator, acts like all feminine legislators, chatting over-comradely in a fur tippet with her colleagues. Under each desk is a spittoon of green glass. The Senators when they speak turn their back upon the President and address each other walking away from their desks. They all look stout, solid, blear-eyed and sulky. Borah[1] is there. He is not what I expected. I expected an ascetic, arrogant, enfevered face: it is just an untidy rather unimportant sort of face, shaking his invincible locks.

We are picked up there by Elizabeth Lindsay[2] and she and Viti drive on to the White House. Negro footmen in dark livery with silver buttons. Aides-de-camp in white gloves and cigarettes. They are given tea. Two negroes stand behind Mr Hoover at attention like eunuchs.

DIARY   *29th January, 1933*
                                                   New York

Find letters from V. who passed through here yesterday. She is indignant because a gossip-column writer in a Chicago newspaper has invented a story that we abused the United States, and New York particularly, at a dinner party. This is irritating (a) because we would be neither so ungrateful, so bad-mannered nor so unintelligent as to abuse this country even if we felt like it. (b) Because we do not feel like abusing it in the least. On the contrary, we find it fascinating and congenial. Anyhow she had written to the paper in indignant repudiation which they will not print.

V.S-W. TO H.N.   *31st January, 1933*
(in Stockbridge, Massachusetts)   *Niagara Falls*

Niagara is really some waterfall! It falls over like a great noisy beard made of cotton-wool, veiled by spray and spanned by rainbows. The rainbows are the most unexpected part of it. They stand across like bridges between America and Canada, and are reproduced in sections among the boiling foam. The spray rises to the height of a sky-scraper,

[1] William E. Borah, a Senator from 1907 continuously until 1942, and Dean of the Senate.
[2] Wife of the Ambassador.

shot by sudden iridescence high up in the air. There is a strange and impressive alliance between the works of God and the works of man: factory-chimneys line the cliff; great pylons stretch away across the country. It was a sunny day, and only remnants of snow lay about. But there were grand icicles on the cliffs.

I think it is very good for you and me to have come to America. I am glad we did. I am getting a lot out of it. There may be moments when we are tired and nauseated and bored. But on the whole it is infinitely valuable.

DIARY   *7th February, 1933*
                                                       Chicago

Wake up to find a blizzard blowing outside. The whole place howls and whirls and boils. It is like smoke billowing upwards. Lake Michigan is frozen right up to the beach and in ridges in the shape of breakers. The lake further out, where it has always been frozen, is a dark scabby colour. A few cars struggle along Lake Shore Drive, twist and stagger, and then get stuck. The snow banks against their mud-guards and radiators. V. has to catch the 11.30 for St Louis. She will not let me go to the station. She disappears into a revolving snow landscape through a revolving glass door. I return wretchedly to my rooms. I shut her door.

V. S-W.'S DIARY   *7th February, 1933*
                                                St Charles, Missouri

Wake to find Chicago under snow and a blizzard. Hate leaving Hadji in it, but have to catch the 11.30 to St Louis. Dreary journey across snow-bound plains interrupted only by grim towns and occasional bumps of broken motors sticking up out of the snow. Two women from Linderwood College meet me. I escape from reporters by saying that I am late. I am indeed, for my lecture is timed for 8, and we do not reach St Charles till 8.45. I wash but do not change and give the lecture at once: 'Modern Spirit in Literature'. Audience mostly the college girls. I am introduced to all of them afterwards and made to sign books. I observe that copies of *All Passion Spent* have changed from the 9th edition to the 10th. Am given some dinner which I had not had. Get a telegram from Hadji and ring him up. Long to go to bed, but am kept up talking: with all their kindness, these people have very little imagination. Go to bed finally at 12.

DIARY   *8th February, 1933*
                                                  Chicago

The storm has abated. I wake to find huge tanks with caterpillar wheels digging out the stuck motors. It is said to be 10° below zero. Have breakfast and read the paper. There are pages about the storm. I find the following: '*Crime wanes during storm.* Chicago's radio-equipped police cars were all kept in during the day, but there was a slackening, rather than an increase, of crime, the criminals finding it as difficult to travel about as the police. Only twenty-nine automobiles, about one third the usual number, were reported stolen up to 4 p.m.' Good for the windy city.

This morning I was bothered by reporters. Then Miss Dennett, or whatever her name was, said, 'Oh, Mr Nicolson, I took the liberty of asking two girls of the Ellesmere Institoot to come up and be photographed with you.' 'Certainly, Miss Dennett—delighted—but what is the Ellesmere Institute?' 'Oh they look after tarts.' 'Rescue work, I suppose?' 'Of course not—only tiny tarts.' 'Tiny tarts?' 'Yes, wash and dress them, you know, and give them their bottles.' 'But surely, Miss Dennett—oh, I see, you mean a crêche, you mean tiny tots.' The girls then arrive and I was photographed with them in positions of great affection.

H.N. TO V.S-W. (*in Chicago*)   *16th February, 1933*
                                   British Embassy, Washington

Lunched with Alice Longworth.[1] My word, how I like that woman! There is a sense of freedom in her plus a sense of background. That, I feel, is what is missing in this country. Nobody seems to have anything behind their front. Poor people, they feel it themselves, and hence all those pitiful gropings after manor-houses in Wiltshire and parish registers and Daughters of the Founding Fathers. But Alice Longworth had a world position, and it has left her simple and assured and human. It was a pleasant luncheon: you know, the sort of luncheon where one feels mentally comfortable and warm.

I then walked down to the site of the old [British] Embassy. It has been completely cleared of buildings and the large triangular site is

---

[1] Mrs Longworth was the eldest daughter of President Theodore Roosevelt. In 1906 she married Nicholas Longworth of Cincinnati, Speaker of the House of Representatives, 1925–27. He died in 1931.

now occupied by second-hand cars standing cheek by jowl in the mud. I felt rather sad about poor B.M.,[1] and those distant happy days when she was young and successful and a belle. I stood there reflecting on the mutability of human affairs, and thinking of that encumbered bedroom at Brighton, and all the rage of disappointment hanging in the air. Oh my sweet, pray God that you and I need not prepare ourselves for so tragic an old age.

H.N. TO V.S-W. (*in Columbus, Ohio*)   *17th February, 1933*
Charleston, South Carolina

I feel rather guilty, as I have been enjoying myself these days, and you must be having an absolutely foul time. That's what comes of being a celebrity and having a husband and two children to support.

The hotel here is southern in feeling—stone floors and open windows. There is a wide bay like Southampton Water and below my windows a grove of ilexes. There are gardens everywhere. Public squares with statues of Pitt among palm-trees. Green grass. Azaleas in bud. Little quiet cobbled streets with the neatest of houses. And above all, they have walls everywhere, and iron gratings disclosing lovely gardens. And all around stretches of water.

DuBose Heyward,[2] author of *Porgy*, picked us up. A very thin, quiet, interesting man. He motored us out to Middleton Place. We drove out through avenues of huge ilexes draped in Spanish Moss. It drapes every branch, hanging down like huge cobwebs. In detail it is ugly and untidy: in the mass it is strange and impressive.

Middleton Place was one of the great plantation seats. It is as romantic in its way as Sissinghurst. Enormous ilexes, eighteen feet round in the trunk, flank a wide lawn cut up into high beds of camellias in flower. The terraces drop down to dark lakes, thirty feet below. In front stretches a wide marsh intersected by a river. Six elderly Negroes in blue were mowing the vast lawns with tiny mowing-machines. The camellias blazed. The air was damp and heavy with the scent of *Olea fragrans*, a sprig of which I sent you. We went into the little house. All very simple. Three rooms with Empire furniture and shuttered as

---

[1] *Bonne Mama*, the family name for Lady Sackville. As a girl she had acted as hostess for her father, Lionel Sackville-West, who was the British Minister in Washington, 1881–88.

[2] DuBose Heyward was born in Charleston in 1885. His novel about the deep South, *Porgy*, was published in 1925.

if it were blazing hot. Not a touch of the *Lady's Journal*. The gardens are beautifully kept, and when the azaleas are out it must be amazing. We came back, and I came face to face with Elizabeth Lindsay. We fell into each other's arms. I said I had been to Middleton. She said, 'Now, what did it remind you of?' I said that it reminded me strongly of something but I could not remember what. She said, 'Well, it's Vita's poem *Sissinghurst*'. Of course it was. She is no fool, that Elizabeth.

I gave my lecture in a lovely Adam hall with old pictures. The whole thing is so effortless and unaffected here. No strain. No noise. I delight in it. They are all longing to see you. Great passion-spenters.

H.N. TO V.S-W. (*in Cincinnati*)   18*th February, 1933*
Charleston, South Carolina

Charleston is really delightful. It is not merely that there are a few old bits and lovely houses. It is that the whole place is old in character and southern. The atmosphere is lazy, untidy, dignified, lotus-eating. Even their voices are as soft as the feet of the negro-woman selling narcissus in the street. It would be impossible to understand America's falling-off unless one sees this place.

H.N. TO V.S-W. (*in Newark, Delaware*)   23*rd February, 1933*
Cincinnati

I confess that I find all this slushy adulation very trying and irritating, in the sense that all unrealities are irritating. Of course I know that you and I are very gifted and charming. Only we are not gifted and charming in the sort of way these people suppose. One should remember, however, that if we were lecturing at Cheltenham, Roedean, Bath and Harrogate, we should be faced with just the same vapidity of compliment, by just the same uniformity of faces. It is not that these people are less civilised than similar sorts of people in England. It is just that at home we should be bored stiff by that sort of person, and that here we have a feeling (which may or may not be justified) that there simply does not exist the sort of person whom we like. If you cut out the territorial aristocracy and the types that have gathered round them in England, and also cut out our scholars and intellectuals, one would be left with a residue which would be no better, and possibly worse, than our audiences. What appals me is that the only alternative to these audiences over here is the vulgarity of big business or the morons of the farming community. America seems to have so few alternatives: England so many.

DIARY   24th February, 1933
                                                        Washington

Breakfast with the Ambassador. He says that what the Americans lack is *patina*. I say that not only have they no sense of the past: they have no sense of the future. They do not plant avenues for their great-grandchildren. This gives them not merely an absence of past roots but of future roots also. It gives a ghastly feeling of provisionality: 'Chicago's ever-changing sky-line.'

DIARY   2nd March, 1933
                                                    Cleveland—Buffalo

They simply do not know what will happen to their banking situation.[1] The whole country seems very close to a smash. But I get money cashed all right at the Express Company and then on to the book-shop again where I sign more books. Young Hallé[2] comes in. He says it is terribly difficult to pay his pay-roll. He cannot leave his people short and yet he has no cash. Everybody here is drawing money from neighbouring States, with the result that the run will spread widely.

Leave Cleveland at 12.43—I for Buffalo and Viti for Indianapolis. Another farewell. A dinner-party and journalists in Buffalo. A lady journalist says, 'What does it feel like being the husband of a famous wife?' Also, 'Have you and Mrs Nicolson ever collaborated on anything?' 'Yes', I answer, 'we have two sons.' 'And what age are they?' she asks.

DIARY   3rd March, 1933
                                                      Niagara Falls

On to Niagara Falls. We cross the Peace Bridge between America and Canada. A tiny little bridge. Above the Canadian end of it is a Union Jack. I take off my hat. I show my passport to an official. 'From the Old Country?' he asks. I get a lump in my throat. I am no

---

[1] This was the height of the economic crisis, two days before President Roosevelt took office. By 2nd March twenty-three states had suspended or drastically restricted banking operations. By Inauguration Day virtually every bank in the U.S.A. had been closed, and the hoarding of currency set in on a large scale.
[2] Of Hallé's Stores.

longer on foreign soil. We then motor along the Canadian side till
we get to the Falls. They are small and disappointing. A fine flow of
water and much steam and spray. But a fraud really. Then motor
back to the United States. At the frontier-post the man asks me how
long I have been resident in Canada. 'Between twenty and twenty-
five minutes', I answer.

DIARY   *4th March, 1933*
                                                          Toledo, Ohio

Inauguration Day. I reach Toledo at 7.40 and am met by Mrs Hineline
who takes me to see Viti who has arrived from Indianapolis by an
earlier train and has been having coffee and orange-juice in the restaurant. A charming woman. We drive off to the Commodore
Perry Hotel where a suite has been reserved. Breakfast and wash.
The bank crisis has now spread to New York. The whole country is
paralysed. Two interviewers and a photographer come to see us. As
usual we have to ask all the questions. We are then fetched and give a
joint lecture on marriage in a cinema. It goes well enough.

We adjourn to a huge Department Store where we have luncheon
with a Women's Club. Daffodils and wall-flowers on the table. The
rest of the guests at little tables all around. I sit next to a woman in
purple silk. 'Well, Mr Nicolson, and are you going right out to the
coast?' 'Yes, Mrs Strachey,[1] we go to San Francisco, Los Angeles and
Pasadena. We then visit the Grand Canyon.' 'That is swell for you,
Mr Nicolson. When I first saw the Grand Canyon I said, "My, if only
Beethoven could have seen this". You see, I am very musical. I do
not know how people can see life steadily unless they are musical.
Don't you feel that way, Mr Nicolson?'

Meanwhile the inauguration of President Roosevelt was proceeding
in Washington and a huge voice was braying out across the daffodils
in their art-ware. '*And now*', yelled the voice, '*the historic moment is
about to arrive. I can see the President-Elect . . .*' The band strikes up at
that moment *Hail to the Chief*. My neighbour pauses for a moment
while we have the President's inaugural address. It is firm and fine.
'It is such a pity', twitters Mrs Strachey beside me, 'that you are only
staying such a short time in Toledo, Mr Nicolson. I would wish to
have you see our museum here. We have a peristyle of the purest
white marble—a thing of utter simplicity but of the greatest beauty.

[1] I have changed the name for obvious reasons. N.N.

I always say that the really beautiful things in life such as the Sistine Madonna are beautifully simple.' *'Small wonder'*, boomed the voice of President Roosevelt, *'that confidence languishes, for it thrives only on honesty, on honour, on the sacredness of obligation, on faithful protection, on unselfish performance ...'* 'You see', whispered Mrs. Strachey, 'the peristyle is lit by hidden lights in the cornice. And they change colour, Mr Nicolson, from the hues of sunrise to those of midday and then to sunset. And at night it is all dark blue. Very simple.'

I strive to catch the historic words of Roosevelt: *'With this pledge, I assume unhesitatingly the leadership of the great army of our people dedicated to a disciplined attack upon our common problems. ... In the event that Congress should fail to take one of these two courses, and in the event that the national emergency is still critical, I shall not then evade the clear course of my duty that will then confront me.'* 'You see, Mr Nicolson', whispered Mrs Strachey, 'our peristyle is a dream in stone. Now I mean that literally. The architect, Mr J. V. Kinhoff, dreamt of that very peristyle. And one day ...' 'Mrs Strachey', I said firmly, 'do you realise that your new President has just proclaimed that he will, if need be, institute a dictatorship?' 'My,' she said, 'now isn't that just too interesting? Not that I care for the radio, Mr Nicolson. We have one, of course, at home above the bathing-pool. It sounds so much better out of doors.' *'We do not'*, Mr Roosevelt was saying, *'distrust the future of essential democracy. The people of the United States have not failed. In their need they have registered a mandate that they want direct, vigorous action.'*[1]

Afterwards, Viti and I have to stand up to say a few words. I get back upon them by stating that they have just listened to the most important announcement in American history. We then go to the station and entrain for Detroit.

13th March, 1933
                                                                     Cleveland

The banks have opened in most places and the people are pouring in with their hoarded gold. Partly patriotism, partly fear of being shown up, but mainly the effect of Roosevelt's wireless address. No man has ever enjoyed such sudden prestige as Franklin Roosevelt. His stocks

[1] This was the famous 'the only thing we have to fear is fear itself' speech. The words attributed by H.N. to Roosevelt were not his exact words, but they give their sense and mood.

are right at the top. Even the Senate dare not delay his activity. This will lead to great jealousy on their part once the crisis is over. They will never forgive him for appealing to the country across their heads.

DIARY   *16th March, 1933*
Denver—Salt Lake City

Wake up on a lovely morning. Viti can see that it is a lovely morning by raising the blind beside her bunk. I can see it because the fan-shaped ventilator throws a four-leaved clover of sunshine on to the ceiling above mine. We are approaching Denver. We get up. The landscape is different. The foreground is tawny like the Persian *biaban* and starred with little cactus which look like dried cistus bushes. Rolling sandhills, and then beyond the indentations of the Rocky Mountains. They are rose-madder and blue. It is exactly like Persia and we are delighted. We skirt the mountains for a bit, going south to Colorado Springs and Pueblo. The mountains are lapis-lazuli behind the sand-hills. There are a few cattle and horses about. We see Pike's Peak. It is all very wide and sweeping and coloured. We are excited.

DIARY   *25th March, 1933*
Los Angeles

We drive to Hollywood. We are taken into the luncheon room where there is a table with flowers and four directors. They are quiet cultured people—not in the least the noisy boasting lot we had supposed. Gary Cooper[1] comes to join us. He is like Paul Hyslop[2] but with an arched eyebrow. The beginnings of a double chin and the hint of greying hair indicate that he may cease to be the *jeune premier*. Yet he is a nice shy quiet modest young man, devoid of any brains. They talk about the earthquake[3]—how frightened they were. About Charlie Chaplin, his moodiness, his affectations, his genius for mimicry. About the life of a film—not more than three years; the film which they thought was an innovation in 1930 now seems to them as old-fashioned as 1886.

The stage-hands and property-men greet Gary Cooper with "'lo Gary, how's life?' He is very nice to them. He then leaves us to look for a house with a huge fence where he can live in peace.

[1] The most famous and masculine of the Western film-stars, then aged 32.
[2] The English architect.
[3] There had been a serious earthquake in California a few weeks before.

DIARY   26th March, 1933
                                                              Pasadena

Mrs John Balderston[1] motors us to her house at Santa Monica. It is a
nice site with huge Eucalyptus and a view over the ocean. On the way
there she tells us that Gary Cooper must look after his laurels as the
great favourite among the picture fans is now Leslie Howard.[2] We
find that Adonis at tea—he looks like an assistant master at some in-
ferior private school. Glasses and bad teeth. But he is a nice man.
Walter Lippmann[3] is there: a sensitive attractive face.

We then go on to Clemence Dane[4] across the gorge. She has a small
bungalow and supper consists of a table at one end with cold food to
which one helps oneself. She has become large but is still matronly—
a Roman Empress who has opened a school for the daughters of
gentlewomen. She talks to me about the difficulty of giving advice
to the young. She says one cannot do so. All one can do is to throw it
out daily like crumbs for the birds and hope that they may peck at it
sometimes when there are no worms about. G. B. Stern[5] is there,
looking like a bright Tahitian—a great shaggy mop of grey hair and
clever eyes underneath. She is a nice person, and we get on. And
Diana Wynyard[6] is there, with her legs swathed in bandages having
got burnt sun-bathing. She is the most lovely woman I have ever
seen. I gaze entranced. Her face, though perfect, is not empty since
there are little bits of it which have strange upward angles, little
upward puckers which suggest individuality and humour. We then
motor back the twenty-five miles to Pasadena. A lovely party.

DIARY   28th March, 1933
                                                   Smoke Tree Ranch, California

We drive out into the desert past Palm Springs. We reach Smoke
Tree Ranch and are shown our cottage—an asbestos hut with bedrooms, shower-bath and kitchenette. Mr Doyle, the owner of the
ranch, comes to visit us. The desert is all around us with sage bushes

[1] John Balderston (1889–1954), the American author and playwright.
[2] The English actor and film-star, 1893–1943.
[3] Already the most distinguished political commentator in America, then aged 44.
[4] The English novelist and essayist.
[5] The English author, who also wrote film-scripts for Hollywood.
[6] The English actress, then aged 27. She had just finished making Cavalcade in Hollywood, and was playing in the film Reunion in Vienna.

and verbena in flower. The hills across the plain are pink and crinkled as in Persia. We are very happy. We then cross to dinner in the main cottage. There is a young man of extremely dramatic looks dressed as a cowboy. He has a black silk scarf round his naked throat fixed with a little horn ring. He is very proud of being dressed as a cowboy and makes up to the ladies. We sit down to the table d'hôte. Good food. We return afterwards to our own cottage. Light the fire. Write letters and read. To bed early. I do not sleep well as the desert air is too exciting. The coyotes howl in the hills.

DIARY *29th March, 1933*
Smoke Tree Ranch

We are aroused by bells ringing and have a huge and excellent breakfast in the main cabin. V. walks south looking for flowers and I do ditto north. It is very hot. The verbena is everywhere and there is a grey bush with orange flowers. When we get near the oasis we are overpowered by the smell of orange blossom.

At 6.15 the whole party gets into cars and on horses and drives to a gorge some three miles away off the road. They light a fire over a grid and cook steaks. Asparagus and coffee. We then sit round the camp-fire under the rocks and the cowboys sing. There is one song—a lullaby to the young cows which they call 'doeghies' or 'dôgies'—and there is another one called *Out on that Utah trail*. They have a real background of homesickness and romance. One of the boys on the ranch called Bob comes and leans against a rock and sings with the firelight on his fresh face. He sings *Ole Man River*. It is very Walt Whitman. The moon dips behind the mountain and the stars are warmed across the drifting smoke. Clara the maid comes and sings her little songs. There is something rather splendid about that side of American life. The way the servants mingle with the masters without self-consciousness and with complete equality. Bob and Clara would have giggled and felt awkward in England. We then return. A happy day in marvellous air.

DIARY *1st April, 1933*
Grand Canyon, Arizona

The Grand Canyon gets less like Dawlish as one looks at it after breakfast, twenty Matterhorns blazing with alpine glow and situated many thousand feet below one. We find some seeds of unknown plants and a saxifrage. We then walk back to the hotel and are just in time for a dance of Hopi Indians.

A fat chief in feathers explains, in that flat voice assumed by orientals when they know English very well, that the Hopis are a very peaceful tribe and as such have no war-dance, but that he will show us the sort of war-dance that they would have had had they been a less peaceful tribe. Having given us this bright explanation he starts to yell out loud and to shake a cardboard shield and a bow and arrow. Being a stout man, and his assistant brave not being very well, the dance is defective in vigour. There is also an eagle-dance and a cow-dance—neither of which carries much conviction. A good deal of shuffling in moccasins and shaking of bells and feathers. Viti is very impressed by the Grand Canyon. So am I.

DIARY   *2nd April, 1933*
                                                      Grand Canyon

We walk out to Howell Memorial. It is approaching sunset and we get the best view of the Canyon we have yet seen. The shadows are slate-blue and the rocks a dominant *sang-de-boeuf* trailing off to pink in places and in places to orange. We walk back thinking out comparisons. I say it is like a wood-fire—looking into the glow of logs. Viti says it is like nothing on earth. She adds that she feels 'increased'. I say that I do too. We dine hungrily, look out again by moonlight—but there is only half a moon and the Canyon opens a dim cold greenness—and then return to our rooms.

Arizona was a holiday that they had arranged for themselves towards the end of their tour. They returned together slowly to New York via Charleston, gave three or four more lectures, and then packed for home. They embarked in the 'Bremen' on 15th April and sailed shortly after midnight. On the 19th they saw the lights of the Isles of Scilly. It is disconcerting to find that the diary should record so flatly the events of the next day. In the minds of my brother and myself it remains one of the most exciting days of our lives. We were 18 and 16 respectively. We had been staying together in a French pension near Tours. We had travelled up the day before to Cherbourg, risen at 4 am. and embarked on the tug which took us out to the 'Bremen'. It was just getting light as we approached.

20th April, 1933
Cherbourg—Sissinghurst

Wake up at 5 am. to find that we are entering Cherbourg. Dress. The tug puts out in the dawn. We go on deck. See the brown hats of Ben and Nigel. We whistle to them. Go down and greet them at the gangway. Ben just the same, Niggs with altered voice, and grown immensely. Give them breakfast on the Sun Deck and thereafter show them over the ship. We see the Isle of Wight about 10 and come to rest in the Solent about 10.15. Get to London at 4 pm. and are met by Christopher [Hobhouse] and Hilda [Matheson]. Drive to K.B.W.

Viti and the boys pick me up and we motor down to Sissinghurst. A lovely evening. Arrive soon after eight. The arms are on the porch. The grass has grown in the inner court. The grass has been laid in the lawn. The stone path has been laid between the yews. My new wing has been done. The outside is all right but the chimney is too high. The sitting-room is lovely except that the opening is too big. My bedroom, w.c. and bathroom are divine. The primroses are superb. Dine. Bed. Rebecca curled up beside me. Home.

The huge meal of the American tour was soon digested and entered their blood-stream. They returned to the domestic felicities of Sissinghurst, worries about money and Lady Sackville, the advent of Hitler, and the perennial problem of Harold Nicolson's future.

In retrospect he would say that he devoted the years 1932 and 1933 to removing the stains left by 1930 and 1931. In fact, it was not quite so simple. It is true that by his three volumes of diplomatic history he restored his reputation, but he did not wish to settle down to a life of authorship and nothing else. It was too sedentary for a man with his highly developed social and political tastes; and it did not earn him enough money. In the round figures which they both preferred, the Nicolsons were spending at a rate of £6,000 a year and were earning at the rate of £3,000. 'Peacemaking' made no more than £500; the book-reviews which Harold Nicolson now began to write for the 'Daily Telegraph' (five books a week for three weeks a month) brought in another £1,000. Royalties on their past books and the occasional article and lecture-fee made up the rest. They found it strangely difficult to economise. Long Barn was neither let nor sold. A chef and his wife arrived at Sissinghurst on 29th April. There was London. There were quick expeditions to

Paris or Wales, a holiday in Italy, a stream of friends to Sissinghurst, and ambitious plans for extending the garden and the house. Somehow all these things were done, paid for and enjoyed, and became part of the fabric of their lives.

The summer of 1933 was a reflection of the summer of 1932. 'Peace-making' was published on 13th July. 'Curzon, the Last Phase' was started on 1st May, the research-work finished by 21st August, and the book itself written by 14th November. The weather was perfect: the garden was beginning to stretch and colour: they bathed in the lake: they worked: they were anxious but very happy.

DIARY   *23rd April, 1933*

Over to Brighton. Find B.M.[1] very weak. She abuses Nigel unjustly and I lose my temper. I say I shall kill her if she hurts my children. I then ask for her forgiveness. She gives it. We part as friends, but it was hell. Poor Vita, what a strain for her.

DIARY   *5th May, 1933*

Take my proofs[2] round to Michael [Sadleir]. Down to Sissinghurst. Cyril Joad comes over. He is deeply distressed about the Nazis[3] and fears we may end by having *fascismo* in this country.

DIARY   *8th May, 1933*

Up to London in Ben's car. His first experience of London traffic. He is courageous but thoughtful. Lunch with the *New Statesman* people at the Red Lion Tavern. Peter Quennell,[4] Bunny Garnett,[5] Kingsley Martin and others. Talk about America. Kingsley is worried about *fascismo* in England. Says that Tom [Mosley] is making dangerous progress. Peter is doing a book on Byron.[6] Bunny Garnett is keeping on the *Books of the Week* page but will give me any other column I want. This will not mean enough pay for me. London Library meeting. Desmond MacCarthy and E. M. Forster are the new members of the Committee.

[1] Lady Sackville.   [2] Of *Peacemaking*.

[3] Hitler had become German Chancellor on 30th January, 1933. The whole country was rapidly transformed into a one-Party state. On 2nd May the Trade Unions were dissolved and their funds seized.

[4] The author and literary critic. He was then aged 28.

[5] David Garnett, author of *Lady into Fox* (1923), *A Rabbit in the Air* (1932) etc.

[6] *Byron, The Years of Fame.*

DIARY   *27th May, 1933*

Go to tea with the Drummonds. Eustace Percy[1] there. He walks
back with me. He says that the world does not realise how far the
capitalist system has really broken down. I say that it is not the old
question of rich versus poor, but of man versus the machine. He says
that it is merely the old thing of consumption and production in
another form. I say, 'Is it, Eustace, seriously now?' He says, 'No,
Harold, it isn't. It is a new factor.' We discuss whether economics
are a science or an art. We agree that the Victorians regarded it as
fixed as Latin grammar. Now there is something unknown. That has
rendered economics more dynamic and far more respectable.

I ask him whether he thinks I am lotus-eating by living in the
country and doing what I love. He says that all serious people ought to
withdraw from life nowadays as it is so transitional as to entail insincerity. We walk along the lane in the rain. I feel comforted by
him: I am worried about life, and this old, old friend is calm and
sincere. He says that what he likes is administration. He should be
head of a great university. In spite of his pessimistic views I feel more
confident. As long as we keep our intellectual integrity we shall be
all right. I lost it in 1931: I have got it back today. Ben turns up
while we are at dinner. He is very calm. He smashed a telegraph post
in two and wrecked his car. Viti weeps silently with relieved fear.

DIARY   *16th June, 1933*

Work hard at *Curzon*. Lady Curzon says that she is going to write the
life herself. That means that she will do his personal side and use all
the letters she promised me. This is really not such a blow as it sounds,
since the book will be mainly a study of post-war diplomacy and I
do not wish to cram it with personal detail. Moreover it leaves me
free to say what I like. We decided yesterday quite suddenly at
luncheon to go off to Italy for three weeks. These improvised ex-
cursions are best.

---

[1] Lord Eustace Percy (1887-1958). He had joined the Foreign Office on the same
day as H.N., but later left to enter politics. Minister of Education, 1924-29. Rector
of Durham University, 1937-52. He married Stella, daughter of General
Drummond.

DIARY   *21st June, 1933*

Have a long talk with Gladys Marlborough[1] about Proust. She had
known him for years. She said that his snobbishness was just snobbishness and that there is little more to say about it. He would repeat
names to himself succulently. Once she said to him that she thought
the Duke of Northumberland had a lovely name. He was very excited.
'*Tiens*,' he exclaimed, '*je vais l'annoncer*.' And he got up, flung the
door open and yelled, 'Madame la Duchesse de Northumberland!'
This brought on a fit of coughing and wheezing. She also said that
Albert[2] was not, as I had been told, a Syrian waiter, but a boy at the
Lycée Condorcet. He deliberately made Proust jealous. Proust loved
Hardy. He said that *A Pair of Blue Eyes*[3] was of all books the one which
he would himself most gladly have written.

> *On 26th June they motored to Italy, and Ben, who was learning Italian
> in Florence, met them there. They were away until 13th July. Their
> route was Newhaven – Dieppe – Rheims – Simplon Pass – Milan –
> Bologna – Florence – Siena – Perugia – Urbino – Ravenna – Mantua
> – Verona – San Vigilio on Lake Garda – the Aosta Valley, and so home
> through Switzerland and France. They arrived back at Sissinghurst
> to face a sudden crisis.*

DIARY   *13th July, 1933*

Leave Newhaven about 8 a.m. and reach Sissinghurst at 9.40. Heaps
of letters. Have a bath. At 12.40 the telephone rings. It is Nigel's
Dame at Eton. Nigel has a pain and they are rather anxious about
him. 'Then he will not be able to come over tomorrow for Long
Leave?' 'Oh certainly not.' 'Then we shall come across to Eton to
see him.' 'I should rather you came today—in fact at once.' It then
dawns upon me that it is serious. It is pouring with rain and I put
on a great-coat and go across to Vita's tower. We decide to leave at
once.

We have an endless drive in the rain to Eton. Nigel is in bed in his
little room. They know it is appendicitis. He has had it a week and

---

[1] The second wife of the ninth Duke of Marlborough. She was born in Boston.
[2] Transformed by Proust in *A la recherche du temps perdu* into Albertine, the great love
of the hero's (Marcel's) life.
[3] Published in 1873.

ought to have been operated on. We telephone to Barrington-Ward[1] who arranges for a home for him at 18 Bentinck Street. An anxious drive to London, Niggs sitting upright in the back seat in pyjamas and a great-coat. We get to Bentinck Street and he is taken upstairs and put to bed. Barrington-Ward comes and says he must operate at 9.15. Can we come back at 10? We dine at the Wellington. Speechless with anxiety and distress.

At 10 we return to the nursing home and sit in the little waiting-room. Read *Punch* and *Country Life*. The smell of ether and chloroform hangs about the place. At 10.30 we hear the drone of the lift which means that Niggs is being taken upstairs. A few minutes afterwards Barrington-Ward enters looking very grave. He says the appendix was twisted backwards: it was gangrenous and an abscess had formed: the top of the appendix broke off, so diseased was it. He says: 'Ordinary cases of appendicitis are not lethal. But this is not an ordinary case. In fact it is some time since I have seen so dangerous an appendix.' We ask him if there is any hope. He says, 'Yes—of course there is. But for the next thirty-six hours it must be touch and go.' We then leave dumbly.

DIARY   *14th July, 1933*

Niggs is only sick once from the anaesthetic. His pulse and temperature are high all day. Dine with Olive Nation.[2] Too worried to think.

DIARY   *15th July, 1933*

The thirty-six hours are up. Barrington-Ward is more optimistic. Niggs is in great pain at moments. He has two drainage tubes inside him. Temperature and pulse still high.

DIARY   *16th July, 1933*

Niggs definitely better. Allowed to have some jelly. Sit with him. Watch spasms passing across his face. Not much fun.

DIARY   *17th July, 1933*

Niggs almost out of danger. He has a slight cough which causes pain. He is rather weak. Telegraph to Ben.

[1] Sir Lancelot Barrington-Ward (1884–1953), Consulting Surgeon to the Hospital for Sick Children, Great Ormond Street.
[2] A life-long friend of Lord Sackville and the Nicolsons.

DIARY   25th July, 1933

With Niggs all day. His Dame[1] comes up. Lunch with Enid Jones
as a farewell to Albrecht Bernstorff.[2] Wells, Desmond [MacCarthy]
and myself make farewell speeches. He replies with deep emotion.
I discuss seriousness with Desmond. I say that I fear that if one is very
happy in life one becomes superficial. He says, 'Yes, my dear Harold,
I agree that acute unhappiness is a great assistance to nobility of soul.
But it is a mistake to imagine one can achieve nobility merely
by making oneself acutely unhappy.' Wells is very friendly and
amusing.

DIARY   27th July, 1933

Down to Folkestone. Walk up Castle Hill Avenue to the Lees and
sit in the shelter reading. The sea is like Amalfi and the heat is terrific.
The hottest day I remember in England. Stirrings of childhood
memory. To the Grange.[3] It has gone down in the world and looks
small and scrubby. An odd impression revisiting those rooms where
I had been so unhappy and which I had not seen for thirty-four years.
Odd tactile recollections—the feel of the fender in Great School, the
feel of the bell-rope, the feel of the handle of the baize door into what
had been Hussey's[4] study.

Now if, as a little boy, I could have had a vision of myself today I
should have been less unhappy. What oppressed me then was fear
and a sense of failure.

A concert and a dramatic performance in the Gymnasium. Mr
Wodeman is the headmaster. He sings the *Gondoliers*. I give away the
prizes. I make a speech. Afterwards lemonade and tea on the lawn.
A man comes up to me and says he was once my teacher. I remember
his eyes. His name is Nettleton. He seems to remember me more than
I remember him. He says Eric[5] and I were known as 'Rags and
Tatters' owing to our grubbiness. He says my written work was
disgustingly untidy, but that I was keen on it and really good at
Greek. He told Hussey that I was certain to get a scholarship but

[1] Miss Nancy Hichens, who looked after the boys at A. H. G. Kerry's house at Eton.
[2] The Nazis had recalled him from the German Embassy in London.
[3] The private school where H.N. was educated 1895–99.
[4] The Headmaster when H.N. was a boy.
[5] H.N.'s elder brother. He succeeded as third Baron Carnock in 1952.

Hussey would not let me go up for one. He says that Hussey really was rather a bully and that I am not exaggerating.

DIARY   *4th August, 1933*

Work hard at *Curzon* in the morning. Niggs and Vita arrive at 1 p.m. Niggs is carried over to his room but comes down to luncheon.

Wystan Auden[1] reads us some of his new poem[2] in the evening. It is in alliterative prose and divided into Cantos. The idea is Gerald Heard as Virgil guiding him through modern life. It is not so much a defence of communism as an attack upon all the ideas of comfort and complacency which will make communism difficult to achieve in this country. It interests me particularly as showing, at last, that I belong to an older generation. I follow Auden in his derision of patriotism, class distinctions, comfort, and all the ineptitudes of the middle-classes. But when he also derides the other soft little harmless things which make my life comfortable, I feel a chill autumn wind. I feel that were I a communist the type of person whom I should most wish to attack would not be the millionaire or the imperialist, but the soft, reasonable, tolerant, secure, self-satisfied intellectuals like Vita and myself. A man like Auden with his fierce repudiation of half-way houses and his gentle integrity makes one feel terribly discontented with one's own smug successfulness. I go to bed feeling terribly Edwardian and back-number, and yet, thank God, delighted that people like Wystan Auden should actually exist.

DIARY   *15th August, 1933*

Over to see B.M. Her solicitor is there. She is in a foul temper, makes idiotic accusations against Vita and myself, and finally turns us out of the house. She is quite off her head.

DIARY   *23rd August, 1933*

Work hard at *Curzon*. Review von Kürenberg's *Graue Eminenz*. Berners,[3] Bob Boothby and Rex Whistler[4] come over. Bob urges me

---

[1] The poet, then aged 26.
[2] Possibly *The Dance of Death*; but this was a drama. Wystan Auden cannot now (1965) identify the poem referred to.
[3] Lord Berners, the author, painter and musician.
[4] Rex Whistler, the painter, who was killed in Normandy in 1944, was then decorating a room at Lympne for Sir Philip Sassoon.

to join the Conservatives and prophesies that either Walter Elliot or Oliver Stanley will lead, both of whom are liberals.

DIARY   26th August, 1933

After luncheon at Lympne Colonel T. E. Lawrence,[1] the uncrowned King of Arabia, arrives. He is dressed in Air Force uniform which is very hot. Unlike other privates in the Air Force he wears his heavy uniform when he goes out to tea. He has become stockier and squarer. The sliding, lurcher effect is gone. A bull terrier in place of a saluki.

In September, the strain on their finances became so great that Harold Nicolson seriously considered accepting an offer to return to the 'Evening Standard'. At almost the last moment V. Sackville-West discovered that she had accumulated a considerable sum in French royalties. Of course it was no permanent solution, but it was enough to save him from cutting the ties that he most loved and renewing those that he most detested.

DIARY   14th September, 1933

Walk back feeling happier than I have ever felt. A sort of triumphant lifting. Find a message at K.B.W. saying will I lunch with Mike Wardell.[2] He says, 'Would you consider coming back to us?' His idea is that I should edit the Londoner's Diary on my own, having complete control of the Diary staff. I say (a) That I could not consider it before January next as I must finish the Curzon book. (b) That I could not enter into a binding contract, but would take on a renewable three-months contract or a gentleman's agreement. (c) That the moment our finances improved or I was offered a seat in the House of Commons I should leave. (d) That I should want the same salary. (e) That I should want Saturdays off, plus a week in February for my Vienna trip which would not count as leave. (f) That I should not be expected to attend public dinners or to insert into the Diary any society or court gossip. He agrees to all this and I say I shall let him have a definite answer by Monday. Go back and think it all over. On

---

[1] Lawrence, who had inspired and led the Arab revolt in 1916–18, joined the Royal Air Force as a simple aircraftsman in 1925, and changed his name to Shaw in 1927. In 1933 he was still in the Air Force, engaged on motor-boat construction and trials at Portsmouth. He was killed in a motor-cycle accident in May 1935. H.N. had known him at the Peace Conference in 1919. Sir Philip Sassoon, his host at Lympne, was Under Secretary of State for Air, 1931–37.
[2] Editor of the *Evening Standard*.

the one hand it would solve our financial worries and the conditions at Shoe Lane might be a little better than last time. On the other hand it means becoming a journalist again which I loathe and abhor.

DIARY   27th September, 1933

Work hard at *Curzon* chapter v all day. Write close on 5,000 words. Also dictate a huge long letter to Peter Quennell telling him what to look up for me at the Hendon newspaper museum. Measure the central path in the kitchen garden and Gwen[1] helps me. Finally Vita refuses to abide by our decision or to remove the miserable little trees which stand in the way of my design. The romantic temperament as usual obstructing the classic.

DIARY   11th October, 1933

Go to see Tom Mosley at Ebury Street. He has had a bad back and is lying down. One of his fascist lieutenants is there but leaves us. He says he is making great progress in town and country alike. He gets very little money from the capitalists but relies on canteens and subscriptions. His aim is to build up from below gradually, and not to impose construction from above as we did in New Party days. Whenever anything happens to remind him of Cimmie,[2] a spasm of pain twitches across his face. He looked ill and pasty. He has become an excellent father and plays with the children. Cimmie's body is still at Cliveden in the chapel, and he visits it once a week. It is to be buried at Denham in a high sarcophagus in a wood. Irene[3] said that the children, Vivian and Nikki, had said to her, 'We don't cry when you talk to us about Mummy, but we always cry when we talk about her amongst ourselves.'

Then to the London Library. H. A. L. Fisher[4] in the chair. He talks to me afterwards about Curzon. He says that he was above all a *savant* and an historian and not a man of action. That he would bore the Cabinet by endless discourses and when asked for his policy would look disconcerted and astonished. Fisher never once knew Lloyd George to be rude to Curzon.

---

[1] Mrs St Aubyn was now living at Sissinghurst.
[2] Cynthia Mosley had died on 16th May, 1933.
[3] Baroness Ravensdale, Cynthia Mosley's sister. Died 1966.
[4] The historian, and Warden of New College, Oxford, 1925-40.

DIARY   *27th October, 1933*

Viti gets a letter from her French bank saying she has a balance there of £2,600. We decide on this that I shall NOT have to sell myself to Beaverbrook. I am immensely relieved. The dread of the ordeal and humiliation had been hanging over me like a sullen cloud. Work hard and cheerfully at chapter IX. Very cold and damp. In the afternoon plant irises and mark out the path in the kitchen-garden.

H.N. TO V.S-W. (*on a tour of Wales*)   *7th November, 1933*
                                                             4 King's Bench Walk, E.C.4

H. G. Wells' dinner-party was not, perhaps, an unqualified success. I gather that his intention was to announce his engagement to Moura,[1] but for some reason no announcement could be made. That was the first error. The second error arose from the fact that the titled cousin of Moura who was to play to us on the harp has two children, and one of them developed a temperature with the result that the titled cousin of Moura failed to come. The harp was there all right, as once in Tara's halls,[2] but there was no one to play it. The third error was that we dined in a little restaurant in Soho, where there was a large horse-shoe table in imitation of the Last Supper. There were also little snippets of lobster in tomato cocktails, which were among the least successful of *zakouska* that I have ever known.

Then the company was mixed in the sort of way that companies could not, or should not, be mixed. There was Emerald Cunard looking like a third-dynasty mummy painted pink by amateurs. There was Christabel[3] who is going to have a baby. There was Hazel Lavery who looked as though she had stuck on top of her face a caricature mask done by someone else: very ill she was, poor woman. And there was Enid Jones[4] who arrived veiled like the Begum of Bhopal. The men were below their usual standard. There was

[1] Baroness Budberg, who was Moura Benckendorff by her first marriage, and had been the intimate friend of Maxim Gorki.
[2] *The Harp that once through Tara's Halls*
    The soul of music shed,
    Now hangs as mute on Tara's walls
    As if that soul had fled.
                                        Thomas Moore
[3] Christabel McLaren, later Lady Aberconway.   [4] Enid Bagnold.

156

Stutterheim, late of the *Berliner Tageblatt*, David Low the caricaturist,[1] Keeble the botanist,[2] and Brendan Bracken.

After that we adjourned to Wells' flat, which is like a fountain-pen box split into cubicles by the designers of Broadcasting House. Maurice Baring appeared and Max Beaverbrook. We sat around looking at the harp. It was not a successful party. But I rather enjoyed it.

H.N. TO V.S-W. *8th November, 1933*

Yesterday I went to the *Daily Telegraph* to pick up books, and there among them, all careless on the granary floor, were *Collected Poems, vol. I*,[3] looking slimmer than I expected, but very neat and prim and serious.

Lunched with Sibyl Colefax. The Margeries[4] there. She will not like London. She thinks she is going to have a *salon*. She won't. Not a literary *salon*. Our decent literary people are all Bohemians, and our social literary people aren't decent. I told her so. She was a trifle saddened. Margerie is a really nice man.

DIARY *23rd November, 1933*

Read through the whole of *Curzon*. A most disappointing book. It falls between two stools. It is too detailed and historical for the ordinary reader, and not documented enough for the student or as a work of reference. If I could be certain of getting the papers out of Lady Curzon, I should write the whole thing again.

DIARY *20th December, 1933*

Dine with John Sparrow at the Garrick. We discuss the revision of the Peace Treaties and the condition of Europe. I take the line that nothing will content German opinion but 'victory' and that they will treat the Treaty of Versailles as an artichoke, pulling it to pieces leaf by leaf. The bad parts of that Treaty have already revised themselves. What remains is not unjust and its disturbance would lead to disturbance all

[1] David Low, born in New Zealand, was then aged 42, and was approaching the height of his fame as cartoonist for the *Evening Standard*.
[2] Professor Frederick Keeble (1870-1952). He was not a botanist but an expert on scientific farming.
[3] V.S-W.'s first volume of *Collected Poems*, including *The Land*, was published in November 1933 by the Hogarth Press.
[4] Roland de Margerie, First Secretary to the French Embassy, 1933-39.

round. But let us re-examine the Treaties, repair what can be repaired, and then cement them by an open defensive alliance.

DIARY   24th December, 1933

Subconsciously Vita is wounded by feeling (quite wrongly) that Niggs does not admire her poetical gifts and notices only her rational weaknesses. I go to bed rather unhappy about all this. The real difference is that V. and Ben are introverts and Niggs and I are extroverts. Niggs' remorseless logic irritates her as much as Ben's muddle-headedness irritates me. Yet how slight, really, is this irritation! Our happiness and understanding is so complete that the slightest little discordance echoes like a thunderstorm. Yet the problem gives me one of the three or four restless nights that I can remember having experienced.

I blame myself mostly. I have got into the way of taking my happiness for granted. Yet Viti is not a person one can take for granted. She is a dark river moving deeply in shadows. She really does not care for the domestic affections. She would wish life to be conducted on a series of *grandes passions*. Or she thinks she would. In practice, had I been a passionate man, I should have suffered tortures of jealousy on her behalf, have made endless scenes, and we should now have separated, I living in Montevideo as H.M. Minister and she breeding Samoyeds in the Gobi desert.

DIARY   25th December, 1933

I go up to London, and Viti and the boys go to Brighton. I feel dreadfully sad all day. Lunch with Mummy.[1] Very grim. Tea at Gwen's. Rather strained. Come back and change and then return to Gwen's for dinner. Jessica, John and Piers[2] are in evening dress. They are so young and keen and charming that I feel again that life is an adventure. Viti rings up after dinner. The strain and trouble have passed from her voice and I return at ease to K.B.W.

DIARY   31st December, 1933

A year coloured by two anxieties, some disappointment and much pleasure. The first anxiety was Niggs' illness, which caused us agony at the time but which has left no traces. The second has been money

---

[1] Lady Carnock.
[2] The three eldest of the five St Aubyn children. They were then aged 15, 14 and 13 respectively.

worry. By giving up what B.M. ought to pay us under settlements we are flung back upon what we can make. We have some £2,000 in Paris on which we can draw—but once that is expended we shall be in a bad way. It is quite clear that as long as B.M. lives and unless we begin to make more money by books we are in for a very difficult time. This for me is a constant anxiety. Vita takes it more calmly. B.M. is likely to live five more years at least[1] and to become more and more of a paranoiac. No job that I could get in London would really make the difference unless I sold myself to Beaverbrook which I cannot face. Thus at the back of all our life is a sense of worry and possible disaster.

In addition to all this there is the sad feeling that I have not made the best of my life. I cannot write better than I write now, and my best is little more than hack-work. My three books on diplomacy will have a certain value since they represent experience, study and a certain amount of practical reflection. But they are not good enough to justify my having cut adrift from public service. Had I remained in public service I should have had at least the illusion of progress. The horrors of age would have been compensated by material rewards. I should have been soothed by the fallacy that 'Minister', 'Ambassador' etc. did represent some sort of progression, some rising scale of achievement. Yet would I really have been lulled by such a fallacy? I do not think so. The constant work might have given me the illusion of creative activity, whereas the self-centred work that I do now seldom gives me that illusion. On the other hand, I should have ruined my domestic happiness and sacrificed much personal enjoyment. It would not be true to say that I 'regret' having left diplomacy. What I regret is that I did not from the first devote my energy to some profession which could have been combined with my present sort of life.

---

[1] Lady Sackville died in January 1936.

1934

Journey to Italy and Morocco – H.N.'s idea for a major autobiographical work – Somerset Maugham – an illness – journalism and lecturing – invitation to write the life of Dwight Morrow – first visit to the Morrow family at North Haven and Englewood – meeting with Charles and Anne Lindbergh – the Hauptmann case – Thor and little Jon – visit to Pittsburgh in search of Morrow material – H.N.'s affection for the Lindberghs – return to England

On 26th January V. Sackville-West and Gwen St Aubyn went to Portofino on the Italian Riviera, where in a spasm of romantic extravagance they took a fortnight's lease of the Castello overlooking the harbour. Harold Nicolson joined them on 8th February, having travelled out by Paris, Munich and Vienna.

H.N. TO V.S-W. (*at Portofino*)   *31st January, 1934*
                      4 King's Bench Walk, E.C.4

I dined with Clive [Bell]. The Peter Quennells and Desmond [Mac-Carthy] there. The latter was in his very best form. We talked about John's book,[1] about Pound,[2] about Tom Eliot, about Byron. Desmond evolved a theory that Mallarmé wrote in his opalescent manner because he did not know English well enough to understand it, but well enough to see the colours of the thing. He then changed his mind and said that Pound and Eliot made a mistake in thinking that they knew Latin because they didn't: that a line like 'Love and the fine Greek hills' was a bad line to us because we knew how far the words and phrases were hackneyed, but that only a great scholar could tell whether a line in Virgil was or was not a great line, because only a great scholar would know the background of the words used. He then said that no foreigner could or should criticise another language. In fact he got himself tied up in a lot of nonsense. But how we laughed! You know, that asbestos laughter which does one such a lot of good. And what remains of it all? I mean, even to you who know Desmond I cannot reconstruct the thing. No wonder that people like Sydney Smith[3] seem to enjoy or have enjoyed an exaggerated reputation. Dr Johnson is the only conversationalist who triumphs over time.

H.N. TO V.S-W. (*at Portofino*)   *1st February, 1934*
                      4 King's Bench Walk, E.C.4

Your telegram arrived saying that you have taken the Castello. Well, I am all for that sort of thing, as you know. I liked being turned out

[1] *Sense and Poetry* by John Sparrow. Constable. 1934.
[2] Ezra Pound, the American poet.   [3] The cleric and wit, 1771–1845.

163

of my dear little suburban home[1] and made to sleep in a ruined tower on a camp-bed. And I see no reason why, in the present state of our finances, you did not buy the Castello outright. You might also lease the Carnarvon Villa in case Olive Rinder comes to stay with us. But I am glad all the same. It all comes from Gwen reading the Tauchnitz edition of the works of Elizabeth Russell.[2] I hope you are both very uncomfortable and happy. Bless you both.

H.N. TO V.S-W. (*at Portofino*)   *4th February, 1934*
                                                                           Munich

I found that Jim Lees-Milne[3] was going over to Paris on the Friday, so I decided to go with him, as it was more or less on my way. He had never been to Versailles, so we went out there for lunch. It was quite empty and very cold and magnificent. I picked up several hints for Sissinghurst. The *Bassin de Neptune* would do well in Mr Nicolson's rondel.[4] Jim is such a charming person. He has a passion for poetry and knows masses about it. I like my friends to be well-read and well bred. Jim is such an aristocrat in mind and culture. You would like him enormously.

I walked to James Joyce's flat in the Rue Galilée. It is a little furnished flat as stuffy and prim as a hotel bedroom. The door was opened by the son. A strange accent he had, half-German, half-Italian—an accent of Trieste. We sat down on little hard chairs and I tried to make polite conversation to the son. Then Joyce glided in. It was evident that he had just been shaving. He was very spruce and nervous and chatty. Great rings upon little twitching fingers. Huge concave spectacles which flicked reflections of the lights as he moved his head like a bird, turning it with that definite insistence to the speaker as blind people do who turn to the sound of a voice. Joyce was wearing large bedroom slippers in check, but except for that, one had the strange impression that he had put on his best suit. He was very courteous, as shy people are. His beautiful voice trilled on slowly like Anna Livia Plurabelle.[4] He has the most lovely voice I know—liquid and soft with undercurrents of gurgle.

[1] Long Barn.
[2] Elizabeth Mary, Countess Russell, published in 1898 her immensely successful novel *An Enchanted April*, which had the Castello at Portofino as its setting.
[3] The architectural historian.
[4] A circle of yew hedges at Sissinghurst.
[5] A section of James Joyce's novel *Finnegans Wake*.

He told me how the ban had been removed from *Ulysses* ('Oolissays', as he calls it) in America. He had hopes of having it removed in London, and was in negotiation with John Lane. He seemed rather helpless and ignorant about it all, and anxious to talk to me. One has the feeling that he is surrounded by a group of worshippers and that he has little contact with reality. This impression of something unreal was increased by the atmosphere of the room, the mimosa with its ribbon, the birdlike twitching of Joyce, the glint of his glasses, and the feeling that they were both listening for something in the house.

He told me that a man had taken Oolissays to the Vatican and had hidden it in a prayer-book, and that it had been blessed by the Pope. He was half-amused by this and half-impressed. He saw that I would think it funny, and at the same time he did not think it wholly funny himself.

My impression of the Rue Galilée was the impression of a very nervous and refined animal—a gazelle in a drawing-room. His blindness increases that impression. I suppose he is a real person somewhere, but I feel that I have never spent half-an-hour with anyone and been left with an impression of such brittle and vulnerable strangeness.

DIARY   *5th February, 1934*
                                                                   Vienna

Leave Munich very early. An effect of winter dawn in snow-steeped streets. Lights in the top windows of baroque palaces. As the train draws out of the station a great red sun rises over the fields. Then the frost gathers on the windows and it is not till we reach Salzburg that I can see through them. The sun has by then melted the flowers. Reach Vienna at 3.20. Met by Walford Selby,[1] Frau Jacobi of the *Kultur Bund* and the chairman of the Anglo-Austrian Association.

To a dinner with the Rohans. Party consists of Selbys, Prince and Princess Rohan, Prince Schwarzenberg, Countess Palfi and the historian Selick. Afterwards many people come in—including Kastner and Neumach, who is supposed to be the future Hitler of Austria. There is in fact a sense of revolution in the air. We and France and Italy have said that Austria must at all costs 'preserve her independence', or in other words must not join with Germany or become Nazi. Yet most of the country is Nazi in feeling and if they turned out

[1] Sir Walford Selby, British Minister in Vienna, 1933–37.

Dolfuss there is no more to be done or said.[1] We cannot send the Atlantic fleet to Linz.

DIARY   9th February, 1934
                                                                            Portofino

Drive to Max Beerbohm's villa.[2] He meets us. It is a shock. He is quite round; his cheeks are chubby with a scarlet nose, like two melons with a peppercorn between them. And his head has sunk sideways a trifle—a very different thing from the neat slim seductive person I remember. Mrs Beerbohm appears straw-coloured and *affairée*. Then Gerhart Hauptmann[3] and his wife. He is more magnificent than ever. A huge grey frock-coat of which the waistcoat buttons up almost to the chin disclosing a little black stock from which hangs a huge *catena* of tortoiseshell at the end of which is (as I later observe) a flat gold watch.

We go upstairs to the little house for luncheon. It is almost unbearably hot, but the food and wine are excellent. Hauptmann talks a great deal and very simply. He talks about that lack of harmony in the German character. 'But you', I say to him, 'seem to be harmony personified.' 'Yes', he answers, '*aber nach siebzig jahre bestrebungen*.'[4] Hauptmann says that Germany will probably liberalise itself even as Italian *fascismo* has liberalised itself. I am not so sure. He says that what they need is *Der Grosse Mann*. If Gottfried Bismarck were older he might be that man. He is now *Landrat* at Rügen. Max, who speaks no German, says little, and in fact I scarcely had a word with him.

---

[1] The incorporation of Austria into a Greater Germany had been forecast by Hitler in the opening pages of *Mein Kampf*. The Austrian Nazis, armed and financed by Germany, kept up a violent propaganda campaign, backed by acts of terrorism. On 25th July, 1934 the Chancellor of Austria, Engelbert Dolfuss, was assassinated by the Nazis and Rintelen proclaimed Chancellor in his place. The *putsch* failed, however, owing to the unrestrained fury of Mussolini and his open support for Austria. Hitler hurriedly disengaged.

[2] At Rapallo. Max Beerbohm was then aged 63.

[3] The German dramatist, novelist and poet, then aged 72. He died in 1946.

[4] 'But after exerting myself for seventy years.'

DIARY   *10th February, 1934*
                                                              Cap Ferrat

To Cannes, where at the Carlton bar we meet Michael Arlen[1] and his wife. Dine with them. Willy Maugham[2] tells me two stories about Lily Langtry.[3] They were crossing to America together and one night on deck she mentioned a man called Eckmühl, or something like that. Willy said he had never heard of Eckmühl. 'But', said Mrs Langtry, 'he was famous in two continents.' 'And why was he famous?' asked Willy. 'I loved him', she answered quite simply. Then there was another story. She had an affair with the Crown Prince Rudolf or the Archduke Leopold or someone—anyhow a potent potentate. They were sitting in front of the fire and had a row. She took off a huge emerald ring which he had given her and cast it into the flames. He immediately dropped down on his knees and began to rummage in the ashes. 'Naturally', said Mrs Langtry, 'I couldn't love him again.'

Michael Arlen is one of those few writers who has had the sense to realise that his great vogue was not permanent and that he must treat his income as capital. At one time he was making about £20,000 a year; I doubt whether he actually earns today more than £1,200. But he has investments. He is a decent companionable person, clever and intelligent. The two so seldom go together.

From the South of France, Harold Nicolson, V. Sackville-West and Gwen St Aubyn went on to Morocco, where his father had been British Minister from 1895 to 1901 and where he had spent part of his childhood. It was during this long holiday that he began to evolve the idea of writing a six-volume autobiography. The idea was conceived and planned with such enthusiasm that it seems strange and untypical that it was never carried further. Perhaps it was due to the serious illness that he contracted from an insect-bite at Fez. Fortunately the infection did not reach its climax until after his return to London, but at one moment, not for the first time in his life, he thought that he was dying. After his recovery, the idea of the autobiography was scarcely mentioned again,

---

[1] The novelist (1895-1956). Born in Bulgaria, lived in New York.

[2] Somerset Maugham, the novelist, with whom H.N. was staying at the Villa Mauresque, Cap Ferrat. He was then aged 60.

[3] The famous beauty (1852-1929), known as the 'Jersey Lily', because she was born the daughter of the Dean of Jersey.

but something of the autobiographical approach which he had intended
influenced the structure and manner of 'Helen's Tower' (1937) and 'The
'Desire to Please' (1943).

DIARY   11th February, 1934
                                                         Cap Ferrat

Since I left Munich—and in this sunshine—an idea has been forming in
my mind. 'I shall', I said suddenly to myself, 'write an autobiography
in six volumes. It will be called F.A. or *Fictional Autobiography*'. It will
be dedicated to Viti as follows :

> *Hunc Librum*
> *Vitae Sicut Omnia Vitae*
> *Vitae*
> D.D.D.
> H.N.[1]

Later I picked up the books that I was reading for review and thought
no more of the idea, imagining it had been induced only by reading
Proust again lately, by the change of air, and by the strange emotional
state created by early rising, snow, sunrise, and lights in baroque
palaces. After that came Vienna and a rush of visits and diversions.
But again, on leaving Vienna in the almost dawn, the idea came back
to me stronger than ever. It seemed to have achieved an outline, almost
muscles, certainly a backbone, in the interval since Munich. A mere
jelly it had been that morning and now it was forming into a foetus.
The fact that Vienna had been a success, that I had been surrounded by
people who had not only read but had been influenced by my books,
that I had spoken well at my lecture, all this, coupled with the change of
air and movement, gave me self-confidence as well as fluidity.

Since then the thing has seldom been absent from my mind, and I
see the whole scheme as a vast undertaking stretching over ten years.
Primarily it will be a study in mutations. But I shall try and give to it a
serious philosophical shape. I may be wrong, but I feel that in the last
year I have found myself. And if only my present mood of energy
and confidence persists, then I shall bring the whole thing off.

Curiously enough, the idea has shown me one thing clearly. I have
been toying with the theory that when B.M. dies I shall go into politics,

[1] 'H.N. dedicates this autobiography, like all things in life, to Vita.' The pattern of
the words is better than their grammar.

and many of my day-dreams have centred upon the picture of my returning to the Foreign Office as Secretary of State. But now that I am obsessed by THE IDEA all this seems perfectly trivial, and is disclosed as an attempt to solace myself for not writing better by the illusion that I am really a man of action. Thus I now see six volumes ahead of me—*à la recherche du temps perdu*. Tangier fits in beautifully for this. But I must try and write a play first, as I must make money. Anyhow the *Mutations* shall never leave my mind—my constant companion. I am delighted to feel that I have become far more intelligent in the last two years. Until now I have regretted that I should only have got real control of my mind after I had left diplomacy and started writing books with which people will identify me. Now they will only identify me with the *Mutations* series.

DIARY   *18th February, 1934*
                                         Marrakesh, Morocco

Begin taking notes for my *magnum opus*. Rather appalled by its hugeness. After luncheon go down to the town. The mountains are visible and it is very warm. Walk about the market. There are story-tellers and snake-charmers and conjurers. The whole atmosphere is unchanged since thirty years ago. It is hot. A lovely new moon in the evening. Please God make me able to do my *magnum opus*. I feel this evening my inability present in front of me like a huge piece of furniture in a servant's bedroom: *le bureau de Louis XV* in the attic of a housemaid.

DIARY   *19th February, 1934*
                                         Marrakesh

In the morning go on planning my *magnum opus*. My difficulty is to decide how far I can go. Is the book to be fictional or accurate? There is much that I do not mind saying about myself but much which would, if truly told, cause trouble to other people. The only standard, I think, is to expose myself to any amount of shame but to disguise other people so that they will not be involved in my humiliations. Yet the book will be nothing if it is not true. The temptation to make it half-true will be a constant temptation and I must fight against it with all the vigour within me. I sit on the little terrace with the sun very hot on one side and the shade on the other very chilly, thinking of all this. Proust was not honest enough. If I do not possess his talent, I do possess far more courage. I have a good memory, an observant nature, and I have lived through one of the most interesting fifty years in the history of human civilisation. If I can reproduce those years in a really sincere form I shall have contributed something to human understanding. But can I be sincere without wounding people less pachydermatous than myself? And once I start introducing fictional situations, I may end by just writing a bad novel. The only thing about which I know anything is myself. Yet I was not alone: I was surrounded by people to whom a true account would be painful. That is the problem. I feel I have energy enough and even talent enough, but am I sufficiently ruthless? That may be the *pierre d'achoppement*.[1] Then obviously I must be slow about it and not skate over thin ice. My impatience may be a difficulty. I am so apt to take short mental cuts. And writing of a sort comes so quickly to me and so fluently. But it is a great adventure, perhaps the most important thing that I have ever essayed.

DIARY   *23rd February, 1934*
                                                              Casablanca

I have been bothered whether to make my book an autobiography or a biography. Am I to say 'I' throughout, or am I to talk of 'he', making my hero Gerald Tomkinson? If I say 'I', I shall sacrifice all alibis and discretions; if I say 'he', I shall lose reality. I think I shall say 'I', making certain central figures wholly fictional.

We have tea at the Moorish café. Coffee and almond cakes. The storks clatter their beaks in the turrets, laying their heads backwards in order to do so. From time to time they clumsily make love—huge legs agitated at untidy angles. There are musicians who play an endless Moorish tune, and around are the wives of French minor officials with their restless children. The sun sets upon the river estuary and the storks wheel away to Salé to fetch frogs. We return to the hotel. The lights fuse and we have only one candle between us. Gwen feels tired and goes to bed.

Vita and I walk out on the front for a bit. There is a school opposite and we can see through the window the master walking from group to group beating time. 'A', 'I', 'O', 'U', 'é', 'è', 'ê', shout the little boys in unison learning French. There is a thunderstorm over the sea and the lightning flashes towards the Cape Verde Islands. Vita and I discuss whether women enjoy their freedom. I state that women who

[1] Stumbling-block.

170

would have been quite happy and contented as married in 1910 are now feeling restless and nervous. V. says that in every revolution there is a transitional stage. That women have for centuries been suppressed and that one cannot expect them to slide quite naturally into freedom. This saddens me. I know that there is no such thing as equality between the sexes and that women are not fulfilling their proper function unless subservient to some man. But I do not say so, as it would hurt Vita's feelings. Love seems so wide a thing to women that unless their emotions are canalised by some sort of social discipline they get lost. With men there is always the discipline of action. Gwen, for instance, thirty years ago would have felt herself fortunate at having a faithful husband and five adoring children. But now she feels that these obligations limit herself, that there is a more important function for her somewhere beyond the function of mother and wife. V. regards this new feeling as a revolt against the centennial domination of the male. But the male always had a sense of responsibility. Women seem to lack that sense and only to have a feeling of possession or belonging.

DIARY   *6th March, 1934*
                                              Fez

A marvellous day. Walk up in the evening to the cemetery above Bab Guissa. There is an old man praying and beyond a story-teller with the Arabs arrayed round him upon the tombs and rocks. And to the west is the valley of the Oued el Fez, the edge of the town and the distant snow mountains, with the dust of goats returning hanging in the evening sun. As lovely an evening as I have ever seen.

DIARY   *10th March, 1934*
                                           Tangier

My ear, which was stung at Fez, has been suppurating. I do not know how to treat it and send for the doctor. Spend the morning working on my proofs.[1]

DIARY   *19th March, 1934*
                                   4 King's Bench Walk, E.C.4

Go to see Knuthsen.[2] As I enter he says, 'You're ill!' 'No', I answer, 'I am not ill. In fact I have just eaten the largest luncheon I have ever eaten.' 'Sit down', he says, taking my pulse and at the same time

[1] Of *Curzon, The Last Phase*.   [2] His doctor, Sir Louis Knuthsen.

171

thrusting a thermometer into my mouth. 'Thought so', he says, releasing the pulse. 'Over 100.' 'Thought so', he says, glancing at the thermometer, '101. Now let's look at that ear.' He thinks I have got staphylococcus poisoning and tells me to go straight to bed. In the early morning my temperature is down to 98°. I therefore get up, intending to see him again at 2.30. But by then I feel groggy, take my temperature again, and find it nearly 104. I telephone to Knuthsen saying this. He fixes me up with a room in a nursing-home in Manchester Street where I am to go at 4 p.m.

Spend the interval writing my Will, instructions to Christopher Hobhouse etc. These may be the last words I ever type on my beloved Tikki.[1] I am not really jumpy, which is strange, but rather excited and amused. I wish V. were here, but it would fuss her terribly to telegraph tonight when she is so far away.[2] If I am not well, I shall telegraph to her tomorrow morning. But even if I am a corpse before she arrives, I have nothing to say to her which she doesn't know—immortal love, immortal gratitude.

Finis Vitae Meae
Deo Gratias

How lucky I have been! That is my only feeling.

DIARY   *24th March, 1934*
                              17 Manchester Street, W.1

I am better during the day, but in the night the crisis comes. I am sick and feverish and pour with sweat. Very apprehensive and nightmarey. Dim edges of consciousness flickering like a battlefield. Very horrible. In the morning I recover. My temperature drops to normal.

DIARY   *25th March, 1934*
                              17 Manchester Street, W.1

Viti spends all day with me, bless her. I read voraciously, including *The Silver Spoon* by Galsworthy. He is even worse than I imagined —shallow and self-righteous. I cannot understand why he has such a reputation. He is far worse than Hugh Walpole. John Sparrow comes to see me.

[1] His three typewriters were known as Rikki, Tikki and Tavy.
[2] She was motoring home slowly through Provence.

DIARY   *29th March, 1934*
                                                  Sissinghurst

Viti comes at 3 and we motor down with Gwen to Sissinghurst.
Rebecca very pleased to see me. Go straight to bed. Heaps of parcels
and letters. Delighted to be home. Louise[1] leaves us in tears. Mrs
Staples[2] comes.

*He recovered very quickly, and resumed his life at Sissinghurst, gardening,
drawing plans, reviewing books for the 'Daily Telegraph' and writing
a weekly article for the Paris 'Figaro'. 'Curzon' was published on 10th
May after a number of instalments had been serialised in 'The Times',
and it received superlative reviews. Two days later he went to Stock-
holm to lecture on Democratic Diplomacy.*

H.N. TO V.S-W.   *13th May, 1934*
                        On board Svenska Lloyd 'Suecia' in the North Sea

A nice clean boat with dryad chairs and waitresses instead of stewards.
I washed. I brushed my thinning hair. I entered the saloon. 'Skilje-
tecken utstrykning sasom sarskilda konditor bud', said the head-waiter.
'That', I answered, 'would be delightful.' So I sat at the Captain's
table. He, poor man, was threading the intricacies of the Thames
estuary and did not appear. But two Swedish matrons appeared and
I rejoiced to find Lord Peel,[3] whom I like very much indeed. No
food came. 'Gong-gongen gar ej', said the head-waiter. I translated
to Lord Peel (I have picked up Swedish very quickly): 'The gong', I
said, 'has not sounded yet.'

H.N. TO V.S-W.   *15th May, 1934*
                                     British Legation, Stockholm

I had such a nice surprise. When I came downstairs there was no one
here, and I picked up the *New Statesman* expecting to read that rather
snuffy business on the part of Kingsley Martin.[4] It was less snuffy than

---

[1] Louise Genoux, V.S-W.'s French maid. She retired and lived at Dover.
[2] Mrs Staples, the cook, had been with the Nicolsons since May 1926. She was
  widowed, married for a second time to George Hayter, and left Sissinghurst for a
  year. Now she returned, and remained there until her retirement in 1966.
[3] The first Earl of Peel (1867–1937), Secretary of State for India in 1922–24 and
  1928–29.
[4] A review of *Curzon, The Last Phase.*

I had gathered. And then I turned the page and there was a long review by Richard Church[1] about my own angel. Oh, I *was* pleased! It was such an intelligent review and so praiseworthy. I nearly sent you a telegram saying 'Congratulations on being churched', but I thought the better of it.

But I was so pleased and left it lying about turned upwards, so that when Archie[2] came in a few minutes later and said, 'Hello, what a eulogy of Vita!' I said, 'Is there?', blandly; 'I must read it'. But I knew that to you it would give pleasure to have such a review in the *New Statesman*, the only paper that really counts much in these things, and the only book about which you have seriously cared. You know how pleased these things make one. I mean a sort of warm doughnut inside for the rest of the day, sweet outside, soft all round, with a fid of jam in its little gentle belly.

DIARY   *12th June, 1934*
                                        4 King's Bench Walk, E.C.4

To luncheon with Malcolm Bullock to meet Brüning.[3] David Balniel,[4] Archie Sinclair, Bob Boothby and Wheeler-Bennett[5] there. They all say that the House of Commons is up in arms against the fascists and that something will be done about them. They think this is a good thing, as it will render it difficult for the Socialists in future not to take steps against the communists if the Conservatives have suppressed the fascists. Brüning talks well. He says that he would have liked to get back the Hohenzollerns in the shape of Louis-Ferdinand,[6] or even the old Kaiser. I suggest that the only way to restore democracy is through constitutional monarchy. He agrees, and adds that Germany has suffered from the fact that there has been no sense of 'legitimacy' in any Government since 1918. He says that a reaction against Hitlerism is already beginning among the young people of 18 to 21. The Reichswehr will establish a purely military dictatorship if Nazism

---

[1] The poet, novelist and literary critic. The review was of V.S-W.'s *Collected Poems*.
[2] Sir Archibald Clark Kerr, later Lord Inverchapel, British Minister in Sweden, 1931–35.
[3] Heinrich Brüning had remained German Chancellor until 30th May, 1932, when he was removed from office by President Hindenburg.
[4] He succeeded his father as the Earl of Crawford and Balcarres in 1940.
[5] Sir John Wheeler-Bennett, the historian. He was the author of *Munich, Prologue to Tragedy*. Macmillan. 1948.
[6] The second son of the Crown Prince; then aged 26.

breaks down, and when the military dictatorship fails, then there will
be communism.

*1934 had not so far been a very productive year. Harold Nicolson had
started no new book, and V. Sackville-West's latest novel, 'The Dark
Island',[1] he thought 'morbid and distressing', a view that was shared
by the majority of critics. The 'Mutations' idea had faded. He had firmly
refused a new offer to rejoin the 'Evening Standard'. His broadcasts
and journalism took up only a small part of his time. It was therefore
with some excitement that he received an invitation to write a biography
of Dwight Morrow, the American statesman.*

*Harold Nicolson had only once met Morrow, at the time of the London
Naval Conference in 1930, and had never met his widow, who personally
chose him as the author for her husband's 'Life'. It was a brave gamble on
her part to commission an Englishman, and Harold Nicolson was well
aware of the double pitfall of misinterpreting American sentiment and
upsetting his widow-patron. Besides, Morrow had spent much of his
life with the firm of J. P. Morgan and Company, and finance had never
been among Harold Nicolson's strongest subjects. It would also mean a
long absence in the United States. But he was attracted to the idea for
precisely the same reason as had prompted Mrs Morrow to invite him: it
would give him a splendid opportunity to write about American diplomacy,
and add a fourth volume to his diplomatic trilogy.*

*The blurb attached to the American edition (Harcourt, Brace, 1935)
illustrates how the finished book was presented to the American public
and gives a summary of Morrow's career:*

*'There is no biographer better equipped than Harold Nicolson to
write the biography of Dwight Morrow. Mr Nicolson's experience
of diplomacy, the skill with which he told the story of his father's life
in "Portrait of a Diplomatist",[2] the objectivity of all his biographies,
have prepared him to write of a man whose name has come to symbol-
ise the increasingly significant role of the United States in international affairs.*

*'Dwight Morrow was born in Huntington, West Virginia, in
1873. He entered Amherst College in 1891, and upon graduation,
studied law in New York. For fifteen years he distinguished himself
in the profession of law. With the outbreak of war, his partnership*

[1] Published by the Hogarth Press, 1934.
[2] The title given to the American edition of *Lord Carnock*.

with J. P. Morgan and Company brought him increasing responsibility. In the years that followed, through his work in Cuba, on post-war reconstruction, the London Conference in 1930, and finally his achievement in Mexico, the character of Dwight Morrow steadily emerged. As Walter Lippmann has said, "He was a public figure of the first magnitude."

'At the very height of his career, on 5th October, 1931, he died.' Neither the life nor the book was quite so arid as this sounds.

DIARY   *26th June, 1934*

Lunch with Morgan, Grenfell[1] at 23 Great Winchester Street. After luncheon Teddy Grenfell takes me into another room and shows me a letter to him from Mrs Dwight Morrow. 'Will I write the biography of her husband?' I reply that the idea appeals to me: that, however, it will entail visiting New York and Mexico: that this means loss of income here and expenses there. I should have to be indemnified for these expenses. He asks me to think it over. I am attracted to the idea as I admired Morrow and I want to write a book about an American. It will have small success here but should go well in America. The difficulty is that if I have my expenses paid I shall lose something of my independence, and that unless I have my expenses paid I can do nothing.

DIARY   *30th June, 1934*

Write to Francis Rodd[2] saying that I will do the Morrow book provided that they can pay my expenses. I shall not take a penny more than my actual out-of-pocket costs.

DIARY   *13th August, 1934*

Finish the main skeleton of my Morrow notes. I can now begin on the bricks.

DIARY   *15th August, 1934*

Niggs and I decide to create an island in the lake as a bird-sanctuary. We decide that it shall be a Greek island and an exact model of Ithaca. Vita is not at all pleased. She calls it a waste of time: she calls it

[1] Morgan, Grenfell and Co. was the London finance-house associated with J. P. Morgan and Co., New York.
[2] A Director of Morgan, Grenfell and Co. Later Lord Rennell.

mud-larking: she says we shall never finish it: she says it will be washed away. We transport five or six stones down to the lake. Vita says it is a waste of her precious stones. We get Abdul[1] to help us. His knees wobble. Then Uncle Charlie[2] and Lionel Sackville-West[3] come over and we cease discouraged. The outline of Ithaca straddles the bed of the lake like the Loch Ness Monster with stones in its mouth.[4]

DIARY   *22nd August, 1934*

At the Garrick I met Constant Huntington[5] who, as an American, gave me glum advice. He says I shall never be able to capture the American background and that if I try to do so, they will think I am being patronising. I must expect great prejudice in the U.S.A. against my doing it at all. I felt diffident about that side from the first. God grant that I make a good book of it, mainly for Mrs Morrow's sake. It is so bold of her to suggest me and I know all too well that her friends and family will reproach her for it. I must try and make this the best book I have written.

I have left active life too soon. I could have done this biography business when 60, and devoted these thirteen years to real active work.

Harold Nicolson left for the United States on the 'Berengaria' on 14th September. He was not to return until 8th December. At the start, he felt very homesick.

H.N. TO V.S-W.   *16th September, 1934*
                      On board S.S. 'Berengaria' in mid-Atlantic

It was slightly foggy as we approached Cherbourg. We swung into the outer harbour and I watched the tender approaching. I remember how in the *Bremen* I had leaned over and seen Ben and Niggs on that tender. *J'avais pitié de moi.*

Darkness was descending and the *triste patience des phares* throbbed painfully along the parapets of Europe. For half-an-hour I paced the deck seeing the lights fling out sudden appeals.

[1] A donkey which they had sent back to Sissinghurst from Morocco.
[2] Charles Sackville-West, who had succeeded his elder brother Lionel (V.S.-W.'s father) as Lord Sackville in 1928.
[3] Lord Sackville's nephew, then aged 21, and now (1966) sixth Baron Sackville.
[4] Ithaca is still there, but obliterated from view under a sea of reeds.
[5] Chairman of Putnam, the publishers.

I talked to Philip Lothian about his scheme for saving historic buildings. His idea is to get the Government to accept certain places as national possessions in their entirety, including park, garden, furniture and general condition. The Treasury would accept as payment for death-duties the transference of an equivalent value in these possessions. The objects thus transferred would belong to the State who would lend them on trust to the owners. Thus Eddy Sackville-West could pledge the furniture for Knole as payment on death-duties: the furniture would remain there and all the Government would ask is that it should not be sold or otherwise dispersed, that the public should be admitted, and that the owners, as guardians, should take all the proper precautions. He thinks he will persuade Neville Chamberlain to accept this scheme. It would be a magnificent thing for Knole if he could.[1]

H.N. TO V.S-W.
23rd September, 1934
Deacon Brown's Point, North Haven, Maine

We went down to the little pier where something between a yacht and a steam-launch awaited us.[2] The Scotch mist hung over the little harbour of Fockland, Maine, and the spars and rigging of a little yacht at anchor were hung with heavy drops. We hummed out into a satin sea, accompanied by a soft circle of fog. The islands are some eight miles from the mainland and I enjoyed the forty odd minutes which it took us to creep cautiously towards them. Then a buoy appeared with two cormorants on it, and directly afterwards the dim outline of pine-trees stepping gingerly down to the very edge of the rocks. We swung in between two islands and across to a third where there was a landing stage. There we landed, O venusta Sirmio. A station-car was waiting for us. We drove in and out of tiny bays with pines down to the water, and eventually the pines became tidier and there were sweeps of mown grass between the plantations. Then we swept down on to the house. It was built by Aldrich[3] and is charming. It is of wood and has shingle

---

[1] Lord Lothian's scheme was carried out by Section 30 of the Finance Act of 1953. Knole passed to the National Trust in 1946.

[2] The Morrows had two houses in the United States: Englewood, New Jersey, where Morrow had died in 1931, twelve miles from New York City; and a summer home on North Haven Island. H.N. worked mostly at Englewood, but he was taken out to North Haven for his first meeting with Mrs Morrow.

[3] Chester Aldrich, the American architect, and a close friend of the Morrows. He also built Englewood.

sides. Rocks and islands at every angle and the sea splashing in and out of dahlias.

Mrs Morrow advanced to meet us at the gate. A little, neat woman. She is in quite a state of excitement at my arrival. She had not slept all night. I pray that I shall not disappoint her. She worships her husband's memory, but is intelligent enough not to wish to control what I write.

The Lindberghs are in California and are coming back shortly. I gather they will be at Englewood all through the time I am here.

Charles Lindbergh and his wife Anne, Dwight Morrow's second daughter, were at that moment passing through a new crisis in their dreadfully harrowed lives. As so many of Harold Nicolson's letters during this period were concerned with the ordeal and character of these two remarkable people, a brief account of what happened to them is a necessary preface to what follows.

Lindbergh married Anne Morrow at Englewood in May 1929, two years after the flight to Paris which had made him the most adulated man in America. Their son, Charles Lindbergh Jnr., was born on 22nd June 1930, Anne's twenty-fourth birthday. This was the baby that was snatched from his cradle on 1st March, 1932. A ransom was demanded by the kidnapper and it was handed over in circumstances that made it impossible to apprehend him if the boy's life was to be saved. But it was a double-cross. The boy was already dead: his body was found in a wood near the Lindberghs' home a few weeks later, and it was clear that he had died within a few minutes of being taken from his crib.

The American people were profoundly shocked. The whole police resources of the country were mobilised for tracking down the murderer, but it was largely owing to the skill and patience of one detective, Arthur Koehler, a timber specialist, who traced the source of the wood used in the ladder which the kidnapper had left behind him, that the man was eventually caught. He was Bruno Hauptmann, a German carpenter who lived in the Bronx. He was arrested on the 19th September, 1934, two days before Harold Nicolson landed in New York.

The publicity given to these events in the newspapers, and the search for new personal angles by reporters harried by their editors, had imposed on the Lindberghs a strain that was becoming almost unendurable. By nature shy and sensitive people, they were now dragged through the fire all over again. They were forced daily to re-live the events of two-and-a-

half years before. On top of it all, they became nervous for their second son, Jon, born in August 1932. 'From the moment of Jon Lindbergh's birth', writes Lindbergh's biographer, Kenneth Davis, 'his parents had been the recipients of a stream of letters containing clear or implied threats against the child.' They guarded him carefully at Next Day Hill, Englewood, where they had come to live with Anne's mother soon after the finding of the body of their murdered son. It was here that Harold Nicolson met them on his return from North Haven.

H.N. TO V.S-W.   30th September, 1934
                                      Next Day Hill, Englewood, New Jersey

As we approached Epping Forest (since it is in such terms that you must visualise this place—the same distance from New York as Epping from London, the same effect of street lamps, the same idea that in the recesses of those trees lie sardine-tins and rain-soaked copies of the *Daily Mirror*), a man at the gate waved us on with an electric torch. To be accurate, there is no gate, only two piers and a little hutch in which the detectives group and grouse. The car hummed up the hill between dripping trees. Banks, the butler, was waiting. 'Mrs Morrow', he said, 'is dining out with Mr Lamont. Colonel and Mrs Lindbergh are here.'

He led the way through the hall to the boudoir. There were Anne and Charles. Anne like a Geisha—shy, Japanese, clever, gentle, obviously an adorable little person. Charles Lindbergh—slim (though a touch of chubbiness about the cheek), school-boyish, yet with those delicate prehensile hands which disconcert one's view of him as an inspired mechanic. They were smiling shyly. Lindbergh's hand was resting upon the collar of a dog. I had heard about that dog. He has figured prominently in the American newspapers. He is a police dog of enormous proportions. His name is Thor. I smiled at him a little uncertainly. Not for a moment did Lindbergh relax his hold upon the collar. It is this monster which guards Jon Lindbergh.

'What a nice dog!' I said.

'You will have to be a little careful at first, Mr Nicolson,' he answered.

'Is he very fierce?'

'He's all that. But he will get used to you in time . . .'

'Thor is his name, is it not? I read about him in the newspapers.'

I stretched a hand towards him. 'Thor!' I said, throwing into the word an appeal for friendship that was profoundly sincere. He then made a noise in his throat such as only tigers make when waiting for their food. It was not a growl. It was not a bark. It was a deep pectoral regurgitation—predatory, savage, hungry. Lindbergh smiled a little uneasily. 'It will take him a week or so', he said, 'to become accustomed to you.' He then released his hold upon the collar. I retreated rapidly to the fireplace, as if to flick my ash from my cigarette. Thor stalked towards me. I thought of you and my two sons and Gwen and Rebecca, and my past life and England's honour. 'Thor!' I exclaimed. 'Good old man!' The tremor in my voice was very tremulous. Lindbergh watched the scene with alert, but aloof, interest. 'If he wags his tail, Mr Nicolson, you need have no fear.' Thor wagged his tail and lay down.

I had a stiff whisky-and-soda and talked to Anne about Mrs Rublee. Feeling better after that, I turned to Lindbergh. 'What happens,' I asked, 'if Thor does not wag his tail?' 'Well,' he said, 'you must be careful not to pass him. He might get hold of you.' 'By the throat?' I asked—trying, but not with marked success, to throw a reckless jollity into my tone. 'Not necessarily,' he answered. 'If he does that, you must stay still and holler all you can.'

By the time you get this I shall either be front-page news or Thor's chum. I have a lovely suite here. Large sitting-room, superb bathroom, I shall be supremely comfortable. I am here all safe with a super police-dog to protect me against gangsters, and detectives behind every bush.

H.N. TO V.S-W.   *1st October, 1934*
                                                          Englewood

Yesterday I spent the morning preparing for my intensive attack on the Morrow papers. After luncheon I drove out with Mrs Morrow to the Palisades above the Hudson River where Tom Lamont[1] has a villa or home.

Tom Lamont is a nice intelligent man. Norman Davis[2] was there. He is the big noise now in American diplomacy and the adviser of Roosevelt. At tea, he talked. Now, the oddest thing about Americans is that they never listen. Davis was telling us what he felt would be the

---

[1] Chairman of the Board of J. P. Morgan and Company.
[2] Chairman of the U.S. delegation to the Geneva Disarmament Conference, 1932; Head of the U.S. delegation to the London Naval Conference, 1935.

prospects of the Naval Conference. He was talking seriously and earnestly. His idea is that the Franco-Italian pact and the Russo-French understanding will force Germany to come to heel. He discussed whether the true pacifist should not be strong and forceful rather than weak. What he said was thoughtful, well-expressed and immensely important as coming from him. But did they listen? Not for one moment. 'Now let me get you another cup of tea, Mr Nicolson. I am afraid that our tea here is not as good as the tea you get in England . . .' Chatter, chatter; interrupt, interrupt. If I understood the explanation of this, I should understand more about American civilisation.

I suspect that it has something to do with the position of women, or rather with the vast gulf which separates the male and the female in this continent. Women are supposed to discuss art, literature and the home. Men are supposed to discuss business. It is as though Sir John Simon were lunching at Sissinghurst and explaining his policy to Venizelos, and then you interrupted by talking about the Russian Ballet. You would not do such things. Why do they?

Mrs Morrow has gone for two days up to Cleveland to see her mother. I am alone with the Lindberghs. He amuses and puzzles me. On the one hand he is a mechanic and quite uneducated. On the other hand he is shrewd and intelligent. He has also got a sense of humour. Mrs Morrow mentioned that Mrs Lamont, who is not air-minded, said that she would only fly if he took her up. 'Now isn't that just like those old dames', he said. 'Just because I flew alone to Paris, they think I am a safe pilot. That's just silly.'

He has an obsession about publicity and I agree with him. He told me that when Coolidge presented him with a medal after his Paris flight, he had to do it three times over: once in the President's study, which was the real occasion; and twice on the lawn of the White House for the movie cameras. 'The first time', he said, 'I was kind of moved by the thing. After all, I was more or less a kid at the time and it seemed sort of solemn to be given that thing by the President of the United States. But when we had to go through the whole damned show again on the lawn—me standing sideways to the President and looking an ass—I felt I couldn't stand for it. Coolidge didn't seem to care or notice. He repeated his speech twice over in just the same words. It seemed a charade to me.'

An odd thing. We have breakfast together. The papers are on the table. The Lindbergh case is still front-page news. It *must* mean something to him. Yet he never glances at them and chatters quite happily to me about Roosevelt and the air-mail contracts.[1] It is not a pose. It is merely a determined habit of ignoring the Press. I like the man. I dare say he has his faults, but I have not yet found them. She is a little angel.

H.N. TO V.S-W.   *2nd October, 1934*
                                                      Englewood

The American, in spite of many qualities, is incurably suburban. Isn't it strange? I wish I could get to the bottom of it. They simply do not possess our idea of country. Even North Haven, which was as wild and rugged as one could wish, was tamed and trimmed to look suburban. The estate here is rather superb in its way. It is a wood about the size, I suppose, of our own beloved wood and sloping along a hill. A real stream dissects it, falling in little waterfalls quite naturally. But there the resemblance stops. Great asphalt motor-roads sweep round the wood, a huge drive sweeps through it, the stream is crossed three times by the driveway over imposing bridges, the grass under all the trees is mown, any untidy tree is immediately removed—and the result is merely a clump of trees in Regent's Park.

But it is a marvellous place to work in. Yesterday I worked all day from 9 a.m. till 10.30 p.m., with a short break for luncheon and a short walk in the afternoon. Today I hope to do the same. Once a week I shall go up to New York to see people. Do not fuss. I have a huge Cadillac and an aged Scotch chauffeur called MacFarlane. If I sleep the night, I shall sleep at the Knickerbocker Club of which Copley [Amory] and Kermit Roosevelt have made me a member for two months.

H.N. TO V.S-W.   *5th October, 1934*
                                                      Englewood

I went a walk in the park. Thor came with me. He likes me now. He will even allow me to play with Jon, whom I have taught to say, 'Halloa, old boy!' Such a dear little mar.[2] It is so difficult to think of

[1] Lindbergh, himself a former air-mail pilot, had openly opposed Roosevelt in the row that had blown up about the profits allegedly made by certain firms to which air-mail contracts had been awarded.

[2] See note 3, p. 48.

tragedy associated with a little thing in overalls who toddles about picking up chestnuts and stuffing them into his pocket. Charles Lindbergh adores the baby, and is so attractive with him. It is all nonsense people saying that Lindbergh is disagreeable. He is as nice as can be. This morning he opened his heart to me on the subject of publicity. He absolutely loathes it. He says that the worst about this trial[1] is that he has again become front-page news and that the persecution is again beginning. I confess that it is irritating to see the reporters who hang gingerly in the roadway outside being frightened of Thor. But he says that he cannot walk down the street unless disguised, and that it is quite impossible for Anne and him to go to the theatre together. 'It's all right', he says, 'for your Prince of Wales and people like that, because they have an organisation to protect them. I haven't.' Then he paused and thought carefully. 'But then, of course, they have to be polite whereas I don't, so it works out either way I suppose.' He is absolutely naïve about all this.

H.N. TO V.S-W.   9th October, 1934
                                                                Englewood

Yesterday Hauptmann was identified by Lindbergh as possessing the voice he had heard calling in the cemetery.[2] Yet this dramatic event did not record itself upon the life here. Lindbergh was at breakfast as usual and thereafter helped me to unload my Leica camera. He is very neat about such things and I am clumsy. He then said, 'Well, I have got to go up to New York—want a lift?' I said no. Then I worked hard at my files and at luncheon there was only Anne and me, as Mrs Morrow had gone to some charity committee. Towards the end of luncheon Lindbergh arrived and we chatted quite gaily until coffee came. We had that in the Sun Parlour, and when it was over I rose to go. The moment I had gone, I saw him (in the mirror) take her arm and lead her into the study. Obviously he was telling her what happened in the court. But they are splendid in the way that they never intrude this great tragedy on our daily lives. It is real dignity and restraint.

At 3 p.m. I went out for my walk in the garden. The paths wind in

[1] The trial of Bruno Hauptmann for the murder of the Lindbergh baby was to begin on 2nd January, 1935.
[2] St Raymond's Cemetery, New York, where the ransom money had been handed over on 2nd April, 1932.

and out of the property and over the stream. Anne and Jon join me. Jon is bad at going down steps and has to turn round and do them on his tummy. He is a dear little boy with the silkiest fair curls. I think of his brother. It is a ghastly thing to have in one's life and I feel profoundly sorry for them. The best way I can show it is by manifesting no curiosity. But it is awkward and rather farcical when I take up the paper at breakfast and it is full of nothing else. 'Things seem to be getting rather dangerous in Spain', I say. But I am sure that is the best attitude.

H.N. TO V.S-W.   14th October, 1934
                                                  Englewood

I am sending you Anne Lindbergh's article[1] on her flight round part of the globe. I want you to read it carefully and to keep it carefully. I know you will adore it as a narrative of adventure, but I think (unless I am blinded by my real affection for those two people) that it is something more than just interesting. Anne is so modest and diffident, and was so anxious to appear scientific and geographical and unstuntish. But underneath her modesty pierces, I think, something very real and literary. I want your opinion as I am urging her to write it up in a real book plus her other journey.[2] She says, 'Oh yes, but the papers here would take it up as a Lindbergh stunt and spoil it all for me—and it was so lovely: you can't think how free one felt ...' How you will understand her fear of vulgarizing what was an acute and dangerous experience. She sets such store by your judgement, being a Landite.

H.N. tO V.S-W.   24th October, 1934
                                                  Englewood

Darling, I am sorry I don't like The Dark Island.[3] But then if I just said I liked all your books, it would detract from the ones I do like.

[1] In the National Geographic Magazine. After their marriage Anne Lindbergh became navigator, radio-operator and co-pilot in flights with her husband to many parts of the world. This article dealt with their journey from Africa to Brazil, which she later described more fully in Listen! The Wind, published in 1938. It is one of the most moving books about flying ever written.
[2] To China via Alaska in 1931. Anne Lindbergh described this flight in North to the Orient, published in 1935.
[3] V.S-W.'s novel, published on 10th October, 1934 by the Hogarth Press.

I think I like *Sissinghurst*[1] the best of anything you have ever written
—but that may be personal. But I think nonetheless that it *is* the best
you have ever written. Then *The Land*. Then *Knole*. Then Lady
Anne. Then Marvell. Then *Challenge*. Then *Heritage*. Then Dragon.
Then G.W. Then *The Heir*. Then King's Daughter. Then A.P.S.
Then *The Edwardians* . . . thenthedarkisland. I cannot judge of the
two Persian books[2] since they mean so much to me, but I think I should
put them after Lady Anne. I think I should put *Family History* after
the Dragon. Thus you see, I put *The Edwardians* and this book last
on the list.

H.N. TO V.S-W.   *26th October, 1934*
                                                            Englewood

My God! What a difficult job I have taken on. It seems more and
more difficult as I get deeper. And therefore more and more fascinating.
Morrow is a Protean figure. There was about him a touch of madness,
or epilepsy, or something inhuman and abnormal. Very difficult to
convey, but certainly there. He had the mind of a super-criminal and
the character of a saint. There is no doubt at all that he was a very
great man.

V.S-W. TO H.N. (*at Englewood*)   *30th October, 1934*
                                                            Sissinghurst

I went to Long Barn today. I had rather dreaded going, thinking that
it would bite, but it didn't bite: I just thought, 'Thank God for Sissinghurst!' Long Barn seemed just smug. Of course, it was looking its
worst: that sodden autumn feeling about the garden. But I didn't
regret it for one moment; there wasn't a single stab. I only longed to
get back to Sissinghurst. Honestly, Hadji, Simon Peter though it may
be, I am thankful we left, and I am sure you would feel the same.[3]

---

[1] A poem published by the Hogarth Press in 1931. The full titles of the other books
he mentions, with their dates of publication, are: *The Land* (1926); *Knole and the
Sackvilles* (1922); *The Diary of Lady Anne Clifford* (1923); *Andrew Marvell* (1929);
Challenge (1923); *Heritage* (1919); *The Dragon in Shallow Waters* (1921); *Grey
Wethers* (1923); *The Heir* (1922); *The King's Daughter* (1929); *All Passion Spent*
(1931); and *The Edwardians* (1930).

[2] *Passenger to Teheran* (1926); and *Twelve Days* (1928).

[3] Long Barn had now been let to Mr Sidney Bernstein, the film-producer.

H.N. TO V.S-W. *7th November, 1934*
Englewood

There was a reception for the Englewood neighbours. It was just like the King's Birthday party for the British colony at St Petersburg or Berlin. In they poured, about eighty of them, and I was introduced to each single one. I got an ache in my face. But how undiscriminating are Americans! A sickly looking dotard in huge glasses assured me of the immense interest taken by Morrow in music. 'But surely', I suggested, 'he was not really musical?' 'So people have said, Mr Nicolson; but I assure you that it is not true. He would come to our glee-club evenings and beat time with his hand. There was a song called *So Let's Have Another*—it went like this:' (dotard sings drinking-song in undertone with gestures of his right hand as if clinking tankard against tankard). 'Not of course that Dwight was in favour of excessive drinking, but he liked the swing of the thing.' (Further spectacle of dotard humming and carousing.) 'And then he felt it made people feel human, Mr Nicolson. He was always one for the human side. So that always at *alumni* dinners he would ask the glee-club to sing that song and he would keep time with it with his fork or knife. I can tell you he was a real man right through.' This sort of thing makes me loathe Morrow.

Finally they began to drift away. They went. Mrs Morrow, Miss Shiff,[1] Anne and I were left alone in the big room. We agree that it had all gone very well. A sepulchral voice broke in on us from outside the window: 'Have they all gone?' And in vaulted Lindbergh who had been watching outside. Miss Shiff gazed at him with lustre eyes. He handed her what remained of the caviare sandwiches. 'You look all in, Miss Shiff. Have a bite.' She bit lovingly.

H.N. TO V.S-W. *8th November, 1934*
Englewood

I dined alone with the Lindberghs. Charles was more communicative than usual about his personal affairs. He told me that the Western Union had got out a telegram-form with alternative messages of congratulation to him. All one did was to choose No. 8, which ran 'Welcome to America's hero'; or No. 9, which read 'Greetings to the Lone Eagle'; or No. 12, which ran 'Lindy does it again'. One paid

[1] Madelon M. Shiff, who acted as H.N.'s secretary at Englewood.

187

twenty-five cents to have one's number telegraphed by Western Union in one's home town and then the message corresponding to the number was typed out at the other end and delivered to Lindbergh. In one day he got 52,000 such telegrams, and the next day 63,000. And so on. They had to be delivered in special vans. This was after his pan-American trip.[1]

Since then, of course, they have organised a regular system. All letters of whatsoever nature addressed to them by name are sent down to an office in New York and gone through there. Sometimes there is a great delay, because when the Lindbergh case gets on to the front pages they get about 100,000 letters a day. Many important letters and invitations never reach them. But if the thing were to be done properly they would have to have a trained staff and it would cost them at least £2,000 a year. So they just have office-boys and trust to luck. Of course their nearest and dearest write to them at an accommodation address without their real names. But it must be hell.

V.S-W. TO H.N. (*at Englewood*)   *9th November, 1934*
                                                        Sissinghurst

In London yesterday I went to try on my new clothes at Jay's. They are all right, I think. But I hate women's shops and all the clothes-talk. Also I hate seeing myself in mirrors, and being asked to look at myself. I do so absolutely loathe my own appearance, and to be forced to look at myself in a long mirror is real distress to me.

Then I went to luncheon with Virginia [Woolf], who gave me an imitation of Yeats[2] telling her why he was occult. He has been confirmed in this theory because he saw a coat-hanger emerge from his cupboard and travel across the foot of his bed; next night, it emerged again, clothed in one of his jackets; the third night, a hand emerged from one of the cuffs; the fourth night—'Ah! Mrs Woolf, that would be a long story; enough to say, I finally recovered my potency.'

[1] December 1927 to February 1928.   [2] W. B. Yeats, the Irish poet.

H.N. TO V.S-W. *17th November, 1934*
British Embassy, Washington

Alice Morrow[1] and I went by train to Pittsburgh.[2] We drove together visiting sites. The difficulty was that whereas I was anxious to make the background as horrible as possible (wishing to paint Morrow's childhood in dark colours), Alice was anxious that I should see it in terms of dear little homes nestling amid vines and roses. The actual habitat of the Morrow family was across the river in Allegheny. Factories smoke on every hand and the sluggish waters of the Ohio are fringed with coal-dust. The little street where they lived runs down to the river edge; no boulevard there, but a somewhat disused railway track along the edge and coal-laden reeds. A little red house near the Presbyterian chapel. A dull wooden porch, an aspidistra behind the muslin curtains of the best room. Thereafter the Morrows, owing to their son's prowess, went up in the world. The second house was larger and higher up the hill and the last house was quite a big horror of stone. It was sad and dull.

For three-and-a-half hours I sat in a lounge while a procession of school-marms arrived and kissed Alice on the lips and talked of dear old Pittsburgh friends. Not once did I get anything out of them of the slightest value as Morrow material. They were all so true, so staunch, so loyal. 'You have a beautiful subject, Mr Nicolson, and you should write a beautiful book.' There is something about the smarminess of Americans which makes me see red. It arouses in me not merely protest, not merely impatience and irritation, but actual unkindness. I wish I understood better how this happens. I am generally a benevolent person, but sentimentality awakens in me something quite definite and hostile. I feel a sharp, cold knife coming up within me and I want to cut and slash. It is something nastier than any mere intellectual annoyance at the eternal superficiality of the American race. It is something really *unkind*. I longed to say, 'But this is all nonsense and you know it. Dwight Morrow was a shrewd and selfish little *arriviste* who drank himself to death'. It was not merely that I had a longing to contradict them; it was also that I was conscious of a temptation to cause pain.

---

[1] Dwight Morrow's sister, born in 1871.

[2] Dwight Morrow was born in 1873 when his father was President of Marshall College at Huntington, but in 1875 he was appointed a teacher at Oakdale Academy near Pittsburgh.

When I feel that angry sword within me, I understand why people think I am a cruel person. I could have smashed and bashed their silly heads. I merely sat there glum and silent. I know that it might be possible to excuse my feelings in terms of intellectual impatience or hatred of the sham. But it was more than that. It was something almost brutal which rose up in me. I feel rather ashamed of it looking back. But I see that there is in me a vein of intellectual brigandage, a rather mean little hawk swooping on the doves, and it is that, I think, of which people like Hugh Walpole are conscious and which gives the impression that I am unkind. I must try to work it out of my system. It is not a pretty thing.

H.N. TO V.S-W.   *23rd November, 1934*
Englewood

I have just got back and am faced with another tragedy. Some terrible fate does hang over this family. Elisabeth,[1] who had survived her appendicitis, has now developed pneumonia. They have telephoned for Mrs Morrow to fly there. She leaves in an hour. I feel quite bruised with pity for her. She seems so lonely in her misery, poor little thing. I do admire that woman. She never breaks down under these blows. For the first time tonight she mentioned the baby and in such a pathetic way. I said something about her control and courage. 'Courage?' she said, 'Do you know that I cry about that baby of ours every night even now. That is not *courage*!'

I wrote the above last night. I was really upset by this tragedy. Lindbergh got back and started telephoning to air companies. His own company[2] did not think it safe to fly, and in fact there was a gale and rain. But another company offered to fly her. Lindbergh was really fussed but thought she ought to risk it. So at 8 pm. poor little Betty[3] was bundled into a car and driven to Newark. I shall always think of her in the doorway with her little hat and bag. A gale outside and the rain lashing down. There she was about to fly three thousand miles in the night.[4] And she loathes flying in any conditions. So small and pathetic she looked. But what guts that woman has got! She is the real pioneer type. I confess that I was deeply impressed. God!

[1] Anne Lindbergh's elder sister, who married Aubrey Morgan, a Welshman, in December 1932. She died on 3rd December, 1934.
[2] Transworld Airlines.   [3] Mrs Dwight Morrow.
[4] To Pasadena, California, where Elisabeth lay ill.

How I admire courage—I have none myself. Would I face a thing like that with her superb dignity? I hope so. I know you would, but then you are also magnificent.

H.N. TO V.S-W.   *25th November, 1934*
                                                      Englewood

In the afternoon I sat with Anne in the Sun Parlour and she went through the notes she had prepared for me. You know, Viti, there is a great difference between an observant and a non-observant person. An observant person is a person who observes. An unobservant person is a person who does not observe. 97 per cent of humanity belong to the second category. Anne belongs to the first. She noticed every detail about her father and remembered it. She sat there graceful and shy upon the large chintz sofa reading her notes slowly with precision. 'He would rub his right forefinger over the back of his left hand as if feeling a lump.' 'When he threw away his newspaper it never fell flat upon the carpet but always remained standing upwards.' 'He would tear off little bits of paper while talking, roll them into spills, and then work the spills into his ear. These spills would lie about the floor. We hated them.' 'On Sunday evenings we used to have family prayers. As we got older these prayers became more and more embarrassing and therefore fewer.' And then there was a description of family breakfast which was so good that I told her to write it down and I shall produce it in the book[1] just as I produced your piece in father's book.[2] Whatever you say, that girl has real literary ability.

[1] He did so, on pp. 168–72 of the English edition.
[2] In the last pages of *Lord Carnock*, H.N. included V.S-W.'s description of his father in old age.

1935

Second visit to America – result of the Hauptmann trial – Cuernavaca, Mexico – visit to President Calles – an Hellenic cruise – third visit to America – the House of Morgan raises difficulties – H.N. makes temporary decision to devote his life to literature – fourth visit to America – Ben and the Lindberghs – 'Dwight Morrow' finished – H.N. homesick for the Foreign Office – a visit to Venice – H.N. invited to stand as National Labour candidate for West Leicester – the General Election – his hatred of electioneering – his triumphant victory by 87 votes – takes his seat in the House of Commons – Churchill's welcome – Ramsay MacDonald's leadership of the National Labour group – the Hoare-Laval pact over Abyssinia – H.N.'s maiden speech on the subject

Harold Nicolson returned to England for December and January. On 6th February he was on his way back to America, which he was to revisit twice more during the next six months. On none of his books did he expend greater energy, yet 'Dwight Morrow' is one of his least known. It forms an admirable example of his conscientiousness as a biographer and of his methods of work. The physical basis of the biography was a huge loose-leafed notebook into which he inserted, in the strict chronological sequence of Morrow's career, the notes of his reading and conversations with Morrow's friends. At the back were many pages labelled collectively 'Character', and subdivided into humour, personal habits, mannerisms, dress, family relations, attitude to money, and so on. He formed the skeleton of the notebook by typing out from the best existing biography of his subject the essential dates and appointments. Then he filled in the picture by reading every printed source. Next came the personal papers, which in Morrow's case were very extensive indeed and formed the bulk of the material which he used. Then came the interviews with Morrow's family and colleagues. All this information was transferred to the notebook, usually by typing, sometimes in manuscript, and always in full, for he would say that his intention was to make the notebook so comprehensive that it would be possible for him to retire to a Greek island and write the entire book without any other work of reference.

Normally the notebook would be completed before a single word of the biography was written. But in the case of 'Dwight Morrow', he was obliged to leave until his second trans-Atlantic trip the period of Morrow's career when he was American Ambassador in Mexico, a period which fortunately came at the very end of his life. So Harold Nicolson was able to start the book soon after his return to England in December. By the time he landed back in New York, he had completed fifteen out of eighteen chapters, up to the point where Morrow went to Mexico in 1927. On the five-days outward voyage in the 'Berengaria', he wrote 20,000 words.

He was in sight of the end when he rejoined Mrs Morrow and the Lindberghs at Englewood on 13th February, and was greatly looking forward to his trip with Mrs Morrow to Mexico, where they were to stay in the lovely little house which Morrow had bought at Cuernavaca, some fifty miles from Mexico City, halfway between the central plateau and the tropical regions of the coast. This working-holiday was clouded by the usual despair which overcame him when he re-read what he had already written; and by the coincidence that he reached Englewood on the very day when Bruno Hauptmann was found guilty of murdering the Lindbergh baby.

H.N. TO V.S-W.   *14th February, 1935*
                                   Next Day Hill, Englewood, New Jersey

Dinner yesterday evening was rather strained. You see, that morning Judge Trenchard had summed up in the Hauptmann trial.[1] He did it very well and his statement was one of which even an English judge need not have been ashamed. Lindbergh tells me that it reads more impartial than it sounded. For instance, he kept on saying to the jury, in going over some of Hauptmann's evidence, 'Do you believe that?' Now that sounds all right when read in print. But what he actually said was, 'Do *you* believe THAT?' Anyhow the jury had been in consultation for five hours when we sat down to dinner and a verdict was expected at any moment. They knew that the first news would come over the wireless, so that there were two wirelesses turned on— one in the pantry next to the dining-room and one in the drawing-room. Thus there were jazz and jokes while we had dinner, and one ear was strained the whole time for the announcer from the court-house. Lindbergh had a terrible cold which made it worse.

Then after dinner we went into the library and the wireless was on in the drawing-room next door. They were all rather jumpy. Mrs Morrow, with her unfailing tact, brought out a lot of photographs and we had a family council as to what illustrations to choose for the book. This was just interesting enough to divert, but not to rivet, attention. Then Dick Scandrett[2] came over to see me. It was about 10.45 pm. The Lindberghs and Morgans with Mrs Morrow left us alone. We discussed Dwight for some twenty minutes. Suddenly Betty put her head round the huge Coromandel screen. She looked very white. 'Hauptmann', she said, 'has been condemned to death without mercy.'

We went into the drawing-room. The wireless had been turned on

[1] The trial, which had been going on since 2nd January, was held at Flemington, New Jersey.
[2] Dwight Morrow's nephew.

to the scene outside the court-house. One could hear the almost diabolic yelling of the crowd. They were all sitting round—Miss Morgan with embroidery, Anne looking very white and still. 'You have now heard', broke in the voice of the announcer, 'the verdict in the most famous trial in all history. Bruno Hauptmann now stands guilty of the foulest . . .' 'Turn that off, Charles, turn that off.' Then we went into the pantry and had ginger-beer. Charles sat there on the kitchen dresser looking very pink about the nose. 'I don't know', he said to me, 'whether you have followed this case very carefully. There is no doubt at all that Hauptmann did the thing. My one dread all these years has been that they would get hold of someone as a victim about whom I wasn't sure. I am sure about this—quite sure. It is this way . . .'

And then quite quietly, while we all sat round in the pantry, he went through the case point by point. It seemed to relieve all of them. He did it very quietly, very simply. He pretended to address his remarks to me only. But I could see that he was really trying to ease the agonised tension through which Betty and Anne had passed. It was very well done. It made one feel that here was no personal desire for vengeance or justification; here was the solemn process of law inexorably and impersonally punishing a culprit.

Then we went to bed. I feel that they are all relieved. If Hauptmann had been acquitted it would have had a bad effect on the crime situation in this country. Never has circumstantial evidence been so convincing. If on such evidence a conviction had not been secured, then all the gangsters would have felt a sense of immunity. The prestige of the police has been enormously enhanced by this case.

Poor Anne—she looked so white and horrified. The yells of the crowd were really terrifying. 'That', said Lindbergh, 'was a lynching crowd.'

He tells me that Hauptmann was a magnificent-looking man. Splendidly built. But that his little eyes were like the eyes of a wild boar. Mean, shifty, small and cruel.

H.N. TO V.S-W.   16th February, 1935
                                                                    Englewood

I went through the book yesterday and am terribly discouraged. It is as heavy as lead. What was interesting about Morrow was his character and his method. But the actual things he did were very dull. I fear that the book falls between two stools. I have tried to make it the same sort of thing as my book on my father, but whereas father was dealing with great historical and dramatic events, Morrow was dealing with the New York Underground Railways. I am very disappointed in the book now that I read it *en masse*. I fear it will have largely to be re-written. I console myself by thinking that one always goes through a stage of gloom and that re-writing is never as serious a business as it seems. The real work is getting the facts down on paper. It is not very hard work titivating them up a little once they are in some sort of form. It is odd, really; I was not conscious that the book was dull when I was writing it. I never felt stale or bored with it. But the resultant effect is something which does not live at all. It just crawls along in prose.

H.N. TO V.S-W.
22nd February, 1935
Casa Manana, Cuernavaca, Mexico

I cannot tell you the beauty of the mornings and the evenings in this place. My little cottage, which is only one room really and a bathroom, is at the bottom of the garden and the main house is three terraces higher. I have two little windows with blue shutters and little blue wooden bars. The centre of the room is taken up by large folding doors, which, when opened, turn the room into a loggia. I shut them at night.

When I wake I see a square of sunshine from the little east window upon my wall. I then look at the clock. 7 a.m. I then wait till 8.15 a.m. I then rise, open my two doors. That is the excitement. The first impression is a puff of cool datura smell—not hot datura smell. The second is of ringing sunshine and blue sky. The third is of tropical creepers tumbling up into that sky—magenta and scarlet and blue. In my own little walled garden there is a tree called Jacaranda, which is quite naked of leaves, but from which burst huge plumes of blue-like enormous wistaria blooms. On the wall, which must be twenty feet high, is a vast *Thunbergia* with blue morning-glory flowers. On the higher terrace I can see plumbago, white oleander and hibiscus.

I put on my dressing-gown and soon I hear flip-flap on the steps and Carmencita appears carrying my shaving water in a tin cruche. I then shave and dress, walking towards the door the whole time and gazing out upon this piled and terraced Gauguin. (Bananas when fruiting are very rude. They hang like a stallion.) I then climb up the several flights

of staircase, past the pool, to the upper loggia where there is breakfast.
I then come down again to find my room swept and garnished and
heavy with the scent of Bermuda lilies. I then write to you. I then
work. I then lunch. I then sleep. I then work again. I then have tea.
I then work again. I then have a bath. I then dine out on the terrace.
I then play nap which is a good game. I then go up on the Mirador
and look out over the view. I then go to bed.

I should like never to move out of this enchanted garden but I
suppose I shall have to. It is incredible that this should be the New
World. I cannot believe that I am not in Spain. But there is also a
Tahiti flavour about it.

H.N. TO V.S-W.   *26th February, 1935*
                                                            Cuernavaca

This really is the most lovely country in the world. Yesterday we went
to Taxco, and stayed there the night. It is fifty miles away and we went
by car. It is as though one went down from Fiesole, across a huge
plain, and then up to another Fiesole fifty miles opposite. The plain,
when we reached it, was scorching. There were one or two villages
with pink Spanish churches and huts made of thatched reeds and
hedged with cactus—very African. The Indians are small and slight
like Abamites. They have a strong Mongolian look—sometimes
Eskimo. They are the colour of coffee-beans with straight black hair
like Navaho Indians and again like Japanese. They are a comparatively
clean race and the whole place, when there is water, is neatly cultivated.

We climbed up, after some forty miles, again into the mountains.
In and out we went among foot-hills covered with oak scrub, and
suddenly we saw a building of pink stone like Palermo Cathedral and
then lost it again behind a high conical hill. Behind rose tier after tier
of cliff like the south of France, but larger with a pinkish tinge. Then
suddenly we reached the little town or village and drove into the
market square.

We had been lent a house by an American. It was a tiny little house
above the town and we had to leave the motor and climb almost
perpendicular cobbled streets. There were horses tied to rings in hot
walls and draped with elaborate bits and saddles. I thought of you.
I know how much you love strange equine accoutrements. The house
itself was on a steep terrace cut into the hill-side. It was only an L-
shaped cottage, containing a large living-room with tiled floor and

two bedrooms. There was a loggia on each side of the living-room with white pillars. The one to the west looked upon a little scoop of garden planted with datura, *poinsettia*, and mango. The one on the other side was flush with the terrace edge and looked right down upon the roofs of the town, upon the church, and out towards the jumble of plain and mountain beyond.

I slept out on the terrace. Just as I was going to bed there was a sound below us and they began to serenade. I leant over the edge and listened. There was music coming up from all over the village, echoing the closer music below our terrace. When they had gone I lay and looked at the stars. I had already said goodnight to my V star, which was on the west side of the house. They were so close and seemed detachable. I woke later when a little moon came over the mountain. Then I slept again and woke to see a blur of green behind the ridge, deepening into pink and then lightening to gold. The datura tree at the end of the terrace was still smelling as dawn came. I saw one of the white bells shaking and found that a huge dragon-fly was poking at it with its nose. Then suddenly I realised that it was a humming bird. I sat up in bed all excited. It fluttered off shimmering to perch on a *poinsettia* and at that moment the sun rose with a lance of flame. Now that is one of the moments that I shall never forget.

We drove back after breakfast reaching here at 1.30. In front of us all the way soared Popocatapetl and Ixtaccihuatl.[1] The attendant mountains are all of different kinds, crinkled pink as in Persia, dotted grey as in Provence, or tumular or tabled as the *mesas* in Arizona. It was terribly hot and dusty, and when we arrived back in this cool garden there was iced cup waiting for us, a plunge in the pool, and, best of all, a fat fid of letters from home.

H.N. TO V.S-W.   *7th March, 1935*
                                                      Cuernavaca

I have finished the book! Morrow is dead. I have had to leave a tiny gap in the chapter on the Naval Conference as I cannot finish that part until I have seen Massigli. But it is only about 3,000 words of a gap in book of 110,000. Yes, it is done. I am relieved.

---

[1] Mexico's two volcanoes.

H.N. TO V.S-W.   *9th March, 1935*
                                                              Cuernavaca

On Friday morning, as I told you, I finished the last chapter. I did not have a sense of release exactly, as I had skipped a chapter on the London Conference or at least half of that chapter, since I shall have to add to it after my conversations in Paris. But this missing half worried me so much that yesterday I sat down to it and finished it in such a form that if I am killed tomorrow the book can be published. I shall have to re-write that section after seeing Léger and Massigli but that will only take me a day. Apart from that hang-over, the life of Dwight Whitney Morrow is finished. It is dull. But I have enjoyed writing it and I think it is a perfectly solid piece of work. It has *taught* me so much in many ways, and, apart from anything else, it has brought me a real friendship with the Morrow family and this wonderful visit to Mexico. I am absolutely determined to come back here with you sometime. It is certainly the loveliest country I have yet seen. I am soppy about it.

H.N. TO V.S-W.   *11th March, 1935*
                                                           Culiacan, Mexico

We arrived here by train from Mexico City. There was Calles'[1] A.D.C. and the local captain. I was pushed into a car with the Director of Agriculture who was to translate. We drove some thirty miles through scrub and then came to huge fields with peons cultivating and a distant factory. Rather a shock in these untamed deserts. But Calles believes in progress and the factory is a sugar factory which mushes up the sugar cane which was all around us. He owns 50,000 acres—so there.

Round the factory a sort of village has grown up, and what I first took to be the school-house turned out to be the Villa Calles. There were a few guards about with pistols but no other sign of dictatorship. The house, when one enters it, is nicer than I thought. A huge patio with a fountain like a swan. It was all rather oriental—elderly bare-footed women scuttling around. His daughter appearing suddenly, a person very like Cimmie Mosley. Then the Dictator appeared. He is a fine featured man just like Mustapha Kemal to look at. Rather shy.

---

[1] Plutarco Elias Calles became President of Mexico in 1924. Dwight Morrow had established with him close personal relations which were to benefit both Mexico and the United States for a generation.

Rather impressive. A gentle voice. I asked him questions about Morrow. He could not remember. He kept on saying, 'Senor Morrow was a man of great judgement and friendliness.' No good at all. Then I got up and took leave and he accompanied me to the motor. I thought, 'Really, that was not worth a 6,000 mile journey.' But then Mexico itself is worth a million-mile journey.

Sandwiched between the second and third of his four journeys to America within ten months, was a cruise to Greece in April. This trip had long been promised to his younger son, who had acquired at Eton the same deep interest in the classics which remained with Harold Nicolson throughout his life. The cruise was organised by the Hellenic Travellers Club on the ship 'Letitia', and was accompanied by scholars of the quality of Sir Richard Livingstone, Stanley Casson and Dr Cyril Norwood. Among the Nicolsons' own friends on board were Hugh Walpole and Lady Ravensdale. They visited most of the main sites of classical Greece, and for two days were stranded on a sandbank outside the entrance to the Gulf of Corinth, while tugs from Patras and Piraeus strained to pull the ship clear. The passengers were in no danger, as the weather remained calm throughout the small adventure, and the ship's bottom was found to be undamaged. Harold Nicolson took the opportunity to give a lecture on Byron, pointing out from the top deck the site of Missolonghi on the port bow. The cruise was then completed as planned, and on the last day of April they arrived back in England via Naples and Rome.

May was spent at Sissinghurst, where the structure of the garden and the making of a long library within the old stables were approaching completion. Then came a minor setback. J. P. Morgan and Company objected to the passages of Dwight Morrow which dealt with Morrow's long connection with the firm, and Harold Nicolson was obliged to hurry to New York to arrange some sort of compromise. It proved less difficult than he had feared. After a fortnight in England, he returned again to America in late June, this time accompanied by his elder son Ben, in order to revise with Mrs Morrow the final proofs of the American edition. They stayed with the Lindberghs at North Haven, and Ben was also able to visit some of the major museums of the east coast, extending his knowledge of art-history which was to become the central interest of his life. At the beginning of August they returned home, and 'Dwight Morrow' was at last off Harold Nicolson's hands.

H.N. TO V.S-W. (*returning from Italy*   *4th May, 1935*
    through France)   *Sissinghurst*

I got my typescript[1] back from America yesterday with the comments
of those to whom it had been submitted. They are rather helpful.
But my real relief is that Betty and Anne are delighted with the book.
So long as they are pleased, I do not care about other people.

DIARY   *16th May, 1935*

Betty Morrow telephones at noon to ask me to come over at once.
Evidently the House of Morgan are raising difficulties. Very annoyed
and depressed—but I shall have to go.

H.N. TO V.S-W.   *1st June, 1935*
                        RMS. 'Aquitania', in mid-Atlantic

I tackled a large section of the Morgan dossier yesterday. It is easier to
meet them on points of fact. But it is points of interpretation which
will be difficult. It all boils down to the difference between my conception of banking and theirs. There was one comment which amused
me. I had written, in describing the immense expansion assumed by
Morgan's bank at the outbreak of the war, 'It ceased to be a private
firm and became almost a Department of Government.' I meant that
as a compliment. Old J. P. Morgan appears to have regarded it as an
insult. He has added a little note on his own, 'I have no right to ask
you to alter this, but it will be interpreted as if we were reduced to the
status of a department subordinate to the Government'. This is
characteristic of both of us. *I* feel it the highest compliment to compare
Morgan's to the Foreign Office. *They* regard it as an insult to suggest
that they have any connection with the Government, or any Government. But, you see, the whole point of view is different. I regard
bankers and banking as rather low-class fellows. They regard officials
as stupid and corrupt. Anyhow I continued my emendations this
morning and should finish the whole Lamont dossier before I reach
New York.

---

[1] Of *Dwight Morrow*.

H.N. TO V.S-W.   *2nd June, 1935*
                                                       RMS. 'Aquitania'

I worked practically all yesterday on the Morgan dossier as I want to finish it completely. As you saw, it is immense. Every single partner of J. P. Morgan and Company has been allowed to have his fling. But it all boils down to the fact that they are furious with the tone I have adopted towards the House of Morgan. Not that I have said a word against it. It is merely that I have not treated it with the awed respect to which they are accustomed. But I dare say that I shall manage to tone it down a trifle. I do not want to create unnecessary ill feeling for Mrs Morrow.

Having worked all morning at the beastly thing, and having emerged upstairs with my feathers all the wrong way, I sat down in a huge arm-chair in the lounge and started reading the letters of Proust before going down to luncheon. And while so engaged the smoking-room steward descended upon me in glee. 'You've won, sir', he exclaimed. 'Won what?' I asked. 'The sweep.' I was very British and imperturbable and went on with Proust's really appalling letters to Robert de Montesquiou. Then, all aloof, I strolled into the smoking-room to see the extent of my gain. £127—exactly the cost of Ben's ticket there and back in July. Now it will have to be spent on that. I have felt guilty about it—a sort of corner-Turfey.[1] Now I shall feel quite a clear conscience.

DIARY   *4th June, 1935*
                                                       Englewood, New Jersey

I find on arrival a memorandum by Reuben Clark[2] bitterly attacking the whole Mexican chapters and saying the thing will do harm. The result is that Betty Morrow has lost all confidence in the book and in me. I shall either have to withdraw the book or insist on its being printed as it stands. We sit up talking till 1.40 am. and I retire to my

---

[1] Turfey (originally Turf) was an old black spaniel who had died at Long Barn in 1929. In his last years he smelled dreadfully, and V.S-W. would whisper 'Corner, Turfey!' when guests showed that they had become aware of his presence in the room. The phrase came to be applied to any unpleasant subject which one knew one should face squarely, but tucked away into a corner of one's mind.

[2] Legal adviser to the State Department, who had accompanied Morrow to Mexico in 1927.

room only to lie awake in torments of rage. How seldom do I get as angry as this and how seldom do I feel unable to sleep! A horrible night.

DIARY   5th June, 1935
                                                        Englewood

Up to New York and lunch at the River Club with Walter Lippmann. I have three hours with him. He is intelligent and sympathetic and tells me some 'favourable truth' with which I can sweeten the Morgan passages. It is a great relief to be able to talk to an American of such intelligence and knowledge on this subject. Most of them feel kindly but are so ignorant and stupid that they do not understand my point of view. Then back to Englewood. Feel very depressed and disheartened before dinner. But then George Rublee[1] dines and we go through the Reuben Clark memorandum very carefully. It really reduces itself to complete nonsense. Betty who assisted at our séance was I think completely happy. She went off to bed all gay again. George Rublee spoke of the book in very high terms. I go to bed completely restored in nerves and sleep perfectly.

DIARY   7th June, 1935
                                                        Englewood

Devote today to revising the whole book in the light of final criticisms. As I read it again, it seems to me to be very sugary sort of stuff. The influence of American caution and sentimentality has pervaded my style. My fear of hurting Betty's feelings has made me a trifle sloppy. And then the excisions have removed from the book any tang it may have had. Thus the result is soft and flabby. But in spite of all this Morrow does emerge as a real person, not as a legend. I am not really discontented with the book.

DIARY   19th June, 1935
                                                           London

Christopher [Hobhouse] tells me that I have 'not got a political mind'. I ask him to explain what he means. He says that I am too fastidious and too critical to have the essential faculty of belief in democracy. He is right.

[1] He had been Morrow's chief assistant in Mexico and later at the London Naval Conference of 1930.

I then lunch at the Travellers with Rex Leeper to discuss the book or article on Allen.[1] He tells me that Michael Sadleir had said to him that he thought that I would survive as one of the leading writers of this age. True it was that my public was at present small, but then a faithful minority was proof of permanent literary reputation. That this belief was no politeness on his part is shown by the fact that this most cunning of all bibliophiles has made a corner in my first editions and that his daughter has done the same.

Odd that these two remarks should have been made to me within an hour of each other. Not that I believe either. Yet they occur at a moment of acute hesitation and may well tip the balance. Christopher with his usual insight realises that my desire to go into politics is motivated by feelings other than real political ambition or aptitude. He knows that I wish to enter public life partly from a sense of curiosity, partly from a feeling of duty, and partly because I have not sufficient confidence in my own literary gifts. Obviously I should rather be the Proust of England—*si qua fata aspera rumpas Tu Marcellus eris*. Yet I hesitate to devote what remains of my life to literary composition unless I feel sure that such work will really be more than an indulgence in a hobby.

Now all this coincides with a real perplexity on my part. I think it odd that I who have worked so hard and have written so many books should not have a serious literary position. I have been thinking that this must be due to the fact that I do not possess essentially a literary gift. I therefore desire politics as a sort of alibi from literary failure. And then come these two chance remarks, one telling me that I am not suited for politics, and the other encouraging me to believe that my failure to achieve an established literary reputation is due more to my contemporaries than to any lack of talent. I do not think I am conceited about myself. Vain and proud I am; but not conceited. The actual conjunction of these two remarks may in fact prove determinant in my future decision. If Michael and Christopher are both right, then there is only one alternative. I must devote such years as may remain to me to my *magnum opus*.[2] And that is evidence of how little

---

[1] Allen Leeper, a contemporary and close friend of H.N. in the Foreign Office, had died on 24th January, 1935 at the age of 48. His brother, Rex Leeper, later British Ambassador in Athens, asked H.N. to write a memoir, which he did in the form of a long article.

[2] See pp. 167-70.

one knows oneself. Having felt this finger of fate indicating in one direction, I realise that it was in that direction only that I have wished to go.

DIARY
25th June, 1935
Sissinghurst

Motor over to Brighton for luncheon. B.M. weak and pathetic. When I get back, Charlie[1] telephones to say the Sevenoaks Conservative Association have not chosen me as their candidate.[2] Vita is in the room but pays no attention at all, and merely plays with Martha the puppy whom I had brought from Uckfield. Nor does she ever refer to the matter again. It is as if she hadn't been aware in any sense that this may mean a final decision regarding politics versus literature. Strange, very strange.

H.N. TO V.S-W.
11 July, 1935
North Haven, Maine

We had an almost perfect day yesterday. The sun was very hot but the air was scented with fresh seaweed and pines. I must say, this island is a divine spot. It must be exactly like the Western Highlands with distant mountains, a whole archipelago around us, morning mists, and heavy rain-drops on the pines.

Ben and I worked all morning in our little cottage. He is doing Bismarck and is very interested. I was doing the final revisions to my proofs and starting on the index. After luncheon we watched Lindbergh doing stunts in his little scarlet aeroplane. It is a divine little instrument and he plays with it as one plays with a canoe in a swimming pool. Up there in the high air he flashed and dived and circled above the sea and islands just like a boy plunging in the sea. The scarlet wings flashed in the sun and then darkened to shadow.

Then he came down and we played tennis, or rather Ben and the Lindberghs played tennis. I sat and watched with a book. Ben plays a good style but inaccurately. Like my handwriting, it looks efficient from a great distance.

Our dear Benzie—what a strange person he is! He is so absolutely

[1] Lord Sackville.
[2] Just before leaving on his third trip to the United States, H.N. had heard that a bye-election was impending at Sevenoaks, and on a sudden whim, had allowed his name to be put forward for the Conservative candidature.

himself. It was a lovely day and as we sat on the terrace looking down on the sea and the islands, Anne said to him, 'Would you like to come sailing this afternoon?' 'No,' said Ben, 'sailing bores me.' I confess that I was rather taken aback. I reproved him afterwards, but he said, 'I think it wrong to pretend to like a thing which I don't like. You always say, Daddy, that you hate music.' I then explained that he had put on 'his voice' and that his remark sounded not merely like a curt refusal but like a snub. He was terribly distressed by this and brooded over it. I asked Anne afterwards whether she had thought him rude, and what one does between telling people to be absolutely frank and yet training them to observe social conventions. She said that she had liked him for it. But all the same Ben does lack zest. It is so beautiful here and the bathing and tennis and general charm of the place render him happy; but he does not show it. I know that he is not bored in the very least. But they, who expect high spirits and affability in the young, must feel him very 'dumb' and very 'effete'. But perhaps not. One is unduly sensitive about the impression people whom one is very fond of make on other people of whom one is very fond. He loves Anne, who is angelic to him. He likes Mrs Morrow. He is thrilled by Lindbergh.

H.N. TO V.S-W.   *12th July, 1935*
                                                    North Haven

Already by breakfast it was very hot and the flag on the mast hung limp in a cloudless sky. We returned to our cottage and worked hard. Ben really does work hard when he gets down to it. Four hours at a time without a word and with neat and careful notes entered in a *cahier*. At 12.30 there was a knock at the door. Charles Lindbergh appeared. 'It is a perfect day for flying: would you like to go up, Ben?' Ben said he would, and we walked out to the front where the flying-field had been cleared. There was the little aeroplane scarlet as sealing-wax. Ben was quite calm and brave and aloof and slow and distant and drawly and incompetent. They climbed in. Off they went over the sea and islands and then high, high up in the ringing air. I watched my poor son and heir up there, a tiny point in the stratosphere. In half-an-hour they came down and there was Ben safe and aloof and lethargic and drawly and incompetent. But even he expressed something which in someone else would have been indicative of slightly aroused interest but which in him was passionate en-

*Vita Sackville-West and Harold Nicolson at Smoke Tree
Ranch, California, March, 1933*

*Charles Lindbergh with the 'Spirit of St. Louis' at
Le Bourget, Paris, 1927*

thusiasm. I did so envy him, damn you.[1] That perfect summer's day, that lovely island-studded sea, those distant mountains and that vault of blue above the scent of pines. Damn you.

Then in the afternoon we went down to the harbour and took out the *Muette*, the motor-launch. From that launch we cast a surf-board and one by one we dived over the side, clambered on to the surf-board and then turned on the motor full speed ahead. It dashes through the waves and one clings on like hell. Gradually one attains a certain balance and is able to rise on one's knees. The next stage is to stand up clasping the ropes and driving the surf-board as Apollo the chariot of dawn. Ben almost got to that standing stage when he collapsed backwards with a swish, ceasing to be a person riding the waves and becoming a lonely and rapidly outdistanced head bobbing in the sea. I almost got on to my feet when I also swished backwards from a rush of motion into just paddling in the sea with a motor-boat flashing miles away towards the coast of Maine. Then Anne and Charles tried and were triumphant. For miles they drove the chariot of the sun. It was like skiing. I loved it.

H.N. TO V.S-W.   *17th July, 1935*
                                                  North Haven

I worked and worked and at four-thirty there was the whole thing beautifully finished and at five-thirty there was the beach-wagon going down to the village with my final proofs for Harcourt, Brace. I watched it turning the corner with deep relief. No book has caused me such fuss and worry as this one. It is a relief to see it turn tail and go.

Ben leaves tomorrow for Boston, Washington and Philadelphia. He has got museums opened for him all along the route. He gets on very well with Lindbergh who seems to enjoy talking to him. Lindbergh has the reputation of being an extremely silent man, yet with us he chatters the whole time. Yesterday he made a huge bonfire, cutting down whole pine trees to improve his landing-ground. I puffed and puffed. Ben very languidly stooped, picked up a pine cone, and with infinite forethought flung it on the bonfire. I was goaded by his example to wield an axe. He stood there, watching. The smoke was all resinous and drifted in a huge yellow turban out to sea. The sea-

[1] This refers to the promise V.S-W. had extracted from H.N. after a near-escape in 1923 that he would never fly again.

gulls yelled. Little Jon from a safe distance watched us entranced. Lindbergh hewed and hacked. The sea-gulls yelled all the louder and the fir-cones clattered in the cinders. It was an odd occupation to render one so happy; but it did.

Anne told me a story which I find strange. They were asked formally to the White House after their flight to China. Much against their will they went. Mr and Mrs Hoover were very polite. But Mrs Hoover called them 'Mr and Mrs Lingrün' throughout. 'Please sit here, Mrs Lingrün, and Colonel Lingrün, you go over there.' Now isn't that very odd indeed? What would Freud have said to that? It is as though Lady Pembroke called Mr Baldwin 'Mr Baldock'. That is the sort of story I really enjoy. An insoluble problem in human conduct. Now you see, that's what comes of foreign travel. Had I stayed at Sissinghurst I should never have learnt that Mrs Hoover called Lindbergh Lingrün.

Harold Nicolson returned from America for the last time at the beginning of August. 'Dwight Morrow' was published on 10th October. Between those two dates he remained at Sissinghurst writing book-reviews for the 'Daily Telegraph', while V. Sackville-West was absorbed in her biography of Joan of Arc. The boys went abroad, Ben to Vienna to study pictures, Nigel to Hanover to learn German. With no new book on hand, the old doubts returned. What was he? What were his real gifts— politics or literature? What was he to do? The crisis caused by Mussolini's threatened invasion of Abyssinia deepened his sense of exile from the Foreign Office, and even a hectic visit to Venice in early September failed to restore his spirits. Then suddenly on 3rd October came a telephone-call which settled the five-year old problem once and for all.

DIARY   *16th August, 1935*

I dreamt that Vansittart wrote and asked me to join the F.O. again. My disappointment when I woke up and found that this was only a dream is a measure of how much I really mind having severed my connection with the F.O. I must seriously consider, now that I have finished my diplomatic books, and now that politics offer no opening and journalism is horrible to me, if I could not creep back somehow into the Service.

DIARY   *19th August, 1935*

I feel terribly out of it all down here and in a backwater.

DIARY   *21st August, 1935*

I lunch with Emerald Cunard. I arrive early. I am ushered into the little ground-floor sitting-room and open *New York Life*. Then a lovely lady arrives, rather shy, whom I afterwards identify as Lady Jersey.[1] Then in comes Sir Arthur Wauchope, High Commissioner in Palestine. And then a slim young man of the name of Davison. And then Emerald herself very glad about everything. Then Anthony Eden.[2] Then Walter Elliot.[3] We go into luncheon. I sit between Walter and Davison with Eden on the other side.

Emerald is at her best. She well knows that Anthony Eden and Elliot are not able to disclose what happened at the Cabinet this morning. Yet she also knows that by flagrant indiscretion she may get them to say something. 'Anthony', she says, 'you are all wrong about Italy. Why should she not have Abyssinia? You must tell me that.' As the only guest whom I have not mentioned was de Castellane of the French Embassy, Eden's style was cramped. He just reacted flippantly. They therefore discussed English women and how they were no help to their husbands whereas the merest French cocotte at Toulon moved heaven and earth in favour of her *commandant de frégate*. As I was one off Eden, I was able to ask from time to time leading questions: e.g. 'What attitude will Switzerland adopt?' 'She has her constitutional difficulties, but we do not think that land frontiers matter very much.' He then said that Lloyd George had been summoned that morning into conference. He had explained that Italy in 1919 had been offered far more than she could absorb. This is true about Eregli, Adalia and Albania. Eden asked me whether this was true. I said it was. I asked what other people had been called into consultation. He said old Lansbury, Herbert Samuel and Winston. Also Bruce of Australia and the other High Commissioners. He said that Winston was all out for blood and thunder. I referred to the unhelpful attitude of the French press, instancing the *Figaro* of yester-

[1] First wife of the ninth Earl of Jersey. She was born in Australia.
[2] He was then Minister without Portfolio for League of Nations Affairs, with a seat in the Cabinet, and was to become Foreign Secretary in December in succession to Sir Samuel Hoare. He was aged 38.
[3] Then Minister of Agriculture.

day. He said, 'Yes, it would be simple enough if the French were really with us.' From which I gather that he himself and the F.O. are out for sanctions but that the French and the Beaverbrook and Rothermere Press over here are a doubtful quantity. Walter Elliot hinted that we might remove the embargo on the export of arms to Abyssinia and I suggested that this would not be understood in the U.S.A.

I felt that I had touched the fringe of the centre of the problem. But I also felt that in the F.O. I should have been in the centre of the problem. I was very sad.

Then back by the 5.42 to Sissinghurst. The posters of the evening papers bear headlines, 'Ramsay MacDonald says "Worst crisis since 1914".' 'Ll. G. and Lansbury summoned to F.O.' 'Opposition consulted' etc. etc. A general crisis atmosphere. It is very hot in the train. I read the silly books I collected at the *Daily Telegraph*. A guidebook to Morocco. A book on English phonetics for foreign readers. I feel more out of it all than ever.

H.N. TO SIR LANCELOT OLIPHANT[1]   *24th August, 1935*
                                                                  Sissinghurst

I rather wished, when I got back on Thursday night, that I had never mentioned to you my ambition to creep back into the F.O. It was selfish of me to do so and was not quite fair on you. I have found that one is seldom at one's best after broadcasting. The mere ventriloquial effort of addressing millions through a little machine is bad for the nerves. Nor was my jumpiness lessened by reading Rothermere and Beaverbrook upon the Abyssinian question. People inside the Office never know how deep is the outsider's longing for authoritative information. It is like thirst to the marooned.

But I really do understand the position. I am not in the least impressed by the fervour of the obituary notices which I still receive, knowing that there is a wide gulf between the thought 'He ought never to have left' and the thought 'He ought to come back'. I see also that the congestion in the Service renders it quite impossible, without actual unfairness, to put in people such as me while chucking out people such as Horace Rumbold. Nor am I blind to the fact that my journalistic, literary, Mosley and *Action* expeditions have rendered me damaged goods.

[1] Assistant Under-Secretary of State at the Foreign Office.

So on the whole I think it would be better if you never mentioned the business to Ronny[1] or anyone else. I have had such wonderful luck in life that a little run of misfortune will do me no harm at all. After all, I am still bursting with energy and there should be no reason why I should not do something even now with what remains to me of life.[2]

H.N. TO V.S-W.   *3rd September, 1935*
                                              Palazzo Vendramin, Venice

We went to the Regatta and the *Bucentaur* passed and other state gondolas and Canal police turned on two hoses to prevent the gondolas crowding too far up the course and the cousin of Angelo won which made him wave his hand in the air and there was a girl alone in a little row-boat like Grace Darling in and out of the crushed jumble of gondolas and the royal crew wear top hats with gold bands. So that when all the shouting was over we went to Harry's Bar which was crowded and there was a Pekinese being fed with crisps so that we came back and dressed and J. A. Spender came to dinner and talked about the Titians which are bad and about the early days of Robert Greg and he is escaping to Switzerland as he wishes to read the papers and he asked me about Stephen his nephew. But he went away before the party arrived and the first arrival we didn't know as Myrtle [Erlanger] hadn't come and Peter [Rodd] was too sleepy already and Victor [Cunard] was having a button sewn on in the other room. But the Infante came quite early and Mary Baker curtsied to him and Peter Rodd said that one ought not to curtsey to the Infante even out of snobbishness since he had been deprived of his royal status by King Alfonso so that the Infante cried a little and said he had been outraged and they took him away with tear-furrows draggling down his purple powdered face and I sat on a sofa with Baby Goldsmith Rothschild who asked me why I disliked her so much and said that Lord Reading had behaved admirably but not so Philip Sassoon—'*qui est snob enfin*'— and then Myrtle came up with an Austrian Baron and asked me to comfort Mary Baker who had a yellow canna plant put in her hair by a Pole and had liked it at first but had then seen that she looked stupid so I told her that she didn't and by then the singer who had gone off with the Infante came back and sang *Ramona* and *The Isle of Capri* in Italian and I talked to Serge Lifar about Diaghileff; Serge has

[1] Sir Ronald Lindsay.   [2] H.N. was then 48.

grown a beard a little peaky thing which disguises the fact that he has completely lost his looks. I had some white chianti at that stage since I realised that everybody except Victor and I and Sylvia [Thompson] were getting rather drunk and then a female acquaintance of Oscar Wilde came and said she thought I ought to take a chance; my last chance; I asked her what sort of chance; she made me sit on an old Venetian *cassone* while she told me what sort of chance and as this alarmed me rather I crept down the staircase under huge lit arches to the mezzanine but there were two people in my bedroom examining the stucco and so I came up again and there she was still on the *cassone* having been to the lavatory and come back. So that when Myrtle came up and asked me about Gwen it seemed so domestic like and then Smith broke a whole bottle poor man and it was 3 am. and my bedroom was all empty now so I locked the door and snuggled behind the mosquito curtains and while the noise upstairs bumped and screamed I slid off into calm and dark.

DIARY   *3rd October, 1935*

Lunch with Mummy and on to the Foundling Site where Gwen makes a pretty little speech. Motor back to Sissinghurst afterwards. Buck De La Warr[1] telephones to say that if I will agree to contest West Leicester in the National Labour interest he thinks he can give me a safe seat. I answer that I must think it over.

The constituency of West Leicester, which both Ramsay MacDonald and Winston Churchill had fought in past Elections, had been represented since 1931 by a Liberal, E. H. Pickering. He had been elected as a National-Liberal with a 12,000 majority, but after a few months had crossed the floor of the House and became an Opposition (Samuelite) Liberal. This action had greatly displeased his National-Liberal and Conservative constituents, since both had given him their support in 1931. They determined to replace him by a new candidate whom both parties could jointly sponsor. Lord De La Warr, a cousin of V. Sackville-West, suggested Harold Nicolson. The latter agreed to stand at the forthcoming General Election in the interests of National Labour, the

---

[1] The Earl De La Warr, then Parliamentary Secretary to the Ministry of Agriculture and Chairman of the Coordination Committee set up to allocate seats between the three wings (Conservative, Labour, Liberal) of the National Party. He was himself National Labour.

small Party still headed by Ramsay MacDonald, whom Stanley Baldwin had succeeded as Prime Minister in June.

It is no wonder that the electors of Leicester found the situation confusing, for Harold Nicolson did not quite understand it himself. He was to stand as a candidate backed by National Labour for a Liberal constituency with Conservative and National Liberal support. He firmly refused to call himself Conservative, although he supported Baldwin's leadership, and had offered himself only recently as Conservative candidate for Sevenoaks. He attacked the record of the 1929–31 Labour Government which Ramsay MacDonald had led. He was known to have been a member of Mosley's New Party. He had strong leanings towards the Liberal Party, but he was opposed by a Liberal in a three-cornered fight. To add to the confusion in his own mind and in the minds of his electorate, he was eventually billed as 'The National Government Candidate' (in other words, as a supporter of Baldwin without qualification), and he woke up one morning to find the whole of Leicester placarded with posters describing him as 'The National Conservative Candidate'. The printers apologised for the mistake and his opponents jeered. There was much talk of his 'chameleon' activities in search of a seat, and W. B. Jarvis, the indefatigable Chairman of the West Leicester Conservative Association, went to great pains to explain that his man was a supporter of the National Government, that he was a person of independent mind, and that one day they would be proud of him. They were.

The General Election took place at the height of the Abyssinian crisis. Mussolini had invaded Abyssinia in early October, and the League of Nations, following Anthony Eden's lead at Geneva, had voted for economic sanctions against Italy. Mussolini nevertheless persisted with his invasion, and British opinion was then almost unanimous in supporting strong action by the League up to a point just short of actual war. 'There will be no wavering over our support for the League', stated the Conservative Election manifesto in unequivocal tones. The Labour Party under Mr Attlee was only slightly less categorical. So Harold Nicolson did not find himself challenged on the ground that he knew best. He was obliged to defend the National Government's home policy, of which he knew little, and explain away his chequered political past. He had never known Leicester before, nor indeed any other town like it, and he found the actual process of electioneering as distasteful as he had found daily journalism, and for much the same reasons.

*'I hate and loathe every moment of it', he wrote on 7th November
to V. Sackville-West; and one cause of his distress was her refusal to
make even a single appearance at his side. Their exchange of letters
on the 28th and 29th October records one of the few serious disagreements
that ever clouded their marriage. She hated politics. She did not understand it, and deep down she resented it as a male preserve. She passionately wished him to succeed in anything he undertook and was overjoyed
at his victory. But she would not contribute towards it by the simple
gesture of sitting on one of his platforms, where she would have been
regarded as 'the candidate's wife' and not as V. Sackville-West in her
own right. He told 'the magnificent lie' that she was ill.*

*All this was forgotten on the night of 14th November, when he ex-
perienced the greatest single moment of triumph in his whole life.*

H.N. TO V.S-W. (*at Domremy, Lorraine*[1])   *10th October, 1935*
                                                          4 King's Bench Walk, E.C.4

Having dressed soberly but not unimpressively, I went to see Buck
De La Warr in the Ministry of Agriculture. He was very pleasant
and cousinly. I told him that I was in a difficulty. I knew nothing
whatsoever about the rules of the game. In fact my ignorance of even
the elements was as if a man sitting down to play bridge with Mrs
Keppel were to exclaim brightly, 'Tell me, Alice, are those clover-
shaped cards spades or diamonds?' I was perfectly willing to stand as a
National Candidate under any of the minor labels, Tory, Liberal or
Labour. By nature I was an Asquithian Liberal much improved and
purified by twenty years of war and post-war. I had offered myself to
the National Liberals two years ago. I had offered myself to the Tories
at the time of the Sevenoaks bye-election. I was now offering myself
to him.

Anyhow, at that stage Buck pressed the buzzer for his secretary
(a pale young man, anxious to please). He told him to get on at once
to Mr Jarvis at Leicester. Now I do not really know who or what Mr.
Jarvis is. He seems to be the person what runs the Conservative
Association—but why he should have the deciding voice as to whether
your old bumbles should stand for a Liberal seat as a Labour candidate,
simply passes my comprehension. Anyhow he told Mr Jarvis that I
was willing in principle.

[1] Where she had gone with Gwen St Aubyn to visit the birthplace of Joan of Arc.

H.N. TO V.S-W. (*at Domremy*)   *11th October, 1935*
                                                4 King's Bench Walk, E.C.4

I went back to see Buck yesterday and was sent upstairs and into the waiting-room. There I read *The Times* newspaper. While thus employed a brisk man entered and hung his bowler briskly on the peg. I went on reading *The Times* newspaper. After about five minutes, the office-keeper entered and said that Lord De La Warr was free. At which both I and the brisk man rose briskly and I realised that he must be the man Jarvis. Thus from the first he must have put me down as a bad mixer. We got terribly mixed up moreover entering Buck's door. 'You go first', I said. 'But, please', he answered, and then we both advanced. Obviously he must have concluded that I was not a man of the world.

Anyhow Buck then greeted us and we sat side by side on the sofa with Buck at the writing-table. Jarvis is aged about 35; high colour; high morals. He is Chairman of the Conservative Association for West Leicester. He began by saying that it was most important that I should stand as 'The National Government Candidate' and not as 'National Labour'. I let Buck answer that point as I am all at sea about these labels. Buck said he agreed. I said, 'But supposing people ask me what party I belong to, what am I to say?' Buck said that I must say that I was a follower of Ramsay MacDonald. The conversation went on this way with me sitting all good and quiet on the sofa. Then I realised that something must be done. I said that it was no use asking me about these things, but that what was important was that I should not get a single vote under false pretences. I would be anything they liked except all things to all men. I would not pretend to be a Tory to catch the Tory vote and so on. I would get muddled if my own position was not quite clear and straight from the start. 'I am very bad,' I said, 'at *prolonged* deception.' Anyhow they agreed and told me not to fuss about MY HONOUR.

As regards expenses, headquarters will pay one third, local organisations one third, and (what may strike you as unexpected) V.S-W. one third. (She does it by raising a mortgage on Long Barn.) I shall ask for £500 from you under this head, pay you interest on it, and repay the mortgage when I become First Lord of the Treasury. I made it quite clear that you could take no part. I said that I much objected to the 'Candidate's Wife' stunt, that you were not interested in politics and that it would be humbug to pretend that you were, and that although you might come for the last flurry to see the fun, you would only come out of curiosity and that they were not to expect you to play any part in the constituency. They said that that would be all right. It would go down very well if I explained that in advance. What would not go down well would be if you came up all smiling and with huge rosettes on Martha's collar, and then turned tail when it was all over and never saw West Leicester again.

By this stage you will be saying, 'But I don't understand. Has Harold (since you will not have liked that bit about the mortgage, nor in fact any part of this letter[1]), has HAROLD been elected already? Does it mean that he has got to take his seat or something?' No, nothing of the kind. I have not even been adopted, being still a completely orphan child.

H.N. TO V.S-W. (*at Chinon*)   *17th October, 1935*
4 King's Bench Walk, E.C.4

I have not heard quite definitely yet whether I am adopted for Leicester. I am to go down there this afternoon for the final decision.

Dearest Viti, do not be cross with me about the Election. I know you think I have been impulsive about it, but in fact I have been brooding over the problem for a year like an old hen.

H.N. TO V.S-W. (*at Orléans*)   *18th October, 1935*
4 King's Bench Walk, E.C.4

Buck De La Warr telephoned to say he was sending round one of his organisers to see me. Mr Flaxman he is by name. And Mr Flaxman shortly afterwards arrived, with a huge wild rose made of canvas in his buttonhole—why in October? Why didn't Gabriel get a lily? He looks like a bookie. He talks with a strong cockney accent. He is very pushing and affable. He is a dreadful man.

Anyhow, when Mr Flaxman was with me, Mr Jarvis telephoned from Leicester. Would I come down at once? And would I bring someone from Headquarters? So I said that Mr Flaxman would come. Oh my God! He did.

We entered the train. Mr Flaxman started talking. He has been a parliamentary agent for many years and thinks entirely in terms of bamboozling electorates. He started serving questions at me much as a

[1] Normally she called him Hadji. He became Harold when he was in disgrace.

tennis pro serves balls. I returned these services as well as I could. 'No that will not do at all, Mr Nicolson. You must not say that, it would offend the Catholics. You must say that it will be for the people themselves to determine at the General Election ...' 'But mayn't I ever say what I think?' 'Most certainly not, Mr Nicolson, very dangerous indeed.'

When we arrived at Leicester there was Mr. Jarvis on the platform. He took us first to see the Chief Conservative organiser for the East Midlands. It seems that the Liberals are determined to put up against me an independent candidate of their own, which is a bitter blow. I fear it means that the seat will go to the Socialists. They then discussed in what form I should be presented to the voters of West Leicester. I sat there twiddling my hat while I was discussed as if I were not present. They decided that I should stand as British Government candidate. Then I intervened. I said that was all very well. But that in fact I was standing as National Labour. I was quite prepared to call myself the 'National Candidate', but if asked, I should reply that I was a supporter of Ramsay MacDonald. They said that this would lose me votes. I said that if I suppressed the fact, I should be getting votes under false pretences. I would never agree to that. They looked down their noses. Mr Flaxman said angrily, 'But surely, Mr Nicolson, you do not suppose that a General Election is a vestry meeting?' I said that I would not stand as a candidate unless I started on an open and honest basis. Mr Flaxman cast up his hands in horror. Jarvis said, 'Yes, you're right, quite right.'

After this we walked across to the Conservative Club. When we entered, the Executive Committee were already in session. A rather worn Union Jack was draped across the radiator and in front of it were three chairs and a table complete with carafe. Facing this platform were three rows of Windsor chairs occupied, as to the front row, by leading Conservative ladies, and as to the two other rows, by leading Conservative men. Mr Jarvis made a little speech introducing me and saying that I would answer questions. Luckily nearly all the first questions were about Abyssinia which I could answer off my hat. Then a man asked whether I had studied the mining question. I said that my ignorance of that question was as wide as it was deep. They looked startled at that and then the central lady said, 'Well, I am sure, Mr Nicolson, that if you smile like that, it doesn't matter what you know or don't know.' Then they asked me to go outside and

I and Mr Flaxman went on to the landing while they discussed me.

Finally the door opened and we were led back. I resumed my seat, managed not to ask 'Animal, vegetable or mineral?' and waited while Jarvis cleared his throat and read out what they had resolved. It amounted to the fact that the Conservatives of Leicester pledged themselves unanimously to support me. After expressing words of appreciation and gratitude I descended from my chair and mingled with the throng of my supporters.

H.N. TO V.S-W.   *23rd October 1935*
                                                 Grand Hotel, Leicester

It is nice to feel that this evening you will be back in the same old island as I am.

I fear, darling, that you will have to come up twice, as they are very pi[1] here and will think that we are divorced. I have spoken vaguely about your not being very strong and having gone to France for a few weeks. But you will have, I fear, to appear at least twice and to sit on the platform.

I make my first big speech this evening to the Conservative Association. Meanwhile I have opened Committee rooms, organised my workers, engaged halls, had a tiff with my Labour opponent[2] and set everything in motion for the real fight on 1st November and the following days. Agents and political organisers always tell the most awful lies. They say I have 'an even chance'. But I do not really believe that they think I have a chance at all, with a Liberal taking half my votes. I should have romped in had not the Liberal come and made it a three-cornered fight. But I expect he feels the same about me, poor man.

V.S-W. TO H.N.   *28th October, 1935*
                                                 Sissinghurst

My darling Hadji,

I fear you have gone away hurt[3] and I mind that dreadfully. It is no good going over old ground, so I won't. Only to say that apart from what you called 'principle', I do genuinely think that an isolated

---

[1] 'Pious', 'respectable'.
[2] John Morgan. The tiff was about the allegation that H.N. had been a fascist.
[3] H.N. had returned for a night to Sissinghurst to welcome V.S-W. home from France.

appearance at Leicester would be worse than none, because of its inconsistency, and that it would also lead to bazaars and things *after* the Election, if you get in, as I do very truly and sincerely hope you will.

Still, I am more sorry that I can say to have hurt you, but do remember, darling, that we had always been agreed on this matter even before you got adopted, and I quite thought that your views coincided with mine[1]—as I still think they did until agents and people started badgering you. Do you remember also what I said last night, that I have always cared very, very deeply about your writing and even your broadcasting (don't murder me!); and my admiration for your very rare gift, which I rate far higher than you do, is great and has always been accompanied by the very deepest interest. So don't run away with the idea that I 'have never taken any interest', as you said, in the things which mattered to you. You know as well as I do, if you stop to think, that this is an absurd contention! Darling, don't let this make a rift?

MAR

H.N. TO V.S-W.   *29th October, 1935*
Grand Hotel, Leicester

Darling,

Of course I wasn't 'hurt'. Only puzzled and disappointed and rather cross. I really do not understand your point of view, but I don't think it is a selfish motive in the ordinary use of that term—only selfish in that it does ignore my need and difficulties.

I simply don't know *how* to explain it. But I shall try not to tell a lie. Don't expect letters, as I shall be very rushed.[2]

Bless you, my dearest.

HADJI

H.N. TO V.S-W.   *1st November, 1935*
Grand Hotel, Leicester

In the evening I had two meetings, both in the communist quarter. A school-house with maps on the wall. Some 100 people there, all working men and women lowing in disgust and hatred. A nervous chairman, who from the very start is howled at. Then the local

[1] There was much truth in this. See pp. 217–18.

[2] That he could say this indicates the depth of his disappointment. Nevertheless he did write to her every day as usual.

speaker. They howled and yelled, 'We don't want you', they shouted. 'SIT DOWN!' they yelled. He went on quite bravely for a bit, but then I saw that he was flinching. Another five minutes he struggled on while the yells increased in volume and a man in the front row shouted, 'I'll bash your face to pieces'. To my dismay, he then collapsed. He said, 'You people are not worth talking to!', sat down, fumbled for his hat, and left the hall while they sang the *Red Flag*. It was then up to me to talk to them. I was greeted by a storm of boos as I rose. But I stepped right up to the man who threatened to bash my face. Oh dear, never has Hadji been so frightened or so quite unexpectedly brave. I started to speak and went on the half-hour which was the scheduled time. Most of the audience yelled all the time; but some of them in the middle distance heard what I said; and towards the end I managed somehow to impose silence and when the questions came it was almost a good audience. Then at the end they sang the *Red Flag* again. The meeting then adjourned. But the odd thing was that the people who had yelled loudest came up to me and said they hoped I hadn't minded, and that they wished I was on their side.

H.N. TO V.S-W.   *2nd November, 1935*
                                        Grand Hotel, Leicester

Duff [Cooper] came over with the Duchess of Rutland. Duff made an amazing speech and then went on to another hall where he made another speech. I followed in the intervals. I am really very grateful to Duff and the Duchess for having come. It has made all the difference with my Tory supporters, who were frightened at my calling myself a Liberal, I mean a Labour, man, and now are completely reassured. Moreover I learnt a lot from Duff's technique, which I shall imitate. He is really amazing.

H.N. TO V.S-W.   *7th November, 1935*
                                        Grand Hotel, Leicester

The position is really more or less as follows:

(1) I have about a 48 per cent chance—just a little below even chances. In other words, the odds are really against me, but there is just a chance I may scrape in. (2) If I fail, I shall not feel that it was due to any mistakes on my part, to any lack of organisation or lack of energy. (3) If I succeed, it will be a great personal triumph.

Were I a young man, it would be worth it. It is always to one's credit to have fought a really stiff Election and to have got through with it. But of course I cannot pretend that at my age it is pleasant to have a failure and to spend all this money and energy for nothing. Generally in experiences such as this there is something, some isolated moment, which one enjoys. I hate and loathe every moment of this Election. Not that the office work or the interviews are very irksome; but the evening meetings are such absolute HELL that they hang on one's soul all day like a lump of lead. It reminds me of the days when I was frightened at night and felt a horror of the afternoon declining towards sunset and bed-time. When the lights come out in the streets here, I have a terrible sinking feeling—'the hour draws near'.

H.N. TO V.S-W.   *10th November, 1935*
                                                 Grand Hotel, Leicester

I got back late to my office. The woman downstairs said, 'Oh, Mr Nicolson, a gentleman has just been in to see you—a friend he said he was.' 'What was he like?' I asked. 'Oh, he was very tall and thin, and a little blind I should say from the glasses he wore, and he is round at the hotel waiting for you.' So round to the hotel I went, and there was Aldous Huxley wearing the strangest clothes. I gave him some tea, and he talked for an hour. I have never heard him talk so readily or so brilliantly. It was like the most perfect hose compared to a teapot with a broken spout. He seemed to think it perfectly natural to find me standing National Labour, and he encouraged me enormously just by taking it all for granted and saying that he admired me for doing it. I shall always like him more for that visit. He took me right away from the Turkey rugs of the Grand Hotel and the mud-baths of ignorance and meanness in which I have been wallowing of late.

H.N. TO V.S-W.   *13th November, 1935*
                                                 Grand Hotel, Leicester

This is probably the last letter I shall write before my defeat. Don't feel, darling, that I shall be disappointed. The disappointment came ten days ago when the Liberals put up Crawfurd against me and I knew that he would do me down. Of course, there is always the slender chance that the floating vote may swing away from Labour and that I shall creep in. But I can see from the manner of my canvassers who have toured the streets that they do not believe for one moment that I shall be elected.

DIARY   *14th November, 1935*

One of the strangest days in my life. It pours, the rainwater sluicing
down on dark streets. Copper has come up and we decorate the cars
with posters, streamers and lucky horseshoes. I spend all day going
round the Committee rooms. By the evening the voting becomes
hectic and my fleet of cars are much in demand. Sam[1] does wonderful
work transporting people.

At about 10 p.m. we go on to the de Montfort Hall and find the
counting in progress. Long trestle-tables with people counting in rows.
On the stage is the Lord Mayor and the Town Council officials plus
the Returning Officer. The voting papers are separated into little
bundles of fifty and I and my supporters stroll round the tables watching
the size of the piles. By about 11.30 p.m. it is clear to us that Morgan
will be first, I second, and Crawfurd third. I go out into the lobby and
listen on the wireless for other results. A rumour flies round that
Stafford Cripps has been beaten at Bristol by Church and we are all
delighted. This rumour is then contradicted. We then hear that
Herbert Samuel is out. More delight. I return to the main rooms and
find my supporters very glum and sad. Morgan is triumphant. 'It's
a bad system of counting, this', he exclaims. 'The first thing I shall do
is to get some alteration to the ballot law.' He says this openly,
assuming that he will get in.

Then come the announcements for East and South Leicester. Lyons[2]
and Waterhouse[3] both in. Applause and cheers plus two short speeches.
By that time my own tables are handing their bundles up to the
platform. Jarvis comes to me in the hall and says, 'You ought to be
up on the platform by now'. So up I go. There is a group round the
central counting table, including the Returning Officer and my agent
Tuthill. Morgan sees me, and comes up to me. 'Well,' he says, 'you
have done splendidly—a rare fight for a first Election. But do not be
discouraged: we want men like you in the House of Commons.'
'What', I ask him, 'is your majority?' 'My tellers', he answers, 'estimate it at between 1,200 and 1,500.' I shake his hand in congratulation.

I then walk to the back to think out my speech for seconding the

[1] Francis St Aubyn, later Lord St Levan, H.N.'s brother-in-law.
[2] A. M. Lyons, Conservative M.P. for East Leicester, 1931–45.
[3] Captain Charles Waterhouse, Conservative M.P. for South Leicester 1924–45 and
for South East Leicester, 1950–59.

*Harold Nicolson after his election as Member
for West Leicester, November 14th, 1935*

*Vita Sackville-West and Harold Nicolson in
his sitting room at Sissinghurst*

ote of thanks. I catch Tuthill's eye as he stands there at the table. He winks at me and jerks his head. I imagine that he wants to ask me ome question and I go up to him. *'You're in'*, he whispers, *'by 150.'* My first thought is, 'Poor Morgan—I must show no sign of triumph'. retire again to the back and I hear Morgan's voice, 'I claim a recount, claim a recount.' The bundles are then handed down again to the main room. I stand there looking up at a sea of excited faces, including my Ben, my Niggs and Sam. I give them a slight affirmative motion of the head and see the colour rush to Niggs' face. Never shall I orget that second. The recount goes quickly. Waterhouse, imperturbable always, comes up slowly to me, smoking a cigarette in a long holder. 'Well', he says, 'you must be feeling pretty proud. The greatest fight of the whole Election.' The bundles are then returned and the Socialists query many defective papers. I give them all they want. That leaves me with 87. Tuthill moves away from the table very quietly. 'Well', he says, 'we're in.'[1]

The news communicates itself to the crowd in the hall below and here is a hum rising like a swarm of bees. The Press buzz round me. The Clerk of the Council steps forward and makes his announcement. As my majority is announced, a wild yell goes up from the hall. People rush towards the platform. I step forward and make a short speech. Morgan follows, and then Crawfurd. I then descend from the platform and am seized—Flaxman in tears, Mrs Jarvis ditto, Mrs Pearce[2] ditto. I kiss her. Then photographs outside and on to the Constitutional Club. They are waiting for me in the street in the rain and as I draw up there are shouts of, 'Here he is!' Out they drag me and hoist me up the stairs. Pandemonium let loose. I am dumped on the staircase and say a few words. Then back to the hotel—champagne with Waterhouse. To bed at 2.30 am.

---

[1] The result was:

Nicolson, H. (National Labour)	15,821	
Morgan, J. (Labour)	15,734	
Crawfurd, H. E. (Liberal)	4,621	

[2] Chairman of the Women's Committee of the West Leicester Conservative Association.

H.N. TO V.S-W.   *15th November, 193*
                                                                   Travellers Club, S.W.

I shall tell you all about it when I come down. I confess that I am over
joyed. It was *such* a battle, and I really do not think I said a single
thing of which I could ever feel ashamed.

I know that it was a great personal triumph, and of course I am con
ceited and up in the air. But I am not really conceited, as you know
I think my real pleasure is that I put all my philosophy of life into tha
Election, every inch of it (in spite of all the pleadings of my supporters)
and I won. I feel justified in my ideals—that's what I feel, darling, an
that is why the sense of triumph which I have is not one of conques
but of solemn joy.

V.S-W. TO H.N.   *15th November, 193*
                                                                   Sissinghurs

I am *so* glad. What a triumph! My heart stood still when I hear
'Leicester, West' on the wireless. Oh darling, I do congratulate you

On the strength of his majority of only 87, Harold Nicolson was to
remain the Member for West Leicester for the next ten years.

Baldwin had won the Election with 425 seats, of which 385 were
Conservative, 32 National Liberal and 8 National Labour. The Opposi-
tion had 180 seats, of which 154 were Labour. The National Labour
Party had more than its fair share of offices: Ramsay MacDonald (Lord
President of the Council), J. H. Thomas, Lord De La Warr and Malcolm
MacDonald were all in the Government, and this made it unlikely that
Harold Nicolson would soon obtain a job. The declining health and
capacity of Ramsay MacDonald lost for the Party any sense of identity
that it might have possessed; its vague intention was to represent
'Tory socialism' and to take a semi-independent line on foreign affairs.

The New House of Commons met to elect a Speaker on 26th November,
and the King's Speech was delivered on 3rd December. Harold Nicolson
had intended to lie low for several months, but the Hoare-Laval crisis
impelled him to make his maiden speech on 19th December.

Sir Samuel Hoare, the Foreign Secretary, met Pierre Laval, the
French Foreign Minister, in Paris in early December and discussed with
him a plan to partition Abyssinia between Italy and the Emperor of
Abyssinia. This plan was approved by the British Cabinet on 9th

December. On the 13th the full text was laid before the League, but it had leaked a few days earlier, and an immediate outcry arose in Britain against this cynical abandonment of the victim of Mussolini's attack, when Britain had taken the lead in proposing sanctions and Baldwin had won the Election on a strong pro-League policy. The Cabinet gave way to the strength of Parliamentary and public feeling, and Hoare was obliged to resign. Baldwin himself, wrote Winston Churchill in the first volume of his history of the Second World War, 'fell almost overnight from his pinnacle of acclaimed national leadership to a depth where he was derided and despised'. It was in these circumstances that Harold Nicolson first addressed the House of Commons. His speech, as National Labour's spokesman on foreign affairs, was a great success.

DIARY   *20th November, 1935*

Dine with De La Warr at Windham Club. Ramsay MacDonald was there. He is tired, yet he dramatizes his position as always. The defeated statesman surrounded by his devoted flock; the devoted father having narmed his brilliant son; Cincinnatus longing to return to his plough but restrained by public duty. He talks about the Luttrell Psalter and the *Codex Sinaiticus*. Yet always there is something histrionic and therefore fraudulent about him. I respect and admire him in many ways. But I do see why many people regard him as a complete humbug.

After dinner Ramsay discourses to us about the future of the National Labour Party, which he does not call a 'party' but a 'group'. He advises us to sit together as a group and to communicate with the Speaker through a 'secretary' who would otherwise be called a Whip. Then off he goes to Hampstead with Malcolm.

DIARY   *21st November, 1935*

Poor Hadji, *aetatis suae* 49. To lunch with Sibyl Colefax. Vincent Massey there: he has just come as High Commissioner for Canada. He looks very ill. Rob Hudson, Hannah Hudson, Rob Bernays,[1] Clemmie Churchill,[2] Thelma Cazalet,[3] Kenneth Lindsay,[4] the R. A.

[1] National Liberal M.P. for Bristol. He became H.N.'s closest friend in the House, but was killed in 1945.
[2] Mrs Winston Churchill.
[3] National Conservative M.P. for East Islington, 1931-45.
[4] Independent National M.P. for Kilmarnock Burghs, 1933-45.

Butlers.[1] Clemmie tells me that Winston has not yet been approached.
It looks as if he were going to be left out till February. He wants the
Admiralty. But he has got tickets for Bali, where, if not offered a
Cabinet job, he proposes to spend the winter. Rob Bernays talks to
me solemnly afterwards, advising me to lie very low at first. He says
the rather dramatic circumstances of my election may arouse some
jealousy in that old hen the H. of C. I must do the new-boy for six
months at least. That accords wholly with my own desire.

H.N. TO V.S-W.   *4th December, 1935*
                                              4 King's Bench Walk, E.C.4

Yesterday the House was opened at 12 noon. I went down and stood
in the lobby. There was a crowd of visitors and the wail echoing
from the recesses of the House, 'Speaker! Speaker!' impressed them
almost as much as it did me. Then came the mace and everybody
bowed low and the Speaker followed. After which the doors were
locked and poor old Black Rod tottered across and struck with his
staff on the doors. At which they all poured across to the House of
Lords and I climbed up to the Members' gallery. It was a poor show
and the Lord Chancellor read the speech[2] and then we all went back
again. Poor Wakefield[3] had to move the Address and he sat there
looking very wretched in an airman's uniform with his white gloves
twisting themselves. But when the moment came he spoke very well
and modestly and quite captured the affection of the House. Then
rose Attlee—such a poor speaker, so precise and school-maidish. And
then Baldwin, experienced and sedate. There is something very
strange about Stanley Baldwin. At first sight he is a solid English
gentleman, but then one observes odd nervous tricks. He has an
extraordinarily unpleasant habit of smelling at his notes and licking
the edges slightly as if they were the flap of an envelope. He scratches
himself continuously. There are russet patches across his head and
face. And a strange movement of the head, with half-closed eyes,
like some tortoise half-awake smelling the air—blinking, snuffy,
neurotic. Thereafter rose Archie Sinclair as Liberal Leader and shortly
after that I had to run away.

[1] R. A. Butler was then 36. He was Under Secretary of State, India Office, 1932–37.
[2] The King did not open Parliament in person because of the death of his sister,
Princess Victoria, on 3rd December.
[3] Sir Wavell Wakefield, National Conservative M.P. for Swindon, 1935–45.

I went in first to the smoking-room, which was an unwise thing to have done. I wanted to see if I could find Ralph Glyn[1] with whom I am supposed to be lunching today. But the smoking-room was full of old boys sitting round tables and drinking whisky. It is not in the least like the smoking-room at the Travellers Club. It is far more like the bar of a pub. Shouts and laughter and an almost complete absence of decorum. Having got in, I could scarcely get out, and I tried that business of walking rapidly through with head turning right and left and eyes bearing that far-away look which signifies, 'I am not in the very least bit shy. I am merely looking urgently for someone of immense importance'. Then to my horror from the extreme end of the room came yells of 'Harold!'—and there was Winston Churchill and Robert Horne and Oliver Stanley waving at me. I had to go towards them feeling stared-at and conspicuous.

Winston rose tubbily and stretched out great arms. 'Welcome! Welcome!' he yelled. You know how overwhelming his charm can be, but I would rather it had occurred in greater privacy. 'Well', he shouted, 'when I saw your result on the tape, I said to myself, "That means he goes straight into the Cabinet", and then I remembered that all of your Party were already in the Cabinet and that they must have at least one follower on the back benches. So I realised that you would be chosen as the single follower.' This amused people all round and there was general laughter while I stood there looking a fool. But I do not suppose I really looked so foolish as I felt, and then I sat down with them for a moment and nothing could possibly have been so delightful as they were.

H.N. TO V.S-W.   *10th December, 1935*
                              4 King's Bench Walk, E.C.4

After luncheon I went round to the Privy Council Office for a meeting of our National Labour Party. It is a lovely room with a huge sculptured fireplace and many Queen Anne inkstands. Ramsay sat there in front of the fire and we others sat on either side. There were Malcolm MacDonald, Kenneth Lindsay, Buck De La Warr and Lord Elton.[2]

[1] Sir Ralph Glyn, Conservative M.P. for Abingdon, 1924-53. Parliamentary Private Secretary to Ramsay MacDonald, 1931-37. Later he became Lord Glyn.
[2] Fellow of Queen's College, Oxford, and lecturer in modern history, 1919-39. Expelled from the Labour Party for supporting MacDonald in 1931. Editor of the National Labour *Newsletter*, 1932-38.

We discussed the future organisation and policy of our Party. It was a ridiculous and rather painful discussion. It boiled down to the question of Party funds. We had so much money in hand which would enable us to keep on for such and such a time. How were we to get more money? Ramsay dismissed that question as secondary. 'One can always get money', he said, 'for great political purposes.' Lindsay, who is an impatient and able man, suggested that we might discuss what those purposes were. We all winced at that. 'We shall', said Ramsay, 'be neither red, white nor blue. We stand for Labour within the Baldwin organisation. We shall further the aims of the organisation but we shall remain OURSELVES.' Having said that, he struck the arm of his chair with a clenched fist and gazed upwards to where, above the mantelpiece, God was most likely to be found. 'OURSELVES', he repeated fervently, like a Covenanter dedicating his sword and buckler. We did not even like to look at each other so awkward were our feelings. Then Lindsay again intervened. 'But I should like to ask the Prime Minister—I mean the Lord President—whether we can count on having him and Malcolm both in the House.'[1] 'You may go on that assumption', he answered delphically, and we once again dared not face each other's eyes. It was by then 3.30 p.m., and in acute embarrassment we broke up.

DIARY   *10th December, 1935*

Find the House seething because of the Abyssinian proposals.[2] They have appeared in the Press, and Baldwin, when questioned by Attlee, made the mistake of saying that there had been a 'leakage' in Paris, thus implying that the Press reports were true in substance. Great indignation that after all this fuss we should be giving Italy more for breaking the Covenant than we offered her for keeping it. Eleanor Rathbone makes a very noble speech to that effect. Of course, they are not seeing the thing in its right proportions. Eden and Baldwin make rather feeble replies.

DIARY   *11th December, 1935*

The feeling in the House is still enraged against the Laval agreement. Go to see J. H. Thomas[3] in his room with Buck [De La Warr] and

[1] Both had lost their seats in the Election.
[2] These were the Hoare–Laval proposals to make peace between Mussolini and the League on the basis of conceding to him a large part of his Abyssinian conquests.
[3] Secretary of State for the Colonies.

Kenneth Lindsay. He says that the Cabinet are equally indignant and that Anthony Eden has been told to tell the League that we shall not press them to accept it, i.e. we shall ask them to reject it.

H.N. TO V.S-W.   *12th December, 1935*
                                           4 King's Bench Walk, E.C.4
I have just returned from the trial of Lord de Clifford.[1] It was very strange. The peers filed in with their scarlet and ermine robes and then came the Lord Chancellor[2] with his toby-jug look, and thereat Black Rod advanced bowing low and presented the Lord Chancellor with a wand of office—a thin white stick. At that all the peers put on their cocked hats. A clerk read the indictment: 'We by the grace of God, George V, King, Defender of the Faith, unto our trusted and well beloved Algernon Viscount Hailsham—whereas . . .' On and on it went, talking of *premunire* and 'jettison' and 'barratry' and that sort of thing until it came to the words 'do solemnly indict upon the charge of manslaughter James Allen Curtiss (or whatever his name is), Baron de Clifford, in that he did cause the death, on August 15th 1935, of Douglas George Hopkins of 4 Bellevue Villas, Hoxton.' This was rather an anticlimax, but the peers retained their dignity. They crossed their arms over their resplendent breasts. Freddy,[3] whom I had observed with interest, not to say curiosity, also tried to fold his arms—but such was the intervening space that they would not meet across his robes. So he abandoned the attempt.

After the charges had been read, a voice called aloud, 'Oyez! Oyez! Oyez! Let the Baron de Clifford be brought forward.' At which a door opened and Black Rod or his underling entered followed by a tall and extremely personable young man in a tailcoat. He paused at the Bar, and bowed low to the Lord Chancellor and the peers to right and left. He then crossed the Bar and bowed again. He then entered what I suppose we must call the Lord High Dock. 'My Lord', exclaimed the Lord Chancellor, 'you may sit.' And sit he did. 'Are you, John James etc Baron de Clifford, guilty of this charge?' 'No', answered

---

[1] Lord de Clifford was charged with the manslaughter of a fellow-motorist on the Kingston by-pass by driving in a reckless, careless, negligent manner. It was the first trial of a peer by his peers in 34 years, and Lord de Clifford was unanimously acquitted.

[2] The first Viscount Hailsham.

[3] The second Lord Carnock, H.N.'s eldest brother.

Lord de Clifford. 'How is it your wish that you should be tried?' 'By my peers', answered Lord de Clifford—at which Freddy made another and equally unsuccessful attempt to cross his arms across his chest.

I am really fussed about this Abyssinian business. It seems to me that Sam Hoare has completely and absolutely let us down. I feel very deeply about it and shall certainly not vote with the Government unless I am convinced that they have not done what they seem to have done. But I believe they have. It is really disgraceful—Sam Hoare was certified by his doctors as unfit for public business, and on his way to the sanatorium he stops off in Paris and allows Laval to do him down. My God! Were I on the other side of the House what a chance for a crushing speech.

DIARY   13th December, 1935

I walk back from a Party meeting with J. H. Thomas. He does not think the present Government will last two years—but this may be due to his resentment of Baldwin and the Tories. I ask him whether he foresees a slump once the present building boom reaches saturation. He says that, on the contrary, he foresees great prosperity. I ask him whether he considers my horror of the Laval plan to be exaggerated or emotional. He says, 'No, it is the worst thing that has happened in my experience.'

Dine with Sibyl Colefax. Diana Cooper, Mr and Mrs Simpson,[1] Bruce Lockhart and the Prince of Wales there. The latter is very thin; his complexion has gone and he is brick-coloured, against which background his fair eyelashes rise and fall. He talks a great deal about America and diplomacy. He resents the fact that we do not send our best men there. He knows an astonishing amount about it all. 'What can I do?' he says. 'They will only say, "Here's that bloody Prince of Wales butting in".' One finds him modest and a good mixer.

DIARY   19th December, 1935

After questions Sam Hoare comes in with his nose plastered[2] and sits on the third bench below the gangway. He makes his statement in a precise voice. It is excellent. His voice just breaks at the end : 'I trust

[1] Ernest and Wallis Simpson. The Prince of Wales had first met her in 1930 at Lady Furness' house at Melton Mowbray, Leicestershire.
[2] He had broken it skating in Switzerland.

that my successor will have better luck than myself.' Then Attlee moves the vote of censure, and while he does so Hoare creeps out a broken man. I do not like him but my whole sympathy went out to him. After Attlee, Baldwin makes one of his take-you-into-my-confidence speeches admitting that a mistake has been made. He says the time is past for platitudes and that we now come back to stark realities. Yet he goes on with platitude after platitude, and by the end the House is no wiser than before. Then Archie Sinclair makes a magnificent fighting speech.

The Speaker's Secretary taps me on the shoulder and says that I will be called after Macpherson and Maxton. It is getting near the dinner-hour. I must confess that waiting is torture to me and I am afraid that my knees will knock together when I rise. But eventually Maxton finishes his speech and I find myself on my feet and beginning, 'I crave the indulgence ...' It all goes well enough and members crowd in from the dining-rooms. Baldwin remains on the front bench and leans forwards appreciatively. Very friendly of him. When I sit down there is much applause and Eustace [Percy] comes and says it is the best maiden speech he has ever heard. He is followed by J. H. Thomas who sits down beside me: 'You did fine, Harold, you did fine!' Thereafter many Members cross the House and congratulate me, and one way and another it is rather a sort of demonstration. Duff Cooper is particularly polite. Yet I know that I could have done it better if I had been less nervous. The manner was right enough but the matter was too thin. But it is good enough for a start. I then go out and dine.

My speech had lasted sixteen minutes. Austen Chamberlain congratulates me and I get a message from Baldwin and a note from Ramsay MacDonald. The debate ends up with a good speech by Dalton and a poor speech by Neville Chamberlain. We divide and the Government is saved. Drink afterwards with Bob Boothby, Aneurin Bevan[1] and Seymour Cocks.[2] Then to bed at last. What a day!

---

[1] Aneurin Bevan was then aged 38, and had been Labour M.P. for Ebbw Vale since 1929.
[2] Labour M.P. for Broxtowe since 1929.

DIARY   *28th December, 1935*
Go over to Swifts after luncheon and meet Teenie[1] there. He has seen
much of the P.M. lately. He gathers that the Cabinet were so incensed
at Laval's suggestion that the Hoare plan should be sent to Mussolini
only and not to Abyssinia, that they concentrated upon turning down
that proposal and said nothing about the plan itself.

DIARY   *31st December, 1935*
Externally it has been a superb year. Mexico, Greece (the best holiday
I have ever had), three visits to the United States, a lovely Lido time
at Venice, interesting work, the success of *Dwight Morrow*, and finally
the House of Commons. But for other reasons it has not been an easy
year. I was worried during the early months by Vita's health. Financial
stringency has bothered us throughout. And towards the end there
has been very deep worry about Ben's health and about Gwen whose
operation on January 27th hangs over us like a cloud. We have done
much to Sissinghurst, and next year it should be really beautiful. Ben
has continued to gain golden opinions at Oxford and Niggs has made
a good start.[2] But the year ends rather anxiously owing to Gwen and
Ben. Were it not for that, I should describe it as one of the fullest
and most enjoyable of my life.

---

[1] Victor Cazalet, Conservative M.P. for Chippenham since 1924. He had just bought
Swifts Place, a mile from Sissinghurst.
[2] Nigel had joined Ben at Balliol College in September 1935.

1936

---

*Death of King George V – MacDonald invites H.N. to
become his Parliamentary Private Secretary – death of Lady
Sackville – J. H. Thomas on King George – Hitler re-
occupies the Rhineland – Flandin pleads for strong action –
Anthony Eden and Winston Churchill – H.N.'s visit to the
King of the Belgians – meetings with Mrs Simpson and
King Edward VIII – the Russian Embassy – worry about
Hitler's intentions and Chamberlain's policy of appease-
ment – V. Sackville-West's 'Joan of Arc' and 'Pepita' –
Alfred Douglas – resignation of J. H. Thomas – Lady
Colefax's parties – Cliveden – visit to Paris – Lloyd
George's youthfulness – the Spanish Civil War breaks out –
'Helen's Tower' – a holiday in Austria, Venice and Cap
d'Antibes – the Lindberghs at Long Barn – the crisis leading
to the King's abdication – H.N. seconds the Address – the
King and Mrs Simpson – Baldwin's speech on the Abdica-
tion – H.N. reaches the age of fifty*

*A*t the beginning of the year Lady Sackville died, leaving V. Sackville-
West a small fortune, as well as legacies to her two grandsons which
enabled them to be self-supporting at Oxford. The bric-à-brac in her
house at Brighton was sold, but some of the better pieces of French
furniture were moved to Sissinghurst, and most of the silver and china
was stored in packing-cases in the loft and an upper room of the tower,
for the Nicolsons did not share Lady Sackville's taste for the more fragile
and eccentric objects of the late-eighteenth and early-nineteenth centuries,
and Sissinghurst remained sturdily Tudor within and romantic without.
Lady Sackville's death had one other consequence: it was no longer
necessary to sell Long Barn. Charles and Anne Lindbergh, who had
fled to England from the persecution of the American Press, took a lease
of the house and remained there unmolested for two happy years.

Harold Nicolson was now fully launched on his political career. He
retained some of his outside activities, such as the weekly book-review
for the 'Daily Telegraph' and the London Library Committee of which
he was to become Chairman, but most of his time was spent in the House
of Commons and its satellite drawing-rooms, and in quick dashes to and
from Leicester. The National Labour Party, like the New Party in 1931,
was still in search of an identity, and membership of it was to become
little more than an association of friends and an excuse to take an
occasional line in debate independent of the Government. Ramsay Mac-
Donald, its leader, and Malcolm, his son, had both lost their seats at the
General Election, though Baldwin allowed them to retain their Government posts, and each fought a bye-election in January which brought them
back into the House. Immediately after his return, Ramsay MacDonald
invited Harold Nicolson to become his Parliamentary Private Secretary,
a role which he turned down as tactfully as he could, since MacDonald's
loss of grip on his Party and the House would have made the position one
of some embarrassment.

It was while campaigning in northern Scotland on behalf of Malcolm
MacDonald that he heard the news of King George V's death on 20th
January. The accession of Edward VIII brought him into touch with a
new social world, since he saw much of the new King and Mrs Simpson,

*and watched their friendship build up step by step towards the crisis which
exploded in December.*

DIARY   *13th January, 1936*

Change for dinner. Foolishly I put on a down-turned collar and a
flabby tie, imagining that by this process I achieve comfort and an
A. J. Balfour look. Meet Sibyl Colefax at the Apéritif and have some
smoked salmon and a cocktail. Then on to the Phoenix Theatre for
the first night of Noel Coward's play.[1] Sibyl breaks to me the fact
that the other two members of our party are the Prince of Wales and
Mrs Simpson.

Mrs Simpson is bejewelled, eyebrow-plucked, virtuous and wise. I
was impressed by the fact that she forbade the Prince to smoke during
the *entr'acte* in the theatre itself. She is clearly out to help him. Our
supper-party at the Savoy Grill afterwards goes right enough, but I
find the Prince gazing at my tie and collar in a mood of critical abstrac-
tion—the eye of Windsor blue surrounded by jaundice. Nobody pays
any attention to him, and what is odd is that the waiters do not fuss
unduly. The Prince is extremely talkative and charming. I have a
sense that he prefers our sort of society either to the aristocrats or to
the professed highbrows or politicians. Sibyl imagines that she
is getting him into touch with Young England. I have an uneasy
feeling that Mrs Simpson, in spite of her good intentions, is getting
him out of touch with the type of person with whom he ought to
associate.

Go home pondering on all these things and a trifle sad. Why am I
sad? Because I think Sibyl is a clever old bean who ought to concentrate upon intellectual and not social guests. Because I think Mrs
Simpson is a nice woman who has flaunted suddenly into this absurd
position. Because I think the P. of W. is in a mess. And because I do
not feel at ease in such company.

DIARY   *15th January, 1936*

Albrecht Bernstorff is very outspoken about the present German
régime. He says that Hitler has got cancer of the throat and will die.
He says that the Army are waiting for the succession. He seems to
fear that if the Army use Goering as the screen, Goebbels (who is
sincerely left-wing) may turn against them. In order to prevent that,

[1] *Tonight at Eight-thirty.*

they may engineer a war against Czecho-Slovakia. He says that Goering was shot in the testicles during the 1923 Putsch, and that this has produced a psychopathic megalomania. He begs me to use all my influence to prevent us from identifying ourselves too much with modern Germany. Without us, they would not risk war; the slightest gesture on our part would be interpreted as a firm alliance. Let us keep aloof. I agree with him.

DIARY   *20th January, 1936*
                                                 Dingwall, Scotland

Eventually we get to Tain[1] and go to the little inn where we are received by a man in a kilt and given a dram. We walk across to the Town Hall, where there are the Provost, two ex-Provosts and the local dominie. A good platform. The hall is amazingly full for such a night. The gallery is packed. The Provost makes a speech, and then I talk for 45 minutes. It goes very well indeed. Then we take the old boys round to the inn and have more drams. And then off we go into the night. Twenty-five miles to Dingwall skidding and slithering. The sound of water in the mist. Then the lighted hotel and the journalists in the lounge and warmth and sandwiches.

'How is the King?' is our first question.[2] 'The 11.45 bulletin was bad. It said that His Majesty's life was moving peacefully to its close.' How strange! That little hotel at Dingwall, the journalists, the heated room, beer, whisky, tobacco, and the snow whirling over the Highlands outside. And the passing of an epoch. I think back to that evening twenty-six years ago when I was having supper with Archie Kerr at the Carlton and the waiter came and turned out the lights: 'The King is dead'.

DIARY   *23rd January, 1936*

At 2 p.m. the House meets. Prayers, and then Baldwin advances from the Bar with a message from the King signed by His Majesty's own hand. This message is read by the Speaker and then Baldwin rises to propose a vote of condolence. He speaks perfectly, with great simplicity and with great style. He refers to Kipling, whom he had been burying

[1] In the constituency of Ross and Cromarty, where Malcolm MacDonald was standing as National Labour candidate.
[2] King George V was at Sandringham, and his strength had been ebbing since 15th January. He died at five minutes before midnight on the 20th.

that morning in Westminster Abbey.[1] The end of another epoch. After him comes Attlee (pretty poor) and Archie Sinclair (not very effective). Lloyd George is supposed to have arrived this morning from Tangier, but did not show up.

At 3.20 we walk in procession to Westminster Hall. We enter by our own side-entrance. The centre of the hall is free but for a purple catafalque. Four candles and four Beefeaters draped in black. Behind a slight parapet which runs down the side of the hall are grouped on the north side the House of Lords, with Bishops on the south side and ourselves with the Speaker. The two maces glint in the light. Upon the steps are grouped members of the Court and behind them the choir of the Chapel Royal. We wait silently. At 3.50 the Duke of Norfolk, Lord Cholmondeley[2] and Billy Ormsby-Gore as First Commissioner of Works come down the steps. A great cross is carried to the entrance. Then the Princesses arrive shrouded in black and are grouped near the steps. From outside one hears the words 'Present arms!' and above the catafalque I can see the swing-doors on to Palace Yard open for a minute. I understand that the Queen[3] has come in with her sons. A hush again. Then Big Ben begins to strike four and in the intervals of these reverberations one hears the chink and grating of a gun-carriage outside.

The doors swing open again. I see something rising above the catafalque. It is the end of the coffin with the crown upon it. Six huge guardsmen with bared heads carry the coffin which slips quite easily on to the catafalque although its Royal Standard gets caught for a moment underneath it. The officer in command straightens the Standard, clicks his heels and marches off the steps which raise the catafalque. The coffin remains there, just a wreath of flowers and the crown, its diamonds winking in the candle-light. It is at that stage that I notice that something has gone wrong with the crown. The Maltese Cross at the top is missing.[4] A few very short prayers. A hymn. And then a pause while the Royal Family leave. As they pass the coffin they bow and curtsey. Then in an opposite direction the

[1] Rudyard Kipling had died at the age of 70 on 18th January. He was Baldwin's cousin.
[2] The Lord Great Chamberlain.　[3] Queen Mary.
[4] During the procession from King's Cross station to Westminster Hall the cross on top of the Imperial Crown had fallen to the pavement, from where it was immediately retrieved and pocketed by a Company Sergeant Major of the Grenadier escort.

heralds pass and process up the steps—a sudden flash of gold and scarlet against all those black and dim figures. And then we all file past two by two, some of us bowing as we pass the coffin and others not. The place is then closed—I imagine in order that they may reaffix the cross on the crown. A most terrible omen.

DIARY   28th January, 1936

The King's funeral. I stay in at K.B.W. all morning and do not hear more than the minute-guns firing dolefully in the distance. At 12 I emerge from my seclusion and go to see Betty Morrow at the Ritz. The streets are strewn thick with waste paper, which has got stamped and glutinated into the mud of the roadway. Find Betty and Anne Lindbergh much impressed by the procession, which they had watched from the Ritz. I then walk on to lunch with Emerald Cunard and stop in Grosvenor Square to celebrate the two-minutes silence which was supposed to coincide with the lowering of the coffin into the vault at St George's Chapel.

Go to see Buck De La Warr whom I find in a dressing-gown having just changed from his uniform. We discuss the future of National Labour and agree that there is none. Now that the two MacDonalds have fought [bye-elections] with the aid of the Tory Central Office, we cannot claim any independence. He says that Baldwin is really keen to maintain the semblance of a National Government and wants us to help.

DIARY   30th January, 1936

Dr Broadbent has telephoned to say that B.M.[1] cannot live through the day. Vita goes down by the 12 noon train and I promise to follow as soon as I have put off all my engagements. Reach Brighton at 2 p.m. and go to White Lodge. Go straight up to B.M.'s room and find that she has died some three minutes before, quite painlessly and without recovering consciousness. Take Vita into the other room. Rhind[2] is much upset but behaves well. The solicitor arrives and also the priest. The latter is disgusting and refuses to have a service over B.M. if she is to be cremated. She has left a pathetic little typewritten notice saying that she was to be cremated and the ashes flung into the sea. Vita is much harassed and shattered, but inwardly, I think, relieved.

---

[1] Lady Sackville.   [2] Cecil Rhind, Lady Sackville's secretary.

DIARY   5th February, 1930

Ramsay MacDonald takes his seat amid much booing on the part of the
Labour Opposition and only perfunctory cheers on our side of the
House. I receive a chit to go down and see him. He starts by talking
about his own election, about which he is delighted.[1] He then talks
about Malcolm's election, about which he is uneasy. He then asks if
will be his Parliamentary Private Secretary. I suggest that were I to do
this, it would limit my freedom of action in the House. He says that
on the other hand it would give me enormous insight into the working
of the Parliamentary machine, into the functioning of the Privy Council
Office, and into schemes like radium research and coal-product
research; apart from this it would be very useful to our own group
to have a Secretary (i.e. Whip) who would keep him in touch with
lobby opinion and enable the group as a whole to put up a continuous
and combative fight. I suggest that the group as at present constituted
is not capable of putting up such a fight. Its able men are on the front
bench; its backbenchers are not able, with the possible exception of
Denman.[2] He says that we can get younger and better men elected
that he is astonished at the amount of National Labour feeling in the
country; that we can eventually create a strong nucleus party, when
'the ball will be at our feet'. Now this is simply dealing in unreality
There is no National Labour feeling in the country; there is only
progressive conservatism. But Ramsay would sooner die than enter
into a real alliance with the Tories based on any system of fusion.

DIARY   8th February, 1930

Go down to Brighton. It is a bitter cold day with a strong east wind
I am met by Cecil Rhind and we lunch at the Metropole. We then
go to the oyster-shop of Mr English where B.M.'s ashes have been
preserved overnight. The reason for this strange procedure is that the
Press had got hold of the story, and it was feared that they would
picket the undertakers and take snapshots of us as we carried out the
urn. The latter is placed at the back of the car by Mr English. He is
anxious to come with us in the boat, but I am very firm on the point
'No, Mr English, we really should prefer to be by ourselves.' The boat

---

[1] Ramsay MacDonald had been returned as the Member for the Combined Scottish
Universities.
[2] R. D. Denman, National Labour M.P. for Leeds, Central.

is there on the shingle—a large open fishing-boat with two sailors and a petrol engine. We climb in, holding the little container in its neat brown-paper parcel. We are launched down the shingle in Homeric fashion and chug along the coast until we get opposite White Lodge. Cecil and I sit there huddled in our coats with a most inadequate rug over our knees, bending our heads from time to time as the spray lashes over us. Sun shining and an angry brown sea. 'We're two miles out', says the boatman, at which I undo the string of the parcel. The urn or container is of gun-metal, and one opens it by pressing up the lid with one's thumbs. I am terrified lest the ashes be caught by the wind and I keep the lid on. The two men stand up and take off their hats. So does Cecil. I kneel by the gunwale and spill the ashes over into the sea, saying, 'B.M., all who love you are happy that you should now be at peace. We shall remember always your beauty, your courage and your charm.' It is merely a handful of dust which slides out of the container into the waves.

DIARY   *13th February, 1936*

Go to see Anthony Eden in his room. He says that his aim is to avert another German war. To do this he is prepared to make great concessions to German appetites provided they will sign a disarmament treaty and join the League of Nations. His idea is to work for this during the next three years and then suddenly to put it before the League. I am all in favour of such a far-sighted plan.

H.N. TO V.S-W.   *18th February, 1936*
                                          House of Commons

I went to see Ramsay MacDonald. I told him I would not be his P.P.S. but would be glad to help him unofficially in any way I could. He asked me to 'drop in on him' every morning. Well, if it is only a drop, I don't mind. But I dread an orgy of vain outpourings. He really does want to make the Party into 'a living forrrrce'. Whereas, poor little thing, it is quite dead. I want it to fuse with a real National Party, and that, in the end, will be what happens. But how am I to serve King Lear and Bolingbroke at the same time? The thing cannot be done. Old Jimmy Thomas is no good anyhow. Buck and Malcolm and Kenneth [Lindsay] are the ones who count. I fear that Ramsay is a vain and slightly vindictive old man. Why is it, darling, that I who am the least combative person on earth seem always to be attached to battle-cruisers—Curzon, Tom Mosley, B.M.—but I dare say it is good for me.

H.N. TO V.S-W.   *19th February, 1936*

I gave a lunch-party. I am not a good host. I mean, I am very polite and hospitable and all that, but I forget to ask guests. Now it is very difficult to be a host without having guests. The purpose of the party was to get Sibyl [Colefax] to meet the young Members. I had engaged a room and said there were to be tulips on the table and a soufflé. But I forgot to ask people to come to the party and only realised this omission early this morning. So I telephoned wildly and managed in the end to get Macnamara[1] and Tony Rumbold.[2] I left messages with two others asking them to come. That meant six. But the other two didn't turn up. Sibyl sat with Tony on her left and Macnamara on her right. I sat with an empty place on my right hand, and on my left hand another empty place. I did not feel that this was a masterpiece of successful planning. But it went off all right.

Then I escaped to the innermost recesses of the smoking-room and read a book on Smuts for my review while the House discussed Scotch education. Baldwin came and sat down on the arm of my chair and talked, oh so pleasantly, about life and Baldwin. He has charm, that old snuffy man. He spoke about *The Land*, which is always a sure avenue to my heart.

Then I fussed about my Child Welfare Committee, and before I knew what or where I was the clock stood at 8, and I dashed out undressed to dine with Chips.[3] The Brownlows and the Weymouths there. Oh my God, how rich and powerful Lord Channon has become! There is his house in Belgrave Square next door to Prince George, Duke of Kent, and Duchess of ditto and little Prince Edward. The house is all Regency upstairs with very carefully draped curtains and Madame Récamier sofas and wall-paintings. Then the dining-room is entered through an orange lobby and discloses itself suddenly as a copy of the blue room at the Amalienburg near Munich—baroque and rococo and what-ho and oh-no-no and all that. Very fine indeed.

[1] Captain J. R. J. Macnamara, Conservative M.P. for Chelmsford.
[2] The son of Sir Horace Rumbold, H.N.'s former Ambassador in Berlin.
[3] Henry Channon. He had just been elected Conservative M.P. for Southend. He married Honor Guinness, daughter of Lord Iveagh, but of course he was not, and never became, Lord Channon.

Then back to the House of Commons in time for the division which was late. And dear old Big Ben intoning midnight as I left.

H.N. TO V.S-W.   *20th February, 1936*
                                          4 King's Bench Walk, E.C.4

My new pal Maureen Stanley[1] asked me to come round and meet her father who is just back from hob-nobbing with Hitler. Now I admire Londonderry[2] in a way, since it is fine to remain 1760 in 1936; besides, he is a real gent. But I do deeply disapprove of ex-Cabinet Ministers trotting across to Germany at this moment. It gives the impression of secret negotiations and upsets the French. But we are incorrigibly irresponsible in such things.

Anyhow, when I got in, there was a dear little woman in black sitting on the sofa, and she said to me, 'We have not met since Berlin.' I sat down beside her and chattered away all friendly, thinking meanwhile, 'Berlin? Berlin? How odd. Obviously she is English, yet I do not remember her at all. Yet there is something about her which is vaguely familiar.' While thus thinking, another woman came in and curtsied low to her and I realised it was the Duchess of York.[3] Did I show by the tremor of an eyelid that I had not recognised her from the first? I did not. I steered my conversation onwards in the same course as before but with different sails: the dear old jib of comradeship was lowered and very gently the spinnaker of 'Yes Ma'am' was hoisted in its place. I do not believe that she can have noticed the transition. She is charm personified.

DIARY   *24th February, 1936*

Party dinner downstairs. Ramsay MacDonald, J. H. Thomas, Buck De La Warr, Denman, Malcolm MacDonald and Kenneth Lindsay. Thomas talks out. He says that our group is not consulted; that there is an inner Cabinet which discuss things between themselves and only speak to Ramsay and himself later; that there was a vital telegram (I suspect some Hitler design on Locarno and the Rhineland) which was discussed by the Cabinet last night and only reached Ramsay this

[1] Lady Maureen Stanley, daughter of Lord Londonderry and wife of Oliver Stanley M.P.
[2] Secretary of State for Air, 1931–35, and leader of the British Delegation to the Geneva disarmament conference, 1932–33. He met the Nazi leaders again in 1937.
[3] By the end of the year she would be Queen Elizabeth, wife of King George VI.

morning. There is also an attempt to get Ramsay off on a mission to Australia. Moreover, Baldwin is getting deaf and will have to leave. His place will be taken by Neville Chamberlain, who will then have triumphed over the bullying of his father and the subtle hostility of his brother Austen. Neville is more favourable to MacDonald and Thomas than is Baldwin, and their position will then improve. Meanwhile we must remain in being; not change our name; increase and improve our organization; and link up with the left groups in the House. Malcolm evidently rather wants his father to go off to Australia. I confine my remarks to one of extreme unpleasantness. I point out that a Party which has a meeting of all its members and can only fill a dinner-table with seven, six of whom have Government jobs, cannot be called an ill-used party.[1] Back to the House, where Winston makes a splendid speech on defence.

H.N. TO V.S-W.   *26th February, 1936*
                                              4 King's Bench Walk, E.C.4

Jim Thomas really minds the death of the King. He says he has lost one of his dearest friends. And what makes it so odd is that this is true. The King adored him and he always spent a fortnight at Balmoral every year. I asked him whether he enjoyed that. 'Well, it's a bloody dull 'ouse, of course, and I told the King so. 'E was regretting that the young Princes did not like the place. So I said, "I don't wonder at that, Sir. It's a bloody dull 'ouse." And the King said, "Why?" and I said "because I never get a fourth for bridge"—and after that I got it.'

He talked on and on about the King with real affection, and I thought it all so strange, this railwayman[2] and that dead monarch sitting together upon a bench at Balmoral looking at the Dee. ' "J.H.", 'e says to me one day, "did I ever tell you that my grandmother asked me not to call myself George but Albert? I found a letter on my dressing-table at Windsor saying that it was her dearest wish that I

[1] Ramsay MacDonald was Lord President; J. H. Thomas, Secretary of State for the Colonies; Malcolm MacDonald, Secretary of State for Dominion Affairs; Lord De La Warr, Parliamentary Secretary to the Board of Education; Kenneth Lindsay, Civil Lord of the Admiralty; and Richard Denman, the second Church Estates Commissioner. H.N. himself was the seventh.

[2] J. H. Thomas began work in 1883 at the age of nine. He was at first an engine-cleaner, then fireman and engine-driver. He became General Secretary of the National Union of Railwaymen in 1918.

should change my name. But I said I wouldn't. I had been christened George, and George I would remain." 'E was like that, you know, 'arold, not afraid of people, if you know what I mean. And now 'ere we 'ave this little obstinate man with 'is Mrs Simpson. Hit won't do, 'arold, I tell you that straight. I know the people of this country. I *know* them. They 'ate 'aving no family life at Court.'

H.N. TO V.S-W.   *5th March, 1936*
                                               4 King's Bench Walk, E.C.4

I telephoned to dear old Mrs Woods at the Weald Post Office and asked her to use her influence in the village to see that Charles and Anne Lindbergh were not bothered at Long Barn. She was very flattered at being roped in as an ally. 'No, sir, we shall not stare at the poor people.'

I lunched with Grandi at the Italian Embassy.[1] Well! Well! He does his job excellently and it cannot be easy for him to manoeuvre between Musso on one side and the great British public on the other. What I fear is that the Abyssinians will now collapse and make a separate peace with Italy, leaving out the League completely. What fools we should all look then!

DIARY   *7th March, 1936*

Morning in Leicester. Then down to Sissinghurst. Hitler denounces Locarno and enters the Rhineland zone.

Almost a year earlier Hitler had given secret orders to his Generals to prepare for the military occupation of the Rhineland. He disregarded their advice that France and Britain were bound to react firmly, and that Germany was not yet strong enough to stand up to a determined counter-stroke. His nerve held. He argued that the League's failure to halt Mussolini in Abyssinia was proof that the democracies lacked the necessary will to uphold the Covenant of the League by war: if they would or could not protect an innocent country from Italian aggression, it was unlikely that they would go to war to prevent Germany exercising sovereign rights over her own territory. So he sent his four Brigades over the Rhine bridges, with secret orders to withdraw if the French took military action to stop them.

[1] Count Dino Grandi was Italian Ambassador in London, 1932–39. He had been Italian Minister of Foreign Affairs, 1929–32.

247

Hitler was acting in violation not only of the Treaty of Versailles and the Covenant of the League, but of the Locarno Pact which Germany had freely signed. All signatories to the Pact, including Great Britain, were bound to go to the assistance of France if the Rhineland were refortified by Germany, since it would be 'an unprovoked act of aggression'. The obligation was therefore clear enough, but both France and Britain shrank from the consequences. They were impressed by Hitler's simultaneous offer of a 25-year pact between Germany, France and Belgium, to be backed by the guarantee of Great Britain and Italy, by his proposal for a demilitarized zone on both sides of the Franco-German border (though this would, of course, have wiped out the Maginot Line), but most of all by his offer to return to the League if these conditions were agreed.

Harold Nicolson's diaries and letters reveal the confused reaction of Government and Parliament to these events. He was coming more and more under the spell of Winston Churchill, who held no office at the time but used his immense influence to persuade the House that if Germany were not stopped now, it would be very much harder to stop her later. Hitler's prestige would be enormously enhanced, and with a West Wall confronting the Maginot Line, he could turn with relative security to deal one by one with the countries of Eastern Europe. Pierre Etienne Flandin, the French Foreign Minister, flew to London to implore Britain to fulfil her agreement under the Locarno Pact and stiffen French opinion by declaring herself determined to uphold the Treaties. He received from Mr Baldwin the answer that 'if there is one chance in a hundred that war might result, I cannot commit Great Britain'. In the end, nothing was done except to promise staff-talks between the Powers on Germany's western borders, and all Churchill's prophecies were fulfilled.

DIARY   *9th March, 1936*

Vita's birthday.[1] Great excitement about Hitler's coup. House crowded. Eden makes his statement at 3.40. He reads it with his hands on the box. Very calm. Promises to help if France attacked, otherwise negotiation. General mood of the House is one of fear. Anything to keep out of war.

DIARY   *10th March, 1936*

Eden is in Paris. I have a long talk with Ramsay MacDonald in the morning. The country will not stand for anything that makes for war.

[1] She was then 44.

On all sides one hears sympathy for Germany. It is all very tragic and sad.

H.N. TO V.S-W. (*Postcard*)   *10th March, 1936*
                                                    House of Commons

I am too rushed to write a letter. There is NOT going to be a war. Only humiliation and rancour.

DIARY   *11th March, 1936*

The French know that the invasion of the demilitarized zone was only decided on against the advice of the German General Staff and Foreign Office, and therefore they feel that if we show firmness we may discredit Hitler with his own people. On the other hand, if we do nothing, then finally the League and Collective Security will cease to have any meaning. All this is indisputable, but what is also indisputable is that the country will not allow us to take drastic action in what they regard as a purely French interest.

Have a talk with Eustace Percy.[1] He asks whether I see any way out. The French insist on not negotiating until Hitler has withdrawn his troops from the Rhine. And why should they? As things stand at present, they have a practical alliance with us and can block any further action. I suggest that it might be possible to internationalise the Rhineland situation by sending in some British and Italian troops as in the Saar.

H.N. TO V.S-W.   *12th March, 1936*
                                                    House of Commons

The French are not letting us off one jot or tittle of the bond. 'The Covenant of the League has been violated. Locarno has been violated. We merely ask you to fulfil your obligations under those two treaties.' We are thus faced either with repudiation of our pledged word or the risk of war. The worst of it is that in a way the French are right. We know that Hitler gambled on this coup. We know that Schacht told him it would lead to financial disaster, that Neurath told him it would create a dangerous diplomatic situation, and that the General Staff told him that if France and Great Britain acted together there would be no chance of resistance. Thus if we send an ultimatum to Germany, she ought in all reason to climb down. But then she will not climb

---

[1] He was then Minister without Portfolio with a seat in the Cabinet.

down and we shall have war. Naturally we shall win and enter Berlin. But what is the good of that? It would only mean communism in Germany and France, and that is why the Russians are so keen on it. Moreover, the people of this country absolutely refuse to have a war. We should be faced by a general strike if we even suggested such a thing. We shall therefore have to climb down ignominiously and Hitler will have scored. We must swallow this humiliation as best we may, and be prepared to become the laughing stock of Europe. I do not mind that very much. We can rebuild our shattered name. But it does mean the final end of the League and that I do mind dreadfully. Quite dreadfully.

H.N. TO V.S-W.   *17th March, 1936*
                                              4 King's Bench Walk, E.C.4

The members of the December Club gathered to greet Flandin in the House of Commons. He arrived a trifle late, extended to us an Inter-parliamentary hand, and sat down at the dining-table. A few daffodils enlivened the board and I sat bang opposite to Flandin, a stout and British-looking man with shrewd little blue eyes. There were about twenty of us present, and at first the conversation was hushed but general. Towards the end we managed to get Flandin to expound his case, which he did in a conversational tone, fixing blue eyes now on me, now on Louis Spears, now on Bob Boothby. He has got all his thoughts perfectly in the right order, and he deploys his procession of argument quite gently but firmly, like a nun escorting a crocodile of foundlings to church. The result is overwhelming.

His argument was somewhat as follows: 'I have heard it said over here that France is being "obstinate" or "difficult". I confess that in our former treatment of Germany we made some mistakes, and we ourselves have suffered for it. But ever since Locarno we have done everything we could to establish with our neighbour relations of equality and trust. Why, only the other day, the moment I read in a newspaper that Hitler had pronounced his desire for better Franco-German relations I telegraphed at once to François-Poncet[1] asking him to ascertain from the Führer what exactly he desired. Hitler informed my Ambassador on 29th February that he would send him a considered memorandum, and asked him meanwhile to make no mention of the interview. The memorandum when it arrived a week later announced

[1] The French Ambassador in Berlin, 1931–38.

the occupation of the Rhineland and the destruction of the Locarno system. France would have been well within her rights in at once occupying the demilitarized zone by force, even as you, in the Abyssinian question, sent your fleet into the Eastern Mediterranean. We refrained from any such provocative action. We decided to let the machinery of the Treaties themselves work automatically. All that seemed necessary was that the Council should meet, declare that the Treaty had been violated, and then leave it to the Powers which guaranteed that Treaty to obtain a settlement. But on reaching London I find that the British Government wish to break their word. We are not asking you to do anything more than what we did for you in the Italian dispute. We know that Hitler is bluffing and that if you remain faithful to your engagements we shall be able to obtain satisfaction. But if you break your word, then indeed the world will be shown that violence is the only political factor which counts, and Germany, as the most powerful single force on the Continent, will become the mistress of Europe. In that case France will leave the League.'

A slight gloom was thrown over the company by this discourse. I then asked Flandin whether he would agree to British troops being sent in as sentries to the Rhineland even as they were sent into the Saar. He said he would welcome them. I then asked him whether if a new zone were created under a new Treaty, he would allow the Germans to construct fortresses. He said he would not, since that would deprive France of any chance of intervening to save Austria etc. In reply to another question he said that whereas he would never criticise the British Government when in London, yet he had been wounded by their carrying on telephone conversations with Hitler behind his back.

After which he rose, grasped us all warmly by the hand and departed, leaving us like schoolboys who have been given a pi-jaw. I went to see Ramsay MacDonald in his room and told him of all this. He sighed very deeply. When I emerged from his room, I found all the lobbies and corridors buzzing with people getting signatures to various resolutions, the first to the effect that nothing would make us go to war, the second to the effect that nothing would induce us to break our word. Then Winston gathered a group together in the smoking-room and talked about funk versus national honour and our duty to generations yet unborn. I thought of my sons and my sons' sons with a wish that it was all easier and that no such thing as Germany had ever existed.

Sadly I went to get my hair cut. Miss Farman, the manicurist, talked brightly to me about her Easter holidays—should she go to Brighton again, or try some quieter place?

I dined at the Belgian Embassy. A man's party to meet Van Zeeland, the youthful Prime Minister of Belgium. The party consisted of Van Zeeland, Anthony Eden, Winston Churchill, Austen Chamberlain, Herbert Samuel, Major Attlee, Lord Snell, Archie Sinclair. We had delicious food and wine. I sat next to Winston who was in superb form. Anthony Eden, who looked haggard with exhaustion, his lovely eyes rimmed with red and puffy with sleeplessness, expounded his policy. I shall not put that down on paper because that is not what one ought to do. But it seemed to me wise and honourable and clear. We all agreed. Winston said, 'Now here we are, elder statesmen plus heads of Opposition. We could sign a manifesto this very minute pledging ourselves to an agreed policy. Yet the world outside imagines that the House of Commons and the Government are torn by dissension.' 'And so they are', said Anthony in a low, sad voice.

DIARY   17th March, 1936

To see Massigli[1] at the Savoy. He is very bitter with us and regards us as traitors. In the afternoon a meeting of the Foreign Affairs Committee in the House of Commons. It is packed. The debate is opened by Raikes[2] who urges that sanctions in any form against Germany would mean war and that the country is not prepared to fight for France. I reply by saying that we are bound morally by Locarno and that while we must restrain France from any rash demands we must never betray her. Leo Amery[3] calls this 'a powerful speech', and in fact I do believe it made some slight impression. Austen Chamberlain also speaks, and the general feeling at the end could be summed up in the words 'restraint but no betrayal'. I dine with Mary Hutchinson. Maynard Keynes and Guy Burgess[4] there. Keynes is very defeatist.

[1] René Massigli, Assistant Director of the Political Section of the French Ministry of Foreign Affairs, who had come over with Flandin to London.
[2] Victor Raikes, Conservative M.P. for South-East Essex.
[3] L. S. Amery, the former Secretary of State for the Dominions, held no office at this time.
[4] Guy Burgess, who was to fly to Russia in 1951, was then working for the B.B.C.

H.N. TO V.S-W.   *22nd March, 1936*
                                              British Embassy, Brussels

Dieckhoff[1] received me in the Carlton Hotel before I left London. He was in a littered room heavy with cigarettes and the smell of carbon paper. He sat down on the sofa with that studied leisure of a man who can only give you three minutes of his time and wishes not to appear rushed. I told him that if the Germans missed this chance they were ninnies, that they must not believe all they were told regarding the pro-German feeling in this country, and that opinion would swing against them if they were unreasonable. He grinned and said that he had just telephoned to his wife and she had said that Germany must have its *Gleichberechtigung*,[2] which is the sort of thing a German wife would want to have.

I got to Brussels this morning and was taken to see the King.[3] We went inside to one of the interior *porte-cochères*, where there were red-piled carpets clamped by shining brass to the stone steps, and butlers in correct evening dress with silver chains and frequent bows. I was led across a hall into a Burgundian-looking room with 1860 portraits of Belgian kings and queens. The aide-de-camp entered and we made desultory conversation until some distant clock struck noon. Then one of the butlers entered, bowed low, and we crossed the hall again to where two large sliding doors of Brave New World appearance and great stainless steel handles barred all further progress. The A.D.C. grasped these handles and noiselessly the two doors swung apart disclosing an enormous room with a table at the end of it and a young officer seated alone at the table.

The A.D.C. said 'Monsieur Harold Nicolson, Votre Majesté', and I advanced quite gaily across the long stretch of carpet, stopped and bowed, then advanced further and grasped the young man firmly by the hand. He begged me to be seated. He is extremely handsome and very shy, and terribly pathetic. He speaks English almost perfectly. It was all rather *cercle* at first. 'You were born in Persia, were you not?' 'Yes, your Majesty, at Tehran.' 'And then you were not at Eton, I think, but at Wellington?' 'That also is true, Sir.' 'Then you entered the diplomatic service?' 'Yes, Your Majesty,

---

[1] Hans Dieckhoff, Chief of the Political Department of the German Foreign Office.
[2] 'Equal rights.'   [3] King Leopold III.

I was there for twenty years!' 'Twenty *years?*' 'Twenty-one years to be exact, Sir.' 'But you look scarcely older than I am!'

Obviously I was pleased by that remark and determined from that moment to put the young man at his ease. So I asked him about Eton and he lost his shyness and even laughed in a pathetic little way like a faint dash of sunshine through a mist of rain. I asked him whether he remembered Eddy [Sackville-West] and he said, 'Oh yes, he played the piano beautifully. He was like a little mouse.' Then he discussed what they taught at Eton and why was it that nobody made anybody work there, and wasn't it better really than cramming boys as they do in Belgium and France, and how he had loved it all, and he sighed, poor lonely young man. 'I made great friends there, but now it is so difficult', with a forlorn gesture of his hand. One felt that he half-liked being a King and half-loathed it.

DIARY   *23rd March, 1936*

The feeling in the House is terribly 'pro-German', which means afraid of war.

DIARY   *26th March, 1936*

Foreign Affairs debate. Eden makes a fine speech saying that he is not going to be the first Foreign Secretary to break his word. Dalton replies at length and in a school-master tone. Archie Sinclair comes third. While he is speaking, the Speaker sends me a message that I come next. I am terrified. My knees knock together. I gaze in agony at the packed House and at the crowded gallery. My line is that the present pro-Germanism is a wave and not a tide; that it is only a fluctuation, since when was England pro-German when Germany was weak? Is it not the line of least resistance? Let us base ourselves on certainties, namely on France. The speech is interrupted frequently and creates a blue face. Lloyd George follows and pays me a graceful compliment on my 'hereditary ability' (which *Hansard* gets as 'healthy'). In the lobbies afterwards I have an impression that my speech has been a flop. I bump into Eden who says nothing. Dine with Lady Astor, Massigli, Philip Lothian. Back to the House. Same sense of a floater having been committed.[1]

---

[1] But *The Times* next day said that his speech had made a deep impression.

DIARY   *2nd April, 1936*

I dine with Mrs Simpson to meet the King. Black tie; black waistcoat. A taxi to Bryanston Court; an apartment dwelling; a lift; butler and maid at door; drawing-room; many orchids and white arums. The guests consist of Lady Oxford, Lady Cunard, Lady Colefax, Kenneth Lindsay, the Counsellor of the U.S. Embassy at Buenos Aires plus wife, and Alexander Woollcott.[1] Mr Ernest Simpson enters bringing in the King. We all bow and curtsey. The King looks very well and gay. It is evident that Lady Cunard is incensed by the presence of Lady Colefax, and that Lady Colefax is furious that Lady Cunard should also have been asked. Lady Oxford appears astonished to find either of them at what was to have been a quite intimate party. The King passes brightly from group to group.

He asks me to tell Lindbergh to come and see him. I bow. Then dinner. I sit between an indignant Emerald [Cunard] and the wife of the U.S. Counsellor at B.A. Opposite is Woollcott, and both ends of the table go gaily enough but for continued fury on Emerald's part. The King talked to Mrs S. and Lady O. all the time. Emerald cannot bear it, and begins shouting 'Your Majesty' aloud. That doesn't go at all. Sibyl then starts telling a funny story which goes even less well. Then the women go and we sit on for hours talking to our Sovereign over the port. I must say, he is very alert and delightful. Then back to the drawing-room where Margot Oxford gets more and more sleepy, and at last at 1 a.m. the King retires.

Something snobbish in me is rather saddened by all this. Mrs Simpson is a perfectly harmless type of American, but the whole setting is slightly second-rate. I do not wonder that the Sutherlands and the Stanleys are sniffy about it all.

H.N. TO V.S-W.   *7th April, 1936*
                                        4 King's Bench Walk, E.C.4

I lunched yesterday at the Soviet Embassy. It is in a grim Victorian mansion in Kensington Palace Gardens. The door was opened by a gentleman in a soft collar and a stubby yellow moustache. I was ushered into a room of unexampled horror where I was greeted with effusion by Mr Maisky the Ambassador,[2] Mr Pavloff the Counsellor,

---

[1] The distinguished American radio-commentator and journalist, 1887–1943.
[2] He was Soviet Ambassador in London from 1932 to 1943.

Mr Vinagradoff the first secretary, and the correspondent of *Pravda*. Evidently Mr Maisky thought the time had come to collar the *Daily Telegraph*, since the luncheon consisted of Lord Camrose, the Editor of the D.T., the Foreign Editor of the D.T., and Hadji. What a foolish thing to have done to have asked us in a bunch like that! We stood in this grim ante-room while we were given corked sherry, during which time the man with a yellow moustache and a moujik's unappetising daughter carried tableware and bananas into the room beyond.

We then went into luncheon, which was held in a winter-garden, more wintery than gardeny. We began with caviare, which was all to the good. We then had a little wet dead trout. We then had chicken in slabs surrounded by a lavish display of water-cress. We then had what in nursing-homes is called 'fruit jelly'. There was vodka and red wine and white wine and curaçao. Maisky filled his glass with each separate form of liquor but never drank anything but water. Why did he do this? Was it to manifest his self-control, or to put us at our ease, or to show the lavish temperament of the commissar? I sat next to Vinagradoff who has an inferiority complex. I asked him whether he was any relation of the celebrated professor of that name.[1] 'We have in Russia', he answered, 'no genealogies.' 'Yes, but surely you must know whether a person is your uncle or not?' 'We take no interest in such matters.' What a good idea! Such a help it would be to Jessica and Piers.[2]

During the whole meal, I felt that there was something terribly familiar about it all. It was certainly not the Russia of my memory. And then suddenly I realised it was the East. They were playing at being Europeans, just as Djemal and Kemal used to play at it. They have gone oriental. The propaganda which the Ambassador tried to put across us was childish to a degree. One felt sorry for the little beast.

H.N. TO V.S-W.   *8th April, 1936*
                                              4 King's Bench Walk, E.C.4

Frederick Voigt[3] came to see me. He is as pessimistic as I am myself. He thinks a second German war is inevitable and that all we can hope for is to preserve the West. If only we, France and the Low Countries

[1] The Russian historian.
[2] Jessica and Piers St Aubyn, H.N.'s own niece and nephew.
[3] F. A. Voigt, the political author and journalist. Editor of *The Nineteenth Century and After* from 1938 to 1946.

cling shoulder to shoulder, we may be able to save this little corner of Europe. But the French have such terrible theories about 'peace being indivisible', and if we refuse to agree with those theories they will say that we are being traitors. My argument is: Peace can only be preserved by absolute certainty of intention. If Great Britain has an absolute certainty of intention regarding the League, then universal peace could be preserved. But recent events have shown that the British public will not go to war for the League. What will they go to war for? Possibly the protection of France and Belgium against Germany. We must therefore make that a definite geographical basis for our policy. It is not a question of liking or not liking the French; it is a question of the defence of London. The Channel, which used to be a protection, is now a danger: you cannot organise anti-aircraft defence upon the water; you must have a wide area of land. Thus London is defenceless except from French aerodromes: thus we must rely on France.

But how sad it is that violence in the shape of Goering and Mussolini should triumph so completely over the devices of civilization such as the League and the two western Powers.

Once the Rhineland crisis had ended in Hitler's favour, there was a pause of two years before he took his next major step, the occupation of Austria. In Britain, the search for a new foreign policy went on. The immediate issue was whether to abandon sanctions against Italy, now that the cause of Abyssinia was irretrievably lost (Mussolini's forces entered Addis Ababa on 2nd May), but the bigger problem was the degree of rearmament necessary to meet the new situation in Europe, and the extent of our commitments to France and Eastern Europe. It already seemed almost too late to recharge the batteries of the League of Nations, and when the Spanish Civil War broke out in July, the Dictators seized the chance to throw the policies of France and Great Britain into even greater disarray.

It was not a tidy period of history. Parliament was distracted by the uncertain leadership of Baldwin, by greater divisions within the parties than between them, and by unnerving domestic incidents such as the Budget leak which ended in the fall of J. H. Thomas, the second figure in the National Labour Party.

Harold Nicolson played a very active part throughout this session of Parliament. He spoke far more frequently than he had intended, because the main preoccupation of the House was with foreign affairs, his own subject. He became Vice-Chairman of the Foreign Affairs Committee on the Government side of the House. He quickly gained a reputation as a fluent debater with a flair for translating his expert knowledge into comprehensible and combative terms. And he was very much liked. He continued to write his book-reviews, and to address meetings in many parts of the country. He wrote the main policy-statement of the National Labour Party, which was published under the title 'Politics in the Train'. He contributed extensively to the Party's 'News Letter'. He found time to keep a full diary, of which the extracts quoted below form barely a tenth part of the whole. There was his constituency. There was his sparkling social life. And there was Sissinghurst.

V. Sackville-West took a benevolent interest in what was happening in London and Leicester, but she rarely visited the former and only once the latter. Her 'Joan of Arc' was published by Cobden-Sanderson on 5th June, and she had already started on 'Pepita', that remarkable biography of her grandmother and mother. The remaking of the house at Sissinghurst was now finished, but the garden continued to expand.

DIARY   *22nd April*, 1936

Lunch with Sibyl [Colefax]. Party consists of Mrs Simpson, Victor Cazalet, J. L. Garvin and Winston Churchill. Garvin, with unequalled eloquence, expounds the errors of the Government. He says that to have made an enemy of Italy is a mistake for which we shall pay heavily in after years. He contends that the Mediterranean is now untenable and that our only hope of maintaining our Empire is to have Italy as an ally. Winston, while agreeing naturally with his criticism of the Government, does not agree with the conclusions. Our communications cannot be left at the mercy of so unreliable a thing as Italian friendship. We must retain 'that command of the Mediterranean which Marlborough, my illustrious ancestor, first established'. Victor and I keep quite silent under this deluge of eloquence.

Drive back to the House with Winston. On the way he grumbles about the Budget and contends that Neville Chamberlain has been over-cautious. I say that the Government have been so weak in regard to public opinion that it is not a bad thing that N.C. should take a determinedly unpopular line. He rather agrees.

28th April, 1936
                                                           4 King's Bench Walk, E.C.4

I have been thinking a great deal about your *Joan* book.[1] I really believe it to be first-rate and that it will have a great success. Of course, you will be bothered by endless Joan cranks who will realise that the book is likely to become a standard work and will attack it on these grounds. But you will not mind that. The thing is a very brilliant piece of reconstruction upon factual rather than upon imaginative lines. I believe it will be certain of a great triumph.

I lunched alone with Robert Vansittart at his house. Van was extremely pleasant and friendly. His view is that a German hegemony in Europe means the end of the British Empire and that we have no right to buy Germany off for a generation by offering her a free hand against the Slav countries. Once she has established herself in an unassailable position she will turn round upon us and we shall be too weak to resist her. I think he is right in theory, but in practice it would be quite impossible for us to get the British people to fight Germany for the sake of the Czechs.

Darling, it is a foul world of lunatics and I get so depressed at moments. But to drown oneself in a haze of depression is a bad thing. I must be active about it all, and in truth I am doing a good deal in the way of writing articles and making speeches. I hear a rumour that I am to be elected Vice-Chairman of the Foreign Affairs Committee. If that comes off, I shall get a certain amount more influence. But keep this dark, my angel.

Tell Gwen I do not need Sanatogen at present. What I need is a feeling that we shall avoid a war. And that feeling I do not have at the moment.

5th May, 1936
                                                           4 King's Bench Walk, E.C.4

Jeremy [Hutchinson], David [Wallace], and Stuart Hampshire[2] have

---

[1] *Joan of Arc.*
[2] These three and Guy Branch shared lodgings with Ben at 7 Beaumont Street, Oxford, and together with John Pope-Hennessy and Jasper Ridley, they formed the most intellectually active group of their generation of undergraduates. David Wallace, Guy Branch and Jasper Ridley were killed in the Second World War.
(note continued overleaf)

all been arrested for shooting a policeman with their air-revolver. Ben is a trifle ashamed as he funked taking part in the game and was therefore exempted. The policeman telephoned that he had been shot, and armoured cars gathered around Beaumont Street at 1 a.m. and the house was surrounded by the whole Oxford police force. They then 'effected an entry' and the three foolish boys were dragged out of bed in their pyjamas and arrested. They are to be summoned this week. I do not quite like the idea of Ben being such an old cautious cissie as to refrain from shooting policemen with air-pistols.

Eden made such a dramatic statement yesterday. Nobody knew exactly what had happened to the Emperor [of Abyssinia], and Attlee asked a private-notice question. Eden replied at length, ending by the statement that H.M.S. *Enterprise* had been sent to take him to Palestine. 'He embarks', he added, glancing up at the clock, 'at a quarter-to-four.' It was then twenty minutes to four, and we had a sudden picture of the steaming heat of Djibouti, the untidy French officials, and that strange black family being saluted by midshipmen in white ducks and sailing away from Africa, five minutes later.

DIARY   12th May, 1936

H. G. Wells is delighted with the failure of the League, since it provides him with a perfect illustration of human muddle-headedness. He becomes more of a republican every day, and is in fact the only political thinker I know in England who seriously believes that it would be desirable or possible to abolish the monarchy in this country.

I have a long talk with Masaryk[1] regarding the position in Czecho-Slovakia, and especially regarding Henlein.[2] He is fully aware that Henlein has been corresponding with people in this country, but regards him as an amiable and possibly useful person—but he [Masaryk] is always so intent upon displaying his mastery of American slang that it is impossible really to understand what he is saying.

Jeremy Hutchinson became a leading Q.C.; Stuart Hampshire, the distinguished Professor of Philosophy; John Pope-Hennessy, head of the department of sculpture at the Victoria and Albert Museum, and the author of standard works on the Italian Renaissance. Among Nigel's contemporaries at Balliol were James Pope-Hennessy (John's younger brother), Denis Healey and Edward Heath.

[1] Jan Masaryk, Czechoslovak Minister in London, 1925–38.

[2] Konrad Henlein, leader of the Sudeten German Party in Czecho-Slovakia, which was in the secret pay of Hitler.

H.N. TO V.S-W.   *13th May, 1936*
                                            4 King's Bench Walk, E.C.4

The gentian-bed sounds very professional. I am all for gentians, but if Farley[1] is to spend all his time toying with two square yards of Delos[2] we shall not get much further. What fun we are going to have! I do so love the garden. It is a sort of still backcloth to my rattley ruttley rottley (those words are meant to convey the impression of an elderly Ford lorry bumping along a pavé road. I am a master of language) life.

DIARY   *26th May, 1936*

Alfred Douglas[3] comes for luncheon. There is little trace of his good looks left. His nose has assumed a curious beaklike shape, his mouth has twisted into shapes of nervous irritability, and his eyes, although still blue, are yellow and bloodshot. He makes nervous and twitching movements with freckled and claw-like hands. He stoops slightly and drags a leg. Yet behind this appearance of a little, cross, old gentleman flits the shape of a young man of the 'nineties, with little pathetic sunshine-flashes of the 1893 boyishness and gaiety. I had fully expected the self-pity, suspicion and implied irritability, but I had not foreseen that there would be any remnant of merriment and boyishness. Obviously the great tragedy of his life has scarred him deeply. He talked very frankly about his marriage and about his son, who is in a home at Northampton.

DIARY   *28th May, 1936*

Nancy Astor[4] is terribly indignant at the King for having invited to his first official dinner Lady Cunard and Mr and Mrs Simpson. She says that the effect in Canada and America will be deplorable. She considers Lady Cunard and Chips Channon as 'disintegrating influences', and she deplores the fact that any but the best Virginian families should

---

[1] The head-gardener at Sissinghurst until 1939.

[2] Part of the garden which was now being developed, inspired by memories of the Aegean island.

[3] Son of the Marquess of Queensbury, and the leading figure in the scandal which led to Oscar Wilde's imprisonment for homosexual practices in 1895. Douglas was born in 1870 and died in 1945. He married Olive Custance in 1902.

[4] Lady Astor was the first woman to sit in the House of Commons. She was born in Greenwood, Virginia, and was the member for Plymouth, 1919–45.

be received at Court. I stick up for both Emerald Cunard and Mrs Simpson, but I refrain from saying that, after all, every American is more or less as vulgar as any other American. Nancy Astor herself, by her vain and self-conscious behaviour in the House, cannot claim to be a model of propriety. In any case, she is determined to tell the King that although Mrs Simpson may appear at Court, she must not appear in the Court Circular. I suggest to her that any such intimation would be regarded by H.M. as a gross impertinence. She says that when the dignity of the United States and the British Empire is involved, it is her duty to make such sacrifices.

DIARY   9th June, 1936

Lunch with Sibyl Colefax. Tom and Florence Lamont[1] are there, also the Winston Churchills, Neville Chamberlain and Gerry Wellesley.[2] Winston discusses national character, observing that British people are more individualistic than any race on earth. Tom Lamont is still worried about the American debt, saying that we shall never get good relations with the United States until we at least pay something. Winston explains eloquently that this money was needed to keep the front while the United States was preparing, and that if we had cut down our efforts and merely sat in our trenches, it would have meant that when the Americans did come, they would have had to do much more fighting and would have lost many more men. Tom Lamont agrees with this, but says that a certain proportion of our loans were used to maintain the exchange and therefore for direct purposes of British trade. If we had been unable to maintain our exchange, the Americans would have taken all our export trade for themselves, and therefore at least this portion of the loan should be repaid. Neville Chamberlain,[3] during all this, looks very glum and silent.

Down to the House, which is very full after Whitsun. I go to see Ramsay MacDonald and find him in a deep state of depression. He says that he cannot bear it any more and that he is going to throw up the whole business and devote himself to literature. He says that he was just getting back his health and was able to work continuously for three hours 'without my thoughts wandering in vague rhetorical

[1] Thomas Lamont was Chairman of the Board of J. P. Morgan & Co., New York.
[2] The architect, later seventh Duke of Wellington. One of H.N.'s oldest friends.
[3] He was then Chancellor of the Exchequer.

:ircles'. Now this Thomas disaster[1] has come and he is unable to grip my thoughts any more'. I try to cheer him up, saying that he must stay until after the Coronation. I feel, however, that his mind is et on retiring from politics. I suggest to him that in any case the moment to go would be when Baldwin goes, since this would make a itting end to the 1931 experiment. He seems to take this quite seriously.

I then go into the Private Secretaries' room and am deploring to Ralph Glyn the mental and moral collapse of our leader when the loor opens and in staggers Jim Thomas. He is accompanied by his ?.P.S., the other James Thomas,[2] who has scarcely left his side during all these troubles. He looks very thin and white and is obviously on he verge of a complete collapse. He can scarcely walk or talk and :ould only put his arm round my shoulder, sobbing like a child. He hen staggered into Ramsay's room and I fear that the little good I was able to do the latter must have been undone.

H.N. TO V.S-W. *11th June, 1936*
4 King's Bench Walk, E.C.4

The great event of the day was Sibyl's dinner-party. Poor Sibyl—I had a feeling that it was her swan-song, but nonetheless it was a very :riumphant one.[3] I arrived to find everything lit up lovely and the guests assembling—the Stanleys, the Brownlows, the Lamonts, the Rubinsteins, Bruce Lockhart, the Vansittarts, Buck De La Warr. I sat between Lady Stanley and Lady Brownlow. There were two :ables. Our young King and Mrs Simpson sat at one and the Lamonts sat at the other. Then when the women went, we all sat at the King's :able, and I talked to Stanley about the Navy. Afterwards I took the King downstairs. He said that the Lindbergh dinner had been a great success. Anne had been rather shy at first, 'but with my well-known charm I put her at ease and liked her very much'.

Then we returned to the party. Rubinstein[4] started to play Chopin.

[1] J. H. Thomas had been found guilty by a Tribunal appointed by Parliament of revealing Budget secrets to Sir Alfred Butt M.P., who was also found guilty of profiting by this knowledge.
[2] Conservative M.P. for Hereford since 1931, and Parliamentary Private Secretary to J. H. Thomas since 1932. He became First Lord of the Admiralty in Churchill's post-war Government.
[3] Her husband, Sir Arthur Colefax, an eminent K.C., had died on 19th February, and she was selling Argyll House.
[4] Arthur Rubinstein, the Polish pianist, then aged 48.

More people drifted in—the Winston Churchills, Madame de Polignac, Daisy Fellowes, Noel Coward, the Kenneth Clarks.[1] Madame de Polignac sat herself down near the piano to listen to Rubinstein. I have seldom seen a woman sit so firmly: there was determination in every line of her bum. It was by then 12.30 and Rubinstein (who is sadly losing his looks) had played his third piece. It was quite clear that he was about to embark upon a fourth, and in fact Madame de Polignac was tapping her foot impatiently at the delay. Then the King advanced across the room: 'We enjoyed that very much, Mr Rubinstein.' So that was that, and he then said goodnight all round. But by then more guests had arrived, Gerald Berners and others, and by the time H.M. had got half through the guests, we at our end by the piano had forgotten his presence, and Noel Coward started to strum a jazz tune and to croon slightly. At which the King immediately resumed His Royal Seat. And I much fear that Rubinstein and Madame de Polignac must have thought us a race of barbarians. Nonetheless it was very welcome when Noel sang *Mad Dogs and Englishmen* and *No, Mrs Worthington*, and even if Madame de Polignac failed to smile throughout, the rest of us relaxed somewhat. So that when, an hour later, the King really did leave us, the party had gone with a swing.

I was glad for Sibyl's sake, since I fear it is her last party in that charming house and never has it looked so lovely. She managed it well. She only made one mistake, and that was to sit on the floor with Diana Cooper to give a sense of informality and youth to the occasion. But Sibyl, poor sweet, is not good at young *abandon*. She looked incongruous on the floor, as if someone had laid an inkstand there.

But the important part, my dearest, is the following. I talked to Kenneth Clark. After December there will be a vacancy as Honorary Attaché in the National Gallery. Would Ben take it? After a year he could look about for a paid job. Clark suggests that in the interval he ought to go to Munich, Dresden, Berlin etc., and really master the galleries of Europe. What do you think about all this?[2]

---

[1] Kenneth Clark was Director of the National Gallery, 1934–45.
[2] The proposal matured. It was the first step in Ben's career as an art-historian.

H.N. TO V.S-W.   *12th June, 1936*
                                    4 King's Bench Walk, E.C.4

I lunched with dear wee Maggie [Greville] in Charles Street. 'Oh, dear Harold, how you do drop your old friends.' Whereupon I shook hands warmly with Lady Willingdon[1] who did not recognise me or know me from Adam. I sat next to a German woman who tried a little Nazi propaganda. Poor wretch, she did not know that she had a tiger lurking beside her. 'Do you know my country, sir?' she said. 'Yes, I have often visited Germany.' 'Have you been there recently, since our movement?' 'No, except for an hour at Munich, I have not visited Germany since 1930.' 'Oh, but you should come now. You would find it all so changed.' 'Yes, I should find all my old friends either in prison, or exiled, or murdered.' At which she gasped like a fish. Maggie saw that something awful had happened and shouted down the table to find out what it was. In a slow strong voice I repeated my remark. As Ribbentrop's Number Two was there on Maggie's right, it was all to the good. Old Willingdon, bless his heart, backed me up.

Rather pleased with this little entertainment, I went down to the House and poor Jim Thomas did his stuff.[2] He read it standing just behind me. I felt that the tears would drop on to my head. It was less terrible as a statement than I had expected. When he had finished, he walked out, turned, and bowed to the Speaker. Then his P.P.S. took him by the arm and he left the House for ever. Poor man. Poor man. The House murmured a sort of low sound of sympathy for him.

DIARY   *18th June, 1936*

The House is packed for the debate on sanctions, and it is obvious during question-time that the Opposition are out for battle. Anthony Eden adopts a tone of regretful frankness which, however, rather suggests an embarrassed apology. He is followed by Arthur Greenwood,[3] who makes a second-rate platform speech, which includes a comic poem.[4] It is so bad that one feels actually uncomfortable at the thought that so many foreign diplomatists should be in the Gallery.

[1] The wife of the first Marquess of Willingdon, Viceroy of India, 1931-36.
[2] His resignation speech.
[3] Vice-Chairman of the Parliamentary Labour Party, and Minister of Health, 1929-31.
[4] By A. P. Herbert.

He is followed by Lloyd George, who speaks from the Opposition box. His is a brilliant performance, ending up with a very amusing elaboration on the theme of leadership. He makes one serious mistake by saying that the British people will not fight for Austria. In so saying he obviously abandons the League of Nations point of view.

DIARY   23rd June, 1936

I dash out for dinner at the Savoy Grill with Duff Cooper and Winston. Bob Boothby and Albrecht Bernstorff[1] are there. The latter is extremely courageous and outspoken in his hatred of the Nazis, and I fear he is not long for this world. Winston asks him how we are to prevent a second German war, and he answers with the words, 'Overwhelming encirclement'.

Have a talk with Anthony Eden afterwards. He was grateful for my speech,[2] in which I had defended him warmly. He agrees that the feeling of the House is quite different from what it was on Thursday, and thinks that gradually the country will resign itself to the raising of sanctions.

H.N. TO V.S-W.   28th June, 1936
                                                          Cliveden, Taplow

Cliveden, I admit, is looking superb. I have never seen such *ikkibani*[3] in my life. Great groups of delphiniums and tuberoses, great bowers of oleander. The party also is lavish and enormous. The Speaker[4] and his wife, Sam Hoare and his wife, Arthur Salter, Lothian, Rob Bernays, Leonie Leslie,[5] the Cranbornes, Ancaster, the Vincent Masseys, Bob Brand and some rather forlorn Americans plus endless Astor progeny and hangers-on.

Oh my sweet, how glad I am that we are not so rich. I simply do not want a house like this where nothing is really yours, but belongs to servants and gardeners. There is a ghastly unreality about it all. Its beauty is purely scenic. I enjoy seeing it. But to own it, to live here, would be like living on the stage of the Scala theatre in Milan.

---

[1] The German diplomatist. He was forced to retire from the German Foreign Service in 1933 and was murdered by the Nazis in 1945.

[2] In the House of Commons earlier that day, on an Opposition vote of censure against the Government for abandoning sanctions against Italy.

[3] Japanese term for 'flower-arrangement', incorporated into the Nicolson vocabulary.

[4] Captain E. A. FitzRoy, M.P.   [5] Winston Churchill's aunt.

H.N. TO V.S-W. *1st July, 1936*
House of Commons

When the House of Commons get to know me better, they will know that I am a good old tea-cup really. I do not mind that for the moment they should suppose that I am dynamite disguised as vitriol. I cannot maintain the position I have now acquired. There will be a slump. It is from the bottom of that inevitable slump that I shall build up my authority. My present reputation is fallacious and transitory. It is a March flower. But I shall bloom all right in June. And my roots are deep in energy and faith. You know that—and that is where you help me. Politics I can look after myself. But my faith (in life and integrity and human nature) is something which you alone really understand, and to replenish which I rush to you like a petrol-filling station. We never talk about it, since we never talk about the really vital links between us. But that is where you help.

H.N. TO V.S-W. *2nd July, 1936*
4 King's Bench Walk, E.C.4

Ramsay is now quite a different man. He is acting as Prime Minister during Baldwin's absence,[1] and he feels himself important and useful again. The old flash has come back into his eye and the new whine has gone out of his voice. He stood there talking about my having the ball at my feet if I only kicked it hard enough. I said that it was not a ball but a Carter's Little Liver Pill, which is not by any means an easy thing to kick.

DIARY *4th July, 1936*
Paris

Go to the Quai d'Orsay to see the Under Secretary, Pierre Viénot. He questions me closely about opinion in the House. I warn him that opinion is fluctuating, but that gradually it is swinging away from the belief in friendship with Germany towards the realisation that Germany is the eventual peril. I warn him that it is impossible to forecast how this realisation will interpret itself in terms of policy. I tell him that the French are making a great mistake if they think they will ever be able to get a reliable agreement with us providing for the encirclement of Germany. The most that they can ever hope for is that we should defend our own interests on the Maginot Line, plus our communica-

[1] Baldwin had retired to the country for a few days on the plea of overwork.

tions in the Mediterranean. Viénot says that he agrees entirely with this, that he considers the Laval policy to have been disastrous, and that their one desire is to obtain 'certainty of defence'. He also tells me that he expects Germany to make some declaration shortly regarding the independence of Austria. He anticipates that such a declaration will be taken up in France and England as a sign of Hitler's pacific intentions, whereas in fact it will merely mean that the latter wishes to remove the only obstacle to an agreement with Italy. It is quite evident that the French foresee and dread a German-Italian alliance with the possibility of Japan as a third party. If that occurs, we shall have no alternative whatsoever but to remake the policy of encirclement by an agreement with Russia. He agrees with me that the situation is, as Duff Cooper said, far more dangerous than in 1914.

DIARY
6th July, 1936
Midland Hotel, Derby

In the hotel I found Lloyd George. He had been making a speech in the Drill Hall, and was flushed with pleasure and excitement at the plaudits of the mob. It is almost inconceivable that he should be the same man that I lunched with four years ago at Churt[1] before his operation. He was absolutely bursting with vitality, roguishness, wit and reminiscences. He began by attacking Baldwin for his cowardice and lack of leadership, stating that Austen Chamberlain had told him that when he was Foreign Secretary, he could never get a decision out of Stanley Baldwin who, in fact, never even listened to his arguments. Ll.G. said that this showed his difference from Asquith. The latter always listened, always gave a decision, and never let one down. He was the ideal peacetime Prime Minister, and about the worst War Minister there could be, 'since' (and at this Ll.G. popped a shrewd little eye sideways at me) 'he hated war'.

This led him on to a discussion of Cabinets in general and to a eulogy of his own War Cabinet in the great days. 'Never', he said, 'have I had such great minds around me—Smuts, Balfour, Bonar Law (the public have never realised the creative common-sense of Bonar Law— he was the most constructive objector that I have ever known), and Curzon. Curzon was not perhaps a great man, but he was a supreme Civil Servant. Compared to these men, the front benches of today are pigmies.' He then proceeded, much to my surprise, to give imitations

[1] See pp. 122-3.

of Curzon, Arthur Balfour, and, strangely enough, Attlee. I had never imagined that Ll.G. was a mimic, but he managed in some curious fashion to recall to me the physical presence of Balfour and Curzon, and to render Attlee with a vividness that was unsurpassed.

At last I insisted on leaving and said something about his being the same man as he was in 1917. 'Yes', he flashed at me, 'Gladstone went on till he was 85, and so shall I.'[1]

DIARY   *13th July, 1936*

Ramsay is busy with papers regarding the Coronation. He talks about the problem of the King's appalling obstinacy and the unfortunate Court Circulars in which Mrs Simpson's name figures as a guest. He says it is making a bad effect on the country. He contends that nobody would mind about her were she a widow. The only person who can remedy the situation is Mrs Simpson herself, but there is always the possibility that her head (which as a head is not exceptional) may become turned.

DIARY   *16th July, 1936*

Foreign Affairs Committee. Winston argues from the premise, which everyone accepts, that our main duty is to defend the British Empire and the Rhine frontier. This in itself, in modern conditions, is 'a gigantic task'. What we have got to ask ourselves is whether that task would in the end be facilitated by our telling Germany that she could take what she liked in the East. Were we to say this, Germany, within the course of a single year, would become dominant from Hamburg to the Black Sea, and we should be faced by a confederacy such as had never been seen since Napoleon.

The general impression left was that the majority of the National Party are at heart anti-League and anti-Russian, and that what they would really like would be a firm agreement with Germany and possibly Italy by which we could purchase peace at the expense of the smaller states. This purely selfish policy would to my mind make an Anglo-German war quite certain within twenty years. I do not believe that this mood will last, and I think that eventually Winston will be able to get a solid block for his League of restricted commitments and unlimited liabilities.

[1] At the date of this conversation, Lloyd George was 73. He died in 1945, but he never held office again.

Towards the end of July, just before the House rose for the summer recess, the Spanish Civil War broke out. The Italians, soon followed by the Germans, gave Franco arms and men, while the French felt morally bound to support the quasi-Communist Government. In Britain the conflict was seen as a symbol of Europe's ideological divisions, Christianity versus atheism, fascism versus communism. On the whole, Conservatives tended to sympathise with Franco; on the whole, the Opposition sided with his opponents. But there were many deviations from this line, and many genuine neutrals, of whom Harold Nicolson would have counted himself one, since the brutality and political aims of each side were equally obnoxious to him. Officially the policy of Britain, France, Germany, Italy and Russia was non-intervention: in fact, only the first kept the agreement.

During the summer recess Harold Nicolson began to write 'Helen's Tower', a life of his uncle, the first Marquess of Dufferin and Ava, Viceroy of India, couched in the form of an 'indirect autobiography', or a Proustian approach to biography, which he had conceived in February 1934 but greatly altered in execution. To gather material for this book he went to Northern Ireland and Scotland. In September he went on holiday to Austria, Venice and the French Riviera. In October the shadow of the new session of Parliament was cast ahead.

DIARY   *8th August, 1936*

The Spanish situation is hell. Philip Noel-Baker writes to *The Times* pretending that the Madrid Government is one which should command the support of all democratic liberals. In fact, of course, it is a mere Kerensky Government at the mercy of an armed proletariat. On the other hand, Franco and his Moors are no better. The Germans are fussing outside Barcelona with their pocket-battleships 'making themselves felt'. It is serious in that it emphasises the division of Europe between left and right. Which way do we go? The pro-German and anti-Russian tendencies of the Tories will be fortified and increased.

DIARY   *28th August, 1936*

Up to London. *Daily Telegraph.* Lunch at the Travellers with James Pope-Hennessy. A charming young man. Talk to him about Niggs. He will succeed, if anyone can, in rendering N. a little more human and elegant. Back to Sissinghurst. Bathe. A lovely hot day. Do my reviews.

H.N. TO V.S-W.   *1st September, 1936*
                                                    Clandeboye, near Belfast

This *à la recherche* business is not really much fun when the *temps* is as *perdu* as all that. It makes one feel so beastly transitory. I rode up with Basil[1] yesterday to Helen's Tower.[2] The old caretaker remembered me. 'And what', he asked, 'may you have been doing with yourself, Mr Nicolson, all these many years?' Not a very easy question to answer, but quite a fair question to ask. I climbed up the staircase and was depressed to see that the poems had faded. You will fail to understand that remark. But in the upper chamber are several dedicatory poems let into the walls in 'enlettered gold'. There is one by Browning and one by Tennyson. They used to be very legible and bright. Today they are not. At the top the view was as superb as ever. Right out to the Mull of Kintyre and the whole coast of Scotland, and then Belfast Lough on one side and Strangford Lough on the other, and all the islands and white homesteads and jewelled fields. It is very beautiful, without question, and we could see right across to the Mourne Mountains and Slieve Donard. But, as I said, it made me feel transitory.

But the question remains, what have I been doing with myself these many, many years? *J'ai vécu.* But after all, darling, it seems so odd that I should have lived so long and worked so hard (really, in the last twenty-five years I have worked harder than most people) and have nothing to show for it.

> *Ahi, fu una nota del poema eterno*
> *Quel ch'io sentiva e picciol verso or è.*[3]

Anyhow, I have consoled myself by reading Uncle Dufferin's pamphlets on Irish land tenure.

I feel as if I had been very frightened and had lost all my self-confidence and bounce. Like an old tennis-ball which has been a week in the rain.

I like Basil and Maureen[4] very much indeed.

---

[1] The fourth Marquess of Dufferin and Ava, grandson of the first Marquess. He was killed in action in 1945.
[2] The tower, after which H.N.'s book was titled, was raised in 1861 on a wooded hill near Clandeboye by the first Marquess in memory of his mother.
[3] From Carducci's *Il Canto dell' Amore* (1877).
[4] Lady Dufferin, daughter of Ernest Guinness.

DIARY   *8th September, 1936*
                                                                              Sissinghurst

The Lindberghs, Betty Morrow and Constance [Morrow] come over from Long Barn in the afternoon. Lindbergh has just returned from Berlin where he had seen much of German aviation. He has obviously been much impressed by Nazi Germany. He admires their energy, virility, spirit, organisation, architecture, planning and physique. He considers that they possess the most powerful air-force in the world, with which they could do terrible damage to any other country, and could destroy our food supplies by sinking even convoyed ships. He admits that they are a great menace but he denies that they are a menace to us. He contends that the future will see a complete separation between fascism and communism, and he believes that if Great Britain supports the decadent French and the red Russians against Germany, there will be an end to European civilisation. He does not see any real possibility of our remaining in the centre between right and left.

I point out to him that we are on this point a disunited nation, and that to go wholly red or wholly swastika would split our opinion from top to bottom. He contends that we cannot continue to remain on the fence, that the old political divisions have ceased to count, and that the severance today is between fascism and communism, and that we cannot possibly find a middle way between these two opponents. I very much fear that he is correct in this diagnosis, and that our passion for compromise will lead us to a position of isolation, internal disunity and eventual collapse. Yet I cannot bring myself to envisage any adherence either to right or to left. Isolation seems our only policy. But it is not really feasible. Never have we been faced before by so appalling a problem.

DIARY   *20th September, 1936*
                                                            Schloss St Martin, Upper Austria

The party here consists of Henry and Honor Channon,[1] Lalli Horstmann[2] and Colin Davidson.[3] They are sun-bathing when I arrive.

---

[1] Henry (later Sir Henry) Channon, Conservative M.P. for Southend since 1935. In 1933 he had married Lady Honor Guinness, daughter of the Earl of Iveagh.
[2] Wife of Frederick Horstmann, the German diplomatist. She was a leader of Berlin intellectual society and a firm opponent of the Nazis.
[3] Lt.-Col. C. K. Davidson, who was killed in action in 1943.

Harold Nicolson, 1936

It is very hot. I have some beer. At luncheon we discuss the Nazis. The Channons have fallen much under the champagne-like influence of Ribbentrop and the youthful influence of the Brunswicks, the Wittelsbachs and the House of Hesse Cassel. They had been to the Olympic Games[1] and had not been in the least disconcerted by Goering or Goebbels. They think Ribbentrop a fine man, and that we should let gallant little Germany glut her fill of the reds in the East and keep decadent France quiet while she does so. Otherwise we shall have not only reds in the West but bombs in London, Kelvedon[2] and Southend. I say that this may be expedient but that it is wrong. We represent a certain type of civilised mind, and that we are sinning against the light if we betray that type. We stand for tolerance, truth, liberty and good humour. They stand for violence, oppression, untruthfulness and bitterness. Chips [Channon] says that we have no right to criticise a form of Government or thought in another country. I reply, 'Homo sum, humanum nihil . . .'[3] apart from which I love Germany and hate to see all that is worst in the German character being exploited at the expense of all that is best. Lalli agrees.

H.N. TO V.S-W.
28th September, 1936
Villa Mauresque, Cap Ferrat

I do not believe (if I recollect aright) that you have ever been fired out of a cannon. I have. It happened last night in the station yard of Monaco. Having glanced behind him, the chauffeur turned a switch, at which the car trembled slightly and then shook and gave six loud reports like fifty horsemen of the Apocalypse. It then sprang into the air, cleared the barrier, hurtled sideways past a tram, and flung itself with reckless abandon up the hill by Château Mallet. The moon on my left hung over a silent sea and seemed to swing rapidly westwards as the earth flew below us. Snorting furiously with great raucous snorts, the car crashed through Beaulieu and on to the corniche road. Other humbler cars going in the same direction flashed past my window with a woof as if they were in fact going in the opposite direction. And then we came to the curves. Round we went, the chauffeur leaning out sideways to fling his weight on the inside, in and out, round and

---

[1] Held in Berlin in August 1936.
[2] Kelvedon Hall, the Channons' country-house in Essex.
[3] *Homo sum; humani nil a me alienum puto.* 'I am a man; I count nothing human indifferent to me.' Terence.

round. The precipices, the tunnels, the rock-arches, the great caverns cut above the sea, roared back at us. I thought of you and Ben and Nigel and my poor widowed mother and my little sister. I know I ought to have said, 'Please do not go so fast: *j'ai une petite flébite.*' But I have got Scotch and Ulster blood in my veins. I clenched my teeth. I clung on in grim terror, and suddenly there were the lights of Ville-franche swinging round to the right as if someone were swinging them at the end of a string, and with a scrunch of brakes and a rattle of gravel we crashed into the drive and actually stopped at the front door. Staggering slightly, I entered the white hall, and there were Willy[1] and his nephew[2] and Osbert Sitwell.

DIARY   *5th October, 1936*

Dine with Bernard Berenson[3] at Lady Horner's house. He is very interesting about London in the 'nineties. He used to dine regularly alone with Oscar Wilde. He said that when alone with him the mask of affectation gradually (but only gradually) dropped off. But in public he posed deliberately. Mrs Berenson says that having met him five nights in succession, he said to her, 'Now you have exhausted my repertory. I had only five subjects of conversation prepared and have run out. I shall have to give you one of the former ones. Which would you like?' They said they would like the one on evolution. So he gave them the one on evolution. Berenson asks whether there are any conversationalists of my generation. I am bound to say that there are not. Not that I know of. We have no time.

DIARY   *6th October, 1936*

One of the last Argyll House parties,[4] and the candles flicker a little sadly. H. G. Wells, Rebecca West, Aldous and Maria Huxley, the Berensons, Arthur Salter, Kenneth Clark, and Rob Bernays. Talk to Wells about Spain. He is so intent on finding something quite different to say about it that he might have been talking of dear little Austria.

Later on, when the elders have gone, Rob, Sibyl, Arthur and I have a sad conversation about Wallis Simpson and the King. There is a fine old row on because Mrs Simpson went to Balmoral with her friends

[1] Somerset Maugham.   [2] Robin Maugham, now Lord Maugham.
[3] The great American art-historian. He was then aged 71.
[4] Lady Colefax had sold the house to Lord Crewe.

the Rogers[1] and appeared in the Court Circular. What was worse was that the King drove to meet her at Aberdeen station and drove her back himself. This has shocked the Scotch and British bourgeoisie.[2] The scandal papers, such as *Cavalcade*, have given great publicity to the event. Sibyl says that at any rate up till last July there was no indiscretion at all, and that Wallis seemed really to understand the responsibility of her position. But since the *Nahlin*[3] things have gone more recklessly. There is the new house in Regent's Park. There is that Balmoral episode. Rob thinks that the thing is really serious and will shake the foundations of monarchy. I feel sad about it, since I like Wallis Simpson. The King resents the suggestion that Wallis is not as good as anyone else or that he must confine his friends and guests to those whose names look well in the Court Circular. Nor will he be so disloyal as to cut out Mrs Simpson from the Circular when she comes to stay. But there is seething criticism which may develop into actual discontent.

The House of Commons reassembled on 29th October, and Harold Nicolson was chosen to second the Address in reply to the King's Speech. The occasion, which should have been a triumphant one for him, ended in a small disaster and the loss of any immediate chance of Government office. The session was at first dominated by the situation in Spain, and later by the unprecedented crisis of King Edward VIII's abdication. Like everyone else in public life, Harold Nicolson had long been aware that a constitutional time-bomb was ticking beneath the throne. Unlike most others, his friendship with the King and Mrs Simpson had enabled him to watch the unfolding of the drama.

The main dates should be recalled. On 20th October, the Prime Minister, Stanley Baldwin, first told the King of the Cabinet's anxiety regarding his friendship with Mrs Simpson, and hinted that Mrs Simpson's approaching divorce might bring matters to a head unless the King were able to reassure them. The divorce went through on 27th October. On 16th November Baldwin saw the King for the second time, and was

[1] Katherine and Herman Rogers, in whose villa near Cannes Mrs Simpson stayed when she left England shortly before the King's abdication.

[2] Because the King had refused an invitation from the Lord Provost of Aberdeen to perform a civic function, pleading 'a prior engagement'.

[3] The yacht in which the King, accompanied by Mrs Simpson and, for part of the way, by the Duff Coopers, had cruised in the Mediterranean during August and September of this year.

much more blunt: he told him that the country would not tolerate a marriage between the Sovereign and a divorced woman. The King replied that in that case he was 'prepared to go', as he firmly intended to marry Mrs Simpson as soon as her divorce decree became absolute. Various permutations were considered, such as a morganatic marriage, but these delicate negotiations were overtaken by the Press breaking silence. On 1st December the Bishop of Bradford publicly criticised the King for neglecting his Christian duties. Although he did not mention Mrs Simpson, this speech was widely reported, and on the 3rd the national newspapers came out with full reports of the crisis that had arisen between the King and his Ministers. Mrs Simpson left the country for the South of France the same evening, and on the 8th issued a statement from Cannes saying that she was willing 'to withdraw forthwith from a situation that has been rendered both unhappy and intolerable'. The King replied to her privately that he would follow her to the ends of the earth, whatever she did, and informed Baldwin that he saw no way out of the difficulty other than by abdication. On the 9th the Cabinet agreed to accept this solution, since they had by then decided that a morganatic marriage was out of the question. The next morning, 10th December, the King signed the Instrument of Abdication, and Baldwin, in presenting it to the House of Commons, gave a masterly exposition of the chain of incidents that had led up to it. The Abdication Bill was rushed through all its stages in both Houses the next day, and the ex-King broadcast to the nation that night, acclaiming his brother and successor, the Duke of York, as King George VI. At 2 a.m. on December 12th, as Duke of Windsor, he embarked at Portsmouth on H.M.S. 'Fury', eventually to rejoin and marry Mrs Simpson.

DIARY   28th October, 1936

Dine with Sibyl Colefax for the last of many hundred meals in Argyll House. The party consists of the Winston Churchills, Duff Coopers, Somerset Maugham, the Mountbattens,[1] Philip Sassoon, Arthur Rubinstein, Desmond MacCarthy and others. I sit between an American woman and the Duchess of Rutland. I discuss with the latter the great Simpson question. Mrs Simpson has now obtained her divorce, and there are very serious rumours that the King will make her Duchess of Edinburgh and marry. The point is whether he

[1] Lord Louis Mountbatten was then aged 36. He was working in the Naval Air Division of the Admiralty.

is so infatuated as to insist on her becoming Queen or whether the marriage will be purely morganatic. The Duchess of Rutland is very sensible about the whole thing, and does not believe that he would do anything so foolish. Nonetheless I gather from other people that there is considerable danger.

DIARY   *29th October, 1936*

David Margesson summons me to his room. Will I second the Address on Tuesday? Hell! Hell! Miss Horsbrugh[1] is to move it. We gather together gloomily in the downstairs smoking-room and discuss our misery. It is worse for her as she has to wear evening dress and feels that unless she is calm and brilliant she will be letting down the women of England. But it is unpleasant for both of us.

H.N. TO V.S-W.   *4th November, 1936*
                                    4 King's Bench Walk, E.C.4

I woke up with a sinking feeling, and at 12 I went to the opening of Parliament. It is a fine sight. The King looked like a boy of eighteen and did it well. He referred to the 'Ammurican Government', and ended, 'And moy the blessing of Almoighty God rest upon your deliberoitions'.

I lunched at a snack-bar and got into my uniform.[2] I joined Miss Horsbrugh in the Chief Whip's room and we were conducted to seats exactly behind the Prime Minister and Ramsay MacDonald. The Speaker then read the Speech and called upon Miss Horsbrugh. She delivered her little piece quite beautifully, in a slow voice and without a tremor. She was very warmly applauded.

The Speaker then called on me. I had been told to follow the precedents, and the precedents prescribe that one must allude to one's constituency and then mention previous holders of the seat who have won distinction. That made it essential for me to mention Ramsay. I knew that this might not go down very well, so I prefaced it by saying, 'My constituency, which maybe in a moment of blindness, refrained from electing the Right Honourable Member for Epping[3]....' Winston, at this, flashed out, 'They also refrained from electing the

---

[1] Florence (later Baroness) Horsbrugh, Conservative M.P. for Dundee, 1931–45. Minister of Education, 1951–54. She was the first woman to move the Address.
[2] H.N. wore the uniform of the Diplomatic Corps to second the Address.
[3] Winston Churchill.

Right Honourable Member for the Scottish Universities[1].' The Labour Party let forth a hoot of triumph and thereby broke the solemnity which is supposed to reign on these occasions. Thus it became increasingly awkward when I passed on to my eulogy of Ramsay. They yelled. They hooted. Our people shouted, 'Order! Order!' On I went, heaping on Ramsay's head, which was exactly below me and bowed in acute misery, the compliments which I had prepared. Will Thorne,[2] who is a decent old boy, tried to quieten his companions by shouting out, 'This is not controversial!' but the clamour did not die down until I had finished my bit about Ramsay and passed on to the rest of my speech.

DIARY   7th November, 1936

Many Press-cuttings come in which suggest to me that my speech on the Address was really more of a floater than I had imagined. It is most unfortunate, as I gather that they really did mean to give me a job in the Government when the reshuffle comes in the Spring and I may now lose the chance for ever. Three minutes of blindness and a ruined career! But I do not seriously believe this, although I could kick myself for having exaggerated the Ramsay part. I could easily have fulfilled the requirements of loyalty and courage by a fleeting reference which would not have provoked the outburst it did. Everybody was so embarrassed by the outburst that they ignored the rest of the speech which in itself was good enough. The general impression is not that I was brave and noble, but that I was silly and tactless. I feel depressed about this, and there is no use pretending that I do not. An ache inside me like tooth-ache.

DIARY   12th November, 1936

Debate on Defence. We have to abandon our Foreign Affairs Committee as Winston is to make a great speech. He does. His style is more considered and slower than usual, but he drives his points home like a sledge-hammer. We adjourn rather shaken to Ramsay's room expecting to hear the bombs dropping at any moment. The usual dull drab discussion of Party affairs. Then into the House to hear Baldwin reply. He speaks slowly and with evident physical effort. At one moment he loses his notes. It is all very well done, but he has a poor case. One of the Whips whispers to me, 'This will take three

[1] Ramsay MacDonald.   [2] The Labour M.P. for West Ham since 1906.

months energy out of him', and by the end of his speech his voice and thought limp as if he were a tired walker on a long road. The House realises that the dear old man has come to the end of his vitality.

DIARY   *15th November, 1936*

In the afternoon we go over to Swift's, where Anthony Eden is staying. Prince and Princess Bismarck are also there. Bismarck amuses me by saying that our fear of German air-attacks is somewhat exaggerated, 'since you see what little harm they have done in Madrid'. He is a soft ass. Have a long talk with Anthony Eden. He considers that the international situation has much improved recently, and is not in the least disturbed by Germany's repudiation of the International Rivers Clauses of the Treaty of Versailles.[1] He says that his great fear is the present drift of Europe into two opposing blocks of fascists and communists and of pro-League and anti-League. He considers this wholly unnecessary and he jotted down some notes for a speech he is to make this week in Warwick. We find it very difficult to find an expression for the 'fascist', 'aggressive', 'militarist' or 'dissatisfied' states. We can do nothing better than 'Contented versus Discontented'.

DIARY   *18th November, 1936*

Have a long talk with Sibyl [Colefax]. She had been spending last Sunday down at Fort Belvedere with nobody else there beyond a new naval equerry and Mrs Simpson. She had a heart-to-heart talk with the latter and found her really miserable. All sorts of people had come to her reminding her of her duty and begging her to leave the country. 'They do not understand,' she said, 'that if I did so, the King would come after me regardless of anything. They would then get their scandal in a far worse form than they are getting it now.' Sibyl then asked her whether the King had ever suggested marriage. She seemed surprised, and said, 'Of course not'. Sibyl then suggested that it would be a good thing if certain Cabinet Ministers were told of this, and were in a position to deny the story of an impending marriage. Mrs Simpson readily agreed to this and authorised Sibyl to see Neville Chamberlain. Unfortunately Neville is ill in bed with gout; but Sibyl was able to send him a message through Mrs Chamberlain and

[1] On 15th November, Hitler announced that he was resuming national control of the German sections of the Rhine, Danube, Elbe, Oder and Kiel Canal, internationalised by the Treaty of Versailles.

derived the distinct impression that Baldwin had been told by the King that he was determined to marry Mrs Simpson after the Coronation. Sibyl agrees with me that Mrs Simpson is perfectly straightforward and well-intentioned, and that it is quite possible for the King to have spoken to Baldwin before raising the matter with Wallis herself. Sibyl wants me to do something more about it: but I refuse, mainly because I dislike gossip but also because I remember how badly everybody burned their fingers over Mrs Fitzherbert.[1]

DIARY   26th November, 1936

Diana De La Warr tells me that she had had a long talk with her uncle Lord Willingdon on the subject of Mrs Simpson. He had told her that if the King insisted on marrying, the Privy Council would assemble in force and insist that he either abdicates or they resign. I do not understand the situation. On the one hand you have Mrs Simpson saying that he has never suggested marriage, and on the other hand you have the Privy Council organised for revolt. I believe quite sincerely that the King has proposed to Mr Baldwin and has not proposed to Wallis. I feel unhappy about the whole thing. I got such a sensible letter from her today.

DIARY   30th November, 1936

I go to see Ramsay MacDonald.[2] He talks to me in deep sorrow about the King. 'That man', he says, 'has done more harm to his country than any man in history.' It seems that the Cabinet are determined that he shall abdicate. So are the Privy Council. But he imagines that the country, the great warm heart of the people, are with him. I do not think so. The upper classes mind her being an American more than they mind her being divorced. The lower classes do not mind her being an American but loathe the idea that she has had two husbands already. Ramsay is miserable about it. The effect on America, the effect on Canada, the effect on our prestige. And in particular he is furious because Malcolm [MacDonald] had almost succeeded in persuading de Valera to accept Edward VIII as King, and now the whole thing is torn to pieces.

[1] In 1785 the Prince of Wales, later Prince Regent and George IV, had secretly married Mrs Fitzherbert, who had already been twice widowed.
[2] He was still Lord President of the Council, with a seat in the Cabinet.

H.N. TO V.S-W.   *2nd December, 1936*
                                                  House of Commons

How I hate and detest women. I don't mind women like you who
do their job. But I loathe women who do nothing and get jealous of
the man's job. I am feeling very anti-feminist tonight. I *loathe* women.
The only thing that will make them behave decently is to give them
complete equality and no privileges. Now they claim equality *plus*
privileges. They let us down: they let us down all the time. They are
beasts. I loathe them. How I wish I could talk to you about it. You
are so wise about these things. When I get into a state of rage such as
I am now, I always long for you, just as when I am unhappy or ill.
When I get puzzled or angry or frightened, I want your old shaggy
wisdom and your love.[1]

DIARY   *3rd December, 1936*

The storm breaks. A fine leading-article in the *Telegraph* and a confused muddled jumble in *The Times*. I suspect that when Geoffrey
Dawson[2] sees a vital crisis he writes the leader himself, and the result
is an amalgam of tortuous and pompous nothings. The other papers
write in sorrow rather than in anger.

Down to the House. That note or feeling of expectancy which is
unmistakable hangs over our dear old aquarium. Baldwin rises to
answer some unimportant questions, and is received with cheers from
every part of the House. Members crowd in as question-time draws
to its end and the galleries and gangways are packed. Attlee gets up
to ask whether the P.M. has anything to tell us. Baldwin rises in a
hush of stillness so marked and so immovable that the House suddenly
looks like a print of itself, row upon row of immovable faces. He looks
ill and profoundly sad. He says that no constitutional crisis 'has yet'
arisen.

I dash off without dinner to Islington. There I find the Rev. Paxton
much disturbed at the King crisis. The streets flame with posters,
'King and Mrs Simpson'. I give my address on biography in the
chapel. At the end Paxton asked them to sing the National Anthem
'as a hymn'. They all stand up and there are no protests, but only
about ten people out of 400 join in the singing. Poor Paxton is much

---

[1] This outburst was unconnected with the Abdication crisis.
[2] Editor of *The Times*, 1912–19 and 1923–41.

upset. 'I never dreamt', he said afterwards, 'that I should live to see the day when my congregation refused to sing *God Save the King.*'

I do not find people angry with Mrs Simpson. But I do find a deep and enraged fury against the King himself. In eight months he has destroyed the great structure of popularity which he had raised.

The Cabinet meet all day. I gather that Attlee and Sinclair have both refused to form alternative governments and that the King will be forced to abdicate. The Duke of York will call himself 'King George VI', which indeed he is. We are all staggered with shame and distress. I never dreamt it would come to this.

H.N. TO V.S-W.   *7th December, 1936*
                                            House of Commons

You will be wanting to hear the news, so I will write tonight instead of waiting till tomorrow morning. All is settled for the King's abdication, but Baldwin has given the King 'a few more days' to think it over. In the House today, Winston (whose line is, 'let the King choose his girl') suffered an utter defeat. He almost lost his head, and he certainly lost his command of the House. It was terribly dramatic.

First we had Baldwin—slow and measured. Then Winston rose to ask a supplementary question. He failed to do it in the right form and was twice called to order by the Speaker. He hesitated and waved his spectacles vaguely in the air. 'Sit down!' they shouted. He waved his spectacles again and then collapsed. It was almost painful. And then old George Lambert[1] got up and said, 'Does the Prime Minister realise the deep sympathy which is felt for him in all sections of the House?' At which there was a wild burst of applause.

Oliver Baldwin came to see me this morning. He told me that his father and the King walked round and round the garden at Fort Belvedere discussing the business, and then returned to the library having agreed that H.M. must abdicate. Stanley Baldwin was feeling exhausted. He asked for a whisky-and-soda. The bell was rung: the footman came: the drink was produced. S.B. raised his glass and said (rather foolishly to my mind), 'Well, Sir, whatever happens, my Mrs and I wish you happiness from the depths of our souls.' At which the King burst into floods of tears. Then S.B. himself began to cry. What

---

[1] Liberal-National M.P. for South Molton. He was then aged 71, and had been Chairman of the Liberal Parliamentary Party in 1919.

a strange conversation-piece, those two blubbering together on a sofa!

DIARY   *9th December, 1936*

Luncheon at the House for Ramsay MacDonald. Lindbergh and Thomas Inskip.[1] Lindbergh is shy and his head wobbles slightly at first, but then he gets on to aviation and starts saying, 'See here, sir, it's this way in so far as I can figure it', and his head stops wobbling. Inskip takes notes in a tiny pocket-book. Ramsay is inane. We talk of the Oxford bye-election, and he turns to Lindbergh. 'Now mark my words', he says, 'that Professor Lindbergh is no good at all—I know him—no good at all.' 'Lindemann?[2]' I suggest. 'Of course', Ramsay asserts, with a cursing gesture, as when one has missed a putt at golf. 'Of course I meant Linderbergh.' He is completely gaga.

Lindbergh tells us that there is no known defence against air attack. For the first time in warfare 'all fortification is useless'. There only remain deterrents. We must exploit our deterrents in terms of night-bombers at 30,000 feet guided only by the stars. He and Inskip get off into technicalities, and I observe that Inskip ceases to regard L. as an interesting person to meet at luncheon, and regards him (as he is) as a person whom he wants to talk to again. It is a successful luncheon and for once I feel that I have done some real good.

Get back to find Jim [Lees-Milne] awake and furious at rumours that the King is to abdicate. I say that it is true and that I think it is the only solution. He says, 'Goodnight, regicide', and turns away in rage.

H.N. TO V.S-W.   *9th December, 1936*
                                               House of Commons

I forget whether I told you of Emerald's [Cunard] great betrayal? She came to Maggie Greville and said, 'Maggie darling, do tell me about this Mrs Simpson—I have only just met her.'[3] That has torn Emerald for me. I would not believe the story if I had not heard it at first hand.

What is so tragic is that now the people have got over the first sentimental shock, they *want* the King to abdicate. I mean opinion in the House is now almost wholly anti-King. 'If he can first betray his

---

[1] Minister of Defence, 1936-39.
[2] F. A. Lindemann, later Lord Cherwell, scientific adviser to Winston Churchill.
[3] She had been a close friend of Mrs Simpson during the last few years.

duty and then betray the woman he loves, there is no good in the man.' Thus although he may keep his throne if he 'renounces' Mrs Simpson, he will have lost the respect of his subjects.

Winston collapsed utterly in the House yesterday. Bob Boothby was so funny about it. 'I knew', he said, 'that Winston was going to do something dreadful. I had been staying the weekend with him. He was silent and restless and glancing into corners. Now when a dog does that, you know that he is about to be sick on the carpet. It is the same with Winston. He managed to hold it for three days, and then comes up to the House and is sick right across the floor.' Which is literally true. He has undone in five minutes the patient reconstruction work of two years.[1]

Two things emerge, I think. First the supremacy of Baldwin. A leading Labour man said to me yesterday, 'Thank God we have S.B. at the top. No other man in England could have coped with this.' And, secondly, how unanimous the House really is in times of crisis. There has been no hysteria and no party politics. One really feels that at such moments the House is a Council of State. What a *solid* people we are under all our sentimentality!

DIARY   *10th December, 1936*

Pick up Robert Birley[2] at the Club and take him to lunch with Margerie.[3] The latter is very bright. We discuss German propaganda. I point out that the Germans appeal to the adolescent whereas the French appeal to the adult. Birley points out that this is all very true, but that the adolescent at Charterhouse seldom goes abroad again and that his whole impressions of Europe are derived from that trip to Germany which he took in his last year at school and which was neatly arranged for him by Herr Goebbels. We are all impressed by this, and Margerie suggests adolescent visits to French public schools. They are to work it out together.

I take Birley back with me to the House. We walk through Westminster Hall. At the door we run into Pollock.[4] I introduce my old

---

[1] Churchill had pleaded for delay, to give the King time to think over his decision. There were shouts of 'Sit down!' and he left the Chamber with an expression of thunder on his face.

[2] Headmaster of Charterhouse, 1935-47; Headmaster of Eton, 1949-64.

[3] Roland de Margerie, First Secretary at the French Embassy, 1933-39.

[4] Bertram Pollock, Headmaster of Wellington College, 1893-1910; Bishop of Norwich, 1910-42. He was aged 73 in 1936.

master to the new master. They are suitably impressed. Pollock as an old Carthusian is pleased to meet Birley. Birley is also pleased to meet Pollock. We then go on to the lobby which buzzes like a hive. I say farewell to Birley and enter the Chamber. The Speaker enters, and we proceed to pray for 'Our Sovereign Lord King Edward'.

The House is crowded and rather nervous and noisy. As questions proceed, the galleries fill up in a double row and people begin to sit on the gangways. I am glad to have got my front row of the stalls so early. The Prime Minister comes in, pushing past the encumbered knees of his colleagues, and finds his place. He has a box with him, and on sitting down, at once discovers that he has lost the key. He probes and rummages for a bit and then finds the key. He unlocks the box, extracts some sheets of paper with the royal monogram in red, and with it some flimsy notes of his own, more squalid than a young Labour candidate would dare to produce at a Wapping bye-election. He arranges these sheets of bromo carefully, and rather proudly, on the box in front of him. Questions proceed. There is one to Sam Hoare. He advances pompously to the box and places a file of Admiralty papers on the top of Baldwin's notes. He answers his question, then raises his Admiralty notes, which sends Baldwin's bromo fluttering to the floor. The old man collects them hurriedly and the next minute seizes his red-monographed sheets, walks firmly to the Bar, turns round, bows, and advances to the Chair. He stops and bows again. 'A message from the King', he shouts, 'signed by His Majesty's own hand.' He then hands the papers to the Speaker.

The latter rises and reads out the message of Abdication in a quavering voice. The feeling that at any moment he may break down from emotion increases our own emotion. I have never known in any assemblage such accumulation of pity and terror.

The Prime Minister then rises. He tells the whole story. He has a blue handkerchief in the breast-pocket of his tail-coat. The 'Hear, Hears!' echo solemnly like Amens. His papers are in a confused state owing to Sam Hoare and he hesitates somewhat. He confuses dates and turns to Simon, 'It was a Monday, was it not, the 27th?' The artifice of such asides is so effective that one imagines it to be deliberate. There is no moment when he overstates emotion or indulges in oratory. There is intense silence broken only by the reporters in the gallery scuttling away to telephone the speech paragraph by paragraph. I suppose that in after-centuries men will read the words of that speech and exclaim, 'What an opportunity wasted!' They will never know the tragic force of its simplicity. 'I said to the King ...' 'The King told me ...' It was Sophoclean and almost unbearable. Attlee felt this. When it was over he asked that the sitting might be adjourned till 6 p.m. We file out broken in body and soul, conscious that we have heard the best speech that we shall ever hear in our lives. There was no question of applause. It was the silence of Gettysburg.

I went off to the library to sign some letters. On leaving it, I bumped straight into Baldwin in the corridor. It was impossible not to say something. I murmured a few kind words. He took me by the arm.

'You are very kind,' he said, 'but what did you really think of it?' I detected in him that intoxication that comes to a man, even a tired man, after a triumphant success.

'It was superb,' I answered. 'I regretted only that Hitler, Mussolini and Lord Beaverbrook had not been in the Peers Gallery.'

'Yes', he said, 'it was a success. I know it. It was almost wholly unprepared. I had a success, my dear Nicolson, at the moment I most needed it. *Now is the time to go.*'

I made no answer.

Then he got on to Winston. He said, 'Do you know, my dear Nicolson, I think Winston is the most suspicious man I know. Just now I said that the King had said to me, "Let this be settled between you and me alone. I don't want outside interference." I meant to indicate by that the reasons why I had not made it a Cabinet question from the start. But Winston thought it was a thrust aimed at him, and has been at my Private Secretary within the last five minutes. What can one do with a man like that?'

I suggested that Winston had put himself in a false position. The P.M. flung up his hand. 'We are all in false positions!'

No man has ever dominated the House as he dominated it tonight, and he knows it.

Incidentally, Duff [Cooper] told me a story. Last night, after the Cabinet meeting in the House, the Ministers drifted into their dining-room. Ramsay arrived late looking like King Lear. 'Hallo', said Baldwin. 'You look pretty glum!' 'Yes', said Ramsay, 'my body is here but my soul is elsewhere.' 'Well, I hope,' Baldwin answered, 'that it's not at Cannes.' To do J.R.M. justice, he laughed at this.

11th December, 1936

Round to the House in the morning. The King's Abdication Bill is rushed through second reading, committee stage, report stage and third reading before luncheon. The only opposition are some republican speeches by the I.L.P. on the lines, 'The spell is broken. Why try to weave it afresh?' There is also some contention that the Monarchy is a class business, which draws an impassioned speech from Austen Chamberlain.

I am in the middle of my steak-and-kidney pie when the jigger jigs[1] Black Rod. I nip out and join the tail of the procession. The Commission is read. Then the Clerk rises: 'King's Abdication Bill.' *'Le Roi le Veult'*, echoes the other Clerk. Thus ends the reign of King Edward VIII. Back to my steak-and-kidney pie. Down to Sissinghurst.

DIARY *15th December, 1936*

Ramsay MacDonald insists on my dining with him. In the end we all go and dine with De La Warr. Ramsay says that it has been suggested to him that he should become Earl of Lossiemouth and go to the Upper House. He refused to do anything of the sort. But he declares that after the Coronation he will resign from the Cabinet and become an ordinary member. This fills Buck [De La Warr] and me with blank horror, since we shall never get ahead with our group so long as the old man is with us.

V.S-W. TO H.N. *31st December, 1936*
Sissinghurst

The year ends with the fulfilled planting of the yews on the front of Sissinghurst. I am so glad you said it didn't bore you to hear what was going on at Sissinghurst. I sometimes feel that you are so closely in touch with much more important things, that my small activities must seem insignificant.

And, oh darling, I've got another activity in view: three tiny Hebridean islands for sale, advertised in the *Daily Telegraph* today. 600 acres in all. 'Very early lambs. Cliffs of columnar basalt. Wonderful caves. Probably the largest bird-colony in the British Isles. Two-roomed cottage.' Do you wonder, I have written to the agents for

[1] The electric annunciator, which indicates to M.P.s in the public rooms of the House of Commons what is proceeding in the Chamber.

full particulars and photographs. So far as I can make out from the map, they are about thirteen miles from the northernmost point of Skye. They cost only £1,750.[1]

Oh, Hadji, while I was writing this, I turned on the wireless for the 6 o'clock news, and it suddenly said that you had left for Uganda this afternoon. It made it seem so awfully real. I could hardly bear it.

DIARY   *31st December, 1936*

So ends a full and historic year. I have been well and happy. So has my darling. She has written her book on St Joan and started on *Pepita*. B.M. has died and our financial troubles are over. Ben has left after a successful career at Oxford and enters the National Gallery on 4th January. Niggs is developing quickly. Mummy has been well and happy. Sissinghurst is developing splendidly. A happy year, a useful year, but clouded by menace upon the Continent. I reach the age of fifty. That is a deep sorrow to me. I should not mind so much. But I have dispersed my energies in life, done too many different things, and have no sense of reaching any harbour. I am still very promising and shall continue to be so until the day of my death. But what enjoyment and what interest I have derived from my experience! I suppose that I am too volatile and fluid. But few people can have extracted such happiness from fluidity, and when I look back upon my life, it is as gay as an Alpine meadow patinated with the stars of varied flowers. Would I feel happier if I had stuck to a single crop of lucerne or clover? NO.

---

[1] These were the Shiant Islands. Until 1935 they had belonged to Compton Mackenzie. In that year he sold them to a Colonel Macdonald of Skye, who had intended to breed race-horses on them, but soon realised that they were far too precipitous and difficult of access. They were bought, not by V.S-W., but by her younger son, in whose ownership they still remain.

Sissinghurst: the tower seen from the entrance arch

1937

H.N.'s ten-weeks journey to East Africa as a member of a Commission on African education – Uganda, Kenya and Khartoum – a party at Buckingham Palace – the Coronation – Neville Chamberlain succeeds Baldwin as Prime Minister – the garden at Sissinghurst expands – H.N.'s chivalrous mission to Evreux for the Duchess of Windsor – H.N.'s speeches on Foreign Affairs – his close association with Churchill – breakfast with Lord Baldwin – H.N. on his reputation in politics

Harold Nicolson saw in the New Year in the train between Paris and Dijon, on the first lap of his journey to East Africa. He was a member of a Government Commission sent out to report on African education, and particularly on the affairs of Makerere College, Uganda. The Chairman of the Commission was Lord De La Warr, the Parliamentary Under Secretary of State for the Colonies, who was accompanied by his wife Diana, and among the other members of the Commission were Robert Bernays M.P. and Dr Murray, the head of Exeter University. They were away for ten weeks, and visited Uganda, Tanganyika, Kenya and the Sudan.

He kept a very extensive diary throughout this journey, and at regular intervals posted copies of it to V. Sackville-West instead of his daily letter. Only a very small part of it is here reproduced, because so much was concerned with the details of evidence given before the Commission, all of which was summarised in the eventual Report. The passages selected indicate his attitude towards the country, its peoples, and British colonial administration, which he was seeing for the first time at close quarters. His reaction could have been foreseen: it was a mixture of liberal intent and aristocratic disdain. He confessed that he 'loathed the dark races' but felt acutely sorry for them; he had little in common with the junior and middle ranks of the British Colonial civil servants, but was impressed by 'the good they are doing to the natives'. He enjoyed, as always, the excitement of a new experience and startling scenery. He worked extremely hard on mastering the problems of native education, and was without doubt the leading intellectual force behind the Commission's Report. But except in detail, it presented no new view of British responsibilities, and the tour left no permanent mark on Harold Nicolson's political outlook, except to confirm his life-long belief that true civilization existed nowhere outside the inner circles of certain West European capital cities.

DIARY
23rd January, 1937
Ujiji, Tanganyika

Drive in a procession to Ujiji, the big native centre where Stanley met Livingstone.[1] We go direct to the spot where this famous meeting took place. An old man is brought up in a net and deposited upon the spot—marked as it now is by a monument, the old mango tree having died—and is given an ebony and silver walking-stick by H.E.[2] The reason for this is that as a boy he was Livingstone's servant. We ask him about Livingstone. He raises bleared eyes to us and fumbles in his purple toga, producing a stained piece of paper. It is only a news-cutting from some African paper saying that he (Jumbee Heri) is the sole survivor among Livingstone's servants. We can get no more out of him, and he is put back in his grass net and hoiked on to a pole and carried off swaying slightly and grasping his stick between the meshes of his net.

We then go to the Boma where there is a reception of Chiefs and H.E. makes a speech. We then visit the native school where there is a triumphal arch with a cardboard Union Jack. They sing *God Save the King*. We then visit a White Fathers' Mission School, where it pours and pours with rain on the corrugated iron roof, making all speeches and addresses inaudible. We then return to Kigoma. The natives in this part are far less sophisticated than in Uganda. They are almost completely naked, and lean on spears while they stare at us in respectful amazement.

DIARY
8th February, 1937
Kampala, Uganda

Get up at dawn, the freshest dawn I have ever felt outside of Switzerland. Great miles of dew and early sunshine. We motor to Nakuru[3] aerodrome. The famous flamingo lake is quite near and we fly over it. It looks at first as if it had been edged in a coral necklace, but as we swooped down, the necklace dissolved into a million pelicans flying in wedges. Below us the lake, with this screen of pink flamingoes flying across it, and through them the wake of a vast hippopotamus. And around us plain and mountain in the early light. Probably the

---

[1] In October 1871. David Livingstone died in Africa on 1st May 1873.
[2] Sir Harold MacMichael, Governor of Tanganyika Territory, 1934–37.
[3] In Kenya.

loveliest thing I have seen. We then turn west and after an hour we leave the Rift Valley and drop down to Lake Victoria. Kisumu is below us and then Jinja again, and we land at Entebbe at 10.30, having accomplished a two-day journey in two hours.

DIARY

11th February, 1937
Entebbe, Uganda

We dine with one of the heads of Makerere College. It is not a successful dinner. He is a bachelor and lives in a little bungalow which is hot and dark. He has invited to meet us the prettiest woman in Kampala whose brain is non-existent. She chirps like a canary and makes it impossible for us to talk about the College. Dinner goes well enough, as Rob [Bernays] and I keep the conversation going by serving lobs to each other across the net. But after dinner we go into his ghastly little sitting-room with the faded photographs of college groups each surmounted by some cricket or football cap. Moreover, he has collected local curios in the shape of drums, spears, shields, musical instruments, hatchets, knobkerries and ivory carving. In order to show his enlightenment and modernity he turns on a series of comic dialogues on the gramophone. These dialogues consist of recitations in pantomime metre making fun of the public school and colonial spirit. The old jokes regarding Poonah and pukkha punkhas and the outposts of Empire mingle with similar jokes about the 'varsity and the Oxford accent. We find this profoundly depressing and sit there with our faces buried in our hands.

On returning to the hotel, Rob and I discuss why these comic recitations should have filled us with such gloom. We agree that it was (a) because we wanted to talk shop and were annoyed at being faced by a smart dinner-party; (b) because it is depressing to see elderly people repudiating their own standards; our host was the perfect type of the second-rate school and the second-rate Oxford college; for him to enjoy hearing these things mocked is as ungainly as a clergyman telling a dirty story; (c) because we only enjoy humour when it is related to the facts of life. What amuses me is the contrast between the real and the fantastic. I am not amused by the fantastic in itself. I never laugh at the improbable. If I am to enjoy the fantastic it must be an aberration of recognisable fact. The fantasy woven by these gramophone comedians around the public school and University spirit was not based on recognisable fact. It was as unreal and as unintelligent as those caricatures in the *Tatler* representing leading attendants at the Football Association Dinner in terms of people with large heads and little puppet bodies and legs.

DIARY   *12th February, 1937*
                                                                Entebbe, Uganda

We visit the Gayaza High School for Girls. It is all very false to my mind, and ramshackle. The headmistress is uncertain and perturbed. To all our questions she answers, 'Well, it is difficult to say.' The art school is not bad. The children have some sense of colour and design. Moreover they are not encouraged to imitate Kensington drawings but do Gauguins out of their heads. But this will leave them as soon as they lose their first fine careless rapture. We attend some of the classes, which are not very impressive. The mistress has strips of brown paper on which are printed simple instructions such as 'Go to the door', 'Point to the flowers'. She holds these strips against her body facing the class and with the printed side hidden. She faces the class with a brave bright smile: 'Ready, children?' and then with a rapid gesture, as if she were putting on a lifebelt, she turns the printed side towards the class. A forest of horrid pink hands are raised in response. The printed words were 'Shut the door', but I did not observe them. I observed only extreme embarrassment on the part of the class. This embarrassment was caused by the fact that I was leaning against the door which rendered it difficult to shut. But it was a feeble school, nonetheless, and we were glad to leave.

DIARY   *22nd February, 1937*
                                                                Khartoum

Gordon's old servant, who happened to have gone off on the day before the dervishes entered and thus escaped alive, took us to the place where Gordon was murdered.[1] He says that there is no doubt at all that he was murdered on the steps. He showed us exactly how the present steps and the original steps differ from each other. He says that the picture *The Death of General Gordon* is almost wholly accurate. He added that they did not find Gordon at first, not because he was hiding, since he was in the dining-room, but because they were chasing Coptic clerks in the garden, murdering them and making them squeal.

[1] General Charles George Gordon was besieged in Khartoum by the Mahdi from 13th March, 1884 until the capture of the town on 26th January 1885.

Then they came to the Palace itself. Gordon came out from the dining-room on to the verandah and shouted to the Sudanese guard below in very bad Arabic, 'Kill them! Kill them!' He was leaning over the rail of the balcony shouting, 'Hit them! Hit them!' when a dervish flung a spear which made him spin round and stand for a moment on the top of the stairs before he toppled down. Then they cut off his head and almost cut him to pieces. The remains 'were thrown into the river at the place where the soldiers used to wash', i.e. opposite the Palace gate. The old man was not in the least gaga and became quite excited in explaining it all. But he had small sense of proportion and seemed more anxious to explain to us that there were three lavatories on each floor of the Old Palace than to tell us the details of Gordon's death. He said that although he did not witness the scene, he had obtained full details the next day from someone who had. I expect that this is the most authentic account that can be derived.

Harold Nicolson flew back to England on 7th March, followed by a stream of protests from V. Sackville-West (who was on a tour of Algeria with Mrs St Aubyn) that he did not take the P. & O. ship. There was a safe and happy reunion between them at Sissinghurst a few days later. Parliament was already in session, dominated by the Spanish Civil War, but Harold Nicolson's main preoccupation was with the preparation of the Commission's Report on East African education and with a survey of the colonial problem which was to be published under the auspices of a Chatham House committee of which he was Chairman. He resumed regular broadcasting, continued his book-reviews for the 'Daily Telegraph' and his articles for the Paris 'Figaro', became a member of the League of Nations Union Executive Committee, and spoke very frequently on literary and political subjects in many parts of the country. As a weekend backcloth to this extremely active life, he continued to write 'Helen's Tower' while V. Sackville-West finished 'Pepita'. For the moment he played a smaller part in the House of Commons, and though his affection for it never wavered, there are signs of his awareness that his growing reputation in politics had suffered a temporary check. On 12th May King George VI was crowned, and a fortnight later Neville Chamberlain succeeded Stanley Baldwin as Prime Minister.

17th March, 1937

Proceedings in the House are delayed by speeches on the death of Austen Chamberlain.[1] The Prime Minister makes an adequate oration but rather spoils it by introducing at the end a somewhat unsuccessful play on the phrase 'Who Goes Home?' Attlee follows with a very nice little speech, and is succeeded by Archie Sinclair who for once is short and to the point. Then old Lloyd George gets up and makes one of the most effective speeches I have heard. For whereas the other funeral orations might have been written in *The Times* second article, Lloyd George's speech could only have taken place in the Chamber itself. He reminded us of that famous day on which Austen made his maiden speech[2] and when Gladstone congratulated Joseph Chamberlain on his son. This was the only occasion when Joseph Chamberlain is known to have shown emotion, and it was most effective as told by Lloyd George, since he pointed his pince-nez at the place in the House where the protagonists of that sentimental drama were sitting at the time. The younger members felt that they had been carried back through Lloyd George to Gladstone away to the battlers of the Reform Bill and the administration of the Duke of Wellington.

I go back to K.B.W. and put on my knee-breeches and my silk stockings. I then realise that it was foolish of me not to have ordered a car to take me to the Palace, not so much for the going-in as for the coming-out. It is quite possible, without undue shame, to arrive at Buckingham Palace in a taxi although one's taxi-driver (in an orgy of democracy) insists on throwing his cigarette down upon the red carpet of the steps; but it is difficult when the outer hall is filled with Beefeaters, Gentlemen-at-Arms and Royal Watermen to dash past duchesses in their tiaras and to say to someone (who, for all one knows, may be the Lord Chamberlain or the Master of the Horse), 'Please, do you think I could get a taxi?'

Anyhow, I arrive punctually at 8.20. In the inner hall I observe a stout and stocky figure in conversation with a slim and stockinged figure and see that it is Mr Baldwin talking to David Cecil while they are waiting for their respective wives. I then go upstairs a little alarmed by the fact that upon each fourth step stands a footman dressed in scarlet and gold epaulettes and powdered about the hair. I then enter the first drawing-room: and there stand the equerries and the ladies-in-

[1] He had died suddenly in London on 16th March. [2] In April 1893.

waiting. The party consists of Baldwin, Lloyd George, Halifax, the Duke of Rutland, the Duke of Buccleuch, Ancaster, Montagu Norman, Oliver Stanley and their respective wives. After that we are all arranged in another drawing-room, and at about 8.45 the King and Queen enter silently and immediately start shaking hands all round. When they have completed this procession they walk quickly towards the doorway, and the equerries dash across to Mr Baldwin and the Duchess of Rutland, during which time the latter stand isolated and ungainly in the middle of the room. They are suddenly observed by their Majesties, and the King loops his arm round that of the Duchess of Rutland and the Queen extends her arm towards that of Mr Baldwin. They start to process towards the dining-room, but the unfortunate thing is that whereas the King knows that the dining-room is due east, Mr Baldwin imagines that it is due west. For one moment they start processing in opposite directions, and the danger of a collision is only avoided by the rapid intervention of the Lord-in-Waiting. We then file in behind, I giving my arm to Nathalie Ridley.[1] As we approach the dining-room, the band of the Grenadier Guards, which is in the room beyond, plays *God Save the King*, and there is a moment's uncertainty among the company whether they should continue their slow progress through the drawing-rooms or should stand at attention.

The dining-table is one mass of gold candelabra and scarlet tulips. Behind us the whole of the Windsor plate is massed in tiers. The dinner has been unwisely selected since we have soup, fish, quail, ham, chicken, ice and savoury. The wine, on the other hand, is excellent and the port superb. When we have finished our savoury the King rises and we all resume our procession back to the drawing-rooms. On reaching the door of the fourth drawing-room the equerries tell us to drop our ladies and to proceed onwards to a drawing-room beyond where the men sit down for coffee and cigars. The King occupies that interval in talking to Baldwin and Lloyd George, and I occupy it in discussing with David Cecil the reasons why we have been asked. He says, 'I know why I have been asked. I have been asked as a young member of the British aristocracy.' I say that I have been asked as a rising politician, and I regret to observe that David is not as convinced by this explanation as I might have wished.

1 She was born Countess Nathalie Benckendorff, daughter of the Russian Ambassador in London, and in 1911 married Jasper Ridley, Chairman of Coutts & Co, the bankers.

We then pass on into the Picture Gallery, where we are joined by the women and by the King and Queen. Maureen Stanley is at once summoned by the King and occupies most of his attention. The Queen then goes the rounds. She wears upon her face a faint smile indicative of how much she would have liked her dinner-party were it not for the fact that she was Queen of England. Nothing could exceed the charm or dignity which she displays, and I cannot help feeling what a mess poor Mrs Simpson would have made of such an occasion. It demonstrated to us more than anything else how wholly impossible that marriage would have been. The Queen teases me very charmingly about my pink face and my pink views.

Thereafter the Queen drops us a deep curtsey which is answered by all the ladies present. We then go away, and I cadge a lift from Maureen Stanley. I observe a certain slight hesitation on her part when I ask her to drive me home. She then says, 'This is very awkward. I had hoped that you would think my tiara was my own. I shall now have to disclose to you that it belongs to my mother,[1] and that I have got to drop it at Londonderry House on the way back.' We therefore drive to Londonderry House where we are greeted by the butler who puts the tiara in a small deal box. I then go back to the Stanleys' house and have some beer while we discuss the strange legend of monarchy.

DIARY   21st April, 1937

Mrs Koestler, whose husband has disappeared in Spain,[2] came to see me and sat upon the bench with tears pouring down her cheeks. The Consul at Seville has been assured that Mr Koestler is 'alive and well'. If that were so, he would certainly have communicated with his wife, and I very much fear that he has been shot. I talked to Vansittart about it, and he promised to take the matter up tomorrow and insist on a reply.

A big dinner at the French Embassy for Daladier.[3] I was not impressed by the latter's appearance: compared to our own Ministers, who were resplendent in stars and ribbons, he looked like some Iberian

---

[1] Lady Maureen Stanley, wife of Oliver Stanley, then President of the Board of Education, was the daughter of the seventh Marquess of Londonderry.

[2] Arthur Koestler, the author, was imprisoned by Franco when covering the Civil War for the *News Chronicle*.

[3] Edouard Daladier, Prime Minister of France, 1938–40.

merchant visiting the Roman Senate. It is a man's dinner and consists mainly of the Cabinet and a few Chiefs-of-Staff. I sit between Philip Sassoon and Crookshank[1] and have not only an excellent but also a most agreeable dinner. Afterwards I talk to Lord Derby[2] who is getting to look very old, but is no less amusing than in the old days.

DIARY   3rd May, 1937

I have a talk with George Lansbury. He has just got back from seeing Hitler. He said that at moments one sees in Hitler's eyes an expression of real idealism, and that suddenly this will be followed by a sullen gangster look. He said that Hitler was still obsessed by Russia. Lansbury had suggested to him that this fear was exaggerated. He replied, 'I am not frightened of an open attack; it is their subterranean mining which terrifies me.' 'Well,' replied Lansbury, 'why don't you do as we do? We allow the communists to work above ground where their foolishness is exposed. The moment you do not allow your enemies to work above ground, they will naturally begin to be subterranean.' Lansbury is convinced that Hitler was much influenced by this remark.

DIARY   4th May, 1937

Dine with Sibyl Colefax. Tom Lamont is there, and the party consists of the Winston Churchills, the Duff Coopers, the Channons and Knickerbocker.[3] Churchill takes the view that although in the early stages [of the Spanish Civil War] one might have regarded the conflict as a battle for ideas, it has now degenerated into 'a mire of blood and ashes'. Neither he nor Knickerbocker saw any solution to the problem. Meanwhile the German Press has started a campaign against *The Times* for having published an account of the bombing of Guernica.[4] Winston asks me whether I have heard anything about getting a job. I tell him that if I were offered the Foreign Office,[5] I would take it, but that I would be alarmed at taking any other job in view of the

[1] Captain Harry Crookshank, Secretary for Mines, 1935-39.
[2] The seventeenth Earl of Derby was then aged 72. He died in 1948.
[3] H. R. Knickerbocker, the American journalist, who had just returned from Spain, where he had been imprisoned by Franco for a short time.
[4] Guernica, a small town in the Basque province of Vizcaya, was totally destroyed by German aircraft on 26th April 1937. 1,654 people were killed and 889 wounded. The Germans continued to deny their responsibility, though the evidence was indisputable.
[5] He meant as a junior Minister, not, of course, as Foreign Secretary.

resentment that might be aroused. He answers, 'Don't be a fool. There will be no resentment. Everybody in the House knows that you are entitled to the job on merits.'

DIARY   *12th May, 1937*

The Coronation. I go to see Ramsay MacDonald for a moment and find him sitting in his room punching a hole in his sword-belt and looking very distinguished in a Trinity House uniform. I tell him how well he looks. 'Yes', he answers, 'when I was a visitor to a lunatic asylum I always noticed how well the worst lunatics looked.' I then go across to the Abbey and find my seat in the South Transept. Almost before we are aware of what is happening, the ceremony begins. I am not going to describe it, since the newspaper accounts are full and accurate, and since I shall write something for the *Figaro* myself. I get away about 2.40 and have an excellent lunch at the House. Nigel and I go around to the Hudsons', where there is a large supper. The carriage arrangements for the Abbey have broken down completely, and the guests were stranded until nearly 7. We then go down the river on a launch as far as Greenwich, which is beautifully floodlit. It is very cold getting back, and the party becomes slightly miserable and cross. Get to bed by 12 o'clock.

DIARY   *13th May, 1937*

Busy in the morning finishing my review which I take across to the *Daily Telegraph*. Lunch at the Beefsteak, where I have a talk with Bernard Darwin[1] and Tuppy Headlam.[2] Go to Robin Maugham's coming-of-age party where there are some fifty undergraduates, a few judges, Osbert Sitwell and myself. In the evening we go to the Albert Hall Ball. It is a fine show, and I watch Ben marching round the arena holding a canopy over Margot Oxford. He dances off with Laura.[3]

DIARY   *27th May, 1937*

I arrive at the House just in time to hear Baldwin make his last statement amid loud applause. With characteristic subtlety he does it in

[1] The golf correspondent of *The Times* for many years.
[2] The well-known Eton housemaster.
[3] Laura Bonham Carter, who married Jo Grimond, the future Liberal leader, in 1938.

the form of an answer to a question on Parliamentary salaries, so that his final words are to give us all £200 a year more. This means a lot to the Labour members and was done with Baldwin's usual consummate taste. No man has ever left in such a blaze of affection.[1]

Ramsay also has to answer a question and does it well. He is greeted with cheers. I go to see him afterwards. He had had an interview that morning with the King and had been offered and refused an Earldom. He had also seen the Queen. Poor old boy, he was pleased by the kindness they had shown him. He had told the Queen that the King had 'come on magnificently since his accession'. She had been pleased. 'And am I doing all right?' she asked. 'Oh you . . .', Ramsay had answered with a sweep taking that all for granted. The King had told him that for long periods at the Coronation ceremony he was unaware of what was happening. There is no doubt that they have entered on this task with a real religious sense.

I make Ramsay have tea with me on the terrace. There is Betty Morrow, Raymond [Mortimer], Constance [Morrow], Ben and Laura Bonham Carter. The latter looks pretty in a lovely frock and hat. She is a delightful girl.

Thereafter I work hard at the Makerere Report.

H.N. TO V.S-W.   *8th June, 1937*
                                               4 King's Bench Walk, E.C.4

You were such an angel to take trouble about my old women and it was really worthwhile.[2] I do not know whether this story of a lovely castle will affect the Labour vote. People are so odd. They might say, 'He is a humbug: he talks Labour and lives in a castle.' But they might also say, 'How splendid of him when he lives in a castle to come and worry about our little affairs.'

Anyhow, never has Sissinghurst looked more lovely or been more appreciated. I must say, Farley has made the place look like a gentleman's garden, and you with your extraordinary taste have made it look like nobody's garden but your own. I think the secret of your gardening is simply that you have the courage to abolish ugly or unsuccessful flowers. Except for those beastly red-hot pokers which you have a weakness for, there is not an ugly flower in the whole

---

[1] Baldwin was succeeded as Prime Minister by Neville Chamberlain on the next day.
[2] On 5th June fifty ladies from the West Leicester Women's Conservative Association visited Sissinghurst.

place. Then I think, *si j'ose m'exprimer ainsi*, that the design is really rather good. I mean we have got what we wanted to get—a perfect proportion between the classic and the romantic, between the element of expectation and the element of surprise. Thus the main axes are terminated in a way to satisfy expectation, yet they are in themselves so tricky that they also cause surprise. But the point of the garden will not be apparent until the hedges have grown up, especially (most important of all) the holly hedge in the flower garden. But it is lovely, lovely, lovely—and you must be pleased with your work.

DIARY   *16th June, 1937*

Dine in the Strangers' dining-room with Hugh Dalton and Albrecht Bernstorff. The latter as usual speaks very frankly. He says that we are all wrong in our estimate of the balance of power in Germany. On the one hand we exaggerate the power of the General Staff, but underestimate the intelligence of Goering, and have a rather sentimental feeling about Hitler. He himself considers Hitler a very dangerous, vindictive and sinister figure. He thinks that he is going rapidly mad, and will have to be relegated to Berchtesgaden as a sort of Grand Lama. 'The only way,' he says, 'to remove Hitler is to make him a God.' On the other hand he says that Goering is the only one of them who has learned anything since the Revolution. He is an adventurer pure and simple, and not really a stupid man. He is very fond of the pleasures of life, and has the love-hate complex of the average German bourgeois for England. If he were to be asked to shoot at Sandringham, he would become a powerful influence on our side.

I put to them my idea of a Four Power Agreement between us, Germany, Japan and the United States for the economic development of China. Obviously when these great armament programmes are completed we must have some outlet for surplus steel and factories, and it would be possible for America and ourselves to finance an enormous undertaking in terms of roads, bridges and railways by which we could open up the whole of China, thereby obtaining a vast new market. They do not think this scheme as fantastic as it sounds.

DIARY   *30th June, 1937*

Drive back from the House with Shakes Morrison.[1] He tells me that Neville Chamberlain takes a far more active interest in Foreign Affairs than Baldwin did, and that he is very opposed to a continuance of our policy of retreat. I say that no other policy is open to us, and that if we advance at all, it must be on the Geneva front.[2]

DIARY   *5th July, 1937*

The 1936 Club[3] have a dinner for Inskip.[4] He speaks very frankly about armaments and his own position. He says that it is worked out so that he becomes not Minister of Munitions so much as Vice Chairman of the Committee of Imperial Defence. He says that the first aim is to carry out our 'deficiency programme', and that it is difficult to realise how far behind we had dropped. He also says that whereas there is little recruiting difficulty in the Air Force, Navy and Territorials, the Regular Army figures are perfectly appalling. People absolutely refuse to volunteer owing to the necessity of Indian service. We ask him what is the earliest date by which our 'deficiency programme' can be completed, and he answers 1940. He adds, however, that there is some slight advantage in starting late since we are able to benefit by recent inventions. For instance, the Germans will have to scrap an enormous number of their tanks which offer no protection against modern armour-piercing bullets. Thus although in quantity we are far behind, our quality is second to none. He also says that the whole scheme is based on the assumption that we should only send five divisions overseas and that our main force should be naval and aerial.

DIARY   *9th July, 1937*

I lunch at the Spanish Embassy. It is funny to see those old drawing-rooms of Merry del Val[5] inhabited by people whom he must regard as revolutionaries. The party is already assembled and having cocktails

---

[1] W. S. Morrison, then Minister of Agriculture, subsequently Speaker of the House of Commons.

[2] i.e. by strengthening the League of Nations.

[3] A House of Commons club of Government backbenchers.

[4] Sir Thomas Inskip, Minister for the Coordination of Defence, 1936–39.

[5] Spanish Ambassador in London, 1913–31.

when the door is flung open and in comes a stout self-satisfied little man with a slim dissatisfied wife. They shake hands all round without being introduced, on the assumption that we all know who they are, just as we should recognise the Viceroy if dining at Delhi. I discover eventually that this is Del Vayo, ex-Foreign Minister of Valencia; and my opinion of that Government goes down even further. The rest of the party consists of odd M.P.s and journalists, including Lord Camrose. The bright spots arrive late in the shape of the Lithuanian and Czechoslovak Ministers, who have been attending the Non-Intervention Committee.

Jan Masaryk was very outspoken. He says that during his lifetime he has seen many foolish things and listened to many misplaced speeches, but that never has he heard anything so inept, so arrogant or so senseless as the speech which Ribbentrop[1] delivered to the Committee this morning. It appears that he lectured the whole Committee upon the inner meaning of Bolshevism, and abused the British and French representatives for not realising the danger by which they were faced. He said that had any single one of the twenty-seven representatives come to the meeting with any feeling of sympathy for the German point of view, those feelings would have been destroyed by Ribbentrop's discourse.

That same night Harold Nicolson left for France on a chivalrous mission for the Duchess of Windsor, who had married the Duke at the Château de Candé, near Tours, on 3rd June, 1937. He explained the circumstances in his diary, but so secret was the mission that he did not tell even V. Sackville-West until it was safely accomplished.

DIARY   *10th July, 1937*

The origins of this curious expedition had better be stated. Some time ago Stephen King-Hall[2] told me that when lunching at a hotel in Evreux the proprietor had shown him a piece of paper which had been written on by Mrs Simpson on her dash to the South of France in December last. She had put through a call to King Edward before starting her luncheon, and had then scribbled down on a half-sheet of notepaper the headings of what she was to say. These notes reflect

[1] Joachim von Ribbentrop had been German Ambassador in London since August 1936.

[2] Founder of the *K-H Newsletter* (1936) and of the Hansard Society (1944).

greatly to her credit, since they contain expressions such as, 'Think only of your own position and duties, and do not consider me'. This paper had been carelessly left on the table, and the proprietor had found it and locked it away in his safe.

Thinking this story over afterwards I felt that such a document should not be left in the hands of a French inn-keeper. I therefore wrote to Mrs Simpson, told her the story, and asked her whether I could do anything to help in recovering the document. She replied from Wasserleonburg[1] saying that she had missed the paper when about sixty miles from Evreux and when it was too late to turn back. She would much like to recover it, and could I do all in my power to help? I then wrote and said that I would be willing to go to Evreux, but that she must send me a letter giving me full authority to collect her property. This letter arrived on Friday morning, and at the same time I extracted from Roland de Margerie an official Embassy letter instructing 'all French authorities' to give me every assistance in their power.[2] Thus armed I left for Havre.

I rose at dawn since the saloon was unpleasantly stuffy, and watched the coast of France approaching over a swirling sea. I breakfasted in the train from Havre, and got out at Rouen. I drove to the Hotel de la Poste where I had a bath and ordered a car. I then drove *via* Pont de l'Arche and Louviers to Evreux, which I reached at 11 o'clock. I entered the courtyard of the Grand Cerf, and found my way to the office. The proprietor was sitting there with his two daughters doing accounts. I asked him if I could have a short private conversation with him. He looked somewhat startled, but led me into the visitors' writing-room.

I began by asking him if he had been proprietor of the hotel in December last and whether he remembered Mrs Simpson lunching there on her way to the South of France. He began to look uneasy, and I was afraid that he would deny all knowledge of any paper, a denial which would subsequently be difficult to retract. I therefore

---

[1] Schloss Wasserleonburg, near the Wörther See, Austria, which the Duke of Windsor had rented for the summer.

[2] The covering letter from Roland de Margerie, First Secretary of the French Embassy, began as follows: 'Cher Harold, ou plutôt, cher Don Quichotte. Dans mon enfance, les adventures d'Athos, d'Aramis, de Porthos et d'Artagnan, quittant Paris pour Londres afin d'arracher à Buckingham les ferrets de la Reine, m'empêchaient de dormir: vais-je perdre le sommeil, aussi longtemps que je ne vous saurai point revenu sain et sauf d'Evreux?'

began, 'It seems that the lady in question put through a telephone message from here to the King and that before doing so she wrote out on a piece of paper . . .' I then stopped myself and said: 'But before I go any further I must show you my credentials.' I then handed him the French Embassy letter which Roland had so skilfully worded, even introducing the phrase 'Conseiller diplomatique de sa Majesté britannique'. As I had expected, this letter somewhat alarmed him, since it indicated that if he proved difficult, I could bring in the assistance of the Mayor of Evreux and the Préfet de l'Eure. I then produced Mrs Simpson's letter of authority, which was signed 'Wallis, Duchess of Windsor'. The time taken to read these letters gave him the opportunity to collect his thoughts. I therefore went on rapidly explaining how she had left this piece of paper on the table, that she felt it was a document of great importance to herself, that she believed that it might still be in existence, and that before employing lawyers in the matter, she had asked me, as a personal friend, to come to Evreux and to enlist his assistance.

He replied: 'The general story is correct, but your details are wrong. The paper was not left on the luncheon-table; it was left beside the telephone, where I found it myself. I felt it would be unfortunate if this paper got into wrong hands, and I therefore placed it in my safe. I should, of course, have sent it back to the Duchess; but I feared that she would be very angry with her secretary for having been so careless, and that to return it to her would be unfair to him.[1] Now, however, I shall be delighted to hand it over.' He then left me, and returned in a few minutes with a half-sheet of notepaper in his hands. I took off my glasses, held the paper at arm's length, and was able to see that it bore, in fact, some pencilled notes written in English. I then took an envelope from the rack, put the paper inside, and closed down the flap. I then pocketed the envelope, shook the proprietor warmly by the hand, and walked across to the Cathedral to give thanks, having told him that I should return in half-an-hour for luncheon.

When I got back I found that he was troubled and uncertain. He asked if he could again see my credentials, and he pored over them for a long time. He then asked me if I had gone out to send the document to the Duchess. I said, 'No, I shall take it back with me to England and

---

[1] In fact, Mrs Simpson had no secretary. On her journey to Cannes she was accompanied only by Lord Brownlow (Personal Lord-in-Waiting to the King), a chauffeur and a Scotland Yard detective.

send it by registered post from there.' This increased his anxiety, and I therefore took a postcard from the rack and wrote on it: 'M. Piaccarella, the proprietor, has been most helpful, and has given me the paper.' I then put this card in an envelope and addressed it to the Duchess at Wasserleonburg, having first read to the proprietor the message which it contained. I then gave him the letter and told him to post it himself by airmail to Austria. This removed all his suspicions, since obviously if I had been a journalist obtaining the paper for the *Chicago Tribune*, I should not have written to the Duchess that it was now in my possession.

I then had an excellent luncheon, and parted with M. Piaccarella with expressions of mutual esteem.

DIARY   *11th July, 1937*

Arrive at Southampton at 6.30 a.m., and get down to Sissinghurst in time for luncheon. Read my review books and spend a peaceful afternoon. Write a long letter to the Duchess of Windsor sending her the document and her original letter of authority. My one anxiety is that the paper he gave me may not after all have been her notes, since owing to an excess of delicacy, I did not read a word of it.[1]

DIARY   *15th July, 1937*

The Foreign Affairs Committee discuss Spain. The enormous majority are passionately anti-Government and pro-Franco. The discussion is very useful, as it enables a lot of the younger Tories to blow off steam.

Meanwhile the Opposition have moved the Adjournment for the purpose of discussing the British plan.[2] I had a talk with Anthony Eden about it in the earlier part of the afternoon and told him that I was opposed to recognition of belligerency since I felt that this would enable Franco to blockade and starve the Government forces into submission. He said that he fully agreed that this might occur, and that he himself would only accept recognition when a real evacuation of

---

[1] The Duchess in her memoirs, *The Heart has its Reasons* (Michael Joseph. 1956), acknowledged the service which H.N. gave her, and reproduced the text of the notes as follows: 'On no account is Mr James [her code-name for King Edward] to step down [abdicate]. You must get advice. You must bring in your old friends. See Duff Cooper. Talk to Lord Derby. Talk to the Aga Khan. Do nothing rash.' In fact, the telephone-connection was so bad that the King scarcely heard a word.

[2] To grant belligerent rights to both sides in the Spanish Civil War, once 'substantial progress' had been made with the withdrawal of foreign forces.

volunteers had been secured. I must say, I admire enormously his calm and good temper. Everybody else was indignant that the Opposition had criticised the British plan in a full-dress debate before the other Powers had had time to consider it. Anthony, however, is perfectly calm about this, and although I have to leave the debate in order to make my dinner speech,[1] I gather that his answer to Attlee was simply overwhelming.

DIARY   *19th July, 1937*

Debate on Foreign Affairs. Eden opens with a general review, and Dalton replies with his usual petulant accusations. Lloyd George and Winston both make excellent speeches about the guns mounted in the Straits of Gibraltar, but there is nothing constructive in what they say. For one dreadful moment I am terrified lest I be called upon to follow Lloyd George, but luckily some other victim is chosen, and the debate floats off on to minor points. I am actually called at nine, but am asked not to speak for more than ten minutes. This rather cramps my style, but at least I am not at all nervous, and every time I speak, I feel greater confidence. Cranborne,[2] in winding up, is curiously ineffective. Once these Cecils cease to be crusaders they become parsons.

DIARY   *20th July, 1937*

Lunch with Mary Spears.[3] The party consists of Lady Carlisle, Lady Maidstone, Mrs Ronnie Greville, the Duc d'Harcourt and some young Tory members. Maggie Greville begins by whispering to me how much she dislikes gossip, how much she hopes there will be no gossip at this luncheon and how the one thing she cannot stand in this life is people who say unkind things about other people. Having said this she proceeds to dip her little fountain-pen filler into pots of oily venom and to squirt this mixture at all her friends. Having completed this process she then turns to self-laudation and tells me a long story of how she paid a dentist's bill on behalf of the daughter of the King of Spain, and also how much she regrets the accession of our present Monarch to the throne, since 'I was so happy in the days when they used to run in and out of my house as if they were my own children.'

[1] To the Inns of Court National Labour Group.
[2] Viscount Cranborne, the future fifth Marquess of Salisbury, then Parliamentary Under Secretary of State for Foreign Affairs.
[3] Mary Borden, the novelist, who married General Sir Edward Spears M.P. in 1918.

I try to draw her on the subject of King Edward [VII]. But she merely says that he was the only one of the family with whom she was never intimate. He, at least, had the sense to see that she is nothing more than a fat slug filled with venom.

H.N. TO V.S-W.   *21st July, 1937*
                                        4 King's Bench Walk, E.C.4

My speech on Monday seems to have gone better than I supposed. Many people have come to congratulate me upon it. It is extraordinary how these things seem to affect temperature. If one makes a good speech, even the policeman at the door seems to salute with greater deference. After a failure, it is as if the very pigeons avoided one's eye. This, of course, is mainly subjective. But I think that there really is something in the fact that no institution on earth shows such baro-metric variations as the House. Nor can any triumph be so sweet as a real oratorical triumph in the House of Commons. I wonder if I shall ever have one.

DIARY   *23rd July, 1937*

Dine at the Russian Embassy. The guests consist of Beaverbrook, Mr and Mrs David Low, and Korda the film-director. We have caviare and bortch. The Ambassador talks to me at great length on the iniquities of German propaganda. After dinner I talk to Beaverbrook about isolation. He confesses that he is not an out-and-out isolationist and that he might have to change his policy if Germany becomes too aggressive. Go back with him to Stornoway House and continue the conversation there. The curious thing is that his recent visits to Germany have convinced him that Hitler really means business and have thereby rendered him almost pro-French. He is extremely agreeable and affectionate, and bears me no resentment for past troubles.

DIARY   *27th July, 1937*

The Foreign Affairs Committee is addressed by Anthony Eden. He gives a general review of the problems from Washington to Tokyo. He says that the French really did take the initiative in non-interven-tion and were not put up to it by us. He admits that non-intervention has largely failed, but he says that it has prevented the dispatch of organised consignments of men, and that those who have indulged in it are now sorry that they spoke. He makes a great point of the fact that whereas the difficulties of the dictator states are hidden behind a steel curtain, all our own cards are on the table. We must never bluff. But in fact the position is better than formerly, since both Germany and Italy are abating their former truculent attitude. The foundations of peace, he says, are firmer than we suppose, and our diplomatic position with the neutral countries, in the Eastern Mediterranean and in the United States, is stronger than ever before.

In private conversation with him afterwards he says that he thinks the Spanish War will last another year, and he hopes it will end in deadlock out of which some middle Government will emerge. He points out that if Franco wins he will be able to hold Spanish Morocco, but that if he loses, the Government will not be strong enough to turn him out, and a very difficult situation will arise.

The House rose on 30th July and reassembled after the summer recess on 21st October. Harold Nicolson had no holiday abroad, but worked hard at Sissinghurst finishing 'Helen's Tower', which was published with 'Pepita' as the now usual autumn double. 1937 was 'the year of no surprises'. The Dictators were quiescent except in Spain and in their agitation for the return of their former colonies, and British policy was to hold existing diplomatic positions while building up our military strength.

DIARY   *9th August, 1937*

Another lovely day, although the garden is suffering from drought. Do my review. Stephen Spender, Inez Spender and Wystan Auden come over for tea.[1] Wystan is grubbier than ever and Stephen is as like Shelley as ever. They are very simple and interested and gay. We enjoy their visit.

DIARY   *7th September, 1937*

Revise my book[2] and do my review. The book is dreadful, and I am sad about it. It seems to be childishly frivolous at one moment and bad dullness at others. Discuss the future of the orchard with V.

---

[1] Wystan Auden was then aged 30, and had just won the King George's Gold Medal for poetry. Stephen Spender was 28. He had married Inez Pearn in 1936.
[2] *Helen's Tower.* It was published by Constable on 15th November.

H.N. TO V.S-W. (*motoring in France*) 7*th October, 1937*
Sissinghurst

Look out for two little pictures 18 inches by 12 to replace those made
in sand of stags fighting. I do not care for the Landseer touch even in
oils. But they become the sands of displeasure when executed in a
material which was not designed by God or man for plastic and still
less for pictorial art. I want very much (and I know you agree) to make
the big room a perfect room. I think that the background, now that
we have at last got the right chairs and coverings, is a perfect room.
But then our pictures are not up to the level of our china and cabinets.

I think that about such things we rely on each other's taste. And do
you realise, my dearest Viti (bless you), how much it means that we
should each of us be as excited about Sissinghurst and feel that we have
a chance there which is an enormous chance. I really believe that you
will be able to make of that ramshackle farm-tumble something as
personal and lovely as anything in England. I confess that I am deeply
impressed by your foresight or vision in such matters. I never myself
foresaw how lovely and intimate these dear rooms could become. I
confess that I never foresaw that Sissinghurst would combine dignity
with loveliness. You foresaw these things. And I just take off my hat.
I really believe that you will be able to make it something which will
render all vulgarity foolish. Especially am I puzzled, bothered and
enchanted by the orchard. I think of it all so much, dearest; it is like
a smell of apples in my room. But oh my God in heaven (not excluding
Sainte Thérèse of Lisieux[1] and all the other guys), how I do love that
place! I think only you and I really understand it. Gwen also understands it. The boys only appreciate it. That isn't the same thing at all.
I think it was your poem that made me realise about Sissinghurst first.[2]
That was a good poem. Wasn't it? A very good poem. I wrote a
poem in the train yesterday. Like all my poems it was foul. It was in
the Hopkins manner. You see, poetry takes so much longer than a
book.

Did I tell you (yes I did) that Gerald Barry had asked me to write a
column daily for the *News Chronicle*? I have refused. What I should
like would be to be made Director of the Southern Railway at £600
a year. Something which could release me from pressure but not

[1] V.S-W. had just conceived the idea of writing *The Eagle and the Dove*.
[2] Her short poem *Sissinghurst*, published by the Hogarth Press in 1931.

entail extra work. But I do not grumble. I believe that even if I were deprived of my reviews I should mind.

Enjoy yourselves. Love to Gwen.[1] I am busy and quite happy—no I am very happy really. But I did so love my holiday at Sissinghurst and there is a pang when the flowers die.

DIARY   *10th November, 1937*

Take the 8.53 to London [from Leicester]. The porter tells me as he puts in my luggage that Ramsay MacDonald is dead.[2] I am so shocked by this information that I tell the man to go to the Central Station instead of to the L.M.S.

Otto Kyllman[3] asks me to go and see him urgently and then suggests that I should do the official biography of MacDonald. I say that I don't admire him morally or intellectually sufficiently to justify so much labour. One can never write a biography of anyone for whom one did not have real enthusiasm.

DIARY   *15th November, 1937*

Helen's Tower is published and there are a few scattered mentions.

Lunch with Sibyl Colefax. Down to the House afterwards. Have a long talk in the smoking-room with Winston Churchill. He congratulates me on my intervention in the Foreign Affairs Committee on Thursday,[4] saying that he has seldom seen so short a speech make so much effect in so short a time. I say that I feel terribly hampered in making up my mind about foreign politics, since I have actually no conception whatsoever as to our real defensive power. Obviously, if it is a question between complete defeat and the surrender of the German colonies, there can be no question whatsoever. But if we are in fact able to defend ourselves, I see no reason why we should make concessions without receiving something in return. Winston says that it is of course impossible for the Government to disclose our exact strength at this moment, but that 'he takes it' that Germany's air-force is a little stronger than the French and British air-forces combined.

---

[1] Mrs St Aubyn was travelling with V.S-W. on a motor-tour of Provence.

[2] Ramsay MacDonald had died suddenly on 9th November on a holiday-voyage to South America. His body was brought back from Bermuda and buried in Spynie churchyard, near Lossiemouth.

[3] One of the Directors of Constable.

[4] There is no record in the diary or letters of what this speech was about.

If you add to that the Italian air-force, which is a very excellent striking machine, we are indeed not in a position to go to war without very active Russian assistance. He is in a very quiet, sensible and chastened mood.

DIARY   *18th November, 1937*

Have a talk with Duncan Sandys[1] on the German situation. I say that we cannot form any real opinion unless we know the extent of our own weakness. We know, of course, that we cannot fight Germany, Italy and Japan at the same moment. But we do not know whether an attack by Germany would prove fatal to us. If we are likely to lose our life it is obviously better to sacrifice a few of our fingers. Duncan takes the sensible point of view that if Germany wishes to attack us, she will do so in any case, and her present policy is to get as much as she can meanwhile without war. If we surrender the colonies we shall only gain a very few months respite. Better therefore to put a firm face on it and keep the Germans guessing. Tory opinion is almost entirely on the run and would willingly let Germany take Russia and over-run the Near East so long as she leaves us alone.

DIARY   *25th November, 1937*

Henry Channon asks my advice about his diaries which he has kept at great length since 1917. He says that they are very outspoken and scandalous, but that they record the lives of important people for the last twenty years. He has made a Will leaving them to me plus £500. I say that he must make another Will leaving them plus £1,000 to Christ Church library, with instructions that thirty years after his death the four youngest fellows of the time should consider their publication.[2]

DIARY   *26th November, 1937*

Down to Oxford. Drive to Balliol, where Mr Heath,[3] the President of the Conservative Association, is waiting for me. On with him and Nigel to the Carlton, where we have an amusing dinner, and then to the Taylorian where I address a large and interested audience on the German colonies.

[1] Duncan Sandys, then aged 29, had been Conservative M.P. for Lambeth since 1935.
[2] These diaries were in fact bequeathed to his son, Paul Channon.
[3] Edward Heath, then aged 21, was to become President of the Oxford Union in 1939.

DIARY   *8th December, 1937*

Go to breakfast with Lord Baldwin.[1] I arrive at 69 Eaton Square to find him seated at the breakfast-table opening his letters. He is rather lame with arthritis, but otherwise looks well. He said that he had only got out just in time and that a few weeks more would have led to a real collapse similar to that of Ramsay MacDonald. He said that he had always looked forward to his retirement as a time to read and think, but that for the first three months he had been quite unable to think and only able to read detective novels. He was now beginning to recover and was reading Froude on Erasmus.

He goes on to talk of his mother's family and the Burne Jones–Kipling circle. We then talk about the Abdication. He considers Mrs Simpson to be an admirable woman within her circle of conscience, but to have no conception of proportions outside that circle. He showed me the original of the little pencilled note that King Edward had sent him after the Abdication.[2]

He talked of Winston Churchill and said he lacked soul. I suggested that Winston is very sympathetic to misfortune in others. He answered, 'I don't deny that Winston has his sentimental side.' He then goes on: 'And what is more, he cannot really tell lies. That is what makes him so bad a conspirator.'

I was alone with him for over an hour, and nothing could have exceeded his mellow charm.

DIARY   *9th December, 1937*

Meeting of the Foreign Affairs Committee attended by Anthony Eden. The room is packed. His general line is that there is no imminent likelihood of war and a far better prospect of appeasement than ever before. He draws attention to several favourable factors, such as the progress of our rearmament, the fact that Spain has ceased to be a real source of danger, the improvement of our relations with Portugal and the much closer cooperation which is beginning with the United

[1] He was created Earl Baldwin of Bewdley after his retirement.
[2] There were two notes: one asking Baldwin to state in the House of Commons that Mrs Simpson had tried to the last to dissuade the King from the decision he had taken; and the second pledging his support to his brother, the Duke of York. Baldwin had used the second, but not the first, in his Abdication speech. See *A King's Story*, by the Duke of Windsor, 1947.

States. He also says that the Spanish trouble has shown the increased power of the defence in modern warfare, thereby rendering aggression less tempting. As regards Germany, he takes the line that we must make every effort to come to an agreement, but that it must be a general agreement and not one of 'sops'. As regards Central Europe, he says we cannot disinterest ourselves and will enter into commitments. The general effect of his speech is to encourage all those of us who have been preaching the same sort of doctrine for years.

Dine at Admiralty House. It amused me to see Duff and Diana in this official setting,[1] and strangely enough they were a trifle shy. The party consists of their own friends with two senior admirals and the Italian Ambassador. We arm into dinner and I have to sit next to Madame Grandi who always bores me. I have Maureen [Stanley] on my other side, which is a comfort.

DIARY   *31st December, 1937*

After dinner [at Sissinghurst] I think back on the year 1937. A good year. Vita has been well, written *Pepita* and her flower book[2] and made the garden one of the loveliest in England. Ben has been at the National Gallery and in Florence preparing himself as a *Kunsthistoriker*.[3] Nigel has been at Balliol working hard and managing to rid himself of his shyness. I have been to Africa, spoken in all sorts of places, written *Helen's Tower*, published *The Meaning of Prestige*[4] and *Small Talk*,[5] and been happy and busy.

I have been conscious nonetheless that my political career has suffered a decline. I do not possess sufficient combative instincts to impose my personality upon the House of Commons. Although I am a good platform speaker and a better lecturer, I am not at my ease in the Chamber.

The difficulty is that Foreign Affairs, which is my special subject, is not a subject on which I want to speak. It only does harm. Thus I have remained largely silent and the impression is that I have 'dropped out'. By one good speech I could destroy that impression and recover the general expectation which they had of me before my unfortunate speech on the Address in 1936.[6] But I feel somehow that I am not

[1] Duff Cooper had become First Lord of the Admiralty in May.
[2] *Some Flowers.* Cobden Sanderson. 1937.   [3] Art-historian.
[4] The Rede Lecture, delivered at Cambridge on 23rd April, 1937.
[5] A collection of articles from various journals. Published by Constable.
[6] See above, pp. 277-8.

sufficiently virile to force myself upon the House, and that I am too old to create a gradual impression as Baldwin did.

How much do I mind this? Probably more than I realise. I am so happy in my domestic and ordinary life that I do not notice much that I have not fulfilled high hopes. But I suppose that somewhere I do notice it, since I hate failure. 1938 will decide. At present I am still, for the majority of the House, an open question. This time next year that question will have been answered one way or the other.

1938

Anthony Eden's resignation – H.N.'s speech in support of
Eden – the attitude of his constituents to appeasement –
Hitler's 'Anschluss' with Austria – H.N. forced to resign his
Vice-Chairmanship of the Foreign Affairs Committee –Eden
and Vansittart – H.N.'s lecture-tour of the Balkans – talks
with King Carol of Rumania and King Boris of Bulgaria –
Belgrade – Konrad Henlein – growing sense of crisis –H.N.
on a father's relationship with his sons – and on his marriage –
visit to Somerset Maugham and to the Shiant Islands – the
Munich crisis – emergency meeting with Churchill – the fear
of imminent war – H.N. attacks the Munich Pact – difficulties
in Leicester – he joins the Eden Group in opposition to
appeasement – 'Marginal Comment' – V. Sackville-West
on hating grand parties – 'A foul year: next year will be
worse'

In 1938 the road to war began to slope downhill. It marked the culmination and ruin of Neville Chamberlain's policy of appeasing the dictators. Almost from the moment when he succeeded Baldwin as Prime Minister and began to take more and more into his own hands the conduct of Foreign Affairs, his relations with his Foreign Secretary, Anthony Eden, showed signs of strain. Chamberlain considered the Foreign Office too anti-German, and developed his own means of communication with Hitler through the visit of Lord Halifax to Berchtesgaden in November 1937, and with Mussolini through personal contacts with Count Grandi, the Italian Ambassador in London, and through such amateur emissaries to Rome as Lady Chamberlain, the widow of his half-brother Austen. At home Sir Robert Vansittart was replaced by Sir Horace Wilson as Chamberlain's leading adviser on Foreign Affairs. Eden protested with increasing vigour against this by-passing of the Foreign Office, complained constantly that the slowness of British rearmament weakened his hand, and pointed out to Chamberlain that by this form of personal diplomacy he was diminishing the confidence felt in Britain by France and the United States. We were flattering our enemies and wounding our allies. An open clash between the two leading men of the Government was approaching fast.

In January, when Eden was taking a short holiday in the South of France, Chamberlain replied coldly to a suggestion by President Roosevelt that he, the President, should attempt a reconciliation between the Powers of Western Europe. Eden agreed that the proposal was couched in terms that could be considered diplomatically naïve, but to have waved away the hand proffered across the Atlantic left him, in Churchill's phrase, 'breathless with amazement'. He arrived back in England too late to repair the damage, and Roosevelt's initiative was never publicly made: that it had even been suggested remained generally unknown until after the war. When Chamberlain proposed a few weeks later to open discussions with Mussolini with a view to obtaining a general settlement in the Mediterranean including a de jure recognition of his conquest of Abyssinia, Eden argued that certain conditions must be fulfilled first. Italy must make a substantial withdrawal of her troops from Spain, tone

319

down the anti-British propaganda broadcasts from Italian radio-stations, and reduce the huge garrison which she was maintaining for some unknown reason in L¹bya. To do otherwise would give unnecessary offence to the French and Americans and heighten Mussolini's prestige in the eyes of Hitler. Behind the immediate cause of Eden's disagreement with Chamberlain—the tactics and timing of negotiations with Mussolini— was the mistrust that each felt for the other. Chamberlain believed that there was still time to woo Mussolini away from Hitler; Eden regarded the word of each dictator as equally unreliable. 'A leading democracy', he wrote, when describing the incident in his Memoirs, 'in negotiating with a militant dictatorship, must not go cap in hand in search of fresh negotiations to cover long-standing differences, until there is evidence that the dictator is going to carry out the engagements he has already undertaken.'¹

Parliament and the public were scarcely aware of the impending crisis until a week before Eden resigned on 20th February, having failed to convince his colleagues in the Cabinet. Lord Cranborne, Under Secretary of State for Foreign Affairs, resigned with him. Lord Halifax became Foreign Secretary. In the debate which followed Eden's personal statement to the House of Commons, Harold Nicolson spoke up strongly in his support, as he also did in the Foreign Affairs Committee. His speeches on these two occasions were among the most effective that he ever made in Parliament. The National Labour Party virtually disowned his conduct, but his Leicester constituents gave him a unanimous vote of confidence.

DIARY   *20th January, 1938*

To the Leicestershire Club where I meet Bertie Jarvis. We go over future engagements and I see that he is rather rattled by Janner.² He thinks he will turn me out, but he does not express it in that way. The way he expresses it is to say, 'We shall give him a fine run for his money.' In a way, I think that Janner will make a better Member than I am.

---

¹ Anthony Eden. *Facing the Dictators.* Cassell. 1962. p. 597.
² Barnett Janner, Labour candidate for West Leicester. He defeated H.N. in the 1945 Election.

H.N. TO V.S-W.   *26th January, 1938*
                                                 House of Commons

My visit to the Cambridge Union was great fun. The debate was
'Art must be political'. Stephen Spender said Yes and I said No. I
won by some 230 votes. I had a long talk with Stephen afterwards.
He was as charming as ever, as egoistic and as void of all humour. He
amused me during his speech by saying, 'I fear I cannot make an
amusing speech. I have just been reading a book which says that "all
geniuses are devoid of humour ".' It was said so simply that it did
not appear extravagantly vain.

He is very worried about the young men who join the International
Brigade in Spain. They go out there with deep faith in communism
and in a few weeks they lose all their faith and illusions. But they have
to stay and be butchered for a cause they do not believe in. He says
that only some 40 per cent survive.

DIARY   *3rd February, 1938*

Dine at the St James' with Gladwyn Jebb. Characteristically we do not
touch on the centre of Foreign Affairs. Here I am, Vice Chairman of
the Foreign Affairs Committee of the House, and there he is, Private
Secretary to the Permanent Under Secretary of State[1]—and friends of
long standing—yet such is the tradition of discretion that I dare not
ask him a single question nor even why it is that he has to return to
the Office after dinner. That would not be so in France.

DIARY   *8th February, 1938*

Godfrey Nicholson[2] comes and pours out his heart about how incompetent and useless he feels. I suggest a cold bath in the morning
and a ride in the park. I also suggest great efficiency in minor matters
and allowing nothing to slide. This, added to great punctuality, produces a spurious sense of efficiency and will-power.

V.S-W. TO H.N.   *10th February, 1938*
                                                 Sissinghurst

Powys, our new architect, wants to build the courtyard wall on the
same principle as the garden wall, about 4-feet thick and very elabo-

[1] Sir Alexander Cadogan, who had succeeded Vansittart on 1st January 1938.
[2] Conservative M.P. for Morpeth 1931–35 and for Farnham 1937–66.

H.N.D.   321   X

rately sloped. So unless you cable me, I shall tell him that we only want an ordinary wall. Apart from the question of expense, I think too thick a wall would look wrong in comparison with the other relatively slender walls. After all, part of the beauty of Sissinghurst lies in its slenderness and consequent grace, and a great lumping elephant of a wall would be inconsistent.

DIARY   *15th February, 1938*

The news arrives of the result of the Berchtesgaden conversations between Hitler and Schuschnigg.[1] Guido Schmidt is to be made Foreign Minister and Seyss-Inquart is to be given the police. This means that Austria hands over the direction of her affairs to Berlin. She will retain nominal independence. Mussolini went off to the Abruzzi just in time so as not to be able to answer Schuschnigg's appeal. But what will he be given in return for Hitler's obtaining Austria? This is a bad first symptom of the Axis.

H.N. TO V.S-W.   *17th February, 1938*
                                                          4 King's Bench Walk, E.C.4

I dined with Vansittart and found him in the depths of gloom.[2] But I do not think there is going to be a war yet. Not by a long chance. And if we can gain two years of peace, then we are almost out of the wood. But there is no doubt that Germany is out for *Weltmacht*, and will carry that through with grim determination.

There was a debate on propaganda, and I made a dear little speech, a little modest sensible thing that went well enough. I am sure that if only I force myself to speak more frequently, all nervousness will go. For the moment I am still rather frightened of the House.

[1] On 12th February Hitler summoned Kurt von Schuschnigg, the 41-year-old Austrian Chancellor, to meet him at Berchtesgaden. On arrival, Schuschnigg was presented with a demand that the pro-Nazi Viennese lawyer, Dr Seyss-Inquart, should be made Minister of the Interior with authority over the police, and other pro-Nazi Austrians appointed to leading posts in the Austrian Government. If his orders were not carried out in full within six days, Hitler would send his troops into Austria. Schuschnigg signed.

[2] Sir Robert Vansittart had become Chief Diplomatic Adviser to the Government, but his influence was less than when he had been Permanent Under-Secretary.

DIARY   *17th February, 1938*

Meeting of the Foreign Affairs Committee. I open the discussion by indicating that Hitler has now re-established his legend and imposed the will of the Party on the Army. We must face the fact that adventurism is now in the ascendant in Germany, and the cautious people have been proved to have been wrong. I discuss the implications of the Austrian agreement and indicate that Mussolini must have known in advance and must have been bought with certain promises. What were those promises? And why has he now 100,000 men in Libya? I conclude by suggesting that we should keep a stiff upper lip, not throw sops or slops about, wait, and, above all, arm.[1] There is a good attendance and my speech goes well. Winston Churchill, who is sitting next to me, says, 'A very good speech: a very good speech indeed.' He himself takes a far more truculent attitude than I do. We must call a halt. The whole feeling of the meeting is very different from that of a year ago. They no longer believe that we can buy Germany off with concessions.

DIARY   *20th February, 1938*

The Cabinet meet three times today, and on the late news it is put out that Eden has resigned. We spend much of the morning listening to Hitler's Reichstag speech on the wireless. It is meant to be moderate, but his references to foreign countries, his talk of 'steel and iron', are received with wild demoniac yells.

H.N. TO V.S-W.   *22nd February, 1938*
                                                      4 King's Bench Walk, E.C.4

Yesterday was a terrible day. The papers blazed with Anthony's resignation. On reaching Charing Cross I went straight to the House of Commons and booked my seat. Already crowds were lolling about. I then came here and Hill[2] unpacked the flowers which make my room a sort of sale of Sissinghurst. Then the telephone began and shrilled

---

[1] Anthony Eden writes of this meeting: 'They had shown themselves robust. Mr Harold Nicolson had said that any nervous advances to Germany or Italy would suggest fear and this was not a moment to show the slightest move in the direction of *de jure* recognition of Italy's conquest of Abyssinia. This last remark was cheered by the Committee, which appeared to be unanimous against attempting to buy Italian friendship on this condition.' *Facing the Dictators*, p. 579.

[2] H.N.'s man-servant.

without stopping. Everybody appeared to want advice on what to do. Miss Grey telephoned to say that I *must* get her a seat in the House. I let Miss Niggeman[1] deal with that sort of call.

I lunched early with Kenneth Lindsay who was rather glum. He felt he ought to resign,[2] and he felt he ought not to resign. I said it was better not to resign. We then went to a special meeting summoned by Malcolm MacDonald. He told us exactly what had happened. He thought that Anthony had made a mistake in resigning on what was merely a point of procedure. The Prime Minister had wanted to enter into negotiations with Italy without stating any terms at all. Anthony felt that that would be dangerous, and that we should not begin conversations until we had certain assurances in advance and until we were quite certain what the Italians would ask for. This, according to Malcolm, was merely a point of procedure, and although (had it been a point of principle) he would have resigned with Anthony, yet he could scarcely break up the National Government on so small an issue.

I had to dash away for Prayers, but before I left I said I did not agree. Italy had behaved atrociously and to enter into unqualified and un-defined negotiations with her was not only dangerous but was also letting down morality in international affairs. I added that I should say this that afternoon in the House. They all looked rather glum and said that I might do so if I wished, but that I must dissociate them from any such statement. So I left.

After questions the P.M. came in and was cheered by his supporters. Then Anthony and Cranborne appeared, both looking pale and self-conscious, and sat on a back bench. They were greeted with wild applause by the Opposition and by four or five of us. The rest kept silence. Those who have toadied and grovelled to Anthony all these years just kept silence. I yelled and yelled and waved my order-paper. That was thought very bad taste.

Then the debate began. Anthony did not really make a good speech. It was too restrained in parts and then too unrestrained. Either he should have confined himself to the distressed-colleague point of view or launched out into an appeal for decency in foreign policy. He fell

---

[1] Elvira Niggeman, who had become H.N.'s secretary in January and remained with him until 1965.

[2] He was Parliamentary Secretary to the Board of Education.

between the two stools. Bobbety[1] was better. The P.M. made a prim statement. He slipped up over the Nyon Agreement[2] and a very bad impression was made.

I sat there in some trepidation. Archie Sinclair spoke at great length, but the rest of the Opposition were very ineffective. In the middle I got a note sent down from the Ambassadors' Gallery: 'Please give me some tea.' It was from Maisky, the Russian. I replied, 'Sorry; about to speak; stuck here like an oyster.'

Then I was called. I was not nervous. Only angry. There were yells of pain and pleasure during my speech.[3] I sat down not knowing whether it was a good speech or a bad speech. Lloyd George crossed the floor and came up to me. 'A fine Parliamentary performance,' he said. Then I was surrounded by people congratulating and applauding. I realised that I had made a hit. Winston came up: 'That was a magnificent speech. I envy you your gift.'

I escaped and went to dine at the Reform with Jack Macnamara. Then with Rob Bernays to Bill Mabane's.[4] They were so unhappy. They felt that they ought to have taken a line against the P.M.

This morning my telephone has never been quiet. Congratulations from all sides. But I shall never now get a job in the Government. But truly, darling, I do not care when such vital principles are involved.

H.N. TO V.S-W.   *25th February, 1938*
                                                4 King's Bench Walk, E.C.4

The Government may say what they like, but their policy is nothing less than the scrapping of the ideas which have been built up since the war and the reversion to the old pre-war policy of power politics and

---

[1] Lord Cranborne.

[2] The agreement signed at Nyon, Switzerland, in September 1937 provided for international action against piratical attacks on merchant shipping in the Mediterranean. Italy was invited but refused to attend. In his speech Chamberlain stated that the Italians were present, and was obliged to correct himself.

[3] In his speech H.N. said: 'It is a problem whether a country which has continuously, consistently, deliberately and without apology, violated every engagement into which she has ever entered can be taken back into the fold with a smile; or whether it is better to make a few concrete conditions before negotiations are resumed. . . . However weak we might be, however divided, however muddle-headed, we never defended wrong with cool and planned deliberation as we are doing now. I regret that those great principles of our policy should now lie tattered at our feet. Above all I regret we should see "their sire, butchered to make a Roman holiday".'

[4] National-Liberal M.P. for Huddersfield, 1931-45.

bargaining. This means: (1) that we shall have to buy the friendship of Italy and Germany by making sacrifices. (2) That this friendship will not be worth 2d once it is bought. And (3) that in doing so we shall sacrifice the confidence of France, Russia, the United States and all the smaller countries. I mind it dreadfully.

There are other aspects that I mind equally. First that Chamberlain has been very tricky about it. Secondly that my own Party has behaved like worms and kissed the Chamberlain boot with a resounding smack. And thirdly that all the Tories and die-hards are hugging themselves at having got rid of all the nonsensical notions of the past and having got back the good old Tory doctrines.

My meeting at Leicester went well in a way. When I arrived at the station, I was met by Jarvis who informed me that opinion in the Conservative Association was all on the side of Chamberlain and that I had better say nothing at all. I said, 'Not at all. I have come up here to explain my action to my constituents and explain it I shall.' Being a decent man, he agreed to let me have my way and backed it strongly.

My speech in fact went well. They did not understand most of it but they agreed. They passed a unanimous vote of confidence with real enthusiasm. I was, as the papers say, 'visibly moved'. And this morning I got a note from Bertie Jarvis: 'Sorry, Harold. You were right and I was wrong. The speech was triumphant.'

We had a most unpleasant meeting of the Foreign Affairs Committee. We heard that they were going to ask for our resignation as Chairman and Vice Chairman. Or at least that Nancy Astor was going to ask. Paul Evans[1] and I therefore agreed that we should resign on our own initiative. Thus when the meeting opened, Paul got up and said that he and I and Jock McEwen[2] had determined to resign. The room was packed and there was one great shout of 'No!' That sounds splendid, but what it really meant was that they thought our resignation would embarrass the Government, as indeed it would. Several people go up quite shamelessly and suggested that we should not resign at once but merely do so later when feeling had diminished. At this Winston in all his majesty rose and said that they were being mean and petty. They were not treating us fairly and he must insist on a vote, either Yes or No. They then voted. Those in favour of our not resigning

[1] Paul Emrys-Evans M.P., Chairman of the Foreign Affairs Committee.
[2] Captain J. H. F. McEwen M.P., Secretary of the Committee.

were unanimous except for one little vicious hand against. That hand was the hand of Nancy Astor.

We then adjourned in some excitement. In the corridor a friend of mine called Alan Graham[1] came up to Nancy and said, 'I do not think you behaved very well.' She turned upon him and said, 'Only a Jew like you would *dare* to be rude to me.' He replied, 'I should much like to smack your face.' I think she is a little mad.

DIARY   *28th February, 1938*

Violet Bonham Carter wants me to go all out and oppose the Government. I refuse to do so, saying that it would be egoistic. She says that country comes before party and that I am being unpatriotic. I say that the moment has not arrived and Chamberlain must be given a chance.

We both go on to lunch with Vansittart. He thinks that Eden made a mistake in resigning on a point which, if not really a mere point of procedure, was at least not a clear issue and one which would be difficult to explain to the country. But he is all with Eden in principle and is in terror of the Chamberlain course. His general view is that Italy is just a minor front and that the main front remains Berlin. If from these Italian talks we can obtain some help for the defence of Austria, then indeed we shall have done well. But if they deal only with Anglo-Italian controversies, then the whole thing is just eyewash. He agrees with me that I should lie low for the moment. 'Berlin, Berlin, Berlin', is his constant refrain. There was a certain attitude of reserve about him which I did not quite understand. I have a feeling that he had invited Violet and me to lunch in order to have a rebels' orgy, but that in the meanwhile Chamberlain had asked him to return to the fold.

Up to Leicester, where I propose the health of the City at a dinner of the Leicester house-builders. A ghastly banquet. I chaff Leicester about its architecture.

H.N. TO V.S-W.   *2nd March, 1938*
                                                               House of Commons

I went to such an odd luncheon yesterday. It is called 'The Focus Group', and is one of Winston's things. It consists of Winston, Norman Angell, Wickham Steed, Walter Layton, Robert Cecil,

[1] Conservative M.P. for the Wirrall Division of Cheshire, 1935-45.

Violet Bonham Carter, Clynes and some other of the Labour people. I was made to make a speech without any notice and was a trifle embarrassed. But one gets a thick skin and an easy habit about these things and my speech was rather a hit. Winston was enormously witty. He spoke of 'this great country nosing from door to door like a cow that has lost its calf, mooing dolefully now in Berlin and now in Rome—when all the time the tiger and the alligator wait for its undoing'.

Don't be worried, my darling. I am not going to become one of the Winston brigade. My leaders are Anthony [Eden] and Malcolm [MacDonald].

Hitler had been secretly planning the rape of Austria since as long ago as July 1936. In the middle of March 1938 circumstances were propitious for putting the plan into effect. In Great Britain opinion was divided by Eden's resignation, and in France there was no Government at all during the four critical days 10th to 14th March, since Chautemps had resigned and Léon Blum had not yet succeeded him. Hitler's major anxiety was not that the democracies would come to the aid of Austria, but that Mussolini would once again send his divisions to the Brenner. This fear was removed by Mussolini's assurance that he would stand aloof. Hitler then acted very swiftly.

On 9th March Schuschnigg, the Austrian Chancellor, announced that in four days time he would hold a plebiscite throughout Austria to determine whether his people were in favour of 'a free, independent, social, Christian and united Austria'. Hitler, through his mouth-piece Seyss-Inquart, told Schuschnigg that if he did not call off the plebiscite, German troops would enter Austria. Schuschnigg agreed to postpone the plebiscite, only to be told that this was no longer good enough: he must resign the Chancellorship and hand over to Seyss-Inquart. This condition was also fulfilled. But determined not to be thwarted of his conquest by the concessions which he had demanded, Hitler now fabricated an appeal from the Austrian Government requesting the presence of German troops to put down internal disorders. On this excuse, German troops crossed the Austrian frontier on 12th March and entered Vienna unopposed. Austria was declared annexed to the German Reich and Schuschnigg was arrested.

As expected, neither Great Britain, France nor Italy made a single move to restore Austrian independence, which had been reaffirmed by

Hitler as recently as *12th February. Our diplomatic protest was rejected
by the German Foreign Secretary on the grounds that 'relations between
the Reich and Austria can only be regarded as an internal affair of the
German people which is no concern of third Powers.' Nor were the
Dominions prepared to risk a war on this issue. On 14th March, at the
moment when Hitler was being received in triumph in Vienna, Chamberlain told the House of Commons that 'nothing could have arrested
this action by Germany unless we and others had been prepared to use
force to prevent it'. On 10th April a plebiscite, held throughout Germany
and Austria under Nazi control, showed a 99 per cent vote in favour
of the Anschluss.*

*These events profoundly affected Harold Nicolson. His close associa-
tion with Churchill, Eden and Vansittart, and his previous experience
of German and Italian methods of diplomacy, convinced him that
Chamberlain's policy was disastrous. As a member of the National
Labour Party, he had slightly greater freedom of action than a Conservative backbencher, but he was alone in the Party in speaking openly
against Chamberlain and he was obliged to resign his Vice Chairmanship
of the Foreign Affairs Committee.*

DIARY   *7th March, 1938*

Lunch alone with Maisky.[1] He minds very much the resignation of
Eden, who was really working up to a London–Paris–Moscow triangle.
He says that Chamberlain once in conversation with him referred to
the Moscow Government as 'our enemies'. He feels that we cannot
give way much more about the Spanish question, and his Government will certainly insist on the words 'substantial withdrawal' representing not less than 65 per cent.

The P.M. is bitterly anti-Russian and also anti-American. The soul
of that ironmonger[2] is not one which will save England.

H.N. TO V.S-W.   *9th March, 1938*
                                           House of Commons

We had a private meeting at Chatham House to discuss the present
situation. We came to the unhappy conclusion that now that Russia
has dropped out, we are simply not strong enough to resist Germany.

---

[1] The Russian Ambassador in London.
[2] In his youth Neville Chamberlain was one of the leading figures in the industrial
life of Birmingham.

Or rather we did not come to so extreme a conclusion. But we did feel that 80 million fully armed Germans plus the Italians were more than we and France could safely take on. What tremendous things have happened in these five years! We are suddenly faced by a collapse of our authority, our Empire and our independence. Poor England.

I dined with [Sir Edward] Spears. Vansittart was there. He was most gloomy. He thinks that we can scarcely prevent Germany collaring Eastern Europe, and that when she has done so, she will turn round on us and demand our submission. Well, it may not work out like that. But opinion at the moment is as gloomy as in the days after Austerlitz. Nobody who is well-informed believes that there is any chance of negotiations with Germany leading to anything at all. We may get some little scrap out of Italy, but it will be a mere crumb of comfort and quite unreliable.

Jolly, isn't it? My dearest, do not worry about these things but cultivate your lovely garden. I wish you were here nonetheless. You always soothe all my ruffled feathers.

DIARY   *10th March, 1938*

Lunch with Leo Amery at 112 Eaton Square. The luncheon is given for Franckenstein, the Austrian Minister,[1] to meet the younger Tories. There are Anthony Crossley, Rob Bernays, Godfrey Nicholson, Duncan Sandys, Somerset de Chair and so on. Franckenstein is anxious and depressed. We congratulate him upon Schuschnigg having declared a plebiscite and having been so brave as to stand up to Hitler. He does not seem to think that his courage will avail very much. He confirms the fact that Hitler at Berchtesgaden lied to Schuschnigg in telling him that Halifax had told him definitely that England did not mind if Austria were absorbed.[2]

DIARY   *11th March, 1938*

Hitler has presented an ultimatum to Austria and threatens to invade the country unless Schuschnigg resigns. The latter consents to put off

[1] Sir George Franckenstein, Austrian Minister in London, 1920–38. He was naturalised a British subject after the *Anschluss*.

[2] In November 1937 Halifax had spoken to Hitler at Berchtesgaden of 'possible alterations in the European order which might be destined to come about in the passage of time. Among these questions were Danzig, Austria and Czechoslovakia. England was interested to see that any alterations should come through the course of peaceful evolution'. But the warning was unclear.

the plebiscite but refuses to go. Miklas[1] backs him. Then Hitler mobilises his Munich corps and begins to invade. Schuschnigg gives way. He makes a pathetic farewell broadcast saying that he is yielding to 'brutal force'.

DIARY   *13th March, 1938*

A perfect spring day which shows Leicester at her ugliest. Round to the Newfoundlandpool Working Men's Club. They are all anti-Chamberlain, saying 'Eden has been proved right.' My own stock has gone up greatly over my speech. My broadcast also pleased them. It is amazing how many of them listen in to serious debates. It really encourages one. I go away feeling how far better in mind these men are than the Tories. I wish I did not hate the Conservatives quite so much.

DIARY   *14th March, 1938*

Chamberlain makes a dry statement threatening a doubled rearmament effort but giving little indication of real policy. The Opposition behave beautifully and do not hoot or scream. There is a sense of real national crisis. Winston makes the speech of his life in favour of the League. I deliberately refrain.

DIARY   *15th March, 1938*

A sense of danger and anxiety hangs over us like a pall. Hitler has completely collared Austria; no question of an *Anschluss*, just complete absorption.

Dine with Sibyl Colefax. Desmond MacCarthy is in despair and says that the Government have betrayed the country and that the Tories think only of the Red danger and let the Empire slide. I am in grave doubts as to my own position. How can I continue to support a Government like this?

DIARY   *16th March, 1938*

I am asked on all sides to take part in the debate on Spain. I therefore do so. My speech is well received by the Opposition and not at all badly received by the Government. When I sit down, the Prime Minister passes along a message through Kingsley Wood asking, 'What do you want us to do?' I say, 'Occupy Minorca.' 'Occupy Minorca',

[1] Wilhelm Miklas, President of the Austrian Republic.

Kingsley Wood hisses to Walter Elliot. 'Occupy Minorca', whispers Walter Elliot to David Margesson. 'Occupy Minorca', whispers David Margesson to Chamberlain. The latter flings back his head with a gesture of angered despair.

Go to Pratt's with Winston Churchill, Randolph and Bob Boothby. Winston doesn't fully agree with us about Spain, but mainly because of his personal friendship with Spanish grandees. He says that never has any man inherited a more ghastly situation than Neville Chamberlain, and he places the blame wholly on Baldwin. He says that in his long experience he has never known a Conservative Party composed of so many blind and obstinate men. He says that he will wait for a day or two in the hope that the negotiations which are now going on between Chamberlain, Attlee and Sinclair for a formula of policy that will command the assent of the whole House have either failed or come to fruition.[1] But if no clear statement is issued between now and Wednesday next, he will refuse the whip and take some fifty people with him. The threat should in itself suffice to determine the Government. He says that the situation is worse than in 1914. 'We stand to lose everything by failing to take strong action. Yet if we take strong action, London will be a shambles in half-an-hour.'

DIARY   *23rd March, 1938*

A man told me a story yesterday which had been told him by a Dutchman. A prominent Nazi had lost his temper with the Dutch Minister in Berlin and said to him, 'There will be no neutrality for you in the next war. You are practically a German race, and I warn you that Hitler may be in Holland within two years.' The Dutch Minister replied, 'I agree that such an event is quite possible. We should welcome him. After all, it is for twenty years that we have extended similar hospitality to the Kaiser.'

DIARY   *29th March, 1938*

I have a talk with Malcolm MacDonald about the crisis. I ask him what I ought to do. I say that I regard the situation as one of terrible danger; that I am convinced that Germany and Italy are trying to chloroform us while they occupy strategic points to our disadvantage; that I consider Eastern Europe is now lost with the seizure of Austria; and that we should make our naval strength felt in Spain. We should

[1] It was later denied by Attlee that any such conversations took place.

occupy Minorca. It is madness to suppose that Italy and Germany will not obtain from Franco some sort of secret arrangement similar to that which the Germans got out of the Turks in 1913. When war comes, we shall be unable to defend Malta, Cyprus, Egypt or Palestine.

Malcolm says that although he agrees with this, we are really not strong enough to risk a war. It would mean the massacre of women and children in the streets of London. No Government could possibly risk a war when our anti-aircraft defences are in so farcical a condition. Even if the Germans exploit our present weakness in order to achieve an even stronger position against us, we must take that risk. No Cabinet, knowing as they do how pitiable our defences are, could take any risk. All we can do is by wise retreat and good diplomacy to diminish the dangers being arrayed against us. The Cabinet know full well that we are shirking great responsibility. But they cannot undertake such responsibility. He wants me to meet Chamberlain and discuss it with him. I say that our views are so fundamentally divergent that this would not do. Chamberlain believes in Italy. He really believes that he can acquire their 'friendship'. I say that I do not wish to arrange a meeting on that basis as it would only lead to disagreement.

I go away, devoted to Malcolm as ever. He has a truthful mind. But I am distressed by the whole thing. I quite see that we cannot announce to the whole world that London is undefended against air-attack. But yet the country ought to be told of the danger. I asked Malcolm what attitude I should adopt. He said, 'Go on criticising in details, but give general support, as it is a real national crisis.'

DIARY   *7th April, 1938*

Paul Emrys-Evans tells me that the Foreign Affairs Committee wish me to resign my post as Vice Chairman. I say that I shall do so. But the bore is that I cannot explain it all myself as I have to go off and do a broadcast on Dick Turpin. I come back to find that the F.A. Committee have put Paul through the hoops also, asking whether he is 'pro-Chamberlain' or 'pro-Eden'. He says that new officers will be elected after Easter. This will kill the F.A. Committee. People like Winston and Amery will no longer speak. I knew this to be inevitable, but now that it has happened, I am curiously hurt.

DIARY   *11th April, 1938*

Vansittart is appalled by the line taken by Henderson[1] in Berlin, and says that Henderson is a complete Nazi and that the Foreign Office do not trust him to represent their real point of view. He says that Henderson is stupid and vain and has become almost hysterical in the Berlin atmosphere.

Down to the House where I meet Jim Thomas.[2] We walk on the terrace and he tells me of Anthony Eden's attitude. The latter is very grateful to those of us who have been what he calls 'my violent supporters'. He will not come to terms with Chamberlain or allow the latter to profit by his return to the Cabinet. He regards Chamberlain as having been definitely treacherous. In this, curiously enough, he is supported by Baldwin with whom he was in constant consultation in the South of France. He himself intends to make a few big speeches on such general topics as Democracy and Young England, in which (while avoiding current topics in Foreign Affairs) he will clearly indicate that he stands for postwar England against the old men. He wants us at any cost to keep the flag flying.

Dine with the American Committee to meet Kennedy, the new U.S. Ambassador.[3] He makes a sensible and excellent speech. The P.M. also makes a speech and so does Winston. On to a party at Sibyl's. Talk to Jan Masaryk.

In the second half of April, Harold Nicolson went on a speaking tour of the Balkans. Officially the tour was under the auspices of the British Council, and the subjects of his lectures were, 'Are the English Hypocrites?' (Bucharest and Belgrade), 'The British Empire Today' (Bucharest), and 'Foundations of British Foreign Policy' (Sofia and Belgrade). Unofficially the Foreign Office asked him to do what he could to bolster Balkan morale against Hitler's south-east drift. He discovered, to his slight dismay, that his visits to Rumania, Bulgaria and Yugoslavia were used as occasions for pro-Western demonstrations in the three capitals.

[1] Sir Nevile Henderson (1882–1942). British Ambassador to Berlin from 1937 until the outbreak of war.

[2] J. P. L. Thomas M.P., Parliamentary Private Secretary to Anthony Eden, 1937–38, and one of his closest personal friends.

[3] Joseph Kennedy, American Ambassador in London, 1937–41, and father of President Kennedy.

He was treated more grandly than he thought his position justified. In each capital he was received by the reigning King or Prince, and the Press wrote up his visit as if (as he recorded in his diary) 'I was Anthony Eden himself'.

H.N. TO V.S-W.   *16th April, 1938*
                                    British Legation, Bucharest

On arrival at the Legation I was met by Rex Hoare.[1] A shaggy man and quite pleasant. His wife is a sister of Bill Bentinck and has that discontented look that settles upon the face of English society women who marry English diplomatists. I was given your telegram and an invitation from King Carol[2] asking me to lunch today. It was that which caused the trouble.

'Oh, Lord!' I said, 'I ought to have brought a tail-coat and top-hat.' 'Do you mean to say', gasped Hoare, 'that you have not brought either with you?' 'I'm afraid not', I said. He raised despairing eyes to heaven. 'And the monarch', he said, 'is so particular about such things.' In truth, upon my invitation card were the words '*Tenue-Jacquette*', and I start upon my Balkan tour *manque de tenue*. Hoare was really in despair. He took me up to his room to see whether his tail-coat would fit me. It did, more or less, but wouldn't meet at the front. 'That's better than nothing', he said, gazing at me with marked disapproval.

H.N. TO V.S-W.   *17th April, 1938*
                                    British Legation, Bucharest

At 12.30 I said that I must dress for luncheon. As I walked upstairs I felt strangely giddy. The staircase seemed to shift and wobble. I was appalled. Supposing I came over faint during my luncheon? That would be hell. I arrayed myself miserably in the tail-coat of Rex Hoare which would not, I regret, meet in front. But it looked all right. Then I espied the bottle of Sal Volatile which I had bought at Cambridge when I had to deliver the Rede Lecture after an all-night sitting. I corked it tightly and put it into my pocket, in fact the only

---

[1] Sir Reginald Hoare, British Minister in Bucharest, 1935-41.
[2] King Carol of Rumania. In 1930 he regained his throne from his son Michael, who had reigned in his stead after Carol's elopement with Magda Lupescu. In 1937 he proclaimed a dictatorship, and while he had an admiration for Mussolini, he had a healthy fear of Hitler.

pocket which I could call my own, my trouser pocket. Then off I went.

At the Palace an aide-de-camp in stays and aiguillettes arrived and made polite conversation. Then a lift hummed and two little pekinese darted in barking followed by the King in naval uniform. I bowed. He greeted me with affection and respect. We passed into the dining-room. I sat on his right. The aide-de-camp sat on his left. The pekinese sat on his knee. We started conversation.

He had ordered, he said, a purely Rumanian luncheon. God, it was good! In spite of my feeling so faint, I gobbled hard. I sat there on my pink plush chair and ate the *marimagi* and the *olovienic* and the *gruzaka*. We talked agreeably. He is a bounder but less of a bounder than he seemed in London. He was more at ease. His Windsor blue eyes were wistful and he had something behind them. Was it sadness, or over-work, or mysticism? He spoke with intelligence about Chamberlain and Eden and the Italian Agreement and the French Cabinet and the League of Nations. He was well-informed and most sensible. We kept all debating topics away.

I had been asked nonetheless to try and tackle him about his dictator-ship and the Hungarian minorities. I got on to the former subject by saying how difficult it was for us not having a good Opposition; how the basis of a democracy was an alternative Government; how the Labour people did not offer a possible alternative; and how bad that was for everyone concerned. He rose to the bait. He said that he also was experiencing that difficulty. It had been necessary for him to clear away the old party politicians (and indeed they were a poor lot), and that he must now build up again three more parties. 'Why three?' I asked, my mouth full of *lutchanika*; 'Your Majesty', I added. He replied that two parties were apt to share the spoils between themselves, and a third party was necessary to restore the balance. Quite a good idea.

I was beginning to enjoy my conversation when I became aware of a cold trickle and the smell of ammonia. I thrust my hand into my pocket. It was too late. The Sal had indeed proved Volatile and my trousers were rapidly drenched. I seized my napkin and began mopping surreptitiously. My remarks became bright and rather fevered, but quite uninterrupted. I mopped secretly while the aroma of Sal Volatile rose above the smell of *gruzhenkoia*.

This was agony. I scarcely heard what he was saying. 'Have you', he was asking, 'recovered your land-legs as yet? After three days in the train one feels the room rocking like after three days at sea.' So that was it! Why on earth had he not told me before, and now it was too late. I recovered my composure and dropped my sodden napkin. The conversation followed normal lines. At 2.45 he rose abruptly. I rose, too, casting a terrified glance at the plush seat of my chair. It bore a deep wet stain. What, oh what, will the butler think? He will only think one thing.

H.N. TO V.S-W.   *22nd April, 1938*
                                              British Legation, Sofia

I went to write my name upon the King. There were four books to write in: the King's; the Queen's; the Princess's; and the *Prince héritier*, who is eighteen months. I wrote my name very distinctly in the last as he must have difficulty, being so young, in reading foreign hand-writings.

Then to see the Prime Minister[1] in the Foreign Office. It is the same as in my day and I thought how often father must have waited in that waiting-room.[2] The Prime Minister was not an attractive man. An ex-diplomatist with those overpolished manners, that *boulevard extérieur* elegance, which always faintly annoys me.

Then came the Press in a band. I sat there and they fired questions at me. I was as discreet as I could be. Here again I am front-page news. It is pathetic how these people long for British friendship and how they exaggerate my importance and the meaning of my visit.

H.N. TO V.S-W.   *26th April, 1938*
                                              British Legation, Sofia

Yesterday I had an audience with King Boris [of Bulgaria]. He was not in the least like what I expected. His pictures show him as a glum and solemn person, but he is really just like an amusing Frenchman, all jerks and gestures and jokes. He kept me for nearly two hours, during nearly the whole of which time he was telling me stories of his adventures. He is certainly one of the most delightful people I have ever met. You know that I am not a royalty snob, and that I am generally bored by the artificiality of one's relations with kings. But this man would be delightful if one met him in a *wagon-restaurant* and

---

[1] Dr George Keosseivanoff.
[2] Lord Carnock was British Agent in Sofia, 1894–95, when H.N. was eight.

got into conversation. He reminded me of Attlee. His stories were thrilling. I did a Proust and kept on interrupting him: *'Mais précisez donc, Majesté, précisez donc!'*

Then there was a ghastly luncheon at which the Bulgarians sat dumb and glum, and I heard my own voice echoing alone in the *salle*. It is, I suppose, a relic of the old Turkish idea that one does not talk at meals. But it makes a banquet rather uphill work.

On his return from the Balkans, Harold Nicolson reported fully to the Foreign Office and was then plunged back into the gloom, fear and uncertainty of British politics. He was a member of the back-bench group, aligned more closely with Anthony Eden than with Churchill, which recognised Britain's military weakness but determined to hold the ring as far as was possible until we were fully rearmed. In this lay the difficulty: the Axis Powers could do almost as they wished unless Britain and France were prepared to resist them by force; and resistance was impossible until we had the means to win. This theme recurs constantly in the diaries and letters up to and including the Munich crisis. There was one moment when we thought we had checked Hitler by our warnings, during the weekend which began on 20th May. During the next forty-eight hours, the Governments in London, Paris, Prague and Moscow were convinced that Hitler was about to launch an attack against Czechoslovakia. Hitler certainly intended to do so, but not yet, and the report of concentration of troops in Saxony was false. The Czechs decided on immediate partial mobilization, and the French backed them by a promise of armed support. Lord Halifax, the British Foreign Secretary, warned the Germans that 'in the event of a European conflict, it was impossible to foresee whether Britain would not be drawn into it'. Nothing happened, and there was misplaced jubilation, reflected in the diaries, that the slide to war had been arrested.

H.N. TO V.S-W. 4th May, 1938
House of Commons

Oh my God, what a meeting I had last night at Lichfield![1] Two thousand people yelling, 'You go home!' Now you know me well. Why is it that when I face a yelling audience of 2,000 hostile people, I feel absolutely elated? I *loved* it. Why is that? I who loathe rows to

[1] Where H.N. was speaking in support of the National Labour candidate at a bye-election.

the point of real cowardice. I simply don't know, darling, what explanation there is. All I know is that after it, I felt that extreme exhilaration which people feel after the Cresta Run. How little one knows oneself. I am actually sorry that I am not going back there tonight. Yet I am *not* a combative person!

DIARY   10th May, 1938

December Club dinner. Jan Masaryk is our guest. I sit next to Spears and Bob Boothby. Jan makes what is rather too slangy and simple a speech, facetious: and yet behind it all one has the feeling of a man on the edge of a nervous breakdown. He says that the Czechs are prepared to make almost any sacrifice to avoid war, but will we please tell them exactly where they stand? What he means is, that they will make concessions provided that in return we guarantee their independence, and no British Government can do that.

On afterwards to Randolph Churchill's flat. He is editing a book of his father's speeches which show how right he has always been. His adoration for his father is really touching.

DIARY   11th May, 1938

Luncheon with Margot Oxford in Bedford Square. Lady Leslie, Anthony Eden and H. A. L. Fisher. Anthony Eden is looking twenty years younger. I go away with him and he asks all about opinion in the House. He is terribly worried by the fact that Foreign Affairs are splitting the country into two hostile and even embittered groups. He is himself determined to do everything to prevent such a split. He told me that he is not going to take Cabinet office, at least during this Parliament. He had meant to come down to the House yesterday as a private member, but felt that so long as the Colonial Office question was unsettled, it was better for him to keep away. In regard to the main issue of his resignation, he said: 'Time alone can show whether I was right or wrong. But that was not the real point. The real point was that I could not have signed that Treaty[1] and felt happy in my own conscience.'

---

[1] The Anglo-Italian Pact had been signed in early April. Mussolini pledged himself to evacuate Spain, and we promised to raise at Geneva the *de jure* recognition of the conquest of Abyssinia.

DIARY   *12th May, 1938*

Lunch with Sibyl Colefax. The party consists of the American
Ambassador, the Duchess of Rutland, Hore-Belisha, H. G. Wells,
Diana Cooper, Henry Channon, Maureen Dufferin and Gladwyn
Jebb. Afterwards Gladwyn, Victor Cazalet and I walk up and down
the Embankment Gardens under the statue of the Burghers of Calais
discussing what can possibly be done to avoid war. Gladwyn feels that
we must cut off any controversy at almost any price until our air-
defences are in order. He says that really the issue is one between losing
something of our old magnificence and ceasing to be a Great Power.
We have simply got to throw something to the wolves.

DIARY   *13th May, 1938*

I give a tea-party at K.B.W. for Henlein.[1] I have invited Spears,
Mark Patrick,[2] Duncan Sandys, Macnamara and Godfrey Nicholson.
Henlein arrives at 4.40 followed by Press men. We all sit around, have
tea, have sherry and talk till 6.40. Henlein tells us (1) that his ideal
solution would be a direct arrangement between himself and the
Czech Government, giving local autonomy to the Sudeten Germans
within a defined area. Such autonomy would cover all local interests
but would not affect federal interests such as finance, foreign affairs
and defence. Similar autonomy would be given to the Hungarian,
Polish and Ruthenian minorities. This cantonal system would be
absolutely democratic and upon an electoral basis. (2) That should
these direct negotiations fail, then he would be prepared to accept an

---

[1] Konrad Henlein, a gymnastics teacher, was the leader of the Sudeten German
Party in Czecho-Slovakia. Since 1935 it had been secretly subsidised by the German
Foreign Office. Hitler used the alleged grievances of the Sudetens as an excuse to
grab the whole of Czecho-Slovakia. On the previous day, 12th May, Henlein had
paid a secret visit to Berlin, where he received instructions from Ribbentrop, now
Foreign Minister, on how to hoodwink the British. He was to deny that he was
acting on instructions from Berlin and 'speak of the disintegration of the Czech
political structure, in order to discourage those circles which consider that their
intervention on behalf of this structure may still be of use'. In his speech at Carlsbad
on 24th April, Henlein had demanded full equality of status between Sudeten
Germans and Czechs, and full liberty for Sudetens to proclaim their Germanism
and their adhesion to the 'ideology of the Germans'. In London, where he met no
Ministers of the Crown, these views were considerably modified, and he reported
back to Hitler that Britain was indifferent to the fate of Czecho-Slovakia.
[2] Conservative M.P. for Tavistock since 1931, and a member of the Eden group.

international commission and a plebiscite upon the Saar precedent. He would not wish to join Germany, although many of his followers desire it. If both (1) and (2) fail, he sees no alternative but German occupation, which he well knows means war.

We tell him that British opinion will probably support his (1) and (2) but will turn against him if he makes demands which are impossible of fulfilment. For instance, we do not understand certain points in his Carlsbad speech such as that in which he claims a directing voice in Czech foreign policy, and that in which he expresses sympathy for Nazi *Weltanschauung*. He explains the first by saying that what he meant was that the Sudetens could not approve of a pro-Russian and anti-German policy, and would claim the right to protest against anything in the nature of allowing Czecho-Slovakia to be used for an attack upon Germany. But they did not claim more than to voice their opinion in this respect. They did not claim to overrule the majority. On the second point he said that they approved of the social and class legislation of the Nazis, but not their anti-God and anti-semitic measures.

H.N. TO V.S-W.   *17th May, 1938*
4 King's Bench Walk, E.C.4

We had an excitement yesterday, Swinton sacked.[1] At once I telephoned (or rather got Duncan [Sandys] to telephone) to Winston saying that his motion[2] must be withdrawn. He assented grumpily. But how silly the whole thing is! Here we are at the gravest crisis in our history, with a genius like Winston doing nothing and Kingsley Wood as our Minister for Air with Harold Balfour[3] as his Number Two. It is all due to David Margesson. I admire David, since he is strong and efficient and kind. But I do not believe that he is a good Cabinet-maker. Much sickness left behind. Nobody understands why Euan Wallace[4] is sent to the Treasury. Nobody understands why on earth Stanley[5] (who is amiable but stone-deaf) is given the Dominions. Nobody understands anything. There is a real impression that the whole show is going to crack up. This view is held, not only by pro-

---

[1] As a scapegoat for delays in British air-rearmament. He had been Air Minister since 1935.
[2] A demand for an enquiry into our air-defences.
[3] Later Lord Balfour of Inchrye.   [4] Financial Secretary to the Treasury, 1938-39.
[5] Lord Stanley.

tagonists like Winston, but by the silent useful members of whom nobody ever hears. They think that a new Government will emerge on a far wider basis, possibly a Coalition Government. I lie low. Little crouching head and bright eyes peeping out.

DIARY   18th May, 1938

On my way home I stop at Pratts' where I find three young Peers who state that they would prefer to see Hitler in London than a Socialist administration. I go to bed slowly, pondering upon the Decline and Fall of the British Empire.

H.N. TO V.S-W.   18th May, 1938
                                                              4 King's Bench Walk, E.C.4

What worries me is my lack of elegance. I go to the best hosiers, the best tailors, the best haircutters: I have the most perfect valet in London: I am always washing and scrubbing: my hairwash comes from Floris. Yet, when I mix with the elegant, I feel scrubby. My shirt pops, my tie becomes crooked, my waistcoat bulges, my hair gets deranged, and I look like Lord Aberconway[1] drunk. I suppose it is all a question of shape. If I were concave all these things would fall into, and remain in, place. As it is, they slip off.

These reflections are prompted by the fact that I went to a First Night. Mr Gordon Selfridge was in front of me—how patrician he appeared! Mr. Noel Coward was beside me—how young and distinguished he looked! Mr Ernest Thesiger, Mr Charles Graves— all of them looked as if they belonged. I looked like a hippo in Piccadilly. Incongruous I looked, and ill at ease. But it was a well acted play, and I took Sibyl on to the Savoy for supper. There was I and my girl-friend (a peeress, for all they knew) supping at the Savoy. And yet when I said 'Waiter!' it was of no avail. The waiter just fetched a chafing dish and brewed delicious sauces for someone else, while I just chafed.

I saw Buck De La Warr yesterday and had a long talk. I think he feels that Chamberlain has made a grave mistake in the Italian Agreement. But why did he not think so before? He says that it has cost the Government the floating vote, and Halifax came back from Geneva appalled by the impression made abroad. And then comes Mussolini's speech which has horrified those who thought we were getting 'friend-

[1] The Second Lord Aberconway (1879–1953).

ship' by this policy. Halifax is so supremely honest that he said, 'Anthony was right.' But that's no good.

DIARY   *20th May, 1938*

Jan Masaryk rings up to say that Benes[1] has invited Henlein to open negotiations. I fear it is too late. They are already accusing the Czechs of 'a terror', which is a lie. I am most uneasy. On to see Vansittart, where I find Jan Masaryk. They are not very gay. We are for it, I think.

DIARY   *22nd May, 1938*

Charles and Anne Lindbergh and Mrs Morrow come over from Long Barn. Lindbergh is most pessimistic. He says that we cannot possibly fight since we should certainly be beaten. The German Air Force is ten times superior to that of Russia, France and Great Britain put together. Our defences are simply futile and the barrage-balloons a mere waste of money. He thinks we should just give way and then make an alliance with Germany. To a certain extent his views can be discounted, (a) because he naturally believes that aeroplanes will be the determinant factor in war; and (b) because he believes in the Nazi theology, all tied up with his hatred of degeneracy and his hatred of democracy as represented by the free Press and the American public. But even when one makes these discounts, the fact remains that he is probably right in saying that we are outmastered in the air.

Victor Cazalet comes over and we sit on Sissinghurst Crescent in utter gloom. The Germans may force Henlein to increase his terms to the point where the Czechs cannot possibly accept and will then intervene. That brings in France, and we shall be faced with the alternative of abandoning France or having a disastrous war.

The news bulletin in the evening is slightly more reassuring. 'We have had', the announcer said, 'a perfect summer day.' True it is that it has been cloudless and that the sun has poured itself upon the azaleas and the irises. But on the whole it has been the most anxious and unhappy day that I can remember.

---

[1] Edvard Benes succeeded Thomas Masaryk, the founder of the Czechoslovak state, as President of the Republic in 1935. Benes had previously been Foreign Minister almost continuously from 1918 to 1935, and had played a leading part in the League of Nations.

DIARY   *23rd May, 1938*

A marvellous morning. The news is better. The German troops have not advanced. Go to see Buck De La Warr. He seems to think that things are really better and I beg the Cabinet to keep firm.

My own idea is that there is hope that this incident may mean the turn of the tide. If we manage to bring on a solution without violence, then it shows that Hitler has for the first time been checked. The Czechs, the French, the Poles and even the Russians have shown a united front. If we can carry through this affirmation of strength then it may mean the end of the present terror. We can then negotiate with the Germans on equal terms. But the danger is, of course, that provocation may lead to incidents. I meet Attlee when I return to the House. 'Well,' I said, 'are we seeing the turn of the tide?' 'I think so', he answers, 'so long as the Government do not show cowardice now.'

Dine at the Beefsteak. The Duke of Devonshire, Lord Onslow, Duff Cooper, Reading, Anthony Crossley and Harold Macmillan. Duff hopes things may go well. I urge him to keep the Cabinet stiff. 'That's all very well,' he says. 'But the Germans are so beastly powerful.'

DIARY   *26th May, 1938*

Lunch with Maureen Stanley. The Halifaxes are there, also Ronnie Cartland, Lady Birkenhead, and Edward Stanley. Halifax tells me that Goebbels said to him, 'You must realise how sensitive we are. You have three hundred years' tradition behind you. We have only four.' That means that they really do regard themselves as something quite new. We regard them as a development of Prussian history. They regard themselves as a revolution. They are thus enraged when we suggest that Hitler might go to a better tailor. We are rather arrogant and insensitive regarding that aspect.

We discuss the question of conciliating Goering. Halifax says that he would be pleased by an invitation to Sandringham. Ronnie and I say that we would resent any such thing. It would affect American opinion. It would lower our dignity. No, ask Goering to Nepal as much as you like, but do not expect the Queen to shake hands with him. Halifax is rather startled by our vehemence.

DIARY   *2nd June, 1938*

Coudenhove-Kalergi[1] comes to see me. He is having a great International Congress in Paris next April and wants me to go. I say I will. He is interesting on the subject of Hitler. He claims that he was essentially a coward, that he is of Jewish origin, that his war-record was deplorable, that he funked during the 1923 Putsch, that he will always give way if you abuse him.[2]

DIARY   *6th June, 1938*

I feel we are passing out of the zone of fear, and entering the zone of anger. Our isolationists must see by now that isolation is not enough. The other people will not leave us alone. The violent countries are creating around themselves an iron ring of hatred. The great drama begins to shape itself towards its close.

How difficult it is to determine what is the right counsel. My view is: (1) Our ancient traditions and principles were based upon the theory that we should protect the weak and defy the strong. (2) I know that this theory was founded upon our own security, and was a luxury offered to us by our own invulnerability, and therefore certainty of ultimate victory. (3) Chamberlain (who has the mind and manner of a clothes-brush) aims only at assuring temporary peace at the price of ultimate defeat. He would like to give Germany all she wants at the moment, and cannot see that if we make this surrender we shall be unable to resist other demands. If we assuage the German alligator with fish from other ponds, she will wax so fat that she will demand fish from our own ponds. And we shall not by then be powerful enough to resist.

What am I to do? I see quite clearly that Rome and Berlin hope to drive a wedge between us and Paris. I see quite clearly that Paris, being concentrated upon *la ligne bleue des Vosges*, thinks only of her own safety. I believe that we might possibly secure peace for ten years by breaking with France and Russia and allowing the Germans to do what they wish. But at the end of that period we should stand

---

[1] Richard Coudenhove-Kalergi, the founder and President of the Paneuropean Union. He also founded the European Parliamentary Union in 1947.

[2] Hitler could not be described as 'of Jewish origin', and in the First War he proved himself a brave soldier. But it is true that in the 1923 Munich Putsch he was the first to scamper for safety when the soldiers opened fire.

without friends and without defences. France would have gone: the League idea would have gone: the small states would have gone: Germany would have the food resources of Hungary and above all the oil resources of Rumania. We should be powerless. And then Germany would say to us, 'Stand and deliver!'

Yet if we provoke Germany now (when our defences are in a pitiable state), she will or may destroy us utterly. We all know that at the moment Germany is not prepared for a European War. But if we really oppose her, she may drive us into it. And if we do not oppose her she will become so strong that we cannot face it. There is some truth in the idea that every month gained is a month gained. The Italians are already distrusting Mussolini, and after our Czechoslovak success the Germans are distrusting Hitler. The spell may have been broken, and I know that it is little more than a spell. But what happens if the Japanese involve America in an Asiatic war, involve Russia as well, detach some of our ships—then Germany can strike in Europe.

We have lost our will-power, since our will-power is divided. People of the governing classes think only of their own fortunes, which means hatred of the Reds. This creates a perfectly artificial but at present most effective secret bond between ourselves and Hitler. Our class interests, on both sides, cut across our national interests. I go to bed in gloom.

DIARY   *7th June, 1938*

We have never imposed any sense of filial duty on either Ben or Nigel. They know that they can make any possible claim on us and that we shall never make any claim on them. That is the only basis for a proper relationship between one generation and another. Our love for them is really extended egoism. Vita and I are intelligent enough to realise that. They are intelligent enough to realise that it is something more than that. Thus we harmonise well. It is more difficult for me than for Vita. She is essentially a solitary soul. I try to live my own life again in those of my sons. I know that this drives them to fury, and I try to control it. I know that it is rather grotesque of me (with all my activities) loving them both so much and thinking more about their lives than about my own. But they understand it. Benzie in a gentle way. Nigel in a dutiful way. I know that they are very fond of me. But I am sometimes terrified by my adoration of them. It just isn't cricket. I try to conceal it, but they are spry enough to see that it is there. And faintly, kindly, gently they regard it as *aidoia*.[1] In just such a way did I resent Mummy's adoration of myself. But now that I am older (or is it old?) I feel that her adoration was a sort of compass-rock in my life. Ben and Nigel have hitherto been successful in life and do not know what suffering is. Ben had a sense of it at Eton, and I think we helped him at that moment. Nigel has never really suffered, and if he did, he would rush away from us, fearing soft appreciation, gentle love. Yet if I were wretched, both of them would fly to my assistance and be of the utmost help. I never thought of that before. I cannot do much to help them, but they (if things went wrong) would sacrifice everything to help me. That is true. Hurray! I have untied one knot in our relationship.

DIARY   *15th June, 1938*

Anthony Eden tells me that he will oppose Chamberlain if he tries to make a Four Power pact,[2] and will we all rally round? I say we shall indeed. Then on to see Vansittart, who says that he thinks Chamberlain has had such a lesson over the Italian agreement[3] that he will not think of German negotiations yet.

H.N. TO V.S-W.   *17th June, 1938*
                                    4 King's Bench Walk, E.C.4

I met an Austrian yesterday who had just got away from Vienna, and what he said made me ill. There is a devilish sort of humour in their cruelty. For instance, they rounded up the people walking in the Prater on Sunday last, and separated the Jews from the rest. They made the Jewish gentlemen take off all their clothes and walk on all fours on the grass. They made the old Jewish ladies get up into the trees by ladders and sit there. They then told them to chirp like birds. The Russians never committed atrocities like that. You may take a man's life; but to destroy all his dignity is bestial. This man told me that with his own eyes he had seen Princess Stahremberg washing out the urinals at the Vienna railway-station. The suicides have been appalling. A great cloud of misery hangs over the town.

[1] *Aidoia gerontos*, 'the shame of an old man'.
[2] Between Britain, France, Germany and Italy.
[3] Despite his solemn engagement, Mussolini increased his intervention in Spain, sending four thousand fresh volunteers there in June and July. Consequently the Anglo-Italian agreement did not enter into force.

I might have thought the man exaggerating. His facts were detailed and his manner calm. But still I retained a portion of doubt whether even Germans could behave like this. But I dined with Bernstorff, and when I repeated these stories, he said, 'Yes, they are true. A Nazi friend of mine was attached to German Headquarters. He told me that he couldn't stand it. He said, "I have seen grown men behave like little boys who pull the wings off flies."'

Dearest, what unhappiness there is in this world. I am glad I am in a position to do something, however slight, to help. I simply could not just remain idle and do nothing.

DIARY   27th June, 1938

Anthony Crossley takes me to task for being so anti-Chamberlain. He says I am working for his fall. He says that the Conservatives realise this and simply hate me. I say, 'But surely, Anthony, they are always so polite when I meet them?' 'Yes', he answers, 'that is part of their technique.'

DIARY   30th June, 1938

Denman asks me tactfully why I have dropped out of politics, and why I take no part in the debates. I say it is because I cannot support the foreign policy of the Government and do not wish to say so openly. The result is a glum silence and the general impression that I have 'dropped out'. He says this is a pity.

Dine with Rob Bernays and Miss Mitford, Unity's[1] cousin. She says that Unity does not hope to marry Hitler. It is merely adoration. Hitler likes her because of her fanaticism. She wants the Jews to be made to eat grass. Miss Mitford herself is not in favour of the Jews eating grass.

H.N. TO V.S-W.   11th July, 1938
                                    4 King's Bench Walk, E.C.4

What a nice Sunday I had! Why did you ask me whether I was happy in life? You asked it in such an odd way. I mean, I felt that you imagined that I was not happy. I think I mind more than most people getting old. The compensations of age (respect, power, fame etc.) mean nothing to me, and I only notice the disadvantages. But that is merely a small despair. I love my life nowadays more than I have ever loved it.

[1] The daughter of Lord Redesdale and sister-in-law of Sir Oswald Mosley.

For what, after all, is happiness? 'Occupation in congenial sur-roundings.' Now I have tremendous occupation which, although it may not seem very successful from the outside, is, I know, rather a successful little thing from the inside. I suppose that some mutton-heads might say, 'Harold had a wonderful chance when he entered the House. He had won a dramatic election and had a reputation behind him. His maiden speech electrified the House. And then he casts it all away for some sentimental reason.' I daresay they say that. But it isn't what I say, my dearest guide. It is: 'I could have toadied those in power and exploited my reputation had I wished. I did not do so. I have proved that I did not join National Labour for purposes of self-advancement. And I have done what I wanted, namely, to earn the respect of people whom I respect. The others do not count.'

So much for the 'occupation'. Then comes the 'congenial sur-roundings'. You know how I love the House and what warm friends I have there. But behind the House there is my own life. There are the boys, who mean a great deal to me. There are my friends. And there is you, my dearest—and about that I think that your dear muddle-head gets confused. You believe so much in passion that sometimes you underestimate love. I know that the central thing in myself (the actual main-spring which makes all the little cogs go round and round so busily) is my love for you. It is the rock on which my life is founded. I know it bores you to realise that we are married—and by the way, we shall shortly have a silver wedding. You must admit that I have always respected that side in your eccentricity. But whatever you may feel about it, and whatever I may feel about it, the fact remains that you are the only person whom I should want to be with me were I in pain. Oh my dearest Viti, I do love you so. And as we both know this fact, we evade it. It is the silent secret between ourselves.

But what I really meant this letter to be about was the poem.[1] I was shy about it, and that made me off-hand. But I was so pleased to think that you had written your long poem that I have felt little twiddles of pleasure all day. It is really true that I would rather you finished a long poem than I became Secretary of State. And I know (with absolute conviction) that you would be more pleased if I were appointed to the Cabinet than if you finished a long poem. Yet each of us would hide their pleasure at the other's success. Which, I suppose, is the way that people get on in life.

[1] *Solitude*. Hogarth Press. 1938.

DIARY   *1st August, 1938*

Lunch with Walter Lippmann and Frederick Voigt. Lippmann has just
been in Italy, Germany and Czechoslovakia, and so has Frederick.
Their points of view agree. They think that Hitler is planning an
attack on the Czechs for the third week in August. The question is,
'Will we come in?' The French may only mobilise, and the Germans
count on success in one week. Frederick thinks it will take them
three weeks to take Prague. Lippmann thinks that if we allow the
Czechs to be crushed, America will turn against us, but that if we
intervene, America will be in within six weeks. We agree that the
country has no idea at all what a mess we are in. Frederick thinks the
Prime Minister has no illusions. I am not so sure.

Harold Nicolson took a short summer holiday divided into two parts.
First he stayed with Somerset Maugham at Cap Ferrat, where he twice
met the Duke and Duchess of Windsor: on his return to London on
8th August, he immediately left for Scotland and with Ben visited the
Shiant Islands in the Outer Hebrides, where Nigel had been camping
with Rohan Butler for the past ten days. Back at Sissinghurst, he began
writing 'Diplomacy', a study in diplomatic method, and continued his
book-reviews and regular wireless talks on current affairs.

V.S-W. TO H.N. (*at Cap Ferrat*)   *3rd August, 1938*
                                                                                Sissinghurst

I went to Rodmell[1] for last night, and very nice it was too. We sat
out in the garden watching the late sunlight making the corn all golden
over the Downs. Then I had a long talk this morning with Virginia,
who was in her most delightful mood. Tell your host,[2] if you think
it would please him, that Virginia much admired his autobiography
(*The Summing Up*). She had liked the clarity of his style, and also the
honesty with which he tried to get at the truth. She liked the analysis
of his own methods of writing.

Oh my dear, what an enchanting person Virginia is! How she
weaves magic into life! Whenever I see her, she raises life to a higher
level. How cheap she makes people like —— seem! And Leonard too:
with his schoolboyish love for pets and toys (gadgets), he is irresistibly

[1] Leonard and Virginia Woolf's small house near Lewes.
[2] Somerset Maugham.

350

young and attractive. How wrong people are about Bloomsbury, saying that it is devitalised and devitalising. You couldn't find two people less devitalised or devitalising than the Wolves—or indeed people more vitalising than Roger Fry,[1] for example. I think that where Bloomsbury has suffered is in its hangers-on like ——— and equivalent young men, and of course the drooping Lytton[2] must have done its cause a great deal of harm. I hated Lytton.

H.N. TO V.S-W.   *4th August, 1938*
                                            Villa Mauresque, Cap Ferrat

I am glad I came here. It really is the perfect holiday. I mean, the heat is intense, the garden lovely, the chair long and cool, the lime-juice at hand, a bathing-pool there if one wishes to splash, scenery, books, gramophones, pretty people—and above all, the sense that it is not going on too long.

H.N. TO V.S-W.   *5th August, 1938*
                                            Villa Mauresque, Cap Ferrat

There was a lovely soft warm evening with that marvellous pink light among the pines. I went up and sat alone with Tacitus by the swimming-pool. It is surrounded by great massifs of red and white oleanders. The sun set over Cap d'Antibes. The lighthouses began to wink across a still purple sea. I stayed there until the red oleanders became invisible and only the white oleanders shone in the moon. I meditated.

Then I came down to the villa, had a bath, shaved, put on my best clothes. Because the late King of England was coming to dinner. Willy Maugham had prepared us carefully. He said that the Duke gets cross if the Duchess is not treated with respect.

When they arrived Willy and his daughter went into the hall. We stood sheepishly in the drawing-room. In they came. She, I must say, looks very well for her age. She has done her hair in a different way. It is smoothed off her brow and falls down the back of her neck in ringlets. It gives her a placid and less strained look. Her voice has also changed. It now mingles the accents of Virginia with that of a Duchess in one of Pinero's plays. He entered with his swinging naval gait, plucking at his bow tie. He had on a *tussore* dinner-jacket. He was in very high spirits. Cocktails were brought and we stood around

[1] Artist and art-critic, 1866-1934.   [2] Lytton Strachey, the author, 1880-1932.

the fireplace. There was a pause. 'I am sorry we were a little late', said the Duke, 'but Her Royal Highness couldn't drag herself away.' He had said it. The three words fell into the circle like three stones into a pool. Her (gasp) Royal (shudder) Highness (and not one eye dared to meet another).[1]

Then we went into dinner. There were two cypresses and the moon. I sat next to the Duchess. He sat opposite. They called each other 'darling' a great deal. I called him 'Your Royal Highness' a great deal and 'Sir' the whole time. I called her 'Duchess'. One cannot get away from his glamour and his charm and his sadness, though, I must say, he seemed gay enough. They have a villa here[2] and a yacht, and go round and round. He digs in the garden. But it is pathetic the way he is sensitive about her. It was quite clear to me from what she said that she hopes to get back to England. When I asked her why she didn't get a house of her own somewhere, she said, 'One never knows what may happen. I don't want to spend all my life in exile.'

DIARY   9th August, 1938
                                                    Portree, Isle of Skye

It is strange how excited I am by my first view of Skye. Before going to bed I gaze at the sunset behind the mountains and watch the sea-gulls wheel, and think that perhaps my ill-adjustment to English life has been due to this Celtic strain. I agree with Nigel that nothing is so ridiculous as the Sassenach who pretends to be a Highlander. Yet deep in me is a dislike of the English (it may account for what may seem in me the purely whimsical), and my joy at knowing that by origin I belong to these solemn proud hills is certainly not anything but deeply sincere.[3] I go to bed entranced.

---

[1] Shortly before their marriage on 3rd June, 1937, the Duke of Windsor had received a letter from his brother, King George VI, informing him with regret that the Cabinet had made a formal submission that while the Duke could continue to use the title Royal Highness, this title could not be extended to the Duchess. The Duke was deeply hurt by this action. 'In his eyes,' the Duchess records in her memoirs, 'it was an ultimate slur upon his wife, and therefore upon himself.'

[2] La Cröe, Cap d'Antibes, which they had rented from Sir Pomeroy Burton.

[3] The Nicolsons migrated from Skye to Edinburgh in the 16th century.

DIARY

10th August, 1938
Shiant Islands, Outer Hebrides

I had agreed with the Captain[1] to start at 5 a.m. Sure enough at that hour the winch begins to raise the anchor. I wake up and swing out of my bunk. I climb up on deck. There are the great hills of Skye and on the other side that flat table-mountain of Raasay. At about 11.30 the Captain points ahead. 'There', he says, 'are the Shiants.' A vague rounded outline of a mountain looms through the haze. On we go over pearled waters. By noon the islands are quite clear. As we get nearer we scan the shore through glasses. Suddenly Ben says, 'I see a man.' A tiny figure can be observed waving on top of the cliff. But only one figure. We are alarmed lest it be Rohan Butler,[2] and that he will tell us that Niggs is lying a crumpled mass on the rocks. We get in closer and pass into the bay between the two main islands. And then we see the figure quite clearly and he flings his hair back with a gesture of the head which can only be Niggs' gesture. My heart thumps.

Then we cast anchor. We get into the dinghy, and hum along the placid waters and all the little puffins rise in fury. As we approach the beach, two figures run down to it. Nigel and Rohan. We walk round to his little shieling. Niggs is glad to have a day like this to show me his romance. It is like a Monet, all pink and green and shining. We are very gay. We lunch by the fire on the flat stone. Niggs has conquered his disappointment.[3] I have seldom in life felt so happy. After luncheon we go round the islands in a dinghy. The cliffs are terrible and romantic. We sing for seals and they pop up their anxious little heads. It is lovelier than can be believed.

The section of Harold Nicolson's diary which covers the period of the Munich crisis may perhaps be regarded as historically its most important part. The events of September 1938 are recorded in forty closely type-written pages, about 25,000 words, written day by day as the story un-folded, and sometimes hour by hour, since Harold Nicolson would often snatch ten minutes between interviews and speeches to bring the record

---

[1] H.N. had chartered a small ketch to take him from Portree to the Shiants.

[2] Nigel's close friend at Balliol. Soon afterwards, he became a Fellow of All Souls, and subsequently Editor of *Documents on British Foreign Policy, 1919–39*, and historical adviser to the Foreign Secretary.

[3] At getting a third in his History Finals.

up to date, and complete it late at night or early the next morning.

The diary became a mounting indictment of a policy which he foresaw would lead to war on the worst possible terms for Britain. A strong note of patriotism rings through these pages. He minded as much the betrayal of the old principles of British foreign policy that we should support the weak against the strong, justice against evil, negotiation against violence, as he did the surrender of yet another strategic position to Hitler, the snub to Russia, the endorsement of French defeatism, and the alienation of the smaller states of Eastern Europe. He accepted 'with unutterable sadness but with resignation' Hitler's claim to the German-speaking areas of Czechoslovakia; but what he could not tolerate was the pretence that Chamberlain had brought back peace with honour from Munich and his failure to galvanise the country into a realisation of the extreme danger to which the Munich Agreement exposed us. Harold Nicolson summed up his views in his speech to the House of Commons after the Agreement had been signed:

'I know that in these days of realism those of us who try to keep our election pledges are told that we are disloyal to the Party. I know that those of us who try to be consistent are accused of having one-track minds. I know that principles are considered as rather eccentric and ideals are identified with hysteria. I know that those of us who believe in the traditions of our policy, who believe that one great function of this country is to maintain moral standards in Europe, not to make friends with people whose conduct is demonstrably evil but to set up some sort of standard by which the smaller Powers can test what is good in international conduct and what is not—I know that those who hold such beliefs are accused of possessing the Foreign Office mind. I thank God that I possess the Foreign Office Mind.'

Harold Nicolson, Churchill, Eden and Duff Cooper, were the only members on the Government side of the House who did not cheer Neville Chamberlain as he set out for Munich and on his return. He was bitterly reproached by his Party in Parliament and in his constituency. But as in another crisis eighteen years later, which created equivalent emotions and divisions, there were many who felt in their hearts that the Prime Minister was wrong, but kept silent. Except momentarily, Harold Nicolson did not suffer from his isolation. He was soon proved right. What is more, the Munich crisis brought out all that was most powerful in him, in thought, feeling and expression. It overcame his nervousness and sense of inadequacy in the House, his doubts about the morality and risks of war with Hitler. From this time onwards Germany was an enemy who must be beaten.

The story of Munich is so familiar that only the main stages of the crisis need be recalled here. Hitler intended to crush and occupy Czechoslovakia to open his way to the east. His excuse was to be the 'intolerable plight' of the 3½ million Sudeten Germans on its northern, western and southern borders. Although these territories had never formed part of Germany, he demanded their 'return' to the Reich. France and Russia were bound by treaty to go to the aid of the Czechs if they were attacked, and Britain was bound to France if she became involved in a war with Germany. Chamberlain was determined to avoid war by putting pressure on the Czech Government to give way to German demands. In August he sent Lord Runciman to Prague as a 'mediator' between Henlein and Benes, but in effect to pave the way for handing over the Sudetenland to Hitler. On 15th September Chamberlain flew to Berchtesgaden for his first interview with Hitler, and agreed in principle to the secession of the German-speaking areas. On the 18th, Daladier and Bonnet (the French Prime Minister and Foreign Minister) visited London and drew up with the British the Anglo-French plan by which all areas of Czechoslovakia with more than 50 per cent German inhabitants should be handed over to Hitler without even a plebiscite to ascertain their wishes. Benes accepted this plan under strong pressure.

With this agreement in his pocket, Chamberlain flew back to Germany on 22nd September and met Hitler at Godesberg. Hitler told him that this was no longer enough. The Sudetenland must be occupied by German troops by 1st October at the latest; all military installations in the evacuated zone were to be left intact, and not even the cattle and household goods of the ousted Czechs might be removed. Chamberlain protested against these outrageous terms, but on his return to London he attempted to persuade his Cabinet to accept them and advise the Czechs to do the same. There was opposition in the Cabinet, particularly from Duff Cooper, and from the French, and Chamberlain was forced to tell Hitler through his emissary Sir Horace Wilson that 'if France, in pursuance of her Treaty obligations to Czechoslovakia, became actively engaged in hostilities with Germany, the United Kingdom would feel obliged to support her'. Hitler merely took note of that position. It seemed that war was inevitable. On the 27th September the French army was partially mobilised; so was the British Fleet. 1½ million Czech *soldiers manned their fortifications on the German border. At the last moment Hitler agreed to Mussolini's suggestion of a conference (actually the proposal was drafted in Berlin), and the news reached Chamberlain during the final few moments of his speech to the House of Commons on the 28th.*

The conference met next day in Munich. Chamberlain, Daladier, Hitler and Mussolini were the main participants. Neither Russia nor Czechoslovakia was invited. An agreement was signed at 1 a.m. on the 30th, by which Hitler obtained almost everything that he had demanded at Godesberg. Chamberlain returned in triumph to London, waving a piece of paper signed by himself and Hitler, by which Britain and Germany pledged themselves 'never to go to war with one another again'. From the windows of Downing Street he assured the cheering crowds that he had brought back 'peace with honour'.

The debate on the Munich Agreement occupied four days, 3rd–6th October. It was opened by Duff Cooper, the only Cabinet Minister to resign. Harold Nicolson spoke on the 5th, as did Winston Churchill, who declared that 'we have sustained a total and unmitigated defeat'. In the vote of confidence which followed, between thirty and forty Government supporters abstained.

DIARY   *22nd August, 1938*

Lunch with the Russian Ambassador alone. I ask him what Russia would do if the Germans pressed on to the Black Sea. He says that the old pan-Slav feeling is dead, that Russia has no sympathy for the semi-fascist systems established in the Balkans, and that she is profoundly disillusioned with the western democracies. If we and France went to war on behalf of the Czechs, then Russia would help. But if we abandon Czechoslovakia, then Russia will become isolationist. She is unconquerable and has her own unlimited territory and resources. Even if Germany absorbed a portion of the Ukraine, how would it benefit her? It would create an *irredenta* and perpetuate Russo-German enmity. Germany could not get the Donetz basin since it is too far away. Russia would thus acquiesce in the domination of the Balkans and even perhaps in some seizure of the Ukraine, confident that her own future would not be jeopardised by such minor losses. But she would not consent to Germany establishing her influence over Turkey.

356

57

her own unlimitedterritory and resources. Even if Germany absorbed
a portion of' theUkraine--how would it benefit her ? It would create
an irredenta and perpetuate Russo-German enmity. Germany could not
get the Donetz basin since it is too far away . Russia would thus
acquiesce in the domination of the Balkans and even perhaps in some
seizureof the Ukraine, confident that her own future would not be
jeopardised by such minor losses. But she would not consent to
Germany estaboishing herinfluehce over Turkey.
   Go¼ to a film and then back to K.B.W. Dine at Bourlestin with
Jim Lees Milne. He says there are legal difficulties about putting
Knole under the National Trust Scheme.
   Broadcast aftewwards upon the possibility of Hitler bringing for-
ward a peace offer. It goes well, I think.

Tuesday August 23. A fine day and slightly warmer. I go ddown by
the 8.15 having my breakfast at the station. Read Temperley's
"Foundations of British Policy". Mac is ill with flu. Olive Nation and her General come to luncheon. Vita had forgotten about
them and we have slices of ham and a paté out of a tin. Then the
Womens Institute of Hurstmonceux come over in a charabanc and we
take them round. Ben and Nigel are most helpful. In the evening
we listen to a talk by Colonel Graves upon the future of television. I then explain to them that this daáry, of which they know
the industry and persistence, is not, a work of literature or self-
revelation but a mere record of activity put down for my own
reference only.

Wednesday August 24. A lovely day. Bathe. Revise Chapter 1 of my
Diplomacy book splitting it into two chapetrs, the one dealing
with the origins of diplomatic technique and the other with
the evolution of theory. Vita goes to Burwash to see an old widow
who has dramatised "All Pasion Spent". She also sees Irene Pirrie.
The boys and I pick nuts and then walk round the lake trying to
find a name for my boat. We decide (but only after having rejecta
every alternative) on "The Mar". Viti comes back for dinner.

Half a page of the original diary for August 1938

DIARY   *23rd August, 1938*

In the evening I explain to Vita, Ben and Nigel that this diary, of
which they know the industry and persistence, is not a work of literature
or self-revelation, but a mere record of activity put down for my own
reference only.[1]

DIARY   *26th August, 1938*

Finish chapter II[2], but I am not very happy about it, as it seems ill-
arranged and imprecise. In the afternoon the boys and I go over to
Fisher's Gate to have tea with the De La Warrs.

Buck and I have a long conversation.[3] He says (a) that the Germans
have made up their minds to attack the Czechs, and (b) that they are
planning some incident which will to some extent put the French in

[1] This is the only reference in the diary itself to the purposes for which it was compiled.
[2] Of *Diplomacy*.
[3] Lord De La Warr was then Lord Privy Seal, with a seat in the Cabinet.

the wrong. He says that they have practically counted us out and that they know that France is weakened by internal troubles. Neither the French nor ourselves wish to 'fight for Czechoslovakia', and therefore they imagine they can bring off their coup *in aller Ruhe*.

Buck has no illusions in regard to the importance of Czechoslovakia. He knows that if that barrier falls, Germany gets down to the Black Sea and becomes invincible. He is not sure whether Chamberlain is equally aware of these consequences. He suspects him of regarding the Czechs as a tiresome little Slav state whom we might protect possibly, but only as an act of great generosity. Chamberlain has no conception really of world politics. Nor does he welcome advice from those who have.

I tell him about my conversation with Maisky.[1] He thinks it is so important that he forces me to sit down there and then and write a record of it for Vansittart. The point being that if Maisky can be induced to promise Russian support if we take a strong line over Czechoslovakia, the weak will of the Prime Minister may be strengthened.

DIARY   *29th August, 1938*

I say to Gladwyn [Jebb], 'Well, I suppose it is 51 per cent on peace and 49 per cent on war?' 'I should have reversed those proportions', he answers.

DIARY   *1st September, 1938*

We may just squeak through. On the other hand, we may get into the same mess as in 1914—namely, give the Czechs the impression that we shall fight for them, and the Germans the impression that we shall not.

DIARY   *9th September, 1938*

Dine with Rob Bernays. Buck, Diana [De La Warr] and Colin Coote[2] there. Colin says that *The Times* leader urging the Czechs to surrender their fringes[3] was written by Leo Kennedy[4] and was

---

[1] On 22nd August. See above.
[2] The distinguished journalist. He was Editor of the *Daily Telegraph* 1950-1964. Knighted in 1962.
[3] On 7th September *The Times* had published a leader suggesting that Czechoslovakia might become more 'homogeneous' if it lost its 'fringe of alien population'.
[4] A Diplomatic Correspondent of *The Times*.

merely glanced at by Geoffrey Dawson.[1] He is appalled by the lack of responsible guidance in Printing House Square. Nobody seemed to realise the amount of damage which such an article would cause.

We talk of the general situation. Buck is discreet and loyal, but I gather that the firm strong attitude of Neville Chamberlain in his conversation with Bob Boothby[2] is not as definite as we had hoped. Colin says, 'I bet sixty to one that the Government back out at the last moment.' Buck does not deny this. He looks grim. I have little doubt that if the Government back down, then Buck and Rob will resign. Colin Coote warns them that in that event they will be accused of constituting a 'war-party', and Chamberlain and Simon will be produced as angels of peace. I return home very anxious.

DIARY   *11th September, 1938*

I have a late dinner with Oliver Stanley. His point of view, I suppose, is typical of the better type of Cabinet opinion. What the worst type of opinion may be passes my comprehension. Thus Oliver agrees that the conflict has really nothing to do with Czechoslovakia, but is the final struggle between the principle of law and the principle of violence, and that the two protagonists in this struggle are Hitler and Chamberlain. He also agrees that if Germany were to make an attack on Czechoslovakia and if France were to be drawn in, it would be almost impossible for us to abstain. Yet his incidental remarks show me that at heart he is longing to get out of it. Thus he loses no opportunity of abusing the Czechs and of reviling Benes for being tricky and slippery. At the same time any reference to Russian assistance makes him wince, and at one moment he sighed deeply and said, 'You see, whether we win or lose, it will be the end of everything we stand for.' By 'we' he means obviously the capitalist classes.

DIARY   *14th September, 1938*

The news is even worse. Japan and Italy have announced that they stand by Germany. The Russian fleet is mobilised. The Sudetens refuse to negotiate and maintain their ultimatum. We feel we are on

---

[1] Editor of *The Times*, 1923–41.
[2] In a conversation which Robert Boothby had had with the Prime Minister on 2nd September, Chamberlain had given him the impression of resolution and determination.

the very edge of the railings lining the cliff. I go on working because I have not the heart to listen to the 9.40 news. Then at 10 Viti comes in and says the P.M. is flying tomorrow to Berchtesgaden. My first feeling is one of enormous relief.

DIARY   15th September, 1938

How difficult it is to decide! Vita takes the line that the Sudeten Germans are justified in claiming self-determination and the Czechs would be happier without them in any case. But if we give way on this, then the Hungarians and Poles will also claim self-determination, and the result will be that Czechoslovakia will cease to exist as an independent State. Vita says that if it is as artificial as all that, then it should never have been created. That may be true, although God knows how we could have refused to recognise her existence in 1918.[1] It all seemed such a reality in those days. Hitler has all the arguments on his side, but essentially they are false arguments. And we, who have right on our side, cannot say that our real right is to resist German hegemony. That is 'imperialistic'. Never have conflicting theories become so charged with illusions.

DIARY   16th September, 1938

Meet Vincent Massey at the Club. I say, 'Well, are the Government going to give way?' He says, 'It is better to have smallpox three years from now than at once.' I say, 'Yes, but if we have it now, we shall recover; if in three years, we shall die.'

DIARY   19th September, 1938

Go to see Anthony Eden. I find him in the depths of despair, and ask him what attitude he will adopt. He says it is very difficult to make any formal decision until the full facts are in his possession. He says that probably if he had been in Halifax's place, he might have done the same as he did. Only he adds with a smile, 'But I do not think I should have put myself into Halifax's place.' He says it is very difficult to criticise one link in the chain of events,[2] when the whole chain is

---

[1] H.N. had been on the Committee of the Paris Peace Conference which prepared the clauses of the Treaty of St Germain which defined the frontiers of Czechoslovakia.

[2] The Anglo-French plan for handing over the German-speaking areas of Czechoslovakia had been published that morning.

in itself vicious. He doesn't wish to lead a revolt or to secure any resignations from the Cabinet.

We then discuss the effect of our surrender. He takes the very gloomiest view, feeling that leadership has now passed completely from our hands into those of Germany. He foresees that not merely the countries of south-eastern Europe but also Portugal will now fall irretrievably under German domination. He agrees with me that Hitler really desires two things, first to obtain more Germans, secondly to smash Czechoslovakia, either as a barrier to his own advance or as an advanced post for Russia. He does not however agree with me that we can give way on the first item but not on the second, since he feels that both objects have now been fused into one.

I discuss his own position in the country and suggest that he is losing a great deal of ground. I say that this does not matter in the least, since he will get it back, and I merely mention it in fear that he may be conscious of it himself and abandon the wise attitude he has followed hitherto of remaining quiet. He replies that he does not feel he has lost ground in the country at all, and that in any case he is young[1] and can wait until popular favour returns to him.

We talk of what small comfort it is to have been proved right, and how terrible has been the influence of the Cliveden set. As I leave him he says, 'Well, we shall not be able to avert war now.'

I dine at the Marlborough with Buck De La Warr and Walter Elliot. The latter very ingeniously states the Government point of view. He makes a great point of the desertion of France, saying that when one army runs away, the other army can scarcely maintain its position. He denies absolutely that the Prime Minister was given an ultimatum at Berchtesgaden. He claims that the Russians never promised really to help, and that we could not have asked the country to go to war merely to prevent a few Germans joining their fellow-citizens. He is very charming and plausible, but my heart is no lighter and my anger in no way diminished as I make my way to the B.B.C.

I am met by Guy Burgess and deliver my talk in a voice of ironic gloom. I then go to the Café Royal with Guy, where we meet James Pope-Hennessy who is almost in tears over England's shame.

---

[1] Anthony Eden was then 41.

20th September, 1938

The morning begins by Baffy Dugdale[1] ringing me up. She said she had been sick twice in the night over England's shame, and that at breakfast she read *The Times* leader. She came upon the words, 'The general character of the terms submitted to the Czechoslovak Government could not, in the nature of things, be expected to make a strong *prima facie* appeal to them.' Having read these words she dashed to the lavatory and was sick for a third time. She then returned and wrote a letter to Buck saying that she must resign from the National Labour Party.

I had myself on reading those words decided, if not on similar action, then at least upon a note of protest. I therefore dictated a letter to Buck saying that I hoped he did not suppose that I had been convinced by Walter's plausible charm last night, and I thought it only fair to tell him that if the terms being imposed on the Czechs were such as given in the Press, I might have to consider opposing the Government and resigning from a Party which had not said one word against them.

I lunch at the Beefsteak. There are present: George Gage, Arnold Robertson, A. E. W. Mason and one or two others. They are all appalled by the terms imposed by Chamberlain, and his 'gallant action' has declined into a mere senile visit to Canossa. They are furious with *The Times*. I abuse it too. Then Barrington-Ward[2] comes in. Gage doesn't know him. The latter says to me, 'What was it, Harold, that you said about *The Times* leader just now?' Considering that Barrington-Ward wrote that leader, the situation is awkward. I replied, 'I said it was a masterpiece of unctuous ambiguity, and I do not in the least mind repeating that in the presence of its author.' General embarrassment. Barrington-Ward gets very red, and I fear I do also.

In the Club there is Vernon Bartlett.[3] We discuss the thing. He says that Anthony Eden must come out into the open and that I must go with him. He says that at Berchtesgaden the other day he had been

---

[1] Mrs Edgar Dugdale, a niece of A. J. Balfour, whose *Life* she wrote. She had been prominent in League of Nations Union affairs.

[2] Robert Barrington-Ward, Assistant Editor of *The Times*, 1927–41, and Editor, 1941–48.

[3] Publicist and broadcaster. M.P. for Bridgewater, 1938–50.

accosted by a German General Staff officer whom he has known for years. The latter said to him, 'My dear Bartlett, it is too late'. 'What is too late?' 'Our plan.' 'What plan?' 'But you know of that—about our action.' 'Yes', said Bartlett, 'the Himmler idea?' 'Yes: it is too late now.' The idea was that the General Staff, when faced by war on three fronts, were going to arrest Himmler and Goering, and then go to Hitler and say, 'Either you are with us or we arrest you also'. This had been conveyed to our people. But now that Chamberlain has capitulated, the stock of Hitler and Ribbentrop has soared to such a point that there was nothing more to be done.[1]

DIARY   *21st September, 1938*

I go down to Sissinghurst in a state of leaden gloom. It is raining. I potter about and then start on my chapter IX. I am too depressed to write well. The news is gloomy. Poland and the Hungarians have applied for similar secessions. The Berlin press says that what remains of Czechoslovakia must adopt a more 'positive' attitude to Berlin. That means that she must subordinate her foreign policy to the Wilhelmstrasse. Chamberlain goes to Godesberg tomorrow. I pity him.

DIARY   *22nd September, 1938*

I work on my last chapter as in a narcotic numbing pain. At about 11.30 Winston Churchill telephones. Would I come up to London for a meeting at 4.30 in his flat? I say that I shall be there.

I travel up and go to 11 Morpeth Mansions. As I approach the door, I see the vulture form of Bob Cecil slipping into the flat. While I wait for the lift to descend, Winston appears from a taxi. We go up together. 'This', I say, 'is hell.' 'It is the end of the British Empire.'

We gather in his drawing-room. There are present Lords Cecil, Lloyd, [Sir Robert] Horne, Lytton and Wolmer. The only House of Commons people there are Archie Sinclair, Brendan Bracken and myself.

Winston has just been to Downing Street. He says that the Cabinet

---

[1] The conspiracy was led by Generals Beck and Halder, who planned to overthrow the Nazi régime as soon as Hitler invaded Czechoslovakia, provided that the western democracies acted to stop him. The strange thing is that the conspiracy was known in London, but not to Hitler.

are at last taking a firm stand. Chamberlain is to demand from Hitler
(a) early demobilisation; (b) agreement that the transfer of the Sudeten
territories should be undertaken gradually by an international commission; (c) that there must be no nonsense about Polish or Hungarian
claims; (d) that what remains of the Czechs shall be guaranteed.[1] We
say at once: 'But Hitler will never accept such terms.' 'In that case',
says Winston, 'Chamberlain will return tonight and we shall have
war.' We suggest that in that case it will be inconvenient having our
Prime Minister in German territory. 'Even the Germans', flashes
Winston, 'would not be so stupid as to deprive us of our beloved
Prime Minister.'

We then get down to business. It is interrupted first by a telephone
message from Jan Masaryk saying that the Germans have occupied
Asch and that the Czechs are withdrawing gradually from the Sudeten
areas. Also Hodza has resigned, and a Ministry of Concentration has
been appointed.[2] Secondly, by a telephone-call from Attlee saying that
the Opposition are prepared to come in with us if we like. That is
vague.

We continue the conversation. It boils down to this. Either Chamberlain comes back with peace with honour or he breaks it off. In
either case we shall support him. But if he comes back with peace with
dishonour, we shall go out against him. 'Let us form the focus', says
Winston. We say that indeed we will. But that it would be better to
wait until we hear what has really happened at Godesberg. He agrees
that such a delay would indeed be preferable. He stands there behind
the fire-screen, waving a whisky-and-soda at us, rather blurry, rather
bemused in a way, but dominant and in fact reasonable. I say that there
is a worse thing. 'What worse than worse?' asks Winston. I say this
point in the communiqué about a 'general agreement'. What can
that mean? They all agree that this is a terrifying prospect. It may
mean surrender on fronts far more extended than the Czech front,
and in return for such quite valueless concessions as 'a fifty year peace',
'no bombing of open towns'. We all feel that it is terrifying that a

[1] At that very moment, Chamberlain was laying his plan before Hitler at Godesberg.
He said nothing about demobilisation or the Polish and Hungarian claims, and the
areas with at least 50 per cent German-speaking population were to be transferred
direct, without a plebiscite or Commission.

[2] Dr Milan Hodza, the Czech Prime Minister, was succeeded by a 'Government of
National Concentration' under General Syrovy.

man like Chamberlain should be exposed to such terrors and temptations.

I walk back feeling that we are very near to war. When war comes it will be a terrible shock to the country. The bombing of London by itself will provoke panic and perhaps riots. All those of us who said 'We must make a stand' will be branded as murderers. I know that. But I also know that the real courage is to sacrifice everything for this fight against violence. The feeling against the Government is very bitter. The argument is: 'Either we can fight or we cannot. If we cannot, then the National Government have not only neglected our defences but pledged the honour of the country to a cause which we are not strong enough to defend.' There is no answer to this argument.

Dine at the Beefsteak. This is, I suppose, a more-or-less Tory Club, and they are all in despair about their Government. They admit that at the moment half the Cabinet will resign. I believe no such thing. Knowing more than half the Cabinet, I am well aware that they will not resign. Yet the fact remains that they[1] all feel Chamberlain has behaved with great optimism and some conceit. The Berchtesgaden visit (which we all assumed at the time was a gesture of strength) has been shown to have been a gesture of weakness. Then there is the secrecy side. Everybody was prepared to agree to Chamberlain's secret diplomacy, provided that it would let us out: they are furious with it now that it has let us in. My impression is that these Tories are appalled by the force of opinion in the provinces.

I go back to K.B.W. and write this diary.

DIARY   *23rd September, 1938*

Down to Sissinghurst. I finish my book[2] at 4.45. So that's done. But I doubt whether it will be published. We listen to the 6 o'clock news. Chamberlain has not resumed negotiations with Hitler: all they have done is to exchange letters. Meanwhile Reuter reports that the *Freikorps* have begun to invade Czechoslovakia. War is almost on us.

At 9 the telephone rings. It is Bob Boothby. 'I have just come back from Geneva, and thought you might want a word.' 'What

---

[1] The members of the Beefsteak Club. Present on this occasion were Sir Edward Grigg, Sir Roderick Jones (Chairman of Reuters), Lord Reading, Lord Stonehaven and Ralph Glyn M.P.

[2] *Diplomacy*. It was published in 1939 by the Oxford University Press.

were they feeling there?' 'Complete demoralisation, but I had a good talk with Litvinov.[1] The Russians will give full support. I told Halifax this the moment I returned, and he got on to Litvinov by telephone. That is all right.' 'Well, what about Godesberg?' 'Haven't you heard? Chamberlain is returning.' 'That means war?' 'Yes, it has taken the Germans in their idiocy to push us into this. We gave them all they asked for. Now they go to the point where they will push even us into it.' 'So that's that', I say. 'Yes', says Bob, 'and we are in for four years.'

I suppose that Ribbentrop has convinced Hitler that whatever happens we shall stay out. We cannot stay out now that Chamberlain has sacrificed everything (even our honour) to secure a peace which he has broken. How sorry I feel for the German people! They never wished this, although they are responsible in having yielded to a somnambulist. All the Cliveden set and *The Times* people prevented us from taking a strong line while it could have made for peace. They never understood that what Hitler wanted was (a) domination; (b) the destruction of Czechoslovakia; (c) the Sudeten areas. They thought that (c) was the point. It was not. This confirms me in the thought that diplomacy is based upon a knowledge of foreign psychology and that it is owing to lack of that knowledge (which implies conceit) that the Government have landed us in war. But we must support them without vituperation or criticism. We are all in the same boat now.

DIARY   *26th September, 1938*

They are making the big room at Sissinghurst gas-proof. Apparently the whole colony will collect there whenever there is an air-raid. Martin and Martha, Fay and Nellie, old Mrs Hayter, the farm-hands —all of us will sit in that room for hours without an inch of ventilation. I know one of the party who will not be there. He will be in his bed minus gas-mask and with all the windows open.

I go to Winston Churchill's flat. He is not there when I arrive, as he has been summoned by the Prime Minister. The others are Cecil, Grigg, Archie Sinclair, Lytton, Amery, Lloyd, Harold Macmillan, Bob Boothby and Spears. We begin by discussing whether national

[1] Maxim Litvinov, the Soviet Foreign Commissar, made a speech at Geneva on 21st September, reiterating that the Soviet Union would stand by its treaty with Czechoslovakia.

service should be proclaimed at once. Grigg[1] is very insistent. Lytton[2] wants a Coalition Government immediately, and I agree with him.

At that stage Winston bursts in. He says (as Rob Bernays had also told me) that the Cabinet were in a blue funk last night and that Simon was urging further retreat. But the younger people revolted and the Simon faction began to lose ground. Then came the French, all brave and solid this time, plus Gamelin[3] who restored confidence. In the end the Cabinet were all united in feeling how brave, how strong, how resolute they had always been. Winston gathers that the memorandum or letter which Horace Wilson is to give to Hitler is not in the least a retreat. It is merely an attempt to save Hitler's face if he wants to climb down. It offers a Conference to decide the means of carrying out the Franco-British plan. It warns him that we do not accept his own post-Godesberg plan and that if he insists, we shall go to war. He had urged the P.M. to mobilise the Fleet at once and call up all reserves. He says he will do so at 9 p.m. this evening if Hitler's speech at 8 p.m. tonight[4] is not conciliatory.

We discuss plans. If Chamberlain rats again we shall form a united block against him. We do not think he will rat, and therefore we shall then 'rally behind him' (poor man). We shall press for a Coalition Government and the immediate application of war measures. Above all, the blockade must be put into force at once. Then national service, even if it entails conscription of capital. Then at once we must get in touch with Russia. Winston says (and we all agree) that the fundamental mistake the P.M. has made is his refusal to take Russia into his confidence. Ribbentrop always said to Hitler, 'You need never fear England until you find her mentioning Russia as an ally. Then it means that she is really going to war!' We therefore decide that Winston shall go at once to Halifax and tell him to put out some notice before Hitler's speech. 'We have only got till nine', says Winston grimly.

My first sight of the War of 1938 was a poster in the Strand:— 'City of Westminster: Air Raid Precautions: Gas Masks Notice',

[1] Sir Edward Grigg, later Lord Altrincham, was a National Conservative M.P. He had been Governor of Kenya, and was to become Under Secretary of State for War.

[2] Lord Lytton, Viceroy of India in 1925.

[3] General Maurice Gamelin, Chief of the French General Staff.

[4] At the *Sportpalast* in Berlin. He declared that he would have the Sudetenland by 1st October and hurled venomous insults at Benes.

followed by instructions where to get yourself fitted for masks. My second sight was workmen digging trenches feverishly in the Green Park.

In the evening I go to Broadcasting House. I am taken up to listen to Hitler's speech. It is drawing to an end. He screams quite a lot and there is a touch of hysterical vulgarity about what he says. *'Benes und ich'*, he yells. But it isn't *Benes und ich*: it is *Ego contra Mundum*. I then give my little talk, taking the peace alternative and not the war alternative.[1]

V.S-W. TO H.N.   *27th September, 1938*

I do not at all like the prospect of your staying Friday night in London. If Saturday is really to be the *giorno fatale*, the first raids on London will be launched directly after midnight on Saturday, I mean 1 a.m. on Sunday morning.

In the meantime we are going on with preparations here, as though war were certain. We have all been fitted for gas-masks, and a trench has been dug in the calf-orchard. Everyone is calm, resolute and cheerful. One hears more jokes than ever, although they all realise quite well what it means. I do respect the English, for all their faults! I do not know whether you have found the same psychological experience going on in yourself as I am finding during these dreadful days: a sort of strange calm and resignation, a mood which scarcely fluctuates at all save in brief moments of human weakness. I feel almost exalted, and most strangely part of a corporate body called England, and not merely 'England', but of all whose ideals and principles are at this moment similar. I might put it like this: that the strings of one's being are tuned up to their finest pitch.

DIARY[2]   *28th September, 1938*

I walk down to the House at 2.15 p.m. passing through Trafalgar Square and down Whitehall. The pigeons are clustering round the fountains and there is a group of children feeding them. My companion says to me, 'Those children ought to be evacuated at once, and so should the pigeons.' As we get near the House of Commons there

---

[1] H.N. had written two alternative versions of his broadcast that night—one if Hitler burnt his boats in his speech in Berlin, and another if he confused the issue.

[2] The first part of this entry, up to the point indicated, was dictated on his return from the House, and broadcast on the Empire Service of the B.B.C. that night.

is a large shuffling, shambling crowd and people putting fresh flowers at the base of the Cenotaph. The crowd is very silent and anxious. They stare at us with dumb, inquisitive eyes.

When we got into the Chamber our eyes were riveted upon a strange metal honeycomb rising in front of the Prime Minister's seat. We realised that this meant that for the first time in the history of the House of Commons, a speech was to be broadcast.[1] This filled us with mingled horror and pride in the occasion.

The Speaker began by announcing the death of previous Members, and he had hardly finished with the obituary list before the Prime Minister entered from behind his chair. He was greeted with wild applause by his supporters, many of whom rose in their seats and waved their order-papers. The Labour Opposition, the Liberal Opposition and certain of the National supporters[2] remained seated.

Mr Chamberlain rose slowly in his place and spread the manuscript of his speech upon the box in front of him. The House was hushed in silent expectancy. From the Peers' Gallery above the clock the calm face of Lord Baldwin peered down upon the arena in which he himself had so often battled. Mr Chamberlain began with a chronological statement of the events which had led up to the crisis. He spoke in calm and measured tones and the House listened to him in dead silence. The only interruption was made by the Messengers of the House who, as always happens, kept on passing along the benches the telegrams and pink telephone slips which were pouring in upon Members. Mr Winston Churchill, who sits at the end of my own row, received so many telegrams that they were clipped together by an elastic band. Mr Attlee sat opposite Mr Chamberlain with his feet on the table looking like an amiable little bantam. The first burst of applause occurred when Mr Chamberlain mentioned Lord Runciman's great services, and as he did so, he removed his pince-nez between his finger and thumb, raised his face to the skylight and spoke with friendly conviction. Being an experienced Parliamentarian, he would abandon his manuscript at moments and speak extempore.

The chronological method which he adopted increased the dramatic tension of the occasion. We all knew more or less what had happened in August and the early weeks of September, and we were waiting

[1] In fact, it was only relayed as far as a room in the House of Lords.
[2] Including H.N. himself.

for his statement of what had occurred during the last few hours. He reached the point where he described the fourth plan of President Benes. The mention of this plan was received with loud cheers, and he described it in precise terms, having taken off his pince-nez and holding them between finger and thumb. 'On Friday, 23rd September', he said, 'a Cabinet meeting was held again ...' The House leant forward, realising that he was passing from that part of the story which we already knew to the part that had not yet been divulged. He went on to describe his negotiations with the Czechs and the French and to tell us how he had felt it necessary himself to visit Herr Hitler 'as a last resort'. When he said these words, 'as a last resort', he whipped off his pince-nez and looked up at the skylight with an expression of grim hope. He then described his visit to Berchtesgaden. 'It was', he said with a wry grin, 'my first flight', and he described the whole visit as 'this adventure'. He said that his conversation with Herr Hitler had convinced him that the Führer was prepared, on behalf of the Sudeten Germans, 'to risk a world war'. As he said these words a shudder of horror passed through the House of Commons.

'I came back', he added, 'to London the next day.' The House was tense with excitement. He then told us how the Anglo-French plan was described by Hitler at Godesberg as 'too dilatory'. 'Imagine', he said, 'the perplexity in which I found myself.' This remark aroused a murmur of sympathetic appreciation from all benches.

'Yesterday morning', began the Prime Minister, and we were all conscious that some revelation was approaching. He began to tell us of his final appeal to Herr Hitler and Signor Mussolini. I glanced at the clock. It was twelve minutes after four. The Prime Minister had been speaking for exactly an hour. I noticed that a sheet of Foreign Office paper was being rapidly passed along the Government bench. Sir John Simon interrupted the Prime Minister and there was a momentary hush. He adjusted his pince-nez and read the document that had been handed to him. His whole face, his whole body, seemed to change. He raised his face so that the light from the ceiling fell full upon it. All the lines of anxiety and weariness seemed suddenly to have been smoothed out; he appeared ten years younger and triumphant. 'Herr Hitler', he said, 'has just agreed to postpone his mobilisation for twenty-four hours and to meet me in conference with Signor Mussolini and Signor Daladier at Munich.'

That, I think, was one of the most dramatic moments which I have ever witnessed. For a second, the House was hushed in absolute silence. And then the whole House burst into a roar of cheering, since they knew that this might mean peace. That was the end of the Prime Minister's speech, and when he sat down the whole House rose as a man to pay a tribute to his achievement.[1]

Go back to K.B.W. and dictate to Miss Niggeman the above account, which will serve as my wireless talk tonight as well as a diary. I find an immense sense of *physical* relief, in that I shall not be afraid tonight of the German bombs. But my moral anxieties are in no way diminished. The P.M., when he read out his final message this afternoon, had, it is true, a look of spiritual delight, but somewhere about it was the glow of personal triumph. I believe that he seriously imagines that Mussolini has made this gesture out of friendship for the Chamberlain family. He does not even now understand that what did the trick was the mobilisation of the fleet and our proclaimed alliance with France and Russia. When all his supporters crowded round him to congratulate him afterwards, he showed great satisfaction and even greater self-satisfaction. Winston came up: 'I congratulate you on your good fortune. You were very lucky.' The P.M. didn't like that at all.

Dine with Buck De La Warr, Rob Bernays and Sibyl [Colefax] at Boulestin. Buck is dead tired. Rob comes back with me. He says that he has lost all confidence in this Government, and that nothing will restore it. I then have to go out and broadcast the above to the Empire. I go to bed again depressed.

DIARY   *29th September, 1938*

The papers are ecstatic about Chamberlain. Raymond [Mortimer] rings me up and says, 'Isn't this ghastly?' Eddy [Sackville-West] rings me up and says, 'Isn't this hell?' Margot Oxford rings me up and says, 'Now, Harold, you must agree that he is a great man.' I say, 'Not at all.' 'You are as bad as Violet [Bonham Carter],' she snaps; 'he is the greatest Englishman that ever lived.'

To luncheon at the Savoy in a private room with Winston, Cecil, Lytton, Arthur Salter, Wickham Steed, Walter Layton, Archibald

---

[1] That was the end of the broadcast script. At the end of the last line on the carbon copy, H.N. typed on his own machine these additional words: 'I remained seated. Liddall [the Conservative Member for Lincoln] behind me, hisses out, "Stand up, you brute!" '

Sinclair, Arthur Henderson, Liddell Hart,[1] Norman Angell, Megan Lloyd George, Violet Bonham Carter etc. Lord Lloyd makes the first speech. He says that Chamberlain is going to run away again and that we must stop him. Then Archie speaks in the same sense. Then I speak, saying that if he does run away I shall vote against him. Then Arthur Salter says that he is all for fighting the Germans, but he would first like to know whether we are likely to win. Winston says that he has got a telegram which he proposes to send to the P.M. saying that if he imposes further onerous terms on the Czechs, we shall fight him in the House. He wants to get Eden to sign it. They all agree that the Government is less resolute than the country, and that if Chamberlain runs away now he will be running badly. It seems that my refusal to stand up yesterday when all the rest of the House was hysterical has made an impression. Everybody has heard of it. I was ashamed of the House yesterday. It was a Welsh Revivalist meeting.

I had meant to go down to Sissinghurst, but Winston asked me to stay on in London. At 7 p.m. we meet again in the Savoy Hotel. The idea had been to get Winston, Cecil, Attlee, Eden, Archie Sinclair and Lloyd to join in a telegram to the P.M. begging him not to betray the Czechs. We had been busy at it all afternoon. But Anthony Eden refused to sign on the grounds that it would be interpreted as a vendetta against Chamberlain. Attlee had refused to sign without the approval of his Party. There was thus no time. We sat there gloomily realising that nothing could be done. Even Winston seemed to have lost his fighting spirit. Afterwards I go to Brooks' to look at the tape. So far as one can see, Hitler gets everything he wants.

DIARY   *30th September, 1938*

The news, as it comes through, is vague. Still this great acclamation of Chamberlain, but in it a note of uncertainty beginning to come through. I go to a meeting in Spears' house, bringing with me a letter which Norman Angell[2] has drafted, and which is to go to the Press under the signatures of Cecil, Lloyd and others. I am to get more signatures. The Tories there agree with the terms of the letter, but feel it might do them harm in their constituencies. I telephone their

---

[1] B. H. Liddell Hart in 1937 became personal adviser to the Minister of War, but gave up the post next year in order to press the need for more rapid rearmament publicly. He was military correspondent of *The Times*, 1935–39.

[2] Author of *The Great Illusion* and winner of the Nobel Peace Prize in 1933.

conclusion to Angell in their presence and in so many words. I hope it makes them feel ashamed.

Then back to K.B.W. I find James Pope-Hennessy there. I am glad to see him as I am sick of politicians and he is above all that. The older I get the more I like young people. They are the only source of wisdom. James, with his usual tact, sees that I am on edge and soothes me down. I ring up Buck De La Warr. He says that it is not quite as bad as I think. I say, 'Why not quite so bad?' He says that I must go and see Vansittart. So off I go to St James' at 11.30 p.m. My God, how tired I am!

Van says this. The past is past. It is a terrible past but we must forget about it. The next country that is going to be bumped off is England. If we start recriminations we shall create splits. What we have got to do is to come together for the next danger. Thus if I hoot at Chamberlain for his crass stupidity, it will only mean that Chamberlain will not admit me to the Government of Reconstruction which is now inevitable. I say, 'But I should never serve under Chamberlain in any case!' He says, 'But it is your duty to do so.' Now that is very noble of Van, who has been more ill-treated by Chamberlain than anybody. I really do admire him. But I shall have to hit at the old boy tomorrow, nonetheless.

DIARY   *1st October, 1938*

Our silver wedding. I do nothing about it, since Viti does not like domesticity. I say a little private prayer of thanksgiving to Demeter, who I feel is the most appropriate person to receive it. Oddly enough, everybody forgets about it except Booth and Emily.[1] The boys are wholly unaware of the event. How happy I have been these twenty-five years!

I go up to Manchester by an early train. I have to speak at a luncheon of the local National Labour Group. I foresaw that there might be some publicity, and for once in my life I typed out the more important passages of my speech. My typescript contained an attack upon Simon, Hoare and Horace Wilson. Reading it over in the train, I saw that this was too personal and indeed improper. I therefore crossed it out. What I forgot was that I had sent a carbon to the National Labour office, and it afterwards transpired that they had roneoed it and sent it to the

---

[1] The butler and his wife at Knole. Emily Booth had been V.S-W.'s personal maid before her marriage.

Press. That very passage was the one that the Press hit upon, and therefore I shall get into a row for having said something that I actually never said at all.

I make my speech. I make it well. There is stifled applause since they realise that it was good of me to have come. But I have depressed them terribly. They had all hoped against hope that the Prime Minister was right. Many of them said to me afterwards, 'You have put into words the feeling which we woke up with this morning and which we at once suppressed.'

I go back to London. The posters say, 'Cabinet Minister resigns'. I assume that it is Buck. But not at all: it is Duff Cooper, and his resignation is accompanied by a nasty letter. That is fine of him. He has no money and gives up £5,000 a year plus a job that he loves.

DIARY   3rd October, 1938

A meeting of the National Labour Executive. Buck is in the chair and the whole Executive plus Malcolm MacDonald is present. They draw up a paper pledging the support of National Labour to the Prime Minister. I and Church are the only two who vote against it.

Then down to the House. It begins by Duff Cooper making his resignation speech. He does it perfectly. Then the Prime Minister follows. He is obviously tired and irritable and the speech does not go down well. Then up gets Anthony Eden. I felt at first that he was not coming out strongly enough, but he was getting the House on his side before opening the attack. When it came, it was superb. After that the debate degenerated for a bit. What has really happened is that the Opposition hesitated to hit out too hard and the Government supporters are in a difficulty. On the one hand the more intelligent among them are against the Government. On the other hand, they find themselves in a quandary. It is difficult to say, 'This is the greatest diplomatic achievement in history: therefore we must redouble our armaments in order never again to be exposed to such humiliation.' The best speech is made by Dick Law, against the Government.

DIARY   4th October, 1938

The letters to the Leicester newspapers attacking me and my Manchester speech are really rather disquieting. Jarvis is really rattled.

Down to the House. I try hard to get in, rising with great regularity, but I am not called. The Speaker says, when I ask him, that he is 'trying to spread things out; there are four days of bread and none too much butter.' My patient submission to two days' back-bench discipline will do me no harm at all.

Baldwin in the Lords backs Chamberlain and will thereby rally Tory opinion, which was becoming very wobbly, to his side. But there is no doubt that the mass of Tory Members feel Chamberlain was too weak at Munich and that we have been humiliated unnecessarily.

DIARY   5th October, 1938

A meeting at Brendan Bracken's house to decide what we are going to do. Are we to vote against the Government or are we to abstain? We agree that the effect of our action would depend upon its joint character. It would be a pity if some of us voted against, and some abstained. It would be far more effective (since there is little hope of many voting against), if we all abstained. Winston says he refuses to abstain, since that would mean that he half agreed with Government policy. We decide that we must all do what we think best.

I keep on rising in my place from 3 p.m. till 9.25. This is a good thing. I have achieved a prominence in the House which is unjustified by my juniority. Thus when I am called, there is a burst of applause and people flock in. My speech goes well. I get approbation and notes from many people. I know that it made its effect. Gwilym Lloyd George (who knows as much about the House as anybody) says that he has never heard such a burst of cheering except for a Cabinet Minister.

Then I have a drink with Rob Bernays. He is miserable because Violet Bonham Carter cut him in the lobby. He puts up all the usual stuff about it being far easier to resign than not to resign. But he knows that I feel less about him. He ought to have resigned.

DIARY   6th October, 1938

Our group decide that it is better for us all to abstain, than for some to abstain and some to vote against. We therefore sit in our seats, which must enrage the Government, since it is not our numbers that matter but our reputation. Among those who abstained were Eden, Duff Cooper, Winston, Amery, Cranborne, Wolmer, Roger Keyes, Sidney Herbert, Louis Spears, Harold Macmillan, Richard Law, Bob

Boothby, Jim Thomas, Duncan Sandys, Ronald Cartland, Anthony Crossley, Brendan Bracken and Emrys-Evans. That looks none too well in any list. The House knows that most of the above people know far more about the real issue than they do.

It was clear that the Government were rattled by this. In the first place, the P.M. gave a pledge that there would be no General Election. In the second place he made the astounding admission that his phrase about 'peace in our time' was made under the stress of emotion. The House breaks up with the Tories yelling to keep their spirits up. But they well know that Chamberlain has put us in a ghastly position and that we ought to have been prepared to go to war and smash Hitler. Next time he will be far too strong for us.

DIARY   8th October, 1938

Go up to Leicester. Bertie Jarvis says that I have put the women's vote against me by abusing Munich. I expect that the historians of our decline and fall will say that we were done the moment we gave the women the vote. The men see that I was right and the women feel sentimental about Chamberlain.[1]

DIARY   13th October, 1938

A meeting of members of the West Leicester Conservative Association. Bertie [Jarvis] is in rather a stew as the women are bitter against me for my Manchester speech. But I get a good reception and a unanimous vote of confidence. I am not even forced to pledge eternal fidelity to Chamberlain, but merely say that I shall support him if he really goes in for peace and rearmament. I gather that the women are really enraged. They think that I 'want war'.

During the remainder of the year, nothing much happened to disturb the complacency of the pro-Munich diehards. Those who had been opposed to it noticed that whenever disagreement arose about the detailed application of the Pact to the delineation of Czechoslovakia's new

---

[1] Duff Cooper, another rebel, found the exact opposite. 'At that time,' he wrote in his memoirs *Old Men Forget*, 'I could count among my own acquaintance twelve happily married couples who were divided upon the issue of Munich, and in every case it was the husband who supported and the wife who opposed Chamberlain. Many would have expected that women would have been more ready than men to accept the spurious peace at its face value. But it was not so.'

frontiers, it was always decided in Germany's favour. The encroachment of the Poles and Hungarians on other parts of the border passed without protest by the Western Governments. The persecution of the Jews in Germany and the newly occupied territories aroused distress but not anger in Britain. Chamberlain was still regarded by the majority of his countrymen as the great peacemaker.

In these circumstances it was difficult for a man like Harold Nicolson to know what to do. He found himself out of step not only with the Government which he had been elected to support, but with his own National Labour Party and its two leaders, Malcolm MacDonald and Lord De La Warr. He seriously considered resignation and offering himself to his constituents under a new label at a bye-election. Instead, he openly allied himself with the group of some thirty other Members under the unofficial leadership of Anthony Eden. It was a ginger group, not an opposition group, and they thought of themselves as distinct from the smaller group which gathered round Winston Churchill, whom many of them considered (as Harold Nicolson wrote to V. Sackville-West on 9th November) 'more bitter than determined, and more out for a fight than for reform'.

In his non-political life, Harold Nicolson accepted from the Editor of the 'Spectator' an invitation to contribute a weekly article, which he continued to write under the title 'Marginal Comment' for the next fourteen years. He also did an odd thing: he bought a small yacht of 9-foot draught. He borrowed the purchase price, £2,000, from V. Sackville-West, engaged the services of a skipper named Captain De'Ath and a mate, and named her 'Mar'. She lay at Southampton until the spring came, and he sailed in her only during the single summer which was left before the outbreak of war.

H.N. TO V.S-W.   *9th November, 1938*
                                                 4 King's Bench Walk, E.C.4

I went to a hush-hush meeting with Anthony Eden. Present: Eden, Amery, Cranborne, Sidney Herbert, Cartland, Harold Macmillan, Spears, Derrick Gunston, Emrys Evans, Anthony Crossley, Hubert Duggan. All good Tories and sensible men. This group is distinct from the Churchill group. It also includes Duff Cooper. We decided that we should not advertise ourselves as a group or even call ourselves a group. We should merely meet together from time to time, exchange views, and organise ourselves for a revolt if needed. I feel happier about this. Eden and Amery are wise people, and Sidney Herbert[1] is very experienced. Obviously they do not mean to do anything rash or violent. At the same time they are deeply disturbed by the fact that Chamberlain does not seem to understand the gravity of the situation. Unless we pull ourselves together and have compulsory registration in the next few months, it will be too late. It was a relief to me to be with people who share my views so completely, and yet who do not give the impression (as Winston does) of being more bitter than determined, and more out for a fight than for reform. I shall be happy and at ease with this group.

DIARY   *10th November, 1938*

League of Nations Union meeting. Liddell Hart puts forward an admirable memorandum in which he suggests that as the League is practically dead, the Union should turn itself into some sort of union for the protection of democracy and liberty. His idea is that there is a real danger of fascism in this country, that the Union machinery should be used to oppose it, and that the whole thing would ultimately work into an international maintenance of League principles. This memorandum was not at all liked by the old ladies of the Executive. Gilbert Murray and Lord Lytton damned it by saying that it is an interesting and original point of view. The discussion, as usual, goes round and round, and one had the impression that these ancient League enthusiasts have ceased merely to have bees in their bonnets and have actually become huge bumble-bees themselves. Luckily I sat between Philip Noel-Baker and Violet Bonham Carter who are both reasonable and alert.

Down to the House. Kingsley Wood makes his speech about the Air Force which carries no conviction to anyone, least of all to Kingsley Wood himself. He did it in the tone of a Lord Mayor praising the Corporation budget and paying compliments to the excellent work done by the gas companies and the tramway authorities. It was received by the Government benches in almost complete silence, and this more than anything else made it clear how profoundly anxious and dissatisfied the Party is. There is a good maiden speech by young Thorneycroft,[2] but otherwise the debate rather hangs.

[1] Sir Sidney Herbert had been a Conservative M.P. since 1922. He was Parliamentary Private Secretary to the Prime Minister in 1923–24 and 1924–27. He died on 22nd March 1939.
[2] Peter Thorneycroft had just been elected as Conservative M.P. for Stafford.

V.S-W. TO H.N.   *14th November, 1938*
                                                     Sissinghurst

I know you will never forgive me, but I *can't* go to this party.[1] I
wrote to Jay's and discovered that an evening dress would cost at
least £30, and the adjuncts, (shoes, underclothes, gloves etc) another
£10. Well, that seems to me wicked to spend on personal adornment
for one evening. It was silly of me ever to say that I would go to it.
Gwen [St Aubyn] says that it would be wrong of me to funk it, and
that I *must* go. But I am too shy. And if I went to this party, I should
be being false to myself. I am writing this letter with my jewels
littered all around me—emeralds and diamonds, just taken out of the
bank—and they make me feel sick. I simply can't subscribe any longer
to the world which these jewels represent. I *can't* buy a dress costing
£30 or wear jewels worth £2,000 when people are starving. I *can't*
support such a farce when people are threatened that their electric
light or gas may be cut off because they can't pay their arrears.

H.N. TO V.S-W.   *15th November, 1938*
                                              4 King's Bench Walk, E.C.4

How I do love you, Mar![2] I am glad you are not coming. You are
quite right, as usual. It is wrong to spend all that money merely to go
to a party. That sort of world is dead today. How can a person of
your sensitiveness and imagination doll yourself up in expensive
clothes when there are cultured Jewish women and men hiding like
foxes in the Grünewald? My God! I do admire you so, my Viti.
You are so sound in your values. They ring like a bell. It makes me
feel so confident that if I strike that bell, it always echoes the perfect
note. I shall never forget what you meant to me during the crisis.[3]
You were all that was spiritually perfect during those days. I could not
have stood them had you not been there as a sort of completely selfless
person, right above all the petty fears and jangles.

---

[1] A dinner at Buckingham Palace on 16th November in honour of the King of
   Rumania.
[2] See note 3, p. 48.   [3] The Munich crisis.

DIARY   *15th November, 1938*

I dine with Rob Bernays and Ronald Cartland[1] at his flat. Cartland says that he cannot stand the Tories any more. He loathes their riches and the self-indulgence. He loathes their mean petty Party schemes. He cannot abide them. He says that the Whips are much rattled. The Germans pour out attacks on us and thus completely undo the effect of Munich.

DIARY   *21st November, 1938*

Up to Leicester with Anthony Eden. He tells me that Edward Halifax has been urging him to sink his differences and to get back into the Cabinet, thus admitting that the split over foreign policy is so serious that the Party organisers are alarmed. Anthony said that he cannot go back if the policy is still to be directed towards a Four Power Pact.

DIARY   *23rd November, 1938*

There is a general feeling in the air that the Chamberlain Government is shaking to its fall. The poor old man has gone across to France in a gale to discuss Anglo-French policy.

I go to the Reform to have a talk with Guy Burgess who is in a state about the B.B.C. He tells me that a technical talk by Admiral Richmond about our strategic position in the Mediterranean (which had been definitely announced) was cancelled as a result of a telephone message from Horace Wilson to the Director General. This has incensed him, and he wants to resign and publish why. I urge him to do nothing of the sort.

DIARY   *24th November, 1938*

A meeting of the group at Ronnie Tree's house. Hopkinson[2] is there and tells us the reasons for which he refused the Government whip. It seems that Chamberlain is trying to put all the blame for our disarmament on Thomas Inskip, and as Hopkinson was Inskip's P.P.S., he is leaving him in order to defend him against attacks which he will not counter himself. His account of our unpreparedness is appalling.

[1] Ronald Cartland had been Conservative M.P. for the King's Norton Division of Birmingham since 1935. He was killed in May 1940 at the age of 33.
[2] Austin Hopkinson, M.P. for Mossley, Lancashire, since 1918.

He says that if we had gone to war in September our air-force would have been wiped out in three weeks and our pilots would have gone to certain death. Things may be a little better in a few weeks, but nonetheless we are terribly at Germany's mercy and shall remain so. The Government are really not telling the country the truth. He had seen Kingsley Wood, and the latter had admitted quite frankly that we can do little without a Ministry of Supply, but that to appoint such a Minister would arouse the anger of Germany. That is a dreadful confession. We all sit there very glum—Anthony Eden, Duff Cooper, Amery, Wolmer and the rest. We still do not really constitute a group, and Anthony still hesitates to come out against the Government.

DIARY   *30th November, 1938*

Go to the Junior Constitutional Club for a debate with Roy Wise.[1] Alan Lennox-Boyd[2] takes the chair. I sit between Patricia Guinness (his fiancée) and Freya Stark,[3] a nice foreign little thing. Roy Wise makes the best pro-Chamberlain speech I have ever heard. I reply to it in a 35-minute speech. The audience are naturally hostile to me but quite polite. When I say that Germany has acquired the political and economic mastery of Central Europe, there are cries from the old gentlemen of 'No! No!' We then have questions to which we reply in turn. I am fortunate, as the last of my questioners says, 'What would Mr Nicolson have done had he found himself in the same circumstances as Mr Chamberlain?' There is a lovely answer to that: 'In the first place I trust that had I been a leading Cabinet Minister since 1931, I should not have found myself in Mr Chamberlain's position. Either I should have had a strong country behind me, or I should have resigned long ago. Yet even if I had allowed this country to become so weak that we could not resist German diplomacy, then I should have avoided raising a major issue upon a matter which was not regarded by the people as a direct interest to this country, but should have urged the Czechs to make the best terms with Germany that they could. If, however, I had neglected all these precautions, and had found myself at Munich like a lamb brought to slaughter, then I would have done what Mr Chamberlain did—I should have run away. (Mixed applause.)

[1] Conservative M.P. for Smethwick, 1931–45.
[2] Conservative M.P. for mid-Bedfordshire since 1931.
[3] The traveller and author.

But of one thing I am quite certain. Having run away I should not have proclaimed peace with honour. I should have crept out of the aeroplane at Heston and said to the crowds: "I have given way. I have avoided war, but let there be no jubilation." ' This reply is received in pained silence. I can feel that it has gone home.

DIARY   5th December, 1938

The debate on the Sandys Report.[1] Winston starts brilliantly and we are all expecting a great speech. He accuses Hore-Belisha of being too complacent. The latter gets up and says, 'When and where?' Winston replies, 'I have not come unprepared', and begins to fumble among his notes, where there are some press-cuttings. He takes time. He finds them. But they are not the best cuttings, and the ones he reads out excuse rather than implicate Hore-Belisha. Winston becomes confused. He tries to rally his speech, but the wind has gone out of his sails, which flop wretchedly. 'He is becoming an old man', says Bill Mabane beside me. He certainly is a tiger who, if he misses his spring, is lost.

DIARY   13th December, 1938

To a grand party given by Barbie Wallace.[2] Some of the Cabinet had come on from the dinner given by the Foreign Press Association to the Prime Minister. They were all agog. The forty German guests (including the Ambassador) had not attended in view of Chamberlain's polite protest against their having called Lord Baldwin a guttersnipe. There were forty empty seats and all this created wild excitement. Then came Chamberlain's speech. He had catalogued his achievements. Treaty with Eire (slight applause); Treaty with the United States (loud applause); Treaty with Italy (sporadic clappings); Anglo-German Treaty (you could have heard a pin drop so icy was the silence); with France we had relations which transcended all legal instruments, since our interests were the same (a wild ovation lasting several minutes). As Buck said, it was almost a vote of censure on the P.M.'s policy.

---

[1] Duncan Sandys had put down a question on the state of our defences, which revealed inside knowledge. He was ordered by the Army Council to give evidence on his source of information, and appealed to the Speaker against a breach of privilege.
[2] Barbara Wallace, wife of Captain Euan Wallace M.P.

H.N. TO V.S-W.   *21st December, 1938*

Darling, I am so much more pleased now than I was. I really think
that we have converted the heathen, and that at last they understand the
danger. I *know* that I have done some good on this. And when I feel
that I have done nothing in life, I shall always remember this quiet
but resolute agitation.

DIARY   *22nd December, 1938*

Go at noon to Jim Thomas' house to meet Anthony Eden on his return
from the U.S.A. He says that the suspicion entertained over there of
Chamberlain's policy is widespread and exaggerated. Quite serious
people imagine that he is in the hands of the Cliveden set and is a pure
fascist.

     Lunch at the Reform with Wilson Harris.[1] I agree to do a weekly
article for him.

DIARY   *28th December, 1938*

I work at my Byron lectures with great pleasure. It is a delight after
politics to get down to scholarship. The older I get, the closer I feel
to Byron. I am like him, without his cruelty or genius.

DIARY   *29th December, 1938*

I read *Childe Harold* with more appreciation than before. I feel happier
after I have read it, having been so depressed these weeks. A gloomy
anxiety has brooded over my apparent business. I wonder what is the
real nature of that anxiety? Is it dread of war and a terror lest Ben and
Niggs may be taken from me? Is it horror of violence and an impersonal
wincing-away from the thought of whole families devastated in
Bermondsey? Is it loathing of the thought that this evil *Mein Kampf*
theory, this vulgar violence, may triumph over the gentle elegancies
which we and France have evolved? Or does my depression come from
the fact that I have no power and so little influence? That my lack of
combative instincts make me merely write comments upon states-
manship without being able to influence or to grasp it? Or is it just
that Sissinghurst is not a winter resort, that I am overworked and
know in my inside that I shall never be a good writer or a forceful

---

[1] Editor of the *Spectator*, 1932-53. This invitation was the origin of Harold Nicolson's
famous series of articles, *Marginal Comment*.

politician? Or is it merely a low physical depression at not being young, at becoming an old asthmatic buffer?

I wonder sometimes whether my activity, my ceaseless passion for work, is not merely a device for evading thought. Such is the fate of a frivolous and self-indulgent person who reaches autumn and observes how recklessly he has flung his seed.

DIARY   *31st December, 1938*

It has been a bad year. Chamberlain has destroyed the Balance of Power, and Niggs got a third. A foul year. Next year will be worse.

1939

'This Year of Destiny'[1]

'Diplomacy' – Hitler invades Czechoslovakia – 'war inevitable after harvest' – Churchill and the Russians – H.N. buys the yawl 'Mar' – Grigore Gafencu – Chamberlain introduces partial conscription – attitude of the Conservatives to the Eden Group – Churchill's reply to Ambassador Kennedy – H. G. Wells on the failure of homo sapiens – Chamberlain's diminishing reputation – H.N. sails in the 'Mar' for three weeks in August – he hears of the Russo-German Pact on his return to Plymouth – emergency meeting of Parliament – the character of Hitler – war-preparations – Hitler's invasion of Poland on 1st September – delays in honouring Britain's obligations to help Poland – Declaration of War by Chamberlain – the first air-raid alarm

[1] This heading was typed on 1st January on the flyleaf of the 1939 folder of the diary. H.N.D.

2B

1939

This View of Destiny

International politics continued to dominate both the diary and the letters during the winter and early spring. Harold Nicolson was at his busiest, speaking in many parts of the country and in Holland and Belgium, and reading his review books and writing his weekly article for the 'Spectator' during his train journeys and spare moments in the House of Commons. 'Diplomacy' was published on 9th February. Only at weekends, and not always, did he manage to get down to Sissinghurst. V. Sackville-West, for once, had no new book on hand, but was writing articles for the 'New Statesman' on gardening, and broadcasting fairly frequently. Ben was appointed Assistant Surveyor of the King's Pictures on Kenneth Clark's recommendation, and Nigel was working in Newcastle with the Tyneside Council of Social Service.

These were the months when Neville Chamberlain was slowly and reluctantly abandoning his policy of appeasement. His visit with Lord Halifax to Rome in January was almost his last hope of detaching Mussolini from Hitler, and it failed. At one moment it would seem from his statements to Parliament that he had at last determined on a firmer policy (such as his declaration on 7th February of Anglo-French solidarity, which seemed so significant at the time but left little impression on history), and at the next he would destroy their effect by a relapse into feeble optimism. The Eden Group remained alertly critical, ready to support the Prime Minister whenever his backbone stiffened, but pressing with increasing outspokenness for a truly National Government. The diplomatic and strategic initiative had passed completely into the dictators' hands. The talk in Parliament, when it was not of a détente with Germany and Italy, was of where each would strike next. There were fears of German aggression against Rumania, Holland and Poland; of Italian aggression against Egypt, Tunisia and the Sudan. In fact, Hitler occupied Czechoslovakia and Memel in March; and Mussolini attacked Albania in early April.

The new Czech crisis was the direct consequence of the Munich Agreement by which Czechoslovakia lost her frontier defences against Germany. Hitler was now in a position at any moment to overwhelm Bohemia and Moravia whose frontiers he had promised at Munich to guarantee, but his guarantee was never ratified. He engineered a suitable opportunity by stimulating the Slovaks, partly by promises and partly by threats, to secede from Czechoslovakia on 14th March, and simultaneously built up a false picture of Czech atrocities against German nationals. On 15th March President Hácha of Czechoslovakia was bludgeoned into capitulation by the threat of immediate invasion, and Hitler entered Prague that evening. At the same time Slovakia was taken under German 'benevolent protection', and the Hungarians were given Ruthenia. Czechoslovakia had ceased to exist by the evening of 16th March.

In London and Paris there was no immediate reaction from either Government. Chamberlain announced that our guarantee to the Czechs no longer applied because Slovakia had seceded. 'The effect of this decision by the Slovak Diet', he told the House of Commons, 'put an end by internal disruption to the State whose frontier we had proposed to guarantee. His Majesty's Government cannot accordingly hold themselves any longer bound by that obligation.' He added not a word of reproach for Hitler's action, nor of sympathy for the Czechs.

This cynical response to direct German aggression against a non-German people aroused such anger in Parliament that Chamberlain, urged on by Halifax, felt obliged to say something stronger. On 17th March, in a speech in Birmingham, he asked: 'Is this the last attack upon a small State or is it to be followed by others? ... No greater mistake could be made than to suppose that because it believes war to be a senseless and cruel thing, this nation has so lost its fibre that it will not take part to the utmost of its power in resisting such a challenge if ever it were made.' On 31st March, sixteen days after Hitler entered Prague, he announced in Parliament that if Poland were to be attacked, 'His Majesty's Government would feel themselves bound at once to lend the Polish Government all support in their power.' France associated herself with this firm commitment. It was the virtual end of the policy of appeasement, and the sad triumph of all those like Harold Nicolson who had endured such unpopularity and misrepresentation for their conviction that war with the dictators was inevitable, and that we must prepare ourselves, militarily, politically and diplomatically, to win it when it came.

17th January, 1939

Disquieting news. The Germans are pressing their *Drang nach Osten* through Hungary towards Rumania. The Irish Republican Army are beginning to start Fenian methods here by bombing power-stations. The Italians are at once starting a Djibouti campaign. And Franco advances towards Barcelona. The harvest of weakness is being dumped upon our doors.

I resort to Byron and work at him all day. In the afternoon I go a walk in the rain. The floods have washed away much of our dyke between the upper and the lower lake. Even that is showing obvious signs of disintegration.

But the tragedy of Europe seems to come closer to us in ever-diminishing circles. Dear little Giles[1] chatters about Sir Humphry Davy for whom he has a passion. His sensitive nervous face and his intelligence make me even more unhappy. What will that delightful boy have to create in the world which will be his adult world? To me it does not matter. I can just die. But he and Niggs and Ben have got to live, and all the delicacy of life will have gone. All the truthfulness, all the outspokenness, all the easiness of life will have gone. They will never know *la douceur de vivre*. There is a certain evolutionary charity which has protected them from the major shocks of this disaster. They are born with a dislike of the luxurious and indolent things which seemed to us important. Many of their losses will not seem to them to be losses since they will never have regarded them as acquisitions. But other losses will cut them to the heart. The loss of what is essential in our values which they know to be important values. For instance, Stafford Cripps these days has been fighting for the essentials of social-ism. He is by far the most able man in politics today. Yet he is being countered by the dumb, drastic, fatuous opposition of Transport House. Even revolution is becoming bourgeois. I hate it all. I hate it all.

20th January, 1939

Lunch with Buck De La Warr. He is discreet as usual, but he seems to have been rather shocked by Chamberlain's mood on his return from Rome. Chamberlain discoursed to the Cabinet upon the friendliness

[1] Giles St Aubyn, H.N.'s nephew, then aged 14. In later life he became a house-master at Eton and the author of several historical books.

not only of Mussolini but of Countess Ciano. Buck passed a note to Walter Elliot, saying, 'He does not know the foreign mind.' Walter scribbled below it: ' "Caesar Borgia was most charming, and although I had my doubts about Lucrezia, I found later that I had misunderstood her." Extracts from the memoirs of a Roman Cardinal published *posthumously.*' Buck says that there is no hope at all of altering Chamberlain's foreign policy. All we should do is to concentrate upon increasing armaments and air-raid precautions.

DIARY   *4th February, 1939*

V. and I go round to the Beales[1] where there is a Television Set lent by the local radio-merchant. We see a Mickey Mouse, a play and a Gaumont British film. I had always been told that the television could not be received above 25 miles from Alexandra Palace. But the reception was every bit as good as at Selfridge's. Compared with a film, it is a bleary, flickering, dim, unfocused, interruptible thing, the size of a quarto sheet of paper as this on which I am typing. But as an invention it is tremendous and may alter the whole basis of democracy.[2]

H.N. TO V.S-W.   *7th February, 1939*
                                                    4 King's Bench Walk, E.C.4

Really Chamberlain is an astonishing and perplexing old boy. This afternoon, as you will have heard, he startled the House and the world by proclaiming something like an offensive and defensive alliance between us and France. Now that is the very thing that all of us have been pushing for, working for, writing for, speaking for, all these months. And the old boy gets up and does it as if it was the simplest thing on earth. The House was absolutely astounded. It could not have been more definite. It was superb. I felt more happy than for months. But this is a complete negation of his 'appeasement' policy and of his Rome visit. He has in fact swung suddenly round. What does it mean? I think it can only mean that he realises that appeasement has failed. It is at this stage that his value as a diplomatic asset becomes operative. No ordinary German or Italian will ever believe propaganda telling him that Chamberlain is a 'war-monger'. I am so

---

[1] A. O. R. Beale, the tenant-farmer of Sissinghurst Castle farm.
[2] The B.B.C. television service first began in 1936, but was interrupted during the course of the war. The Nicolsons bought their own set in the same month.

glad that we all lay low all this time and allowed facts to speak for themselves. Yet still I have the awful doubt that he (being so abysmally ignorant of foreign policy) may not have understood what was meant by his statement.

v.s.-w. TO H.N.   *8th February, 1939*
                                                      Sissinghurst

Thank you so much for sending me your *Diplomacy*. I have been reading it with the admiration and amusement your writing always arouses in me, and thinking how very different the subject would have become in anybody else's hands—dry, dead and pompous. How you have contrived to make it so lively, I can't imagine. I think it is because one knows that at any moment one will come on some little twist of phrase which is absolutely your own. And then of course your gift for lucidity; for knowing exactly what you mean to convey, and expressing it perfectly. I can never get over how brilliantly you carry out the very diversified jobs you undertake.

DIARY   *9th February, 1939*

Lunch at the Russian Embassy. A strange party. Bob Boothby, Dick Law, Vernon Bartlett and J. B. Priestley. We start by talking rather shyly about food. Gradually, as the vodka circulates, we approach the less sure ground of politics. Maisky asks us (with his little Kalmuk eyes twinkling round the table), 'What is going to happen now?' We all hope that someone else is going to answer. I suggest gaily that the moment may be approaching when Russia will be forced to join the anti-Comintern Pact. Maisky says that Russia was obviously much wounded by Munich and that we can expect no advances from her side. But (and here he became serious) if *we* made approaches, we should not find Russia as aloof or offended as we might have supposed. Bob Boothby and I have an eye-meet like a tennis-ball across a net. We all agree that we do not know what the Axis is going to do. Maisky says that he is convinced that Berlin engineered the story about the *Drang nach Osten* in order to divert our attention from an impending drive towards the west. Maisky says, 'They will challenge you during the next few months.' We agree that we and France will make concessions about Djibouti and the Suez Canal, but not an inch in Tunis. We also agree that Chamberlain at last realises all this and that the efforts of the anti-Chamberlainites in future may have to be directed

391

into preventing him plunging us into an unnecessary war. 'Hell knows no fury like a woman scorned.'

DIARY   *13th March, 1939*

Everybody is much fussed by the Czech situation. The Slovaks, under German inspiration, have demanded autonomy. Obviously the Prague government will have to give way. Our difficulty is that many people in this country imagined that Munich meant a settlement of the Czech problem. Inskip said in the House that our guarantee to Czechoslovakia was a 'moral obligation'. We cannot fulfil that obligation and therefore we are exposed as immoral. That worries people in the House. Those of us who knew that Munich meant betrayal are not in the least disturbed at this evidence that what we diagnosed as pneumonia has produced a fever of 103. The optimists are distressed.

DIARY   *14th March, 1939*

The House is in a dreadful state about the partition of Czechoslovakia. I am calm. I say that it merely renders explicit facts that since Munich were implicit. But most people really believed that Munich settled the Czech question and are deeply disturbed. For instance Charles Waterhouse (who is usually friendly in personal contact) gets up and leaves when I inadvertently sit next to him in the smoking-room. The ignorance of the Tory rank-and-file in regard to foreign policy is as terrifying as the prospect of a gardener suddenly driving a Rolls Royce.

DIARY   *15th March, 1939*

I work at my Byron lectures. While I do so, Frederick Voigt telephones to say that Hitler has occupied Prague. Go round to Mark Patrick's house for a meeting of the group. Eden says that he is going to speak today, and what is he to say? We all agree that the one thing not to do is to hoot and jeer. We agree that we must support the Government, and that Anthony should speak, and that only our lesser fry should speak also. The rest to keep silent.

The *Manchester Guardian* today carried a leader headed 'The Gift of Prophecy'. There is a passage from my Munich speech.

DIARY   *17th March, 1939*

The feeling in the lobbies is that Chamberlain will either have to go or completely reverse his policy. Unless in his speech tonight[1] he admits that he was wrong, they feel that resignation is the only alternative. All the tadpoles are beginning to swim into the other camp and we find ourself in the odd position of being Mr Chamberlain's loyal supporters. The difficulty is that he himself cannot introduce conscription because he can only do so with a Coalition Government. The Opposition refuse absolutely to serve under him. The idea is that Halifax should become Prime Minister and Eden Leader of the House.

DIARY   *19th March, 1939*

Buck De La Warr telephones in the evening. He says that the Prime Minister's speech only represents half of the action that he proposes to take, and that he is absolutely determined to make a stand against Hitler. We are getting into touch with Russia and the smaller countries, and are definitely trying to create a coalition.

DIARY   *20th March, 1939*

I have a feeling that war will not come at once (mainly because of the spring sowings) but that it is inevitable after the harvest.

DIARY   *30th March, 1939*

A meeting of the New Commonwealth which is to be addressed by Winston. It is with difficulty that we whip up a proper audience. They simply do not wish to hear what they fear will be painful things. Winston merely says that when the war is over, we must build up a League of Nations based upon organised force and not upon disorganised nonsense.

DIARY   *31st March, 1939*

Chamberlain comes into the House looking gaunt and ill. The skin above his high cheekbones is parchment yellow. He drops wearily into his place. David Margesson proposes the Adjournment and the P.M. rises. He begins by saying that we believe in negotiation and do not trust in rumours. He then gets to the centre of his statement, namely that if Poland is attacked we shall declare war. That is greeted

[1] At Birmingham. See introductory note p. 388.

with cheers from every side. He reads his statement very slowly with a bent grey head. It is most impressive.

DIARY   *3rd April, 1939*

The House rises at 10.50 pm. and I am seized upon by Winston and taken down to the lower smoking-room with Maisky and Lloyd George. Winston adopts the direct method of attack. 'Now look here, Mr Ambassador, if we are to make a success of this new policy, we require the help of Russia. Now I don't care for your system and I never have, but the Poles and the Rumanians like it even less. Although they might be prepared at a pinch to let you in, they would certainly want some assurances that you would eventually get out. Can you give us such assurances?' Lloyd George, I fear, is not really in favour of the new policy and he draws Maisky on to describe the deficiencies of the Polish Army. Apparently many of their guns are pre-Revolution guns of the Russian Army. Maisky contends that the Polish soldiers are excellent fighters and that the officers are well-trained. Winston rather objects to this and attacks Lloyd George. 'You must not do this sort of thing, my dear. You are putting spokes in the wheel of history.' The relations between these two are very curious. They have had bitter battles in the past and have emerged from these combats with great respect for each other's talents and an affectionate sharing of tremendous common memories. It is curious that little way that Winston has when he speaks to Lloyd George of calling him 'my dear'.

Devonshire told me a curious story tonight which illustrates vividly the attitude of the British public. On saying goodnight to his chauffeur, he remarked, 'Well, Gibson, and what do you think about Hitler?' 'Well, your Grace', the man answered, 'it seems to me that he should know by now that he is none too popular in this district.'

DIARY   *9th April, 1939*

In the afternoon Viti and I plant annuals. We sow them in the cottage garden and then in the border and then in the orchard. We rake the soil smooth. And as we rake we are both thinking, 'What will have happened to the world when these seeds germinate?' It is warm and still. We should have been so happy were it not for the thought that tugs at our hearts as if some very dear person was dying in the upstairs room. We discuss whether we might be defeated if war comes. And

if defeated, surely surrender in advance would be better? We ourselves don't think of money or privilege or pleasure. We are thinking
only of that vast wastage of suffering which must surely come. All
because of the insane ambitions of one fanatic, and of the vicious theory
which he has imposed on his people.

*It was now the turn of Poland. Since October 1938, within a week of
Munich, Hitler had begun to step up the pressure on the weak, and
hitherto pro-Nazi, Government of Poland for the return of Danzig
(the German Hanseatic port which had been created a Free City by the
Treaty of Versailles) and for Polish agreement to the construction of an
extra-territorial road and railway link between Germany and East
Prussia across the Polish Corridor. Colonel Beck, the Polish Foreign
Minister, warned Hitler that any attempt to alter the status of Danzig
would be regarded by Poland as a casus belli. On 6th April the Franco-
British guarantee of assistance to Poland against German attack was
converted into an Anglo-Polish mutual assistance pact, signed by Beck
in London. On the next day Mussolini invaded Albania, and Britain
and France countered by equivalent guarantees to Greece and Rumania.
To this stiffening in the Western attitude, Hitler responded in his speech
of 28th April by denouncing the Anglo-German Naval Treaty of 1935
and the German-Polish non-aggression pact of 1934. In the same month
he issued a top-secret directive to the Reichswehr to prepare for an attack
on Poland at any moment from 1st September onwards. A measure of
compulsory military service was announced by Chamberlain to the House
of Commons on 26th April. About 310,000 young men were called up,
but the Labour and Liberal Oppositions voted against the Bill.
Hitler's main object was now to detach Russia from the Western
Powers, for he knew that to conquer Poland he must first get Russian
agreement at least to non-intervention. He had sensed Stalin's increasing
irritation with the lukewarm response from Britain and France to his
repeated proposals to halt Hitler's advance in Eastern Europe by a firm
Anglo-French-Soviet guarantee to Poland, Rumania, Finland and the
Baltic States. Apart from Chamberlain's personal antipathy to a military
alliance with Russia, there was the difficulty that the states mentioned in
the Russian proposal feared rescue by Russia as much as they feared
invasion by Germany, and refused to accept the Russian guarantee. The
turning-point came on 3rd May, when the pro-Western Litvinov was
suddenly replaced as Commissar for Foreign Affairs by Molotov, who soon*

began trade-talks with Germany, accompanied by significant political undertones. All through June and July the German-Soviet talks made progress, while the British negotiations, conducted by William Strang in Moscow, hung fire for the lack of any conviction in London that only an alliance with Russia could prevent Hitler from making war in the autumn. Meanwhile German arms were secretly smuggled into Danzig and the pro-Nazi Danzigers were easily persuaded to create an atmosphere of mounting crisis within the city, which was to be Hitler's excuse for invasion. As Ribbentrop confessed to Ciano, it was not Danzig and the Corridor that Hitler wanted, but the whole of Poland. He intended to bring on the inevitable war at a moment when he considered that Germany had the greatest chance of victory.

Harold Nicolson was active in writing about these events and in speaking outside more than inside Parliament. His main themes were the necessity of an alliance with Russia and the strengthening of the British Cabinet by the inclusion of Churchill and Eden. For relaxation he began to use his yawl 'Mar' for cruises along the South Coast and once to France, sometimes alone with his crew of three, sometimes with a friend.

DIARY   *10th April, 1939*

Does Mussolini seriously suppose that he could defeat ourselves and France? Or is he still relying upon that defeatist and pampered group in London who have for so long been assuring him that the capitalists of England are on his side? I do not believe that an intelligent man such as Grandi could have left him under any illusion that the will-power of this country is concentrated in Mrs Ronald Greville. He must know that in the last resort our decision is embodied, not in Mayfair or Cliveden, but in the provinces. The harm which these silly selfish hostesses do is really immense. They convey to foreign envoys the impression that policy is decided in their own drawing-rooms. People such as Simon and Hore-Belisha (who are middle-class individuals flattered by the adulation of what they suppose—with extreme incorrectitude—to be the aristocracy) are also impressed by the social efficiency of silly women such as Mrs Greville and Lady Astor. Anybody who really knows the latter understands that she is a kindly but inordinately foolish woman. Yet these people have a subversive influence. They dine and wine our younger politicians and they create an atmosphere of authority and responsibility and grandeur, whereas the whole thing is a mere flatulence of the spirit. That is always what happens with us. The silly people are regarded as representative of British opinion and the informed people are dismissed as 'intellectuals'. I should be most unhappy if I were Lady Astor. She must realise that her parrot cries have done much damage to what (to do her justice) she must dimly realise is the essence of her adopted class and country.

DIARY   11th April, 1939

Harold Macmillan is enraged that Chamberlain should remain on. He thinks that all we Edenites have been too soft and gentlemanlike. That we should have clamoured for Chamberlain's removal. That no man in history has made such persistent and bone-headed mistakes, and that we shall go on pretending that all is well. 'If Chamberlain says that black is white, the Tories applaud his brilliance. If a week later he says that black is after all black, they applaud his realism. Never has there been such servility.' That Chamberlain must go is the word that is passing through the country.

There is a theory that the appeasers (Simon, Hoare and Horace Wilson) have regained their influence and that Chamberlain is preparing to overlook the rape of Albania and to enter into a new Mediterranean pact with Mussolini, under which we agree not to make an alliance with Greece and Turkey in return for Mussolini agreeing all over again to withdraw troops from Spain and Libya. I do not believe that Halifax would agree to anything so nonsensical, and if Halifax resigns the Government will fall.

H.N. TO V.S-W.   12th April, 1939
                                                    The Yawl 'Mar', Hamble River

The first letter from the *Mar* must be written to the Mar.[1] I am writing in the saloon with the sun pouring into the skylight, and the sound of people scrubbing and pumicing on deck mingling with the sound of aeroplanes. How happy I should be if there were no fear of war, and if I could really believe that in a few weeks I should be cresting the waves. Really this is just the boat I wanted. I didn't really want a swank boat, even as I never wanted a Pekinese.

[1] See page 48, footnote 3.

DIARY   *19th April, 1939*

Dine with Buck [De La Warr], Jeremy [Hutchinson] and Ben at Boulestin's. Buck is always very discreet and I have to judge his views more from the general temperature of his remarks than from anything he says. But I do get the impression that appeasement is again on the ascendant and that Horace Wilson has resumed his sway. For instance, Nevile Henderson is to go back to Berlin.[1] We are also trying to conciliate Mussolini. I have the definite impression that we shall never get anywhere with Neville at the top. The feeling that Winston is essential is gaining strength, and we shall probably see him in the Cabinet within a short time.

H.N. TO V.S-W.   *20th April, 1939*
                                                         4 King's Bench Walk, E.C.4

There is a sort of pause in the crisis which makes me feel uneasy. That is one of the worst things about this tension. If Hitler does nothing we all get alarmed, and when he does something we get frightened.

DIARY   *20th April, 1939*

Lunch with Sibyl Colefax. Duff Cooper is very violent about the Prime Minister and says that we are already dying slowly from the top. He at least sees that the Second German War began in July of 1936 when the Germans started with their intervention in Spain. Today we have hostile military concentrations in the Straits of Gibraltar, which, owing to the fact that we are at peace, we are unable to disperse. The Germans, were we in a similar manner to threaten the Kiel Canal, would not just sit back and see us prepare for their destruction. The propertied classes in this country, with their insane pro-Franco business, have placed us in a very dangerous position.

Down to the House. The P.M. announces the creation of a Ministry of Supply. Loud and prolonged cheers. 'For this post', he continues, 'I have selected my Right Honourable Friend . . .', and then he pauses, '. . . the Minister of Transport.'[2] There are two schools of thought

---

[1] He had been recalled for consultations. He was opposed to any British commitment to Poland, and had told Cadogan that the Poles should 'talk a little less about their bravery', and think a little more about 'the realities of their geographical position'.

[2] Leslie Burgin, Minister of Transport 1937–39. Previously a solicitor, and Liberal-National Member for Luton since 1929.

regarding what then happened. One school says that there was a gasp of horror. The other school says that there was a deep groan of pain. In any case, the impression was deplorable. It is not that Leslie Burgin will not make a good Minister of Supply. He will probably be excellent. It was that the House hoped that the P.M. would take this opportunity of broadening the basis of his Cabinet. There is a very widespread belief that he is running a dual policy—one the overt policy of arming, and the other the *secret de l'Empereur*, namely appeasement plus Horace Wilson. Chamberlain's obstinate refusal to include any but the yes-men in his Cabinet caused real dismay.

DIARY   *21st April, 1939*

The *Spectator* this week suggests that I should be sent as Ambassador to Washington. It amuses me to observe my own reactions to such a suggestion. My first fear is that it will expose me to ridicule, since all we Nicolsons are morbidly sensitive to being placed in a false position. My second impulse is to realise how much Vita would hate it. My third is to feel how much I should loathe the pomp and publicity of an Embassy. My fourth is to agree with the *Spectator* that I might do the job rather well. But it will not occur.

DIARY   *23rd April, 1939*

Dine at the Rumanian Legation to meet Gafencu,[1] who has just arrived from Brussels. It is a large man's dinner including a few scrubby Cabinet Ministers such as Shakes Morrison and Burgin and a spattering of rather seedy diplomats and officials. Afterwards I talk to Gafencu. He had been thrilled by his visit to Berlin. He said that Hitler had been quite polite and had not tried to bully him in the least. He had spoken quite calmly at first, but when he touched on ideology he had begun to scream. He had spent his whole time abusing this country. He had complained that there was no British statesman of sufficient magnitude or vision to agree with him to divide the world between them. He had no desire to possess the British Empire. All that he wanted was that we should not thwart his destiny in Eastern Europe. It was at this stage that he began to scream. He had said that it was grotesque to imagine that he wanted to invade Holland or Belgium. The only small countries that he wanted to dominate were those to the East. Gafencu asked him whether these included Rumania,

[1] Grigore Gafencu, Rumanian Foreign Minister.

and he then stopped screaming and began to be polite. He said that if war came we might be able to destroy three German towns, but that he would destroy every single British town. Gafencu was not impressed. He advised us to reply to him in the same sort of language. I told him to repeat to Halifax tomorrow every word that he had said to me. He promised to read aloud to him the notes that he had taken.

He had also seen Goering. The latter had talked about encirclement. Gafencu had replied that if threatened, neighbouring countries tried to defend themselves, and to find such support as they could. Goering said, 'How long have you been a diplomatist?' Gafencu answered, 'Two months. Up till then I was a soldier and a journalist.' Goering was pleased by that. He said, *'Vielleicht haben Sie recht'*. He added that although he had liked Hess, he had found the others quite insane. Hitler certainly was suffering from megalomania.

I talk to the Polish Ambassador.[1] He says that they would accept the autobahn to Danzig, but that they would not accept complete German rule over that city. They would agree to a condominium. Gdynia, he added, would be at the mercy of any heavy German guns mounted at Danzig. The loss of these two would be the loss of their independence. We misunderstood Beck since we thought him unreasonable. True it was that in the old days he had been obliged to adopt a pendulum policy. All that was now over. He would fight for the right.

DIARY   *26th April, 1939*

The Prime Minister makes his statement on conscription. The House is fuller than I have ever seen it. The Independent Labour Party start making violent protests, and the Labour Party leaders concentrate firstly upon Chamberlain's broken pledges, and secondly upon the fact that he had not consulted them. The Prime Minister does not really deal with the situation in a conciliatory way. He puts on his obstinate face which would be irritating were it not that one sees signs of extreme exhaustion and profound mental suffering. I am of course delighted about conscription, but if I had been Prime Minister I should have ended my speech by saying that the breach of a pledge was not a thing that any Prime Minister could commit, and that once this had gone through, I would retire from public life. I think it is the combination of real religious fanaticism with spiritual trickiness which makes one dislike Mr Chamberlain so much. He has all the hardness of

[1] Count Edward Raczynski.

a self-righteous man, with none of the generosity of those who are guided by durable moral standards.

DIARY *29th April, 1939*

I feel pretty glum and devote myself to reviewing. There is Joyce's *Finnegans Wake*. I try very hard indeed to understand that book but fail completely. It is almost impossible to decipher, and when one or two lines of understanding emerge like telegraph poles above a flood, they are at once countered by other poles going in the opposite direction. I see that at the back of it all there is some allegory turning around the Tristan saga. But the research involved in working out this loose mosaic is greater than any ordinary reader can possibly undertake. I truly believe that Joyce has this time gone too far in breaking all communication between himself and his reader. It is a very selfish book.

In the evening we have the news. It is most menacing. Intrinsically, the whole long snake of development boils down to the issue between trusting Germany and not trusting Germany. I have always contended that Germany wanted only one thing, and that was power. Now power is an expanding ambition and it is impossible to fix its frontiers. Chamberlain and the appeasement folk imagined that you could. I can now see no alternative between early war upon a false issue or the abandonment of the whole of Europe to Nazi domination. These are the effects of Chamberlain and Horace Wilson.

DIARY *2nd May, 1939*

Bower[1] told me that he heard the following dialogue on the part of two Tories on the bench behind him: 'I suppose we *shall* be able to get out of this beastly guarantee business?' 'Oh, of course. Thank God we have Neville.'

DIARY *4th May, 1939*

Have a talk with Gwilym Lloyd George. He says that he had seen Maisky who simply cannot make the Litvinov business out. The left-wing people are very upset. They say that it means that the negotiations with us will be prosecuted with greater speed. But I can see that they are not happy, and that they are not at all sure that Russia may not make a neutrality pact with Germany. I fear this terribly.

[1] Commander R. T. Bower, Conservative M.P. for Cleveland, 1931–45.

31st May, 1939

Jack Macnamara told me an interesting thing. He is an intimate friend of one of the more decent Whips and has discussed with them the Eden Group. It seems that they respect Eden, Duff Cooper, Amery and the big bugs. But they are terribly rattled by the existence and secrecy of the group itself. They know that we meet, and what they do not like is that we do not attack them in the House. If we came out into the open they would know where they stood. What they hate is this silent plotting. It is no use our saying that we are not plotting at all, that we are too patriotic to demonstrate disunity abroad, and that we are in fact merely a ginger group discussing ginger—that does not convince them. They start from the assumption that we wish to upset the present Government, to force them to take our leaders in, and that we juniors imagine that we shall get some pickings from the victory of our leaders. They regard me, it seems, as an able man gone astray. They do not understand how I can be National Labour, regarding that as treachery to my class. But the people they really suspect are Ronnie Tree, Ronnie Cartland and Emrys-Evans. The one thing that never seems to dawn on them is that we have certain principles and convictions and are prepared to sacrifice everything for them. They take it for granted that a person who opposes his party is out for some sinister and egoistic short-cut. Jack assures me that they exclude me from this assumption. They do not question my sincerity, but they think I am slightly odd in the head. Brilliant but misguided.

H.N. TO ROBERT BOOTHBY *7th June, 1939*
Sissinghurst

I have slipped out of gear in the House of Commons. I could give all sorts of explanations of that, but they are not real excuses. The real fact is that old things like myself are capable of bursts of hysterical heroism but are not good at the constant fight. I lack (as do so many of my kind—those possessed of what we may call the literary temperament) a lust for battle. We have no combative qualities.

I am not ambitious. That would be all very well were it not for another thing. I really do not believe (one never knows oneself) that I have any ardent appetite for success. But I do know that failure makes me miserable. I love the House since I am a sociable person and much enjoy observing the oddities of my fellow beings. I find the House rather like one of those marine diving-bells in which one can sit and watch the vagaries of the deep-sea fish. Yet I am also conscious that I ought to devote more time and will-power to my Parliamentary career. I do an immense amount of constituency fuss. But that may be because it gives me the illusion of activity. What I ought to do is to concentrate my central energies on the Chamber.

DIARY   *14th June, 1939*

Dine with Kenneth Clark. The Walter Lippmanns are there: also the Julian Huxleys and Winston Churchill as the guest of honour. Winston is horrified by Lippmann saying that the American Ambassador, Jo Kennedy, had informed him that war was inevitable and that we should be licked. Winston is stirred by this defeatism into a magnificent oration. He sits hunched there, waving his whisky-and-soda to mark his periods, stubbing his cigar with the other hand.

'It may be true, it may well be true', he says, 'that this country will at the outset of this coming and to my mind almost inevitable war be exposed to dire peril and fierce ordeals. It may be true that steel and fire will rain down upon us day and night scattering death and destruction far and wide. It may be true that our sea-communications will be imperilled and our food-supplies placed in jeopardy. Yet these trials and disasters, I ask you to believe me, Mr Lippmann, will but serve to steel the resolution of the British people and to enhance our will for victory. No, the Ambassador should not have spoken so, Mr Lippmann; he should not have said that dreadful word. Yet supposing (as I do not for one moment suppose) that Mr Kennedy were correct in his tragic utterance, then I for one would willingly lay down my life in combat, rather than, in fear of defeat, surrender to the menaces of these most sinister men. It will then be for you, for the Americans, to preserve and to maintain the great heritage of the English-speaking peoples. It will be for you to think imperially, which means to think always of something higher and more vast than one's own national interests. Nor should I die happy in the great struggle which I see before me, were I not convinced that if we in this dear dear island succumb to the ferocity and might of our enemies, over there in your distant and immune continent the torch of liberty will burn untarnished and (I trust and hope) undismayed.'

We then change the subject and speak about the Giant Panda.

DIARY   *15th June, 1939*

Lunch with [Sir Horace] Rumbold. Jim Marshall-Cornwall[1] is there: he is now in charge of our anti-aircraft defences. He is optimistic. He says that in a few months London will be the safest place in the world. But as he is only getting seventy guns a month and has to supply Singapore and Cairo, I do not see that he has so much reason to be glad.

The other guest is Brüning.[2] I ask him whether he thinks war is inevitable. He bows his fine head. 'Yes', he says quietly.

Dine with Sibyl. H. G. Wells starts a long and well-expressed theory that *homo sapiens* has failed. Even as the dinosaur failed because he had concentrated upon size, so we have failed because we have not developed the right type of brain. So we will first destroy ourselves and then die out as a species. Just revert to mud and slime. 'And we shall deserve it', said Wells. Walter Elliot says that surely it won't be as bad as that. 'One thousand years more', says Wells; 'that's all that *homo sapiens* has before him.'

DIARY   *19th June, 1939*

Ralph Glyn shows me a report he has just received (source unnamed) saying that the Germans are succeeding at Moscow and that the Anglo-Russian Pact is in danger. It is true that Strang has not seen Molotov again since Friday. Yet Maisky continues to be optimistic, and Halifax told Winston yesterday that all was well. I confess I am most uneasy.

H.N. TO V.S-W.   *19th June, 1939*
                                                    4 King's Bench Walk, E.C.4

The red roses are really too lovely in that oblong box-vase you gave me. Dearest, why can we not be left alone? We are doing no harm. We care for fine and gentle things. We wish only to do good on earth. We are not vulgar in our tastes or cruel in our thoughts. Why is it that we are impotent to prevent something which we know to be evil and terrible? I would willingly give my own life if I could stop this war. I would go round to the doctor and be put out of this world without a pang. Yet I cannot think enough to stop it. What a little

---

[1] General Sir James Marshall-Cornwall. Director-General of Air and Coast Defence, 1938–39.
[2] The former German Chancellor.

thing my head is, and what a great thing is hatred when unloosed. I am so unhappy about the outside, and so happy in my own little orbit.

H.N. TO V.S-W.   *23rd June, 1939*
                                              4 King's Bench Walk, E.C.4

Such fun yesterday. The House adjourned at 5.15 and we all went out into Parliament Square where the pavements had been kept clear for us. There we stood and chatted for about ten minutes, and then the bells of St Margaret's began to swing into welcome and the procession started creeping round the corner. They went very slowly, and there were the King and Queen and the two princesses. We lost all our dignity and yelled and yelled. The King wore a happy schoolboy grin. The Queen was superb. She really does manage to convey to each individual in the crowd that he or she have had a personal greeting. It is due, I think, to the brilliance of her eyes. But she is in truth one of the most amazing Queens since Cleopatra. We returned to the House with lumps in our throats.

DIARY   *27th June, 1939*

Dunglass,[1] the Prime Minister's P.P.S., collars me in the lobby and takes me down to his subterranean room. He wants to know about my proposal for a Manifesto of Peace similar to Wilson's Fourteen Points. I tell him that in the first place no such manifesto would be anything but disastrous unless it proceeded from such strength as the Germans would recognise as overwhelming. We must first convince them that we shall beat them in war before we offer them any terms of peace. In the second place, I say, such a manifesto should not be framed in such a way as to suggest that we are offering terms to Germany, but should be conceived merely as a Declaration of Rights which would rally our own opinion and opinion in the United States. It was essential that our own conscience should be got into focus. He agrees.

DIARY   *18th July, 1939*

Round to Ronnie Tree's house for a meeting of our group. We all have the feeling that there is going to be another Munich over Danzig

[1] Lord Dunglass, later the 14th Earl of Home, who renounced his peerage when he became Prime Minister in 1963. In 1939 he was 36, and had been Parliamentary Private Secretary to Neville Chamberlain since 1937.

and that Chamberlain will then appear again as the Great Appeaser. In that event we shall be stigmatized as the war-monsters and driven out of politics. If only Anthony Eden would now come out in rage against this subversive attempt, we should be safe. But Anthony does not wish to defy the Tory Party and is in fact missing every boat with exquisite elegance. We drift and drift and pass the rudder into other hands. I am much depressed.[1]

DIARY   19th July, 1939

Mr Maudling[2] comes to see me, a young man from Merton who has got a first and wants to know what political party he should join. I say that he had better wait. Every party today is crushed by its own old men; out of all this there may emerge a party which young men can join with fervour.

The Prime Minister at question time was so buoyant and perky that it looks as if appeasement was going well.

DIARY   20th July, 1939

Go to tea at the Russian Embassy and find a strange collection of left-wing enthusiasts sitting round in the Winter Garden with a huge tea-table spread with delicious cakes and caviar sandwiches, plus a samovar. The Ambassador is however so interested in convincing them how right is the Soviet definition of 'indirect aggression' that he forgets to offer them any tea and they all go away casting regretful glances at the untouched table. Maisky asks me to go into his study where I have a long talk, plus a large quantity of the sandwiches which the other guests have not been offered.

He says that he believes that Chamberlain hopes to get a compromise on the Danzig question, and that if he does that, he will allow the Russian negotiations to lapse. He says that he has a definite impression that the Government do not really want the negotiations to go through.

[1] H. N. now (1965) believes Eden's attitude to have been correct.

[2] Reginald Maudling, who was to become Chancellor of the Exchequer in 1962, had just gone down from Merton College, Oxford, where he obtained a first in Greats. He became Conservative Member for Barnet in 1950. On being shown this extract in 1965, he commented: 'As I recall it, my concern was not quite so vague as the note suggests. I had never contemplated joining the Socialists, but although by temperament Conservative, I was interested in the National Labour concept. In fact, I was thinking of the parties of the centre, or right of centre, and asking advice on this.'

Back to the House where we have a dinner for Philip Lothian who is off to Washington shortly.[1] He says that he will try and adopt the precedent of Mr Bryce[2] and go about the country as much as possible. He says that he will not make any but the dullest speeches and will in fact behave like an 'affable moron'.

H.N. TO V.S-W.   *2nd August, 1939*
                                         4 King's Bench Walk, E.C.4

We have a debate today about whether we should adjourn or not. I had hoped that Anthony Eden was going to take a strong line, but he is now suggesting that we should all toe the line. I would do so were it not that Winston refuses, and I cannot let the old lion enter the lobby alone. But apart from this I do feel very deeply that the House ought not to adjourn for the whole of the two months. I regard it as a violation of constitutional principle and an act of disrespect to the House.

Why is it that I am always in a minority? Is it wrong-headedness? I simply don't know. Or is it really that I am not a trimmer by nature and hate discipline?

DIARY   *2nd August, 1939*

To the astonishment of the House the Prime Minister gets up and after saying that he will not give way an inch,[3] he adds that certain Members had thanked the Whips for not putting on a three-line whip, but that he wished it to be clearly understood that he regarded the vote as a vote of confidence in himself. Ronnie Cartland says that the Prime Minister has missed a great opportunity by not showing his faith in this great democratic institution. He goes on, 'We are in the situation that within a month we may be going to fight and we may be going to die.' At this Patrick Hannon[4] laughs, and Cartland turns upon him with a flame of indignation and says, 'It is all very well for you to laugh. There are thousands of young men at this moment ...' The effect is galvanic and I have seldom felt the temperature rise so rapidly.

[1] Lord Lothian was to remain British Ambassador in Washington until his death in December 1940.
[2] James Bryce, later Viscount Bryce, was British Ambassador to Washington 1907–13.
[3] On the question whether Parliament should adjourn for the summer recess.
[4] Sir Patrick Hannon, Conservative M.P. for Birmingham (Moseley) since 1921.

He is then followed by Macmillan who extracts some sort of promise from the Prime Minister that he will call Parliament should a situation arise similar to that which arose in September last year.

After dinner the lobbies are still humming, and the general impression is that Chamberlain has in fact missed an opportunity and outraged the feelings of the House. Rob Bernays says to me, 'Ronnie Cartland has ruined his chances with the Party but he has made his Parliamentary reputation'. Hannon makes matters worse by attacking Cartland in a short speech for his 'poisonous words'.

There were forty abstentions on the Government side of the House after the debate preceding the Adjournment, and Parliament dispersed in an angry and anxious mood for the summer holidays. The first three weeks of August were outwardly calm, but in Moscow the tussle for Russia's partnership was approaching a climax. It was waged far more assiduously by the Germans than by the Allies. From the British side staff-talks were conducted by Admiral Sir Reginald Plunkett-Ernle-Erle-Drax, whose instructions were to stall until political agreement was nearer. He had no answer to the key Soviet question whether Russian troops would be permitted to enter Poland in her defence should she be attacked by Germany, and the discussions consequently languished. By 15th August Stalin was hinting to the Germans through Molotov that he would welcome a non-aggression pact with them. He told Churchill in 1942 that he had become convinced that Britain and France had no real intention of helping Poland, but his other motive was to gain time to rearm.

Hitler seized the opportunity. A Russo-German non-aggression pact was already in draft by 19th August, and was signed by Ribbentrop in Moscow on the evening of the 23rd. The Pact provided that neither Russia nor Germany would attack the other, nor support a Third Power against the other. By a secret protocol, not made public until after the war, Latvia, and Poland up to the Vistula, were to lie within 'the Russian sphere of interest'. Stalin would not only refuse to help Poland against German attack: he would join in her dismemberment.

Harold Nicolson was sailing in the 'Mar' during these three weeks. Embarking with John Sparrow at Plymouth on 4th August, he had intended to sail round Land's End to the west coast of Scotland. Bad weather more than the political situation was responsible for the change in plan. They doubled back from Penzance to Weymouth, where Nigel joined them on the 13th, and sailed across the Channel to Cherbourg and Guernsey. Meeting dense fog off Brest, they returned to Falmouth. On the 22nd, at Plymouth, Harold Nicolson heard the news of the Russo-German Pact and hurried back by train to London for an emergency meeting of Parliament on the 24th. He was never to sail in 'Mar' again.

H.N. TO V.S-W.   *14th August, 1939*
                                          The Yawl 'Mar'
                                          At Cherbourg

We spent yesterday morning at Portland dealing with correspondence and with stores. We had a council of war with the Captain. He really does not like leaving the Solent, and is about as grouchy as he can be. We call him the crumpled rose-leaf. If the forecast is fair and the wind favourable, he says, 'We can *get* there all right, but we can't get back, not with this weather': and if it is bad he says that we can't get there. We tried all yesterday to cheer him up. We threw a mattress into the sea (not a smile): we shot at jellyfish with the air-gun (not a glance of interest): we fished for jellyfish with the canvas bucket (not the slightest attention paid to us, until we dropped the bucket overboard and it sank: he then said, 'There's the bucket gone and one can't get buckets in France.' 'But you can, Captain; truly you can.')

Anyhow we had a lovely twenty-four hours from Portland here. A dead calm at first and we just floated off the Shambles and watched the sun sink and the water turn to satin of all colours. Then we dined and played patience and went to bed. At dawn I was woken by the sound of rippling and went on deck. A splendid sunrise and a breeze with it. The foam we made went pink. Then to sleep again and breakfast, and soon after a dim line of coast. We got in here about 1 p.m. and are still waiting for the Customs.

H.N. TO V.S-W.   *19th August, 1939*
                                          The Yawl 'Mar'
                                          Off the Lizard

We left St Peter Port, Guernsey, on Thursday morning. It was a marvellous day and we sailed away happily past the island and away towards France. How gay and happy we were! Sea and sunlight and an expedition in front of us. The sails tautened, the sea sparkled into foam at our bows, the dim islands slid behind us. We were young and adventurous. And as the sun turned round the sky, the day continued to be lovely and the sun sank in a purple sea and the new moon hung in the air and the stars came out. Tomorrow morning, we thought, we shall wake up outside Brest.

During the night we came in for the swell of the Atlantic. The sun still shone when I went on deck at 7, but there was a heavy sea and in front of us a slight haze upon the horizon. The Captain said that he had not been able to see the light at Ushant and was afraid it was 'mighty thick' on the coast. On we went. The sun slipped into a haze and then went out. Wisps of fog began to creep round us and suddenly we saw a lighthouse and some rocks. They were at once swallowed up in the fog before we could identify them. The Captain, being a wise man, refused to go any further until the fog cleared. So we turned back, after that fleeting glimpse of one lighthouse, and hove to. Heaving to means that one heaves with one's nose into the wind. It was cold and grey. Niggs and John [Sparrow] retired to the cabin to keep warm. This went on till 1.30. We decided that we should return to Falmouth. Off we went, feeling cheated, frustrated but wise.

I woke this morning after a marvellous sleep and went on deck. It was dawn. Darling, how you would have loved it. Three dolphins were playing round the ship and the spray as they plunged was pink in the rising sun. It is calm and warm. We have just sighted the Lizard and should be in Falmouth by lunchtime. The Captain, when tiresome things occur, is perfectly charming. I am getting to like him.

DIARY   *21st August, 1939*
                                                                       Fowey

We dine ashore at the Fowey Hotel. As we walk away down the corridor, we hear the news coming from the office on the wireless. It looks as if the Germans have arranged with the Italians and the Hungarians and Japanese to stage their coup at once. The Germans are half-mobilising and the French are doing the same. A sense of terrific imminence hangs above us. We row out across a satin harbour to the *Mar*.

How strange it is that this war which I have dreaded for six years and which I have so repeatedly forecast now seems close upon us.

All talk of appeasement is now stilled, although most serious people believe that there is still some chance of coming to a negotiated settlement over Danzig. Or rather there *was* some chance three months ago. We have missed that chance as usual. It looks like war. I am glad that fate has given me these weeks of happiness before the great ordeal comes.

DIARY   *22nd August, 1939*
Plymouth

There is a mist when we wake up and we hang about at Fowey. The morning papers come aboard. They contain nothing that was not on the wireless last night, except that Ribbentrop has left by air for an unknown destination. We leave at 8.55 and reach Plymouth Sound at 3. We anchor off the Hoe. I read *Nicholas Nickleby*. At six I listen to the News. The Germans and Russians have announced that they propose to sign a non-aggression pact and that Ribbentrop is on his way to Moscow for that purpose. This smashes our peace-front and makes our guarantees to Poland, Rumania and Greece very questionable. How Ribbentrop must chuckle. I feel rather stunned by this news and sit on deck in bewilderment with the fishing smacks around me. I fear that it means that we are humbled to the dust.

DIARY   *23rd August, 1939*

The morning papers announce that the House is to be summoned tomorrow. I leave Niggs and John on board, say goodbye with a sad heart and walk grimly to the North Road station.

I dine with Archie Sinclair and the Bonham Carters. We discuss what the Russo-German agreement really means. There are those who take the view that the Russians have been extraordinarily clever and are forcing the Axis Powers to lay their cards upon the table. These people imagine that Ribbentrop (who has already arrived in Moscow) will be kept hanging about and will be humiliated, even as our own people were humiliated. I doubt it. I doubt whether Ribbentrop would have been such a fool as to go to Moscow unless he was pretty certain that he would be exposed to no humiliating delays. Archie had seen the Prime Minister this morning and found him very depressed but resolute. He leaves us to ring up Winston Churchill. The latter has just returned from Paris and is in high fettle. The French are not at all perturbed by the Russo-German Pact and are prepared to support Poland nonetheless. They are half-mobilising. Winston has just rung up Paul Reynaud, who asserts that all is going well: by which he means war, I suppose.

I leave them at 10.15. As I drive back to the Temple, I pass a motorcyclist in a steel helmet. A sinister sight. It is very hot and still.

Having squared the Russians, Hitler now directed his energies to preventing Britain and France from honouring their pledge of assistance to Poland. He was determined to attack, and set the date for 26th August, postponing it at the very last moment until dawn on 1st September. On the 29th August he demanded that a Polish plenipotentiary arrive in Berlin within twenty-four hours, and when none came, Ribbentrop informed the British Ambassador (but not the Poles) of the terms that he would have offered—the surrender of Danzig to Germany, a plebiscite in the Polish Corridor and an exchange of populations. Halifax urged Beck to open negotiations 'on principles', but it was already too late. Hitler opened his attack on Poland as planned, claiming that the Poles had rejected his peace-offer and that Polish violations of the German frontier (fabricated by the Nazis) had become intolerable.

On the evening of the day of the German invasion, 1st September, Hitler was told by Britain and France, 'not as an ultimatum, but as a warning', that unless he withdrew his forces from Poland, the Allies would go to Poland's help. But simultaneously Bonnet, the French Foreign Minister, without consulting Halifax, let Mussolini know that France would welcome a peace-conference whether Hitler withdrew or not. On 2nd September Halifax made the British position clear to Mussolini, that there could be no talks unless Hitler first withdrew. These abortive negotiations with Mussolini and the British Government's desire to keep in step with the French were the cause of the delay in issuing our expected ultimatum to Germany. It led to a furious scene in the House of Commons on the evening of the 2nd, and Chamberlain told Daladier that unless war were declared next day, his Government might fall. Accordingly, the British ultimatum was delivered in Berlin at 9 a.m. on Sunday 3rd September and expired unanswered two hours later. The French ultimatum expired at 5 p.m.

H.N. TO V.S-W. *24th August, 1939*
House of Commons

Just a scribble in the intervals of this debate. The P.M. was dignified and calm, but without one word which could inspire anybody. He was exactly like a coroner summing up a case of murder.

I see mighty little chance of peace. It may be that Colonel Beck will lose his nerve and fly to Berchtesgaden. But even that would be a bad catastrophe.

I gather that the P.M. has offered to resign, but the King won't accept it.

V.S-W. TO H.N. *24th August, 1939*
Sissinghurst

What ghastly hours. If only you were not in London. It makes me physically sick to think of air-raids. I was rung up in the middle of my luncheon and asked if the Buick would take an eight-foot stretcher or 'only sitting-cases and corpses'. I feel sick with apprehension, but I find that I get braver as the day goes on, a curious psychological working which I wish I could analyse. I went to dinner with Mrs Drummond last night. Her only comment on the 9 o'clock news was, 'Most unsatisfactory'. It made me feel that she was rebuking a house-maid. A superb old woman.

DIARY *28th August, 1939*

Bathe. A lovely hot day. Write my *Spectator* article. Ben goes up to London. The 1 o'clock news says that the Mediterranean and the Baltic are closed to British merchant shipping. The Germans have prohibited all private train or even postal traffic. The sun beats very hot and all the autumn mist melts, and the spider-webs also upon the yews.

It looks as if war will burst upon us tomorrow. Again that curious contrast with 3rd August 1914! Then we were excited by all these events and there was a sense of exhilaration. Today we are merely glum. It is not merely my age and experience which silence me under this leaden cope of gloom. Nigel, though calm and cheerful as usual, is not in the least excited.

DIARY   *29th August, 1939*

Go straight to the House from Cannon Street. Tilea, the Rumanian Minister, comes to lunch with me. He has just got back from Rumania. He had found his Government resolute and well prepared. They will declare their neutrality at first, but will work for the Balkan bloc. He says that Turkey is quite solidly on our side, that Yugoslavia will maintain a benevolent neutrality towards us, that Greece will have to be with us from the first, and that Bulgaria is strongly anti-German. He admits that the German pact has much upset Rumanian opinion.

Louis Spears comes up in some excitement saying that he has had a word with the Polish Ambassador who assures him that so far from the situation being desperate, 'things are going very nicely'. There is in fact some optimism in the lobbies. Everybody had expected an attack on Saturday or Sunday and nothing happened. The fact that Hitler has sent Nevile Henderson backwards and forwards with proposals is taken as a hopeful sign.[1] The House is therefore more cheerful than it has been for weeks and looks at the anti-gas doors being fitted downstairs and the sand-bags being heaped on our basement windows with amusement. I think also that they are proud of themselves for having behaved so well, so calmly, so unitedly today.

DIARY   *30th August, 1939*

Lunch with Sibyl Colefax. Lady Cunard and Ivone Kirkpatrick[2] there. Emerald Cunard says that she has had a very nice letter from Grandi. 'Have you also heard from him, Lady Colefax?' 'Only by telegram', Sibyl answers like a flash.

Kirkpatrick is interesting about Hitler. He says that to meet socially, and when he is host in his own house, he has a certain simple dignity, like a farmer entertaining neighbours. All very different from the showy vulgarity of Mussolini. But that once one begins to work with him, or sees him dealing with great affairs, one has such a sense of evil arrogance that one is almost nauseated. He confesses that he has been rendered physically sick by some of the interviews that he has witnessed.

---

[1] This optimism was misplaced. Britain remained firm to its pledge to Poland, and Henderson's interview with Ribbentrop at midnight 30–31st August approached the point of mutual insult.

[2] He had been First Secretary at the British Embassy in Berlin 1933–38, and had accompanied Chamberlain at his interviews with Hitler in 1938.

Evil and treachery and malice dart into Hitler's mystic eyes. He has a maddening habit of laying down the law in sharp, syncopated sentences, accompanying the conclusion either with a sharp pat of his palm upon the table, or by a half-swing sideways in his chair, a sudden Napoleonic crossing of his arms, and a gaze of detached but suffering mysticism towards the ceiling. His impatience is terrific. We asked Kirkpatrick what gave him a sense of actual evil. He said that after Hitler had flown from Godesberg to Munich to murder Roehm,[1] he returned in the very highest spirits, mimicking to his secretary the gestures of fear which Roehm had made. This was told to Kirk by one of those who were present. He says that even the highest Nazis are amazingly disloyal to Hitler at times. For instance, when Henderson was going in for some important conversation with the Führer, the man who conducted him to Hitler's study whispered as he opened the door, 'For God's sake don't let him get away with it.'

On to see Buck De La Warr at his new office in Alexandra House in Kingsway. There had been a Cabinet this morning to draft the second reply to Hitler which has now gone off. I did not ask Buck what it contained, but I gather that it amounts to an offer of general negotiation if only Hitler will do something to show that he is not imposing a solution by force. I do not feel that Buck shares the optimism which is still circulating in London. He says that 'when' (not 'if') war comes, he will try to find some more active job than that of a Cabinet Minister.[2] I have never found him more attractive.

It is curious to recall and analyse the general mood during these dark days since 22nd August. The House when it met on 24th August was in the depths of gloom. People scarcely spoke to each other above a whisper, as if some close relation was dying upstairs. Then when nothing happened on Saturday or Sunday, and when Hitler consented to enter into an argument, hope revived. The City as usual behaved foolishly and stocks went up. Thus when we met on Tuesday, there was considerable optimism and chattiness. And today when war seems a matter of hours, the absolute despair of a week ago seems to have changed into determination, the gloom of anticipation melting into the gaiety of courage. It is as though we had taken our fill of apprehension and sadness and can absorb no more.

[1] Ernst Roehm, head of the Nazi S.A., was murdered at Hitler's orders on 30th June, 1934.
[2] Lord De La Warr was still President of the Board of Education.

DIARY   *31st August, 1939*

It has been decided to evacuate three million mothers and children tomorrow from the menaced areas. It is rather grim. Historic names such as Rochester, Chatham, Southwark, come over at us in the calm cultured voice of the announcer. I read *Nicholas Nickleby* to cheer me up. How unreal Dickens is! Jazz-band sentimentality. The 6 o'clock news is very glum. It has been a grey day but the sun comes out in the evening and we have a calm twilight under which the garden stretches itself at ease. The flag hangs limply on its flag-staff. It is odd to feel that the world as I knew it has only a few hours more to run.

DIARY   *1st September, 1939*

This morning there is a hot mist over everything and not a breath of wind. The sun comes out and I take a deck-chair and sit at the door of the South Cottage so that I can hear the telephone if it rings. I read Gerald Heard and am deep in a passage about the Essenes when Viti comes along the path walking quickly. 'It has begun', she says. It seems that last night Förster,[1] with Hitler's approval, announced the incorporation of Danzig in the Reich, and that hostilities between Germany and Poland have already begun. The House has been summoned for 6 o'clock tonight. It is exactly 10.45 on the morning of today, Friday 1st September, 1939, that I get this news. I go on reading Gerald Heard. Miss Macmillan appears with my gas-mask in a box.

Motor up with Copper to London. There are few signs of any undue activity beyond a few khaki figures at Staplehurst and some schoolboys filling sand-bags at Maidstone. When we get near London we see a row of balloons hanging like black spots in the air.

Go down to the House at 5.30. They have already darkened the building and lowered the lights. The lobby is extremely dark, and the Chamber, which generally seems like a dim aquarium, appears quite garish in comparison. The Speaker arrives punctually at 6 and we all bow to him. Lloyd George and Winston are already in their places facing each other. We have prayers. The Chaplain adds a little special prayer saying, 'Let us this day pray for wisdom and courage to

[1] Albert Förster, the Nazi Gauleiter of Danzig.

defend the right.' The Prime Minister and Greenwood[1] enter together and are received with a loud cheer. A few enthusiasts try to rise and wave their order papers. They then sit down again rather foolishly. People crowd into the Distinguished Strangers Gallery. The Polish and Russian Ambassadors find themselves next to each other. I grin up at Maisky and he grins back. The Dukes of Kent and Gloucester sit above the clock.

Chamberlain rises immediately. He begins by saying that the time has arrived when action rather than speech is required. He then, with some emotion, reminds the House how he prayed that it would never fall upon him to ask the country to accept the 'awful arbitrament of war'. 'I fear', he continued, 'that I may not be able to avoid that responsibility.' He then goes on to say that we have neglected no means of making it crystal clear to the German Government that if they use force we should reply by force, and he raises his voice and strikes the box with a clenched fist as he says, 'The responsibility for this terrible catastrophe lies on the shoulders of one man, the German Chancellor, who has not hesitated to plunge the world into misery in order to serve his own senseless ambition.' This met with a loud cheer from all benches. He then continues calmly explaining the recent course of negotiations, resting the back of one hand upon the palm of the other, and every now and then taking off his pince-nez between his finger and thumb. When he reveals the fact that the sixteen points which Hitler claims to have been rejected were never even communicated to the Poles, a gasp of astonishment rises and Lady Astor exclaims in ringing tones, 'Well, I never did!' He then reaches the climax of his speech, and after saying that the two Ambassadors have been instructed 'to hand to the German Government the following document', he fiddles with his papers for some time and then produces a document which he reads very slowly. He is evidently in real moral agony and the general feeling in the House is one of deep sympathy for him and of utter misery for ourselves.

I am afraid that the Lobby opinion is rather defeatist and they all realise that we have in front of us a very terrible task. The Prime Minister's speech is generally approved, although the Opposition mind very much his having brought in that friendly reference to Mussolini.

[1] Arthur Greenwood, who was acting as Leader of the Labour Opposition in the absence of Clement Attlee, who was unwell.

I dine at the Beefsteak. Devonshire is there and is as sane and amusing as ever. I must say I do admire a man like that, who must realise that all his grandeur is gone for ever, not showing the slightest sign of any gloom or apprehension.

When I leave the Club, I am startled to find a perfectly black city. Nothing could be more dramatic or give one more of a shock than to leave the familiar Beefsteak and to find outside not the glitter of all the sky-signs, but a pall of black velvet.

I go to Queen Anne's Gate where I find Harold Macmillan and Ronnie Tree. We wait for Anthony Eden. He has been kept by the Prime Minister. Amery comes in and says, 'Well, is there any news beyond the fact that the whole Government has resigned?' It appears that Winston will be brought into the War Cabinet and that Eden will be given a ministerial job. When at last he arrives, it is so late that we really do not discuss anything and agree to meet again tomorrow. What we feel is that our Group, which has done so much to ginger the Government up, should in some way remain in being.

I am not clear why no time-limit was given in the intimation to Berlin. It may be that we are trying to gain a few hours for the evacuation of children. Apparently the French too have certain legislation to get through and the actual ultimatum will be sent during the course of tomorrow.

DIARY   2nd September, 1939

The House meets at 2.45 and we get through the Conscription and other Bills. They pass with slight discussion. Strange rumours begin as usual to circulate: that a supposed Havas message has gone out saying that Mussolini has announced that he will mediate and that a Conference must be summoned at once; that there is to be a War Cabinet with Winston in it, without the Labour people, who rightly refuse to join; that the Polish Ambassador in Paris had a meeting this morning with Georges Bonnet which was so unsatisfactory that on his return to the Embassy he wrote a record of it and sent it to Daladier with the words, 'Herewith my record of my interview with your Foreign Secretary'.

At 7.30 we reassemble. The House is packed and tense and we wait there exactly like a court awaiting the verdict of the jury. At 7.35 the Clerks come in and take their places. At 7.37 the Speaker enters from behind the chair and we all rise. There is an unpleasant silence.

At 7.42 the Prime Minister enters with Greenwood. He gets up to speak.

He begins with the chronological method: 'On Wednesday night Sir Nevile Henderson, our Ambassador in Berlin, handed to Herr von Ribbentrop ...'—that sort of thing. His voice betrays some emotion as if he were sickening for a cold. He is a strange man. We expected one of his dramatic surprises. But none came. It was evident when he sat down that no decision had been arrived at. The House gasped for one moment in astonishment. Was there to be another Munich after all? Then Greenwood got up. The disappointment at the P.M.'s statement, the sense that appeasement had come back, vented itself in the reception of Greenwood. His own people cheered, as was natural; but what was so amazing was that their cheer was taken up in a second and greater wave from our benches. Bob Boothby cried out, 'You speak for Britain.'[1] It was an astonishing demonstration. Greenwood almost staggered with surprise. When it subsided he had to speak and did so better than I had expected. He began to say what an embarrassing task had been imposed on him. He had wanted to support and was obliged to criticise. Why this delay? We had promised to help Poland 'at once'. She was being bombed and attacked. We had vacillated for 34 hours. What did this mean? He was resoundingly cheered. The tension became acute, since here were the P.M.'s most ardent supporters cheering his opponent with all their lungs. The front bench looked as if they had been struck in the face.

The P.M. makes a conciliatory speech saying that he does not mean to give way but that we must work *pari passu* with the French. He makes the mistake of saying that he does not believe for one moment that the French are weakening, whereas he must know very well that the better-informed among us already know about Georges Bonnet. He is not telling the truth, and we know it.

The House then adjourns. The lobby is so dark that a match struck flames like a beacon. There is great confusion and indignation. We feel that the German ships and submarines will, owing to this inexplicable delay, elude our grasp. The P.M. must know by now that the whole House is against him. He might (had he been a more imaginative man) have got out of his difficulty. It was not his fault but that of Georges Bonnet. But he is too secretive by nature to be able to create

[1] This historic intervention, usually attributed to L. S. Amery, was in fact made by Robert Boothby, as he confirmed when shown this passage in 1965.

confidence. In those few minutes he flung away his reputation.[1] I feel deeply sorry for him.

I go to the Travellers and dine with Gladwyn Jebb and David Eccles.[2] Gladwyn with his usual discretion tells me nothing, but I with my usual technique give my own views and information. He admits that they are correct. Then Buck joins us. He is still terribly distressed. He says, 'They are escaping us. They are getting away while we dither.' Talk for a bit to Eccles and Kenneth Clark. Then walk home. The black-out is complete. I creep carefully. I foresee that once the habit of order leaves us, there will be a recrudescence of footpads and highway robbery.

DIARY   (Sunday) 3rd September, 1939

The papers announce that we are sending an ultimatum which expires at 11 this morning.

To Ronnie Tree's house. The usual members of our group are enlivened by the presence of Bob Boothby and Duncan Sandys of the Churchill group. We discuss first whether Anthony [Eden] is to accept the offer to join the Cabinet, although he is not included in the inner Cabinet. Some people think that he must refuse to join except as a member of the War Cabinet. Anthony rather writhes and wriggles, from which I gather that he has already committed himself to join, and does not relish all these suggestions.[3] I watch the minute-hand of my watch creeping towards 11 am, when we shall be at war. When the watch reaches that point, we pay no attention. The Prime Minister is to broadcast at 11.15 and we have no wireless. The housemaid has one and she comes and fixes it up in a fumbling way. We listen to the P.M. He is quite good and tells us that war has begun. But he puts in a

---

[1] When H.N. was editing this section of the diary for possible publication in 1941 (a project that did not mature), he struck out this sentence and substituted, 'And he has to work with French politicians who panic.'

[2] The future Minister of Education (1954–57 and 1959–62), who had just joined the staff of the Ministry of Economic Warfare.

[3] At that stage Anthony Eden had not yet been sent for by Chamberlain, but on the evening of 2nd September he had heard from Churchill that the Prime Minister intended to offer him 'one of the major offices of state'. On the afternoon of 3rd September, Eden was invited to Downing Street, where Chamberlain asked him to take the Dominions Office without a seat in the War Cabinet, but to be 'a constant attender at its meetings'. Eden accepted, but as he says in his Memoirs (The Reckoning, 1965), he disliked this 'somewhat anomalous position in the Cabinet. If it had not been for the emergency of war, nothing would have induced me to return.'

personal note which shocks us. We feel that after last night's demonstration he cannot possibly lead us into a great war. One of the group who had come back into the Chamber after the adjournment says that Chamberlain remained on the bench with Margesson. The latter was purple in the face, and the former was as white as a sheet. It must be clear to them that if it had come to a vote at the time, he would have been defeated.

At 11.40 we decide to stroll down to the House. I walk ahead with Leo Amery, and Anthony and Duff [Cooper] walk behind. Hardly have we left 28 Queen Anne's Gate when a siren blows. Amery says, 'They ought not to do that after what we have heard on the wireless. People will think it is an air-raid warning.' Hardly has he said these words when another siren takes it up. 'My God!' I say, 'it *is* an air-raid warning!' Anthony, who was walking behind, catches us up. 'We had better make for the House', he said. 'We still have time.' We walk on trying to make casual conversation. The sirens scream all around us and policemen wave at us. At that moment [Edward] Spears drives up in his car. We tumble in. I sit on Amery's knee and Anthony sits on mine. We reach Parliament Square. As we enter it the crowd, which had massed itself against the railings, breaks up like a flock of pigeons. They run away towards Westminster Hospital. They cut across the grass plot where the statues are. We go on to Palace Yard. We get out of the car and walk quickly but not without dignity into the House. I give my hat up in the ordinary way and mount the stairs to the Members' Lobby. The police there are in steel helmets and tell us to go down to the air-raid refuge. I do so, and find the corridor towards the Harcourt Room blocked by all manner of people from Cabinet Ministers to cooks. It is very hot. People chat to each other with forced geniality. After ten minutes we are released and go on to the terrace. People assert that they heard gunfire and bombs dropping. I suggest that it was merely the carpenters nailing in the asbestos linings to the windows. The terrace is flashed with sunshine, and we watch with disapproval the slow movements of people at Lambeth trying to get a balloon to rise. It has been dampened by last night's rain.

Nobody really knows whether the raid is over, but at noon we return to the Chamber. The Speaker takes his seat with the usual calm procedure. We have prayers. The Prime Minister then makes a speech which is restrained and therefore effective. He looks very ill. Winston intervenes with a speech which misses fire since it is too like one of his articles. The sirens continue during the debate, but we pay no attention to them. They are sounding the all-clear. We learn afterwards that the whole raid-warning was a mistake. It was some strayed reveller returning (*male sobrius*) from Le Touquet. But the effect of this alarm was that nobody was really attuned to listen with any real receptiveness to the speeches that were made.

At 1.50 I motor down with Victor Cazalet to Sissinghurst. There are many army lorries passing along the road and a few pathetic trucks evacuating East End refugees. In one of those there is an elderly woman who shakes her fist at us and shouts that it is all the fault of the rich. The Labour Party will be hard put to it to prevent this war degenerating into class warfare.

When I reach Sissinghurst I find that the flag has been pulled down.

APPENDIX

INDEX

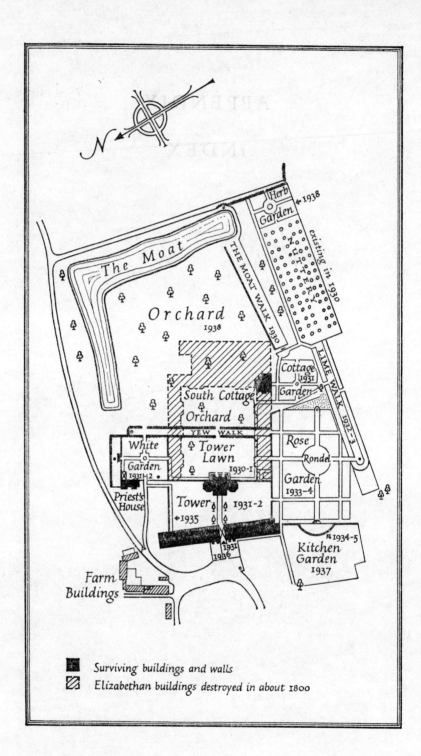

N

Herb Garden ← 1938

The Moat

existing in 1930

Orchard 1938

THE MOAT WALK 1930

LIME WALK 1932-3

Cottage 1931
Garden

South Cottage Orchard

Rose Garden 1933-4

Rondel

YEW WALK

White Garden 1931-2

Tower Lawn 1930-1

Priest's House

Tower ← 1935   1931-2

1931 1938

Kitchen Garden 1937   1934-5

Farm Buildings

■ Surviving buildings and walls

▨ Elizabethan buildings destroyed in about 1800

SISSINGHURST CASTLE, KENT

By comparing the plan opposite with the air-photograph facing page 48, it will be seen that Sissinghurst was a mere relic of the great house of the Baker family which stood entire until about 1800. The long front range, built in about 1485, and the tower (1565), survived, but the central courtyard of the Bakers' house had been pulled down, leaving only one small corner, the 'South Cottage', still standing. Another Elizabethan building, the Priest's House, also survived. When the Nicolsons bought Sissinghurst in 1930, these buildings were in a poor state of repair and some were occupied by farm-workers. The north wing of the long building was a stable. There were only vegetable-gardens, and a vast accumulation of rubbish dating back to the occupation of the castle by French prisoners in the mid-18th century. There were a few old apple-trees, a nuttery (see p. 46) and a single Gallica rose. Otherwise nothing but old brick walls, and the moat which had enclosed a medieval house on the same site.

In 1932, when the air-photograph was taken, the Nicolsons were already living there permanently. The bedrooms and Harold Nicolson's sitting-room were in the South Cottage, the kitchen, dining-room and boys' bedroom in the Priest's House, and V. Sackville-West's sitting-room on the first floor of the tower. Later, a library was made on the ground-floor of the stables, and the boys had separate rooms above it. The south wing was occupied by the cook and the chauffeur. There was no guest-room, and in winter it was most uncomfortable.

Dates have been attached to the plan, indicating when the different parts of the garden were made. Harold Nicolson's basic idea was to form three long axial vistas, creating a sense of distance within a fairly confined space, and within this framework to make several hidden gardens (V. Sackville-West called them 'outdoor rooms'), each different in colouring, scale and flowering-season, and each a surprise. The rose-garden was made from a large cabbage patch, and the lime-walk from the corner of a field. Three new walls were built, and several hedges planted, to create the desired sense of enclosure. The whole garden was finished by 1937, and only in detail and in increasing maturity has it changed since.

V. Sackville-West planted the garden which Harold Nicolson had designed. Much of her inspiration came from Persian gardens, although it remains very English. She was anxious that it should not become too tidy or too garish, preferring tapestry colours, hating rhododendrons or 'herbaceous' flowers, allowing roses to stray and wild flowers to seed themselves naturally in the paths. The garden, in short, was like their marriage—a combination of the classic temperament with the romantic.

INDEX

Abdication of Edward VIII: summary, 275-6; *see* Edward VIII; Simpson, Mrs Wallis; Baldwin, Stanley; House of Commons

Abdul, a Moroccan donkey, 177

Aberdeen, 275

Abyssinian crisis, 211-12, 215, 226-7, 230, 232-4; H.N.'s maiden speech on, 233; 247; sanctions policy, 257, 265-6; Italy's conquest of, 257, 323*n*, 339

Abyssinia, Emperor of, 260

Achoura, Feast of, 31

Action, 78, 80, 85; H.N. becomes Editor, 86-7; failure of, 96-7, 99

Adair, Richard, 49

Addis Ababa, 257

Aeschylus, 28

Africa, H.N.'s journey to, 291-5

Aga Khan, the, 307*n*

Air-raid warning, first, 421-2

Albania, 395, 397

Aldrich, Chester, 178

Alfonso, King, 213

Algeria, 295

Allegheny (USA), 189

Allen, W.E., 66, 82, 90

All Souls College, Oxford, 77, 353*n*

Americans, H.N.'s and V.S.-W.'s opinions of: favourable, 131-2, 133, 135, 136, 137, 138-9, 145, 190, and *see* Lindbergh; unfavourable, 132-3, 134-5, 139-40, 141-2, 181-2, 187, 189; mixed, 130, 137, 205; *see* also United States

Amery, L. S.: on Rhineland crisis, 252; 330, 333; Munich crisis, 366, 375; in Eden Group, 377, 402; on eve of war, 418, 419*n*, 421

Amherst College, 175, 187

Ancaster, Lord, 266, 297

Angell, Sir Norman, 327, 372-3

Anschluss: *see* Austria

Appeasement, policy of, 269, 273, 313, 319-20, 333, 341, 345-6, 359, 360, 361, 366, 388, 390-1, 396, 398, 401, 405

Aquitania, R.M.S., 203, 204

Arizona, 130, 145-6, 200

Arlen, Michael, 167

Army, British, 303; *see* Defence, British

Asch, 364

Ashton-under-Lyne, by-election, 71

Asquith, H. H., 123, 268

Astor, Lady (Nancy), 60, 254, 261-2, 266, 326-7, 396-7, 417

Athenaeum Club, 99

Attlee, Clement: succeeds Mosley in MacDonald's Government, 66; leads Labour Party in 1935 Election, 215; as an orator, 228, 240; in Hoare-Laval crisis, 233; imitated by Lloyd George, 269; in Abdication crisis, 282, 286; on death of Austen Chamberlain, 296; on Spanish Civil War, 308; on all-party policy towards Germany, 332; resembles King Boris, 338; 'turn of the tide?', 344; in Munich crisis, 364, 372

Auden, Wystan, 119, 153, 310

Austria: threatened by Nazism, 165-6; French pledge to, 251; Lloyd George on, 266; H.N. visits, 272-3; Hitler puts pressure on, 322; Mussolini's attitude to, 322-3; *Anschluss*, 328-9, 330-1; Nazis in, 347-8

Bab Guissa, 171

Bagnold, Enid (Lady Jones), 69, 121, 152, 156

Baker, Cecily, 47*n*

Baker, Sir John, 47*n*

Baker, Mary, 213

Balderston, Mr and Mrs John, 144

Baldwin, Oliver, 66, 282

Baldwin, Stanley: Churchill on, 41; neglect of Chequers, 42; on R.101